THE AMERICAN CONGRESS

THE AMERICAN CONGRESS
THE FIRST BRANCH

Abner J. Mikva · Patti B. Saris

A GROLIER COMPANY

FRANKLIN WATTS

New York　　London　　Toronto　　Sydney

Photographs courtesy of:
Architect of the U.S. Capitol: pp. 16, 319;
Library of Congress: pp. 38, 89, 130, 192, 223, 265;
U.S. Senate Historical Library: pp. 116, 139, 170, 214.

Franklin Watts, Inc.
387 Park Avenue South
New York, New York 10016

Library of Congress Cataloging in Publication Data

Mikva, Abner J.
The American Congress.

Bibliography: p.
Includes index.
1. United States. Congress.   I. Saris, Patti B.
II. Title.
JK1061.M54   1983   328.73   82-20153
ISBN 0-531-05422-5

Cover design by Meg Ann Moorhead

CONTENTS

LIST OF TABLES

LIST OF CHARTS

The "Hill" connotes many different places in Washington. It is the neighborhood around the Capitol. It is the Capitol Building, and it is the Congress itself. The authors are grateful to the Hill and its people for making this book possible. In addition to that general acknowledgment, we would like to thank some people for some very specific help.

We are grateful to Allen Schick of the Library of Congress, Mace Broide of the House Budget Committee, and Arthur Hauptman of the Senate for their helpful comments and insights on the budget process; to Lawrence Baskir, Irene Emsellem, and Burt Wides for sharing their Senate expertise; to Ari Weiss and Jack Lew for their insights and expertise on the House; to Dr. Xandra Kayden for her help on campaign financing; to Dr. Constance Schultz for her help on the early congresses; to Brad Simon for his help on ethics in the Congress; and to Gerald Neuman, a distinguished Boston lawyer, for his comments on the entire book.

Zoe Gratsias and Betty Steele were of inestimable help in the typing and copying and keeping track of all the pieces that made up the book. Nancy Dalton and Barbara Caruso did valuable secretarial work.

Professor Flora Davidson of Columbia University gave us thoughtful and constructive criticism at a most important time. She helped us reshape the book for the better. Professor Rita Cooley of New York University was also most helpful. Finally, we are deeply grateful for Will Davison, whose gentleness and kindness made our dealings with our publisher most pleasant.

We appreciate all those people and many more for their help, but candidly acknowledge that the views, errors, and shortcomings are solely the responsibility of the authors.

TO MY WIFE, ZOE, AND THE OTHER WOMEN IN
MY LIFE, MARY, LAURIE, AND RACHEL, FOR
MAKING THE FAMILY THE VERY FIRST BRANCH.
—ABNER J. MIKVA

TO MY FATHER, MORRIS SARIS, WHOSE LOVE
AND CONFIDENCE WILL ALWAYS GIVE ME THE
COURAGE TO STEP BOLDLY IN NEW DIRECTIONS…
AND TO MY HUSBAND, ARTHUR SEGEL, MY MOTHER,
AND THE REST OF MY FAMILY WHO PATIENTLY
(BUT FIRMLY) URGED ME ON THROUGHOUT THE
THREE YEARS OF THIS ENDEAVOR.
—PATTI SARIS

PREFACE

CONGRESS AS
THE FIRST BRANCH
OF GOVERNMENT

Maligned, vilified, scorned, ridiculed, poorly reported by the media, Congress is consistently ranked near the bottom of the list when citizens are polled on their favorite things. Yet this low opinion was not always so. Justice Hugo Black insisted that the First Amendment to the Constitution was first by design, not happenstance—that to the country's founders, speech and press and religion were of primary concern. So too it was not by happenstance but by design that the Congress was established by Article I of the Constitution—for to the country's founders, Congress was the predominant branch.

As with all things, Congress has changed over the years—from Philadelphia to Watergate to the present. As the agenda of national concerns changed, Congress reacted to those changes, sometimes swiftly, sometimes at a snail's pace. At Philadelphia, the arguments pitted small states against large, aristocrats against revolutionaries, advocates of legislative dominance against those of executive power. The compromises reached in establishing the first branch foretold the subsequent countless ebbs and flows of congressional power inherent in the democratic process. People, events, and the evolution of society have stimulated congressional change. Strong presidents (the Jacksons, the Roosevelts) closed the door on congressional power; weaker

1

presidents opened it wide. Every few decades Congress itself engaged in basic structural reform—usually more heralded than real. As the rise and fall of political parties impacted on the congressional branch, the party caucus rose and fell, only to rise again. The input of less formal groups has also been a factor in change, as regional caucuses and issue-oriented caucuses sought and obtained a shaping role.

As the boundaries of the country expanded westward and the representatives of new states swelled congressional ranks, the membership became less homogeneous and the process more unwieldly. The committee system became essential and complicated, as seniority vied with merit as the means for choosing leaders. Subcommittees grew out of the twin pressures to spread the power and action to more junior members and to develop greater expertise. Staffs grew from modest to awesome sizes as modern congresses grappled within and without to meet the demands of a large, complex, heterogeneous America.

The early planned differences between House and Senate assumed varying degrees of importance; other differences derived from tradition, happenstance, and design. Originally intended to serve in part as an adviser to the president, today the Senate often finds itself the antagonist. The function of Congress to oversee the executive branch, there from the beginning, became more important as government by administrative agency became the norm. Constituent services became more important as the federal government expanded to touch the daily activities of most citizens.

When pollsters ask voters about Congress, the institution and its membership as a whole, almost without exception, get very low marks. Almost equally without exception, however, a citizen's own congressman gets high marks. The dichotomy may explain the high reelection success rates of House members who choose to run against Congress.

Despite the frequency of criticism, as expressed in the polls, the media, and common parlance, Congress, as an institution, has worked well over the years. True, it has been touched by every scandal known to the frailties of humankind. Excess and hyperbole have been its first responses to the crises faced by the nation over the years. It has bobbed and weaved to avoid the responsibility for solving crises that persisted. But somehow, some way, Congress eventually managed to rise to the challenge. When the Vietnam War finally ended, it was by congressional action—over the opposition of the executive branch and the refusal of the judicial branch to intercede. When the presidency so fouled its own nest that the whole Republic was imperiled, it was Congress, with a most surprising cast of characters, that restored faith in the ultimate efficacy of government. On the death of presidents or their loss of power, Congress inevitably has filled the vacuum. Congress has indeed taken pride in its primacy, even as it has sometimes refused to accept the responsibilities of primacy. It is unique even in the small family of democracies yet extant in the world.

A cloakroom bromide advises that there are only three ways to leave the Congress, and two of them are very bad: death and defeat. Those who choose the third way frequently write anecdotal books describing the excitement of the Congress. So too was I tempted, because those books are interesting and instructive, but my co-author and I decided that a more structured book about the workings of Congress from a firsthand perspective would better serve the reader who wants to learn more about the American Congress.

The Vietnam War was raging both at home and abroad in 1968 when I was first elected to the Congress of the United States. There seemed no end to the quantity of our resources, both human and material, which that tortured country in far-off Southeast Asia could absorb. At home, assassinations, riots, and bitterly divided political parties led to the election of Richard Nixon as president. And I was elected to the Ninety-first Congress, having ousted the incumbent—the last veteran of the Spanish-American War to hold office—in a difficult primary fight. Washington was the place to solve the problems that were tearing the country apart, so I firmly believed.

The chairman of my first committee was 82 years old; he was first elected with Herbert Hoover. The chairman of the powerful House Rules Committee was 83; when he retired at the end of the Ninety-first Congress, he turned his gavel over to the junior next in line—who was 80. The speaker was a mere 76 years of age, but having led a hard life, he had a cadaverlike look about him that worried us all every time he became too vigorous in gaveling the House to order.

It seemed that those of us who were against the very unpopular war in Vietnam spent the entire term unsuccessfully plotting ways of promoting a debate on the war—even though we knew we did not have enough votes to carry any issue. (Before I had come to Congress, President Lyndon Johnson had taunted the anti-war members in 1964 to vote against the Gulf of Tonkin Resolution if they dared; the resolution, which Johnson used as his authority to greatly expand the war, had passed the Senate with only two dissenting votes. In the House it passed by a thunderous voice vote; five years later House veterans were vying with each other in insisting that they had said "Nay" on the viva voce vote.)

And yet for all those early frustrations, I had no hesitancy in declaring for reelection. When, after two terms, I was gerrymandered out of my safe Democratic district in the city of Chicago, I moved, carpetbags and all, 25

miles to a suburban district that had not elected a Democrat since the Grover
Cleveland landslide of 1892. To no one's surprise except mine, I lost. Instead
of using that happenstance to reappraise my conviction that Congress was
"where it was at," I could hardly wait for two years to go by so that I could
run again. In the interim, I worked for a Chicago law firm. I regained my
seat in the Congress in the post-Watergate election of 1974. (I won by a scant
2,800 votes, my high-water mark in three successful elections in my new
district. In 1976 I won the "landslide" award from my colleagues because
my winning plurality was only 201 votes.)

After working on the Hill for nearly a decade, I resigned from Congress
in 1979 to take a seat on the United States Court of Appeals for the District
of Columbia Circuit. My nomination was controversial, largely because I
advocate gun control. The confirmation proceedings allowed me my first
close (too close for comfort) encounter with the Senate—a body whose
traditions and history are strikingly different from those of the House. On the
other hand, some have commented that my margin of victory in the Senate
(58–31) was my largest ever. As a legislative counsel for Senator Edward
M. Kennedy on the Senate Judiciary Committee, my co-author has seen the
Senate close-up. We have drawn freely on the anecdotes, reminiscences, and
experiences that befell us. The intention, however, is to present a modern
analysis of the Congress as the first branch of government.

ABNER J. MIKVA

INTRODUCTION

T he Congress of today is very different from the Congress of two decades, or even one decade, ago. At that time it huddled in the shadows of the "imperial presidency." Political scientists castigated the Congress for its fiscal irresponsibility, for its glacial legislative process, for its lethargic attention to oversight, for its corrupt campaign finance activities, for its anachronistic committee system, and for its nonexistent party structure. Congress was rated low in national polls. It was common for political scientists to relegate the once proud first branch of government to subordinate status. In 1970 one political scientist had actually proclaimed: "The Chief Executive towers over American politics; he functions at the center of the political state. Congress, like other parts of the overall political system, plays its role in support of the star."*

STRUCTURE OF THE BOOK

There has truly been a resurgence of Congress as a co-equal branch of government. Although only time will tell whether the revival of Congress is due

---

*Leroy N. Rieselbach, ed., *The Congressional System* (Belmont, Calif.: Duxbury Press, 1970), p. 16.

to the prolonged power vacuum in the executive branch, the evidence seems to point in that direction. This nation has experienced in succession three unsuccessful presidents: Richard Nixon, Gerald Ford, and Jimmy Carter. Nixon's name is still anathema in the Congress. Ford is viewed as nice but ineffective, a man who was burdened by an opposition Congress. Carter is regarded with everything from disdain to pity for his incompetence in relating to the legislative process. As an outsider both to Washington and the Democratic party, he had little hope of countering a Congress that understood far better than he the levers of power. But even a president who sustains broad popular support will find, in all likelihood, a Congress reluctant to relinquish the procedural tools it so carefully developed to counter the executive branch, a consensus in support of the president's substantive programs notwithstanding.

History of Congress

This book deals with the history, structure, and functions of Congress. Chapter 1 examines the changes in Congress over the last two decades which have led to the reemergence of the Congress as the first branch of government anticipated by the founders of the country. Chapters 2 and 3 trace the origins of Congress in the prerevolutionary assemblies, the Continental Congress, the Congress of the Confederation, and the Constitutional Convention. This historical perspective is vital to an evaluation of the role of Congress, particularly vis-à-vis the executive branch. The framers of the Constitution anticipated that the Congress would tower above the executive and judicial branches. Despite the verbal and ideological commitment to the premise of "checks and balances," the framers were careful to give Congress the ultimate power to control the purse, to declare wars, to appropriate funds, to override executive vetos, to establish courts, to regulate interstate commerce, to ratify treaties, and to have the ultimate word on judges and other high-level presidential appointees. In short, Congress was given the power to prevail on virtually every policy difference with the executive branch. Indeed, because the founders feared the president would be too weak, a concerted effort was made at the Constitutional Convention to buttress the powers of the office.

Components of Congress

The next five chapters analyze the major structural components of the Congress. Chapters 4 and 5 trace the historical development of the congressional party, the main organizational unit in both houses of the Congress, compare its functions with those of the national and local parties, and examine its integrative role in creating consensus among members of Congress representing constituencies of significantly different interests and perspectives. The chapters examine the nuts-and-bolts of party structure, in particular the role of the leadership, including the speaker, the president of the Senate, the majority and minority leaders and the whips. The leadership structure varies dramatically between the two chambers, particularly with respect to the procedural powers of the House speaker and Senate majority leader. In recent years the congressional parties in both chambers have developed more power as the prestige of their rivals, the committee chairmen, has declined. Nonetheless, as these chapters point out, the party leadership still lacks the weapons (or nerve) to discipline the membership. The challenge of the next decade is to develop a party structure that will be more successful in setting congressional priorities and in minimizing the influence of special-interest groups.

Chapters 6 and 7 examine the pros and cons of the congressional committee system. On the one hand, the committees are essential if Congress is to be co-equal with the executive branch. They permit Congress to specialize in important substantive areas; without this expertise, Congress could not respond effectively to complex, technological national problems. Committee expertise permits the Congress to "check" the executive branch, through its oversight responsibilities. Without the specialized committee staffs, the committees would not be able to compete with the greater staff and financial resources of the administration. Furthermore, the committees provide a rational division of the congressional workload and a system for training new members in the ways of party politics, procedural tricks, and proper etiquette. Finally, the committees provide each member with a soapbox to facilitate reelection. Subcommittee chairmen use congressional hearings to gain national media attention for themselves and their pet issues. Other members use committee assignments to promote benefits for their home district or the special-interest constituencies that form their political base.

On the other hand, committees can be, and traditionally have been, roadblocks to prompt and effective congressional action. By encouraging committee assignments of members with a vested political stake in the substance of the programs within their committee's jurisdiction, committees often represent a parochial outlook that does not serve the national good. Recently the committees have lost much of their immunity from outside congressional pressure. In the House of Representatives, the party caucus and leadership have been given new powers to influence committee activities. In the Senate, there is little disincentive to challenge committee expertise on the floor. Senators frequently, and without hesitation, propose bills as floor amendments that have failed to be favorably reported by the committee—and win. The budget process enacted in 1974, now in full bloom, has contributed significantly to the shift of decision making from the committees to the floor. Finally, the recent development of autonomous subcommittees has contributed to the demise of the power of committee chairmen on the floor of the Congress. These chapters examine the transition of the once omnipotent congressional committee system. Although committees are still fundamentally important to the efficiency of the legislative process, they are no longer the fiefdoms they once were.

Chapter 8 discusses the Hill staff of the Congress, which has witnessed a dramatic increase in number over the last decade. The consequent concern about its role is not without merit. As one senator characterized the aggressiveness of Senate staff: "The Senate is a forum of convenience for Hill staff to legislate." There are four categories of Hill staff. The personal office staff of each member—an administrative assistant, several legislative assistants, a scheduler, a press secretary, legislative correspondents, and mail-room personnel—is a permanent mini-campaign staff, which functions in both the home district and Washington. Usually, also a separate office staff is established in the home district to service constituents, answer mail, perform general legislative work, and most important ensure reelection.

Another category of staff includes the committee and subcommittee staffs, which provide Congress with expertise in various substantive areas. In the Senate, each member is entitled to at least one professional committee staff member for every committee assignment. In the House, members are usually required to rely for such expertise on the staff of the chairman or the ranking minority member—often to their frustration.

The third category of staff includes the General Accounting Office, the Congressional Budget Office, the Congressional Research Service in the Library of Congress, the Office of Technology Assessment, and the Legal and Legislative Counsel offices, which provide essential backup services for congressional activities. Finally, there are the leadership staffs. Serving the party structure in the caucus through the Policy and Steering committees, the leadership staffs provide the information, both political and substantive, to permit the parties to develop the information networks that are integral to their ability to manage floor debate. The leadership staffs of both the majority and minority sides are quite small, compared with the committee staffs, and lack sufficient resources to implement an aggressive approach to legislative activities. Because the axiom that staff means power is widely acknowledged, it is unlikely that more staff members will be allocated to the leadership by Congress, for that action would only challenge the committee and individual prerogatives of the members. Some political scientists argue that the deliberative functions of the Congress have been inhibited by the growth of an entrepreneurial Hill staff. However, the growth of a professional Hill staff has probably helped, more than hindered, the development of an effective Congress.

Functions of Congress

The balance of the book evaluates the main functions of Congress. Chapters 9 and 10 examine the legislative process and trace the stages in the development and implementation of legislation. Chapters 11 and 12 look at the congressional power of the purse. The last three chapters examine the role of congressmen as representatives of the folks back home, and the impact of electoral politics and campaign finance laws on congressional behavior. Less central congressional responsibilities, such as the ratification of treaties and the confirmation of judicial nominees, are treated only in passing. The main thesis of chapters 9 to 15 is that Congress works well as an institution in performing these three functions—noting, of course, that improvements can still be made.

The chapters on the legislative process trace the development of a bill from conception to enactment and from implementation through judicial review and congressional oversight. The objectives of these chapters are threefold. The first, and most mundane, is to provide a nuts-and-bolts description of how a bill becomes law. The second objective is to underline that the legislative cycle does *not* stop with the presidential signature. Rather, throughout the existence of a statute, its substantive impact derives from external political forces. The third objective is to demonstrate that the enactment of any legislation, even the most minor, is a miracle. After surviving many procedural and political hurdles that may take years, a bill may pass both houses only to die in conference or be rejected by the president. Even when signed into law, a bill can languish on the statute books, without any congressional or executive interest.

Chapters 11 and 12 examine the congressional power of the purse, through which Congress can control virtually every activity in the federal government. Although most outside observers consider the enactment of substantive new legislation to be the primary activity of Congress, the bulk of congressional time and energy is devoted to establishing the national budget, raising revenues, appropriating funds, and overseeing executive branch activities. In past decades Congress served more to initiate new programs than to oversee those already in existence. Perhaps as a result of growing inflation, unemployment, and a strong public demand for a reduction in the size of government, later congresses have given far greater attention to wielding the budgetary meat-ax and reallocating a smaller amount of funds among different priorities. Perhaps the most significant contribution of the congresses of the 1980s will be their intensity of commitment to fiscal matters.

Chapter 11 reviews the development and implementation of the new budget process. As pointed out earlier, the new procedures have impacted dramatically on the congressional power structure. More important, they have established a centralized budgetary mechanism to allow the examination of spending in relation to revenues. That the new system has contributed to fiscal "responsibility"—or perhaps, more accurately, to fiscal conservatism—cannot be doubted.

Chapter 12 focuses on the power of taxation and the revenue committees. It also discusses the "new congressional oversight," whereby committees have taken a new interest in overhauling major regulatory programs and overseeing agency decision making. The new oversight is best exemplified by the renewed vigor Congress has displayed in influencing the development of foreign and defense policies.

Finally chapters 13, 14, and 15 examine the role of congressmen as representatives. Most members vigorously fulfill this role as it is the key to their reelection. The new campaign finance laws and the congressional perquisites—the frank, free trips home, and staff resources—combine to make incumbents difficult to defeat. Nonetheless, despite the high rates of incumbent reelection in congressional elections, most congressmen are paranoid about their chances for reelection and devote much of their time and resources to maintaining high visibility in the home district. In contrast, senators, who have easier access to the media and who have to run less frequently—but who have slightly less impressive reelection rates—tend to focus on the home district as a less central, although still important, part of their office function. Members seek committee assignments primarily with a view to representing the home district. For example, members from urban areas want committee assignments that will promote urban development. They propose amendments that will help their constituents. Party leaders do not have the discipline or the incentives to compete with the clear rewards of making the interests of the home district paramount.

Perhaps the greatest dilemma faced by an elected representative is whether to vote his conscience or the will of his constituents. Although each congressman wrestles with the question, inevitably the choice between the needs of home district constituents and the general national good is easy. With rare exceptions, congressmen vote with the home district in the absence of arm twisting by the president or a special-interest group. Theories of pluralism justify this parochialism by positing that the best outcomes derive when district interests are paramount. However, these theories fail to recognize the disproportionate power certain regions acquire by virtue of their members' seniority or as a result of the inordinate financial leverage of certain well-funded groups.

Many congressmen have national constituencies as well to help them gain reelection. Thus, a special-interest voter in North Carolina helps a candidate in Illinois when they agree on certain "hot" issues like abortion or gun control.

These special-interest groups provide needed funds to pit challengers against incumbents or to help an incumbent in trouble. The "moral majority" embodied by the National Conservative Political Action Committee (called NICPAC) targeted certain candidates for destruction in the 1980 election because they disagreed with the NICPAC position—and was successful. Because of the increased reliance on media to gain election or reelection, the clout of well-funded special interests is far greater than the actual votes they can muster. Likewise, the political action committees of wealthy interests, like corporations or labor unions, provide additional leverage to sway key congressional votes. With increasing and distressing frequency, a member's vote on an issue can be correlated with a contribution of PAC money.

It is concluded that, on the whole, congressmen know their self-interests and represent their constituents well—sometimes too well in pressing for relief of local concerns at the expense of the national good. However, the high marks congressmen get for fulfilling their constitutional mandate in representing those who elected them must be tempered by the inordinate influence played by those with access to special-interest funds.

Nonethical behavior in Congress is more likely to be exposed than in the past and less likely to be tolerated. While Congress has enacted numerous reforms in ethics laws and codes, it is still loath to pursue violations vigorously.

GOALS OF THE BOOK

The goal of this book is twofold. Its first purpose is to give the reader a comprehensive sense of how the Congress works. Its ambition is not to present any startling revelations but rather to present a thorough description of the United States Congress—its history, its major structural units, and the three essential functions it performs.

The second goal is to give the reader a sense of the dynamics of the Congress, the dynamics that influenced its past and the dynamics that will function in its future. A thesis that pervades every chapter is that, basically, Congress works, and works well, as an institution. Throughout its history its procedures and practices have responded, sometimes slowly, sometimes with surprising speed, to constitutional and policy problems that impeded its ability to act effectively. When Speaker Joe Cannon's autocratic powers became, in the century's first decade, unrepresentative roadblocks to progressive social change, he was cut down to size, and as a consequence the speaker's authority was considerably diminished. When committee chairmen allowed their seniority to deny political consensus, the party caucus was empowered to expel them from the chair and challenge the autonomy of the committee. Roundly and correctly criticized for fiscal irresponsibility, the Congress responded with passage of the Budget and Impoundment Control Act. When the public demanded a counter to the president's unpopular foreign wars, Congress relinquished its passive foreign policy role and quickly adopted numerous procedures to ensure co-equal status.

Of course, self-interest is not absent from congressional motivation. It is not coincidental that the campaign finance laws protect the incumbent or that the ethics laws are ineffectual. However, when the need arises to buttress the legislative branch in its role as an effective check on the executive branch, the Congress acts aggressively and jealously to protect its own prerogatives and thus fulfills the legislative role anticipated by the framers of the Constitution.

ONE

REVOLUTION IN CONGRESS

The full impact of the revolution in Congress that began in 1973 is not yet clear. The rules, practices, traditions, and norms adhered to just a decade ago are no longer followed. The old power structure has been fragmented and reorganized, and the struggles to grab that power continue. The technology of congressional elections today differs from that of a few decades ago, and legislative "reforms" have radically altered the source and availability of campaign funds. In countless other big and little ways, the Congress has changed. Indeed, in understanding today's Congress a text about the Congress of the 1960s is as helpful as a text describing the Congress of the 1860s.

Ignited at the beginning of the Ninety-third Congress in 1973, the revolution achieved full force in the following years. As with most major changes in congressional personnel and procedures, the internal changes were generated largely by external events. The single most important event was the Watergate scandal, which involved the president and other top government officials in criminal activities and toppled the so-called imperial presidency.[1] It is ironic that the president who had successfully pushed, more than any of his predecessors, the constitutional powers of the presidency to—and sometimes beyond—its limits should have been the instrument of its decline and the reemergence of the Congress. President Nixon acted as a powerful catalyst to unite a disunited Congress. Prompted by the congressional investigation of President Nixon, public pride in the legislative body replaced public contempt. Stimulated by the national disgrace, Congress enacted long-needed reforms that restored its co-equal status. The resignation in disgrace, first of Vice-President Spiro Agnew, who pled "no-contest" to violation of the federal tax laws, and then of President Richard Nixon, who faced a serious threat of impeachment, set the stage for a dramatic Democratic sweep of the House and Senate in the 1974 election. The legislators of 1975 were reform-minded. Their mandate was to shake the status quo, to deny old alignments, and to make the system work.

The Watergate scandal shifted public scrutiny from the universally decried poor performance of the Congress, particularly in the foreign policy areas. The entire Congress had been criticized for failing to debate, and to gain control over, that extremely divisive and unpopular war in Southeast Asia. After overwhelmingly ratifying involvement in the Vietnam War in 1964 in the Gulf of Tonkin Resolution (a brilliantly orchestrated coup by President Lyndon Baines Johnson), Congress had stood passively by as the executive escalated a costly war, costly in lives and money. Watergate highlighted for the nation that the Congress, which had the constitutional power to declare war and appropriate funds for the military, had abdicated responsibility for foreign policy to the executive branch. Moreover, the Congress had failed in a variety of other areas to check the presidency. It had refused to follow budget procedures to correlate federal expenditures to federal revenue and looked passively on as the president impounded monies appropriated by the Congress to fund important social programs. Moreover, it had failed to oversee the activities of the executive branch, which cavalierly ignored or defied legislative mandates. Few political scientists defended the congressional performance. A tremendous shake-up in the congressional power structure was long overdue.

The immediate changes were most noticeable in the House of Representatives. Wilbur Mills, a behemoth of congressional power, both as chairman of the Ways and Means Committee and as a most senior Democrat of great legislative and parliamentary skill, chose that time to escalate a pantry drinking problem into a major national scandal. In what sounds like a grade B movie plot, Mills was detained by the authorities when, in 1974, his companion of the evening jumped into the Tidal Basin while both were "under the influence." Later Chairman Mills was discovered waiting backstage in a Boston theater while his companion performed her striptease. At that point, his drinking problem came out of the pantry, and it became apparent that the power and political base of Wilbur Mills was no longer a factor. When he chose not to run for reelection as chairman of the Ways and Means Committee, the path was clear for the Democratic caucus of the Ninety-fourth Congress to strip the omnipotent Ways and Means Committee of some of its carefully nurtured roles.

But that was only the beginning. Using a procedure that had previously never been effective, the Democratic caucus ousted three senior committee chairmen. Whereas heretofore tradition had automatically elected the most senior committeeman as chairman, now the caucus voted on such nominees by secret ballot. Even Wayne Hays, chairman of the House Administration Committee and the powerful Democratic Campaign Committee, who had total say over the budgets and allowances of both the members and the committees, was forced to two ballots before he could retain his chairmanship, a post he subsequently was forced to resign because of his own scandal involving sex and staff. Philip Burton of California was elected chairman of the caucus, giving the reformers and the other new members who had supported him a strong ally and spokesman in the House councils. The House Un-American Activities Committee, long an embarrassment to the civil libertarians in the Congress but a citadel of patriotism to its supporters, was voted out of existence and its functions were transferred to the House Judiciary Committee.

The most important products of the revolution were not the immediate political repercussions, however, but the vast and sweeping structural changes in the Congress as an institution.

FROM GENTLEMEN TO MAVERICKS

The student of a decade ago would have learned that the Senate was a "Gentlemen's Club." In his famous essay on the folkways of the Senate, Professor Donald Matthews described the frustration of a junior senator who was admonished by his mentors to be "seen and not heard":

> If he gives in to the pressure for conformity coming from the folkways, he
> must postpone the achievement of his liberal objectives. If he presses for
> these objectives regardless of his junior position, he will become labelled
> as a nonconformist, lose popularity with his colleagues and, in most cases,
> his legislative effectiveness as well.[2]

But today the norms of the Gentlemen's Club—reciprocity, courtesy, deference to committee expertise—are largely nostalgic memories of a more genteel past. Freshman senators of the majority party expect not only to chair a subcommittee but to use the subcommittee as a forum to gain national acclaim and even to assert independence from party leadership. In 1957 Bill

Samuel Taliaferro
Rayburn, "Mr. Sam,"
Democrat from Texas,
was speaker of the
House of Representatives
for seventeen years.

Proxmire, a young Democrat from Wisconsin, was elected to replace the infamous Joseph McCarthy. Senate elders shook their heads in disbelief at the maverick when he chose to lead filibusters on the floor.[3] Proxmire even had the audacity to chastise Majority Leader Lyndon Johnson on the floor for his efforts to "dominate" the Senate.[4] Today junior senators participate in, and even initiate, filibusters without anyone so much as blinking an eye. Even Senate leaders no longer adhere to the code of courtesy. Jesse Helms of North Carolina prides himself on the blitzkrieg tactics he uses on the floor of the Senate to spotlight his principles and defeat his enemies.[5] Although House Speaker Sam Rayburn's admonition to junior members "to get along, go along"[6] still is viewed as wise advice, the benefits that party leadership can bestow are insufficient to overcome the political costs incurred in bucking powerful constituencies. To be considered a party maverick was once a useful political characterization. Now virtually all members of Congress are mavericks.

THE DEMISE OF COMMITTEES

The congressional committee, and particularly its chairman, at one time had firm control over the destiny of a piece of legislation. Today, the committee system is a mere shell of its former self. In 1963 a congressman described the committee system:

The committee offers a good example of complete and total dictatorship in action. The chairman runs the committee with an iron hand. He puts people on subcommittees, takes them off, and announces transfers at will. About a year ago a subcommittee was considering something to which he was strongly opposed, but which seemed likely to pass. Just as the committee opened, in walked four additional members of the full committee, two Democrats and two Republicans. Without forewarning to the subcommittee chairman, the chairman of the full committee had added four men to the group. In less than an hour there was to be a vote on a very important issue about which the four could not possibly have been fully informed. The chairman assumed that all four additions would vote with him against the legislation. It looked as though he had won until, much to his distress, one of the four broke ranks. But the action in increasing the subcommittee size was taken solely and arbitrarily by the chairman. Subcommittee chairmen do a lot of grumbling, but when the chips are down they vote with the chairman.[7]

Committee chairmen no longer possess autocratic powers. Although they still retain great influence, chairmen are not empowered to appoint subcommittee chairmen, abolish subcommittees, or unilaterally determine committee agendas. Instead, this authority is exercised by the consent of the party caucus in each committee. The post-Watergate freshman members of the House of Representatives so coveted subcommittee autonomy that the House in 1975 adopted a Subcommittee Bill of Rights, which provided, among other things, that a chairman could not deprive a subcommittee of its jurisdiction over legislation. Committee chairmen are no longer immune from challenge.

WEAKENING OF THE SENIORITY SYSTEM

Prior to the reforms of the 1970s, the most senior congressional members monopolized power in the Congress. Ever since the 1920s, the seniority system had ensured that only the oldest members of the Congress controlled the key leadership posts and committee chairmanships. The rank-and-file congressional membership had little, if any, opportunity to affect national policies.

The reforms of the 1970s "spread the action" to junior members not only by giving the subcommittees new powers but by enhancing the role of the party caucuses and leadership, particularly in the House of Representatives. The House Democratic Caucus adopted new procedures to pressure committee chairmen to adhere to the will of the majority rank-and-file and to control the floor agenda. The speaker also gained new authority to influence committee assignments and determine legislative priorities.

"It's a hell of a way to run a railroad"

From *The Herblock Book* (Beacon Press, 1952)

In short, the revolution of the 1970s resulted in a redistribution of power in the 1980s: The power previously exercised by committee-chairmen is now shared with the subcommittee chairmen, the speaker, and the party caucus. Which power base will prevail is not yet clear.

NEW ERA OF FISCAL RESPONSIBILITY

The greatest change in the power structure in Congress was precipitated by the Congressional Budget and Impoundment Control Act of 1974.[8] Prior to the Budget Act, Congress had no centralized mechanism for setting a national budget. The Appropriations committees set spending levels, and the tax committees (the House Ways and Means Committee and the Senate Finance Committee) raised revenues almost without coordination. As the left hand of Congress often did not know what the right was doing, the result was fiscal chaos. Because Congress could not develop an effective budget process, despite repeated efforts, the executive branch assumed the key role in establishing the federal budget. When Congress found itself on the verge of losing control of the federal purse strings, a power it had cherished since its earliest days, it was prompted to enact the Congressional Budget Act, which transformed a hectic, irresponsible fiscal system into a powerful budgetary machine. This act created a new Budget Committee in each chamber to establish spending and revenue levels. When approved by Congress as a whole in the first and second Budget Resolutions, these limits become binding each fiscal year on the activities of each congressional committee. This new mechanism allows the adjustment of spending and revenue levels in a rational, focused way. In addition, the Congressional Budget office was established to give Congress the information and analytic tools to set a national budget. As it blossomed and matured in the Ninety-seventh Congress, the budget process proved to be an extremely powerful, and perhaps dangerous, tool, for it not only achieves fiscal responsibility but also allows the implementation of entire economic and social programs with record speed.

The main political victims of the new budgetary system were the congressional "prestige" committees. A decade ago political scientists spoke in awe of the prestige House committees—the Appropriations and the Ways and Means committees—whose power derived from their iron grip on the federal purse. Before the Budget Act, the Appropriations Committee had the exclusive power to allocate monies to be executive branch. It was an honor to allocate monies to the executive branch. It was an honor to be selected by the party leadership for membership on the Appropriations Committee. Not only did such an assignment enhance reelection prospects; it also symbolized the esteem with which a member was held by his colleagues. It was sheer joy for a congressman from a farm state to be appointed to the Appropriations subcommittee that controlled agricultural subsidies. Created by the First Congress, the Ways and Means Committee, which raises revenue for the House and to a large extent for the Congress as well, was another coveted committee assignment. Through much of the nineteenth century its chairman was the majority floor leader in the House. For years its Democratic members were the Committee on Committees, which allocated committee assignments until the creation of the Democratic Policy and Steering Committee in 1974. Only those congressmen who were loyal to the party and who came from "safe" districts were considered for a committee slot. Under the chairmanship of empire-minded Wilbur Mills, the committee gobbled up such diverse areas as health care and social security in addition to the traditional revenue measures. The analogous committee assignments in the Senate—the Appropriations and the Finance committees—were similarly coveted.

The passage of the Budget Act severely damaged the autonomy of the prestige committees. Some commentators argue that the once proud Appropriations committees, on some occasions, are now mere rubber stamps of the budget resolutions, which set spending ceilings for every program in the federal government. The resolutions not only set revenue levels but establish explicit directives as to the necessary taxation measures. Although the taxation and appropriations committees remain free to thumb their noses at the budget resolutions, at least in the early stages of the budget process, they are nonetheless under extreme pressure to adhere to the budget resolutions once they have been passed by the Congress. The prestige committees have been toppled from their pedestals.

Although theoretically the budget process is consistent with the jurisdiction of the substantive standing committees (committees that have jurisdiction over specific spending programs), it has become so powerful that it threatens their autonomy as well. Although the Budget committees have no authority to initiate legislation or create new programs, they exert external pressure on the committees to change (or, more accurately, decrease) the size and substance of programs previously immune from general congressional scrutiny. Left to itself, for example, the Veterans' Affairs Committee would have no political incentive to alter the extremely costly system of veterans' benefits. Yet the pressure of the budget process is sufficient to persuade the committee to cut back on its most sacrosanct programs. Of paramount significance, the budget process also altered the entire legislative process. By establishing deadlines for considering budgetary measures, it eliminated the senatorial filibuster for them. Thus senators can no longer propose nongermane amendments or engage in filibusters even though budget measures have the same, or greater, impact than most legislative proposals.

The impact of the budget process in transforming the power structure of Congress cannot be overemphasized. By creating a centralized and expeditious system for setting national budget priorities—a system that circumvents the usual congressional roadblocks of committee jurisdiction and special-interest groups—the budget process accelerates the effective implementation of perceived national mandates. It has partially eroded the time-honored jurisdictional turf of committees.

REAPPRAISAL OF
THE CONGRESSIONAL PARTY

The congressional party system has also experienced substantial change. Historically, the party has been omnipresent but rarely omnipotent. Although political scientists agree that the party is the most important single influence on an individual lawmaker's behavior, they are quick to point out that the party in general is weak and ineffective: "Political power in Congress, all observers agree, is highly decentralized."[9] Indeed, since the earliest years of the Republic, political parties have been viewed with ambivalence. Unlike their counterparts in the British Parliament, the party leadership in Congress has relatively little clout to implement its will.

In the post-Watergate era, the congressional party has developed new powers, particularly in the House of Representatives. The party caucus now elects, by secret ballot, the chairmen of the committees. Through its power to instruct the Rules Committee (which determines when and how a bill may be considered by the entire House of Representatives), it can arrange to expedite and influence the course of legislation. Moreover, by chairing the Democratic Policy and Steering Committee, the speaker has great leverage over committee assignments and can control the congressional calendar. On the Senate side, the role of the party leadership has been less pronounced historically. With its smaller size, the Senate has tolerated greater levels of insubordination, egotism, and individualism than has the House. Senate leaders reign by virtue of cunning, persuasion, better access to information, and crass Machiavellian tactics.

Efforts to revive the congressional party have had limited impact. The national party all but ignores the congressional party—and the feeling is mutual. Each party conducts separate fund-raising activities for congressional seats. Both the congressional and national parties ignore the local parties (except every ten years when redistricting becomes a top priority). The Democratic and Republican parties are integrated units in title only. Because the national party historically has not consulted its elected representatives in forming the national platform, the platform is consequently irrelevant to the legislative agenda. Although reforms are under way, the national party traditionally has not helped members of Congress raise money, forcing them to rely on such external funding sources as direct-mail operations, special-interest political action committees (PACs), and occasionally local party units. The new campaign finance laws, modified several times throughout the 1970s, give PACs disproportionate leverage in obtaining their preferred legislation. How can the party compete for a member's attention?

Although the congressional party can offer few incentives to encourage loyalty, it does have the ability to penalize wayward members. The lack of party discipline has been a serious problem for twenty years. As Professor Charles Clapp said in 1963:

> The congressional parties not only fall far short of being well-disciplined, powerful organizations, possessing the means for permanent enforcement of sanctions against recalcitrant members, but the leaders are reluctant to move against the rebels, generally preferring whenever possible to attribute the deviation to district problems faced by the legislator rather than to reluctance to cooperate on an issue.[10]

The first session of the Ninety-seventh Congress in 1981 witnessed a greater sensitivity to party loyalty than had been seen in recent decades. Senate Democrats—known more for their dissension than cohesion—watched admiringly as a newly elected popular president, with a wide national electoral victory, transformed the Republican party into a military wedge that would have made even Caesar proud—that is, difficult to penetrate and no defections. Because of the new senatorial discipline, President Ronald Reagan's economic package passed in the record time of six months. The Democrats, demoralized by their new minority status in the Senate, began to use the party caucus more effectively to forge compromises within the party instead of bickering publicly among themselves on the floor. (The unity of the Republican party dissolved somewhat in the second session as conservative and liberal wings joined forces in concern over the high Reagan budget deficits and growing unemployment, leaving many observers to conclude that congressional party unity is a short-lived phenomenon.)

On the House side, some saw a need to enforce party discipline in that diverse body. Political commentator David Broder opined that there were many options available to the speaker to deal with Democratic defectors. "The Democrats," he wrote, "do not have to choose between being rigid seminarians of doctrine and discipline or being a bunch of supine dopes."[11] Some suggested that the Democratic caucus should strip recalcitrant Democrats of their committee assignments and chairmanships. As Congressman Gillis Long (Louisiana) pointed out, the seeming impunity with which certain conservative Democrats ignored the demands of party loyalty made it harder for others from the same state or region to vote with their party.[12]

In the next decade, it is likely that the congressional party will see a renaissance. With renewed vigor, the plight of the party has become a cause célèbre, generating much debate in both political and intellectual circles. The parties have begun to raise funds for members in trouble and to train challengers to vulnerable incumbents. The national parties are working more closely with members of Congress with respect to both the legislative agenda and political questions. The toughest challenge ahead will be defining the limits of party discipline.

THE NEW ENTHUSIASM
FOR OVERSIGHT

Perhaps no change has been more pronounced than the new congressional enthusiasm for congressional "oversight"—the process by which Congress examines the manner in which legislative programs are being administered. Ten years ago Congress was widely criticized for its spasmodic efforts at overseeing the activities of the executive branch.[13] Political scientists devised a number of theories to explain this phenomenon. One popular hypothesis, "the iron triangle"[14] doctrine, attributed this inertia to a mutual interest of committee members, agencies, and constituents in not "rocking the boat." Others argued that the political incentive to ferret out waste or expose idiotic policies was negative. In recent years, however, significant change has occurred. Congress has developed into a vigilant, if overeager, watchdog of the executive branch. Oversight is pursued with a vengeance, generated, in part, by a new perception of government as too large and, in part, by the political credits a member can gain from helping a constituent aggrieved by an adverse or infuriating agency decision.[15]

The new focus on oversight has dramatically affected the direction of government policies. Congressional committees no longer limit themselves to examining the minutiae of agency activities; they examine fundamental agency issues as well. The passage of the Airline Deregulation Act[16] in 1978 marked the first deregulation of a major American industry. Deregulation of the trucking, banking, and railroad industries quickly followed. The legislative veto has become an increasingly popular mechanism (if somewhat constitutionally suspect) by which Congress controls the individual exercise of discretion by agency officials.

Congress also began to review the activities of two agencies that were previously "untouchable." For the first time the Central Intelligence Agency (CIA) and the Federal Bureau of Investigation (FBI) were subjected to oversight hearings.

The "new oversight" has impacted extensively on foreign policy. Prior to the Vietnam War, Congress took a back seat to the executive branch in foreign policy matters. The president publicly pronounced the Congress incompetent and unfit to mold foreign policy decisions, and Congress did not so much as object. The Pentagon routinely expended funds for new weapons systems and for aid to foreign nations without notifying Congress in advance. Funds targeted by congressional committees for certain projects were blithely reprogrammed by the military with nary a by-your-leave.

Efforts of the Congress to gain control of foreign policy matters were shrugged off by the executive. However, after the Vietnam War, particularly between 1973 and 1976, the Congress adopted a large number of procedural tools to ensure its role in the foreign policy area. The War Powers Act[17] requires the president to consult with Congress on any decision to introduce American armed forces into hostilities or potential hostilities without a declaration of war or other explicit congressional authorization. In 1974 Congress passed legislation to ensure that the sale of military weapons to foreign nations met with its approval[18] and provided a legislative veto to be used to prevent the sale of nuclear materials to countries that failed to adhere to the nonproliferation treaty.[19] Also, at this time, Congress imposed specific prohibitions on foreign aid to nations that violated human rights (Chile and the Soviet Union) and to countries involved in civil wars where Congress felt American intervention would be unwise (Angola).[20] The committees adopted more rigorous procedures to prevent the Pentagon from thwarting its directives by shifting funds between budgetary functions without congressional approval. In short, Congress assumed a new aggressive role in the foreign policy area, demoting the executive branch from a superior position to that of co-equal.

CAMPAIGN "REFORMS"

Finally, congressional elections differ dramatically from their predecessors of a decade ago. The most important factor in any campaign is money. Without it, challengers are unable to gain name recognition. As a result of campaign finance legislation,[21] incumbents are more likely to be reelected. The strict $1,000-a-person limit placed on individual contributions has greatly impeded the financial ability of a candidate to challenge an incumbent. The legislation redistributed the source of political power from the party and individual donors to the political action committees (PACs), and thereby enhanced the exercise of power in the halls of Congress by well-funded private interests. The PACs, established by special-interest groups including corporations and labor unions to funnel money to candidates for Congress, have enjoyed phenomenal growth and have resisted attempts at limitation.

In addition to the new campaign laws, congressional perquisites are better designed to facilitate reelection. Congressmen are far better staffed than they were ten years ago and much more likely to have large district offices. Most offices have their own press secretaries. More than ever before, every congressional office is a mini-political campaign operation, making removal of an incumbent extremely difficult. Although President Reagan's exceptionally long coattails in the 1980 election created shock waves in the Congress by unseating considerable numbers of incumbents, particularly in the Senate, the statistical trends demonstrate the unlikelihood of defeating a well-entrenched incumbent.

TWO

ORIGINS OF CONGRESS

T he role of the Congress in the constitutional scheme of government is rooted in its origins in early colonial governments, in the role played by the early Continental congresses and the Congress of the Confederation, and in the new state constitutions drafted after the Declaration of Independence.

In light of these roots, it is not surprising that the members of the Constitutional Convention expected the legislature to be the dominant branch. During the colonial period, the popular assemblies provided the main vehicle for popular expression and resistance to royal authority. On the adoption of the Declaration of Independence, the states drafted constitutions giving the legislatures almost unlimited powers. On the national level, the only political institution between 1774 and 1789 was a Congress. There was no independent executive or judiciary. In fact, the early congresses performed functions now thought of as primarily executive: conducting war, managing foreign affairs, providing for national defense, even running the day-to-day details of a national government.

The interesting historical question is why (or whether) the founding fathers made any effort to check the activities of the legislature. To maintain the separation of powers as the foundation of liberty and freedom is, of course, one reason. Another reason may be the failure of the Congress of the Confederation to preserve the peace or promote commerce. However, despite their professed dedication to the doctrine of separation of powers, articulated so eloquently in the *Federalist Papers,* the real answer may be that the authors of the Constitution did not try very hard to establish a truly balanced form of government.

The framers of the Constitution expected that one branch, the legislative, would be more equal than the rest. They readily acknowledged that the legislative branch would "necessarily predominate"[1] because, as James Madison said in the *Federalist Papers*, "the Legislative Department is everywhere extending the sphere of its activity, and drawing all power into its impetuous vortex."[2] Thus it was no coincidence, although indeed symbolic of the preeminent role that Congress was expected to play, that the legislature was the first branch discussed in depth during the constitutional debates and the first to be established by the Constitution.

During the first hundred years of constitutional democracy, political commentators emphasized and analyzed the dominant role played by the legislature relative to the other branches. In the early nineteenth century, French historian Alexis de Tocqueville described the subordinate role of the president to the Congress: "Struggle between President and legislature is bound to be unequal for the latter, if it sticks to its plan, is always able to overcome any resistance he can put up."[3] Almost a century later, a then unknown political scientist at Princeton University, looking with despair at the seemingly impotent executive branch, argued that Congress was predominant "over its so-called coordinate branches."[4] Woodrow Wilson concluded that the vast array of powers Congress possessed under the Constitution quickly constituted it "the dominant, nay, the irresistible power of the federal system, relegating some of the chief balances of the Constitution to an insignificant role in the 'literary theory' of our institutions."[5]

That the framers of the Constitution expected the legislature to be supreme startles most students of American government, who learn almost as a catechism that the Constitution established three branches of government—the legislative, the executive, and the judiciary—with separate, distinct, and roughly equal powers. Each branch was delegated sufficient power to check the abuse of power by the other two branches. This well-known doctrine of "separation of powers" was popularized by Baron de Montesquieu, in his treatise *Spirit of the Laws*. He stated that tyranny could best be avoided by preventing the accumulation of all powers, legislative, executive, and judicial, in the same hands. The chief proponents of the Constitution, during the debate over its adoption, relied on the celebrated Montesquieu doctrine[6] to justify the need for the constitutional distribution of power between three branches.

They argued that the separation of power would protect individual liberties in the newly formed federal government: Ambition would counteract ambition and those who administer each branch would have the "necessary constitutional means and personal motives to resist enroachments of others."[7]

In part, of course, the authors of the Constitution truly believed, with an almost religious fervor, that a balanced government of three equal branches was the best means to protect the public rights from governmental abuse. They were devoted progeny of eighteenth-century European Enlightenment,[8] which relied on the Montesquieu thesis as one of its centerpieces. Moreover, the belief in balanced government was firmly rooted in English and colonial history. In England, the celebrated freedom of the English people was a product of the balanced power of kings, lords, and commons, each representing an order of society; and in colonial governments, built on the same model, the royal governor, the council, and the assembly became the rough equivalents of kings, lords, and commons.[9]

However, even the most vehement advocates of a separation of powers and checks and balances believed that, in practice, the legislature would predominate. John Adams, for example, boasted to John Taylor in 1814 about the "complicated refinement of balances" inherent in the new federal scheme of government. He listed the eight balances:

> In the first place, eighteen states and some territories are balanced against the national government. . . . In the second place the House of Representatives is balanced against the Senate, the Senate against the House. In the third place, the Executive authority is, *in some degree*, balanced against the legislative. In the fourth place, the judicial power is balanced against the House, the Senate, the Executive power, and the state governments. In the fifth place, the Senate is balanced against the President in all appointments to office, and in all treaties. . . . In the sixth place, the people hold in their hands the balance against their own representatives, by biennial . . . election. In the seventh place, the legislatures of the several states are balanced against the Senate by sextennial elections. In the eighth place, the electors are balanced against the people in their choice of the President. Here is a complicated refinement of balances, which for anything I recollect, is an invention of our own and peculiar to us."[10] (emphasis added)

This passage indicates John Adams' skepticism about the effectiveness of checks and balances, since he qualified with the words "in some degree" only the ability of the executive to check the legislative. Moreover, in the *Federalist Papers*, both James Madison and Alexander Hamilton spelled out with great pains the special precautions the authors of the Constitution took to check the powers of the legislature, conceding that it would probably ultimately predominate.[11]

The concern of the founding fathers over an omnipotent Congress and their felt need to buttress the executive branch against legislative encroachment is particularly ironic given the derision to which Congress has been subjected in the last few decades. No institution has come under more attack in recent years for impotence, awkwardness, and general ineffectiveness. Some have called it the "sapless branch."[12] Others have lambasted Congress for the fragmentation of power that prevents effective and prompt response to modern problems. In 1972 former Senator Frank Church commented on the inability of Congress to compete with the imperial presidency: "Thirty years of marathon warfare have nearly transformed the presidency into a Caesardom. Should that exalted role remain unchallenged by a subservient Congress, the American Republic will go the way of Rome."[13] On the other hand Lloyd Cutler, former general counsel for President Carter, analogized the presidency to Gulliver bound by strings imposed by Congress and blamed the constitutional system of checks and balances for the inability of the nation to respond to national problems.[14] Perhaps political scientist Richard Fenno made the most poignant commentary on the low esteem in which Congress is held by pointing out that most candidates run for Congress "by running against it."[15]

The significance of the congressional struggle to reemerge as a co-equal branch of government can be understood only in the context of the supremacy of the legislative branch in the early years of American history. In providing this historical context, this chapter traces the development of the First and Second Continental Congress, the Congress of the Confederation, and the early state legislatures. The following chapter examines the powers given to Congress by the Constitutional Convention, and reviews the early accomplishments of the First Congress under the Constitution.

THE FIRST CONTINENTAL CONGRESS

The formal history of the Congress began more than 200 years ago on September 5, 1774, when delegates from twelve American colonies (Georgia was not represented) met in Philadelphia to form the First Continental Congress. The meeting was prompted by British legislation, the Coercive Acts, which had punished the town of Boston for the Tea Party by closing its port and had altered the constitutional charter of Massachusetts by giving the British governor far more power, at the expense of the colonial assembly, than he had previously enjoyed.[16] The First Continental Congress, which remained in existence for only a month and a half, marked the first step toward the establishment of a permanent Congress fifteen years later in 1789.

The meeting of the First Continental Congress signified the first successful attempt to unify the colonies in some form of ongoing transcolonial government. The idea of a intercolonial parliamentary union was not new. In 1643 the New England Confederation, a regional version of the concept, was established, but it was designed primarily to meet military goals.[17] From 1686 to 1689, James II united the New England colonies administratively in the Dominion of New England, but in doing so he abolished all colonial legislative assemblies. The first proposal for a nationwide union, made by William Penn in 1697, was never seriously considered by the various colonies because each was jealous of its autonomy. The British convened the Albany Congress[18] to unite the colonies during the French and Indian War, but Benjamin Franklin's Albany Plan for unification of the colonies in political and economic matters was unanimously rejected. In 1765 nine of the thirteen colonies united briefly in the Stamp Act Congress to deny Parliament's right to tax the colonies because the colonies had no representation in that body. Although short-lived, this Congress marked the first time that the colonies convened to accomplish nonmilitary goals. Thus, although the advantages of a temporary colonial union were firmly rooted in early political thought, and indeed had been experimented with briefly on a few occasions, no permanent colonial union had been undertaken.

When the colonies adopted resolutions calling for the establishment of the First Continental Congress, they intended it to serve primarily as a mouthpiece in dealing with the growing impasse with London. It was originally designed to be a nongovernmental, nonlegislative entity of limited duration and mandate. Nonetheless, the membership of the First Continental Congress ensured that it would be not only a sophisticated legislative entity but also one that would maintain the respect of its constituents while assertively exercising broad powers. The delegates to the First Continental Congress had learned the art of politics, for the most part, in the colonial assemblies—the only directly elected branches of most colonial governments. Of the fifty-seven delegates, forty-two had been, or were, members of those houses. In general, they were highly educated: More than half had been educated in colleges in America or abroad; one-third were lawyers, and most were men of considerable wealth. Many held important political positions in the colonies. At least eleven had been speakers of colonial assemblies, two had been governors, and six had been judges in colonial courts. John Adams, a delegate to the convention and later the second president of the United States, described those assembled: "The Congress is such an assembly as never before came together, on a sudden, in any part of the world."[19]

As elected legislators, the delegates were generally devoted to the principle of legislative supremacy. Many believed that the most perfect form of government had at least one strong representative branch, a branch that, above all else, controlled the power of taxation and expenditure of the people's money. As a result of the generally bad experiences with royal governors, the delegates manifested repugnance toward a strong executive. Above all most of them distrusted executive power.[20]

All the delegates to the First Continental Congress were elected, although no formal qualifications were required and no election mechanisms were in place to do so. Not surprisingly, the royal governors vehemently opposed the selection of delegates and attempted to adjourn the colonial legislatures and thus block their election. Indeed, in Massachusetts, the members of the General Court (or popular assembly) were successful in electing delegates only by literally locking out the representative of the governor who possessed the order to prorogue[21] the session—an order that was mandatory under the terms of the charter.[22] Other than Massachusetts, only Rhode Island, Pennsylvania, and Connecticut were able to select delegates in the legally established colonial assemblies because in only these colonies were governors not royal appointees but elected. In Maryland, New Hampshire, New Jersey, Delaware, North Carolina, and Virginia, delegates were selected by extraconstitutional conventions or provincial congresses which usually included the same men who had served as delegates to the general assemblies. Other colonies held separate town meetings; South Carolina called a general meeting of the inhabitants of Charleston, and New York held a series of elections in the localities.[23]

Each colony instructed its delegates as to the goals they should seek to accomplish in the Continental Congress. New Hampshire instructed its delegates to "extricate the colonies from their present difficulties"—that is, the Massachusetts conflict.[24] Other colonies directed delegates to eliminate those British statutes and practices that injured the rights of the colonies. For example, South Carolina told its delegates to accomplish the "repeal or withdrawal" of those parliamentary acts, statutes, and instructions that "make an invidious distinction between his majesty's subjects in Great Britain and America."[25] Still others looked to the Continental Congress to establish "with certainty the rights of Americans," in the words of the Rhode Island instructions, "on a just and solid foundation."[26]

These instructions prompted many colonial political thinkers to establish the intellectual foundations for the Revolution. For example, Thomas Jefferson wrote "A Summary View of the Rights of British America" in 1774 to instruct the Virginia delegates to the First Continental Congress. Although substantially modified by the Virginia burgesses, the instructions nonetheless were published immediately in their original form and created an important foundation on both sides of the Atlantic for the principle that Americans "possessed a right, which nature has given to all men, of departing from the country in which chance, not choice, has placed them, of going in quest of new habitations, and of their establishing new societies, under such laws and regulations as to them shall seem most likely to promote public happiness."[27]

These instructions reflect the deeply rooted colonial view that the powers of government should be explicitly set forth and limited by a written document or at least a generally understood set of doctrines. The charters of many colonial governments outlined the distribution of powers among the executive, legislative, and judicial branches and specifically delineated the rights of citizens. Colonies without such a charter developed a set of precedents that established such limitations and protections. The Continental Congress had no such charter or body of precedents to ensure the acceptance of its decisions. Eventually, upon the adoption of the Declaration of Independence, the right to form a representative assembly would be derived from the laws of nature, but this doctrine had not yet been widely endorsed. Therefore, the instructions to the First Continental Congress provided its actions with a legitimacy it would not otherwise have possessed. By drafting instructions to its delegates, each colony provided the Congress with authority. Thus, in a sense, the First Continental Congress was limited by twelve different charters.

At the inception of the Continental Congress, the colonies thought of themselves not as one nation but as many separate sovereign entities. The delegates viewed themselves as attorneys bound to represent the will of the client colony, as expressed in the instructions. Indeed, in some respects, at least initially, they viewed the colonies as independent nations and themselves as ambassadors of those nations. John Adams, for example, referred to Massachusetts, which he represented, as "our country."[28] The delegates seriously examined and felt limited by the terms of their instructions. As one South Carolina delegate stated: "We have no legal authority; and obedience to our determinations will only follow the reasonableness, the apparent utility and necessity of the measures we adopt. We have no coercive or legislative authority. Our constituents are bound only in honor to observe our determinations."[29]

As most delegates considered themselves ambassadors from distinct and sovereign nations, it is not surprising that the first major fight in the First Continental Congress involved rules of procedure—should votes be cast by colonies, population, or property owners? Patrick Henry, understanding the importance of the precedent that this procedural battle would establish and representing a state, Virginia, with 20 percent of the colonial population, argued that the vote should be by not colony but population. His argument was that the governments of the royal colonies had been dissolved by the establishment of the Congress and that the colonies were now existing in a state of nature: "The distinctions between Virginians, Pennsylvanians, New Yorkers and New Englanders, are no more. I am not a Virginian, but an American."[30] (Some commentators have viewed this statement as the first declaration of a nascent national consciousness; it is interesting to note, however, that Henry later opposed passage of the Constitution on the grounds that it impinged too severely on state sovereignty.) The other side of the controversy was argued by states like New Hampshire: Because the sovereign existence of each colony was at stake, each colony should receive equal representation. To prevent stagnation in this procedural quagmire, the Congress agreed that each colony should have one vote but that the decision should not become a precedent for future congresses. (However, this procedural compromise was to have lasting consequences for the distribution of power in the Congress, as established by the Constitutional Convention.)

Although the First Continental Congress lasted only about seven weeks, it established a strong precedent for an activist national legislature. Its decisions were sweeping and dramatic. During its short existence it dealt with a variety of difficult decisions, each one of which was discussed "with a moderation, an acuteness and a minuteness equal to that of Queen Elizabeth's Privy Council."[31] First, the Congress endorsed the Suffolk Resolves of Massachusetts, which declared the Coercive Acts of England unconstitutional and void, and Congress urged the formation of an independent government in that colony.[32] Second, it adopted the Declaration and Resolves, a bold statement of colonial rights and grievances, which unequivocally denied Parliament any authority over the colonies because the foundation of English liberty, and of all free governments, was the right of the people to participate in their legislative council. As the English colonies were not represented in the British Parliament, it stated, "they are entitled to a free and exclusive power of legislation in their several provincial legislatures, where their right of representation can alone be preserved."[33] The Congress tempered this denial with an offer to abide by those acts of Parliament that were genuine regulations of the external commerce of the colonies designed "for securing the commercial advantages of the whole empire to the mother country, and the commercial benefits of its respective members."[34] Third, it created the Continental Association, which would impose economic sanctions against Britain until colonial grievances had been redressed and colonial rights were established on a secure foundation. The Congress also provided for an economic boycott of any colony not implementing the economic sanctions and called for the election of Committees of Safety in every county, city, and town to serve as agencies of enforcement. Fourth, to explain its behavior and seek support, the Congress adopted four public appeals: an Address to the People of Great

Britain, a Memorial to the Inhabitants of the Colonies, an Address to the Inhabitants of the six North American colonies, and a Petition to the King. Finally, and perhaps most important, the Congress voted to meet again on May 10, 1775, thereby creating the authority for future activities.

The First Continental Congress was a huge success. Although it had no formal legislative powers, it passed resolutions that had widespread impact on the political and economic structure of the colonies. Most notable, it authorized the election of local committees to enforce the terms of the Continental Association and in some circumstances called for the election of popular assemblies to fill the vacuum left by the dissolved colonial legislatures. The decision to authorize the election of local quasi-governmental bodies certainly strained the outer limit of the tentative and vague nature of the instructions to the delegates. The high esteem of this Congress is attested to by the reliance of many colonies on its leadership in military matters. Before commencing to build fortifications, the Massachusetts delegates asked Congress for its advice. Massachusetts' revolutionary leaders like Sam Adams were reluctant to have the colony assume legal authority for conducting a war without legitimizing its activities by the approval of the Continental Congress. This request is noteworthy from two perspectives. First, it is significant that a colony that viewed itself as sovereign would ask Congress for its approval and advice.[35] Second, the request to supervise the cause of resistance permitted the establishment of congressional dominance, a precedent that could be established unanimously and with no resentment because it came at the request of a colony. As historian Jack Rakove said: "By asking Congress to judge the legality of their provincial government, the Massachusetts leaders endowed that body with authority they would never have conceded to Parliament."[36]

Realizing its novelty and precariousness as a legislative institution, the First Continental Congress took careful and affirmative steps to ensure nationwide support by pursuing moderate middle-of-the-road approaches for its measures. Controversial decisions were avoided. "Unanimity," the Connecticut delegates wrote home, "was in our view of the most importance."[37] Thus the delegates rejected all proposals that were inconsistent with the mandates received from their colonial constituencies and those that threatened the powers of the legislatures. For example, Joseph Galloway, a delegate from Pennsylvania, offered a proposal to establish a permanent union of the colonies on September 28, 1774, during the third week of the Continental Congress, as a compromise to resolve the diffferences with England. He suggested that a general legislature, called the Grand Council, be established to deal with the administration of the "general affairs of America" and that a president-general be appointed by the king to approve and execute all the acts of the Grand Council. The Grand Council, Galloway proposed, would not interfere with the present power of each colony to regulate and govern. To make this plan acceptable to Britain, Galloway anticipated that the president-general and Grand Council constitute an "inferior and distinct branch of the British Legislature."[38] Because Galloway's proposal went beyond the bounds of the delegates' instructions, most refused, as a threshold matter, to evaluate the merits of the plan. Colonel Richard Henry Lee of Virginia refused even to consider the plan without consulting his constitutents because of the changes it would require in the legislatures of the colonies. John Jay of New York objected that "this plan will alter our Constitution and therefore cannot be adopted without consulting constituents." Joseph Galloway was too soon, and the Galloway plan was soundly defeated.

In its resolutions, the Congress aggressively sought to justify to its constituencies, and to the world, the rationale for each action. In so doing, the delegates began to perceive themselves not as "ambassadors" of several colonies within the British Empire but as delegates to a representative assembly from different sections of *one* nation.

In the Memorial to the Inhabitants of the Colonies the congressional delegates referred to the colonists as their "fellow countrymen." They stated that they had been "authorized and directed to meet and consult together for the welfare of our common country" and urged that their commercial measures were essential to preserve "the honour of your country, that must from your behaviour take its title in the estimation of the world, to glory, or to shame."[39] Thus, by appealing to the newly aroused nationalistic impulses of the colonists, the members of Congress sought to justify their own activities, which were far more intrusive and aggressive than would have been expected, given the limited mandates of some colonial instructions. The members of the Continental Congress were successful in obtaining widespread support for their measures and in preparing the necessary predicate for the activities of the Second Continental Congress.

THE SECOND CONTINENTAL CONGRESS

With the goodwill inherited from the first Congress, the Second Continental Congress convened on May 10, 1775, to deal with the still unresolved problems with England. Hostilities had already broken out on Lexington Green on April 19, and the Congress received a much stronger pledge of colonial support than it had the first time. Seven colonies gave the Congress essentially a "carte blanche," agreeing to be bound by whatever it mandated. Even Georgia sent one delegate, and for the first time all thirteen colonies were represented.

For the first year of its existence, the second Congress served as both the executive and legislative body for the colonies in managing the colonial military struggle with Great Britain. As its first main action, the Congress adopted a Declaration of Causes and Necessity for Taking up Arms. It consequently adopted Articles of War, provided for the organization and equipment of an army, issued paper money to finance military operations, organized a supply system, promulgated military regulations, neutralized or enlisted the support of Indian tribes, opened new channels of trade, made alliances, and further consolidated the union of the colonies.[40] Most congressional activities were executed by committee. For example, a committee was established to draft the Declaration of Independence and another to investigate the failure of the Continental army in the Canadian campaign.

Apart from managing the war, the main focus of the Second Continental Congress was the determination of its future role as a national institution and the definition of its power relative to the powers of individual state governments. On July 21, 1775 Benjamin Franklin[41] prompted the discussion by submitting to Congress a document called the Articles of Confederation and Perpetual Union. His proposal was placed on the back burner, however, until interest in the establishment of a permanent national government intensified after the adoption of the Declaration of Independence. A committee of one member from each colony was established to prepare a formal plan of confederation for the future management of common interests.[42] The committee considered the Franklin plan and several other proposals, which allocated the power of state and federal governments in variety of ways. The Articles of Confederation went through various drafts between April and November 1777. One draft, as proposed by John Dickinson of "the three lower counties" of Pennsylvania (Delaware), identified the Constitution as the central standard by which the rights, powers, and duties of the states were to be measured. The final draft differed dramatically from this formulation: Under the Articles of Confederation, the thirteen states, each of which was sovereign, would delegate certain powers to the federal government only for specific purposes. The official designation of the new government was expressed as "the united States, in Congress assembled." The lowercase *u* symbolized the independent status of the states in the confederacy.

The debates over the form of the confederation reflected the concerns of the various states over the diminution of their powers. According to James Madison, the principal difficulties that retarded the completion of the plan of confederation were the "repugnance" of the states to relinquish power; the "natural jealousy" of its use in the hands of the federal government; the "rule of suffrage" among the colonies whose inequality in size did not correspond to other differences in wealth, military might, or population; and finally the selection and definition of the states' powers.[43]

THE CONGRESS OF
THE CONFEDERATION*

Under the Articles of Confederation, the only organ of national government was the Congress, which had certain enumerated rights that were "sole" and "exclusive." All others were left to the states. The Congress had the authority to declare war, to conduct foreign affairs, to resolve disputes between states and individuals arising from the power of taxation, to compel payment by the states of the public debt, and to regulate foreign commerce. The Congress of the Confederation was not permitted to impose taxes or to regulate domestic commerce. The limitations on the power of the Congress of the Confederation were politically necessary, for without them ratification by the thirteen states would not have been accomplished. Even with the limitations the Confederation was not ratified until March, 1781, nearly five years after the Declaration of Independence.

The structure of the Congress of the Confederation was, not surprisingly, similar to that of the Continental Congress. The Articles in effect legitimized most of what Congress was already doing. The body was unicameral and consisted of delegates (between two and seven) selected every three years by each state government. To ensure continued state control of the delegates, the Articles provided that they were subject to recall at any time by their state governments and that the expenses of the delegation would be assumed by the states. Thus, the incentive was strong for delegates to be responsive to the will of the state legislatures and thus limit federal intrusion into their powers. Each state had one vote regardless of the number of the delegates, and each delegation cast its vote according to the decision of a majority of the delegates. A tie vote within a delegation denied that state a ballot. None of the major powers—including the power to conduct war—could be exercised without the consent of nine of the thirteen states.

Like its predecessor, the Congress of the Confederation (which was still popularly known as the Continental Congress) served executive as well as

---

*Although there were, literally speaking, only two Continental congresses, the use of the title Continental Congress actually continued throughout the Confederation period until the new Constitution went into effect in 1789.

Building in which the Continental Congress
of 1783 held its fall session at Annapolis, Maryland.

legislative functions. The authors of the Articles were fearful of permitting any one person to acquire too much prestige. Thus no person (except the secretary of the Congress) could hold office in Congress for more than three out of six years, and no one could be president of the Congress for more than one year at a time.[44] Fourteen men held the office for varying lengths of time, including John Hancock of Massachusetts, who served for only one summer. The distrust of an executive created a political and philosophical obstacle to the establishment of a strong national leadership. The Articles authorized Congress to appoint a committee of the states to manage the affairs of the union while the Congress was in recess. Congress was also empowered to create separate committees to conduct the general affairs of the United States.[45] Originally the Congress had attempted to perform the executive functions of managing foreign affairs, war, and treasury through committees chosen from its own membership. When the work of these committees proved ineffective, Congress created outside boards of personnel responsible to the committees to manage various substantive areas. Because the boards had no responsible leaders, this arrangement also proved ineffective. Taking the next appropriate step, Congress provided for secretaries to head various departments, such as foreign affairs, war, navy, treasury, and the post office. These boards, or departments, became a part of the established machinery of government under the Articles of Confederation.[46]

The Congress also filled certain judicial functions. Article IX had created an ad hoc judicial process to hear two types of interstate disputes: boundaries on land claims and maritime prize cases. A commission composed of congressmen was established to hear land disputes whenever the states should submit them to adjudication. Of a half-a-dozen potential cases noted in the Journals of Congress, only one was pursued to final judgment; another reached a point where the congressional commission could take jurisdiction; the others were either dropped or settled by direct negotiations between the states affected.

As for maritime prize appeals, Congress set up a standing committee to hear appeals from state admiralty courts. The volume of business was so enormous that in May 1780 the first statute creating a national court of four federal judges was passed by Congress, setting up a special court of appeals in cases of capture. The court heard 118 appeals from the various states, affirming 39 and revising 45. Given the vast sweep of federal jurisdiction today, it is interesting to note that the first federal court dealt exclusively with admiralty cases, which are now a mere fraction of the federal caseload.[47]

Despite the fact that for eight years the Congress successfully directed a draining war effort, the academic literature on the Articles of Confederation is replete with examples of their failure. The Congress was unable to secure from the states the money needed to pay the national debt and current expenses and could not prevent states from issuing paper money. It could not enforce treaties or provide protective tariffs; it could not promote industry at home or prevent states from collecting import duties on goods transported from other states. Most important, because the Congress could not afford to continue to maintain troops after the peace treaty with Britain, it could not control conflicts like the infamous Shays' Rebellion in Massachusetts.

The founding fathers were not shy in their criticism of the Articles of Confederation. James Madison, in his introduction to the constitutional debates, described a main flaw in the Articles of Confederation as a problem in executive management:

> But the radical infirmity of the Articles of Confederation was the dependence of Congress on the voluntary and simultaneous compliance with its requisitions by so many independent committees, each consulting more or less its particular interests and convenience, and distrusting the compliance of others.[48]

He deplored the rapid growth of anarchy and animosity between the states that derived from conflictiing regulations.

In the *Federalist Papers*, Alexander Hamilton blamed the Articles of Confederation for creating "material imperfections in our national system," which are leading to "impending anarchy."[49] He sadly proclaimed: "We may indeed with propriety be said to have reached almost the last stage of national humiliation. There is scarcely anything that can wound the pride or degrade the character of an independent nation we do not experience."[50]

Some historians do not consider the Articles of Confederation a failure; they attribute its demise to the victory of conservative propertied interests over the more radical revolutionaries. Merrill Jensen's work is a strong statement of this point of view. Jensen argues that the conservative and wealthy federalists disliked the Articles of Confederation because they preserved the power of the state governments, which were controlled by radical agrarians: "The mass of the population was composed of small farmers who in the long run could control politics of their individual states."[51] Jensen points out that the conservatives desired a strong central government to protect their property against debtors' rebellions, to regulate trade more effectively, and to control the more radical activities of the state governments. He dismisses the *Federalist Papers* as mere political rhetoric, claiming that "the propaganda of one generation becomes the classic of the next."[52]

When the framers of the Constitution gathered in Philadelphia to form a new government, the only national political institution in existence was the Congress. There was no federal judiciary of any consequence or any formal executive. But the general discreditation of the Continental Congress led to a national recognition of the necessity for another Constitution to deal effectively with competing state sovereignties and the problems common to the various states. The obvious place to seek alternative models of government: the states.

COLONIAL AND STATE LEGISLATURES

Legislative assemblies throughout colonial and early American history enjoyed great prominence which can be attributed to the forum they provided for the expression of popular sentiment. The assemblies served as lightning rods for revolutionary sentiments, and through their tight grip on colonial treasuries, they were effective tools against the royal government.

The four main kinds of colonial government in existence at the end of the American colonial period[53] had one thing in common: an elected popular assembly. The government of Massachusetts typified one type. Under its royal charter, a governor was appointed by the king and endowed with enormous powers. He could veto legislation, disapprove of the assembly speaker, summon, prorogue, and adjourn the assembly's proceedings, and, with the consent of the upper chamber of the legislature, make appointments. The Massachusetts colonial legislature was bicameral. The General Court, or lower chamber, was elected by the freemen of the colonies; it subsequently selected the Council, or upper house. The power of the legislature superseded that of the royal governor on only one count: the authority to control expenditures and to raise revenues—the power of the purse. Thus, although the Massachusetts legislature was dominated by the executive branch, it had sufficient powers to hamstring the royal governor's spending.

In Connecticut and Rhode Island, unlike Massachusetts, the governors were elected by the citizens on an annual basis; the upper house of the legislature was also chosen by popular election, and each town chose deputies to sit in the lower house. In Connecticut, in particular, the legislature had extraordinary powers. Historian Allan Nevins described the second form of colonial government: "In both governments, the salient characteristic was the dominance of the legislature over the executive and judicial branches, a dominance that endured long after the revolution."[54]

In the third and fourth categories of colonial government the central role was played by the royally appointed governor. In the so-called proprietary provinces—Pennsylvania, Delaware, and Maryland—the executive powers were vested in two families, the Penns and the Calverts. Because of the hereditary powers vested in the leading families, these colonies resembled a feudal estate. In Pennsylvania, in particular, the governor and his advisory council retained the right to veto all legislature and make all judicial and civil appointments. The main counterpoint to the governor was the legislature which in Pennsylvania was unicameral and elected yearly. In Maryland, unlike Pennsylvania, the powers of the governor were somewhat balanced by the popular assembly, which controlled public monies and denied the governor's right to veto legislation, and by the governor's council that functioned as a legislative body as well.

The seven royal provinces, which were generally located in the South, provided the fourth form of colonial government. Typically, the governor was appointed by the crown, and executive officials were appointed by the crown or the governor. A House, popularly elected, and an upper chamber, or council, appointed by the governor, comprised the legislature. The power of the governor was great. For example, in Virginia the executive was the commander of the militia and the chief justice, as well as the head of the Anglican Church; he could propose legislation to the assembly, had an absolute veto over legislation, could convoke, prorogue, and dissolve the assembly, controlled the exchange of money, and had large patronage. In most royalist provinces there was no charter explicitly outlining the rights and obligations of governmental entities, although, as in England, a large body of precedents was used to determine proper governmental functions.

The popular colonial assemblies had few characteristics in common. They varied greatly in size. Virginia's House of Burgesses, for example, numbered 110 in 1760, whereas New York's assembly had one-third that number. The property qualifications required to vote and the property qualifications necessary to obtain an assembly seat differed as well. The scheme of representation was generally inequitable. It failed to take into account differences in population and usually was designed to favor one group of voters over another. In Pennsylvania, for example, the five frontier counties had only five delegates, whereas the three more urban counties had twenty-six. In Virginia, the allocation of two burgesses per county provided the gentry with a decided advantage over the small farmers of the upland and Shenandoah Valley.[55] In addition, the means for selecting the members of the upper council varied from colony to colony. In Rhode Island they were elected by popular vote, in Massachusetts they were selected by the General Court, and in North Carolina they were appointed by the governor.

Although the British had two houses of Parliament—Commons and Lords —the colonial governments did not immediately pattern themselves after this model. Instead, the bicameral form of government in most colonies evolved after many years of experimentation. In Massachusetts, for example, the corporate charter originally provided for eighteen "assistants," or "magistrates," who functioned essentially as a board of directors to the governor, who headed the corporation. Later, in 1634, the freemen were permitted to choose representatives from the different settlements to sit with the magistrates in "general court." Although the magistrates were originally elected, they did not serve for a fixed term—it was assumed that they would hold their position for life; the deputies to the general court, on the other hand, were elected periodically. Despite the initial pretensions of the magistrates to have an absolute veto over the decisions of the delegates, and the constant battles between the two kinds of elected representatives over their respective powers, by the mid-seventeenth century it was resolved that all legislation had to be approved by both branches of government. Moreover, the charter was amended to allow the upper branch to choose the lower. Thus the Massachusetts legislature evolved from a unicameral body to a bicameral legislature, in which the upper chamber had more authority than the lower, and finally to a bicameral legislature in which both houses had roughly similar powers.[56]

Most other colonial legislatures experienced a parallel evolution, ending up with a bicameral legislature. Only one major colony, Pennsylvania, shifted from a bicameral to a unicameral legislature.

The evolution of the popular colonial assembly foreshadows the development of the national Congress. Only Pennsylvania, Georgia, and Vermont were governed by a unicameral legislative assembly at the time of the Revolution. In most colonies a popular assembly was elected periodically, usually annually, and a council, or upper chamber, was either appointed by the royal governor or selected by the lower assembly. The upper chamber generally did not have veto power over the lower chamber, and both chambers were viewed as having roughly equal powers in the legislative process. However, the upper chamber was sometimes given advisory responsibility to aid the governor and was, on occasion, delegated quasi-executive powers.

The existence of bicameral legislatures in most colonies signifies the importance of bicameralism as a protection against an overly aggressive, impetuous legislature. In 1776 John Adams in his "Thoughts on Government" expressed the prevailing view that unicameral assemblies were less than ideal because they produced "hasty results," "absurd judgments," and "avaricious tendencies." A single assembly, he said, is "apt to grow ambitious and after a time will not hesitate to vote itself perpetual."[57] Others believed that the slowness of bicameralism would ensure precise and deliberate decisions.

The bicameralism of most state legislatures contrasts with the unicameralism of the Continental Congress and Congress of the Confederation. Not perceived as a threat to individual liberties, the Congress did not need the additional precision and safeguards of bicameralism. However, because the newly created Congress was given significant legislative responsibility, the bicameral model became essential.

In general, the colonial assemblies had little control over the governors. As mentioned earlier, the governor usually had the power to veto legislation, summon or adjourn the popular assembly, and make all appointments. However, despite their lack of formal powers, the colonial legislatures had one major weapon against the encroachments of the royal governor—the power of the purse. Even the governor's salary in most colonies depended upon the appropriation of colonial legislatures. In Massachusetts, for example, at the beginning of the eighteenth century, the legislature allocated annual allowances, rather than permanent salaries, for executive officers. At times the allowances were so meager that the governor himself refused to accept his stipend. In 1728 the General Court of Massachusetts declared that "the undoubted right of all Englishmen . . . to raise and dispose of money for the public service of their own free accord without compulsion"[58] was guaranteed by the Magna Charta.

In other efforts to circumvent royal authority, the legislatures routinely prescribed minutely detailed statutory provisions, bypassed the governor by assigning the execution of laws to administrative commissions, and shortcircuited the governor's appointing power by appropriating salaries not to the offices but to specified persons.[59]

Unlike the legislature, the executive, as a representative of the royal government, got off to a bad start in colonial America. Often the appointment was an award by the king to a loyal subject and a means to revive a family's wealth; sometimes the governor served in absentia, delegating his functions in the colony to the lieutenant governor. In only two of the charter colonies—Rhode Island and Connecticut—was the governor the choice of the electorate. By the middle of the eighteenth century, the popular assemblies had become an integral part of colonial self-expression. With the escalation of British infringement on colonial rights, the governors became the target of public frustration.

When a royal governor exercised his rights under the charter and dissolved the legislature, the colonists devised new forms of representative assemblies to fill the void. In 1773, for example, in response to the British Coercive Acts, the colonies formed a communication network through Committees of Intercolonial Correspondence to carry on the work of the legislatures when they were dissolved. Virginia initiated the Committees of Correspondence when the House of Burgesses was disbanded in 1774. Indeed, the formation of a Continental Congress was first proposed by the Virginia Committee of Correspondence. Popular sentiments found expression in town meetings and, on occasion, in grand juries, which were transformed from judicial to legislative entities.[60]

In time, provincial congresses or conventions were established in nine colonies. The exceptions were Connecticut and Rhode Island, where the popularly elected governors did not dissolve the legislature, and New York and Georgia, which abstained from revolutionary activities. Crudely constituted, most provincial congresses were little more than mass meetings. The delegates were usually the same men who had served in the popular assemblies. Indeed, the creation of provincial congresses was stimulated by the need to send delegates to the First Continental Congress.

As one of its most important acts, the Continental Congress legitimized the provincial congresses by calling for their creation even before the adoption of the Declaration of Independence. In Massachusetts, the provincial congress petitioned the First Continental Congress for the right to operate as a legitimate government under the charter. After obtaining the consent of the Congress, the Massachusetts provincial congress established a general court, or lower chamber, elected by the citizens, and an upper chamber elected by the lower. The governor's position was left vacant. The Continental Congress went one step further. It mandated the creation of local Committees of Inspection to enforce the non-importation provisions of the Continental Association. The Inspection committees often went beyond the terms of their mandate and served as mini-legislatures. Thus the Continental Congress established the legitimacy of representative government when self-expression was denied by the royal charters.

Eventually, on May 10, 1776, at the insistence of John Adams, the Second Continental Congress resolved that all the colonies should provide themselves with permanent constitutions. In a flurry of activity, the provincial congresses acted to comply. In some colonies, the provincial congress itself drafted the document, in others special conventions were called. In general the drafting of the state constitutions was hurried because the congresses were involved in more pressing matters—fighting a war. Thus some governments, like New York, did not adopt a constitution until 1777. Controversy reigned at the constitutional conventions between the more aristocratic representatives, who wanted a balanced government, with equal powers delegated to the executive, judicial, and legislative branches, and the radicals, who believed that the legislature should be supreme.[61] In most instances the radicals prevailed, in part because the aristocratic group was persuaded that the constitutions were temporary, that they would be invalidated, of course, by a peace with England. Massachusetts was the only state to adopt a constitution after calling a constitutional convention and then subjecting its work to popular approval. It was not adopted until 1780. The creation of state constitutions stimulated revolutionary thought about various forms of government based on prevailing political philosophies. The two main European philosophers who provided the framework for the constitutions were John Locke and Baron de Montesquieu. Locke believed that the supreme function of the state was to protect life, liberty, and property—the natural rights of all men. The best way to preserve these natural rights was by a careful separation of the executive and legislative powers. To Locke, however, "separation" did not mean "equal," for he clearly believed that the legislative powers should be supreme, a position that named him the great expositor of the principles of the Whig Revolution in England in 1688. In his *Treatise Concerning Civil Government*, John Locke stated that all men were born free and equal in a state of nature. When they join together, by consent, for the security of all, they are left with the same rights of equality and freedom that they had in the state of nature; but by joining together in a body politic, they have agreed to act by the decision of the majority. While this power may be delegated to one person or many, Locke pointed out that the legislative power was "supreme," could not be "delegated" to another without the consent of the community, and contained certain inherent limitations on depriving a member of the community of his natural rights.[62] John Locke believed that in "well ordered commonwealths" the legislative power should be placed "into the hands of divers persons" who, "duly assembled, have by themselves or jointly with others a power to make laws, which when they have done, being separated again, they are themselves subject to the laws they have made."[63] But because it would be "too great a temptation to human frailty" to give those who make the laws the power to execute them, which would entail the power to exempt themselves from them, the executive power should be placed in other hands.[64]

Baron de Montesquieu took the doctrine of separation of powers one step further. In *The Spirit of the Laws* (1748) Montesquieu asserted that when the judicial, executive, and legislative powers were placed in the same hands there could be no freedom.

Because virtually every New World student of politics was familiar with the works of Locke and Montesquieu,[65] it was logical that these works provided the philosophical underpinnings for the establishment of the new state constitutions. With the call for independence, a debate began over the proper form of the new state governments. Pamphlets and newspaper essays flooded the country. Probably the most influential thinker on this subject was John Adams, who authored the "Novanglus Papers" and the intellectual basis for the arguments against the royal governor used by the Massachusetts revolutionaries. Adams proposed a scheme of government dominated by the legislative branch. He suggested the election of a House of Commons by the people, the choice of an upper legislative chamber by the House, and the annual election of the governor and other executive officers by both houses. The governor would be given the power to veto legislation, command the armed forces, and appoint subordinate officers and magistrates subject to the consent of the chamber. Interestingly, Adams foresaw that the state legislatures might want to provide for the direct election of the governor in more peaceful times.

Another proposal for a scheme of state government came from Thomas Paine's *Common Sense*, which propounded a far more radical, populist view of government. Paine called for the establishment of a unicameral legislature, which would serve both executive and legislative functions. The legislature would be elected on an annual basis, with one representative from each section of the state. Each legislature would elect its own president, have power exclusively in the domestic sphere, and rely on the Continental Congress for foreign relations.

The aristocratic and more conservative colonists circulated a proposal that provided for a bicameral legislature. The lower house would be directly elected by the people. The upper house of twenty-four members would be elected for life by the lower chamber. The governor would appoint all judges, military officers, and inferior civil officers.[66] This proposal received little public support.

Despite a constant reiteration of the need for checks and balances, the first state constitutions provided no real equilibrium between the branches: the preponderance of power was delegated, with few exceptions, to the legislature, which dominated the executive and the judiciary. As historian Allan Nevins stated: "The subordination of the executive branch to the legislature grew out of the memory of hated British executives, and out of precedents set in the hurried work of retiring troublesome governors and giving their authority to the servants of the people."[67] The governor was to be elected by the legislature in all states except New York. The term of office of the governor or president was one year, save in New York and Delaware where it was three and in South Carolina where it was two. In most states the power of the governor was checked by an executive council, varying in number from four to thirteen. In no state did the governor have final veto power over legislation, and in only three did he have partial veto powers. No state allowed him the power to adjourn the legislature. He had no patronage to distribute, and in some states he could not even appoint lower officers. In four states—Pennsylvania, Delaware, New Hampshire, and Massachusetts—there was no governor; the executive power was exercised by a council. In Rhode Island and Connecticut the governor was elected by the people but was subordinate to the legislature.

Indeed, the judiciary did not fare much better. In many states members of the judiciary were elected by the legislature, in some cases for only one-year terms. Generally, the removal of a judge was easily accomplished. During the period 1776–87 the supremacy of the legislatures was supported by the general assumption that they, not the courts, were the sole judges of their constitutional powers. As Nevins said: "Few Americans believed that any state court had the right to declare an enactment invalid on the ground that it violated the constitution."[68]

Although most early constitutions had brief careers—only four lasted more than half a century—they provide a critical window through which to glimpse the perspectives of those men who formed the Constitutional Convention in 1787. Most delegates had served in, or worked with, state legislatures or the Continental Congress. No state government had a strong executive branch, and the national Congress had none. The courts had limited jurisdiction to adjudicate controversies between individual citizens and were powerless to arbitrate between the constitutional prerogatives of various branches. Indeed, the judiciary was often subordinate to the legislature. Thus, the doctrine of separation of powers, in reality, had placed a marked concentration of power in the hands of the state legislatures.

The establishment of state governments contributed to a decline in the prestige of the national congresses. Until the adoption of state constitutions, the Continental Congress had been highly regarded throughout the nation. Overwhelming support for its actions was due, in part, to the cautiousness of the delegates, their adherence to the terms of their mandates, and their success in acting with unanimity. In addition, its success may be attributed to its ability to fill the political vacuum created by the demise of the colonial legislatures. Although some provincial congresses were active, they lacked the widespread support enjoyed by the Continental Congress, which provided the main and most forceful vehicle for revolutionary thought. With the creation of new state governments, and in particular of local popular assemblies, the Continental Congress found itself with thirteen jealous rivals jousting for its power.

With the regained confidence in and popularity of state government, the Continental Congress increasingly found itself at loggerheads with the states over differences in policy. In 1776 the Continental Congress experienced its first major disagreement with the new governments. When the states failed to fill their quotas for the Continental army and confidence in the efficacy of the state militias diminished, Congress felt compelled to pass a resolution requesting the states to draft men to fill the quota. However, a mechanism for enforcing this resolution was not available.

During the debates over the Articles of Confederation, the friction between the state legislatures and the Continental Congress was exacerbated. Under the enormous pressures of the financial and other demands made on it by the necessity of conducting a protracted war, the Second Continental Congress and its successor, the Congress of the Confederation, suffered severely from limited powers and declining public support. When the war emergency ended with the signing of the peace treaty in 1783, the state legislatures attracted the most intelligent men and public luminaries, whereas the Continental Congress attracted lesser men whose prime qualification was that they were willing to live away from home. The Congress became increasingly an advisory body with precatory powers. As historian Jack Rakove concluded, the rivalry of the states destroyed the rough national consensus in support of the Congress and necessitated a new constitutional scheme to revitalize the federal government.[69]

THREE

THE CONSTITUTION AND THE NEW CONGRESS

THE CONSTITUTIONAL CONVENTION

The ostensible goal of the fifty-five men who met in Philadelphia in 1787 for the Constitutional Convention was to amend the Articles of Confederation to permit the Congress to regulate more effectively both foreign and domestic trade. The men of commerce believed that the Congress of the Confederation had failed to preserve domestic peace, establish a uniform navigation policy, promote trade both among the colonies and with foreign nations, enforce treaties, and pay the public debt. In short, as James Madison described in the introduction to his notes on the constitutional debates, the political conditions induced "gloom" among the commercial men of the new nation; they believed that a new constitutional scheme was requisite.[1]

To generate interest in the inadequacies of the Articles of Confederation, commercial leaders, particularly those from Virginia, had suggested a convention in Annapolis to discuss ways to improve domestic and foreign commerce. Contemporary commentators reveal that the call for a trade convention was a clever ruse to obtain a mandate for a more general convention on the problems inherent in the Articles of Confederation. One French representative wrote home that there was "no expectation and no interest" in accomplishing anything at the Annapolis Convention beyond preparing the way for a more general meeting.[2] Although ten states had appointed delegates to the convention, only twelve delegates from five states (New York, New Jersey, Pennsylvania, Delaware, and Virginia) actually attended. They accomplished their goal: passage of a resolution demanding a future meeting to discuss commercial problems and "other matters respecting the Confederation." Assured that the convention would be concerned primarily with amending the Articles for "commercial" purposes, the Congress of the Confederation adopted a resolution in June 1787 calling for the Constitutional Convention.

The delegates to the Convention were, for the most part, wealthy: members of the propertied classes, lawyers, merchants. Three-quarters had gained their political experience in either the state legislatures or the national Congress. Generally well educated, they were described by one historian as "learned ones" whose "ideas and ideals . . . were partly formed or strongly matured by the books they knew—Greek and Rome Classics, Locke, Hobbes, Grotius, Machiavelli, Blackstone, Montesquieu, Hume, Adam Smith and others of similar experience."[3] They were intellectually excited about the opportunity to rethink the constitutional scheme of government. John Adams articulated the prevailing sentiments: "You and I, Dear Friend, have been sent into life at a time when the greatest lawgivers would have wished to live. How few of the human race have ever enjoyed an opportunity of making an election of government . . . for themselves and their children."[4]

Despite their lofty ideals, the first tasks of the delegates were much more mundane. As in the Continental Congress and the Congress of the Confederation, each state was to have one vote. The proceedings were to be strictly secret and no notes were to be taken. The delegates appointed working committees, like the Committee on Detail, to draft the provisions and adopted many parliamentary procedures to govern the proceedings. Most debates and votes, like those in Parliament, were to be considered first in the "Committee of the Whole" before being voted on by the whole body of delegates. George Washington was elected to serve as a kind of speaker to conduct the proceedings and rule on points of order and motions.

It is not surprising that the First Resolution before the Constitutional Convention—that a national government should be established consisting of a supreme legislature, executive, and judiciary—passed, virtually without debate, with only one dissenting vote. Most states had endorsed this concept in drafting their state constitutions, and the tripartite division was firmly founded on the political theories of John Locke and Montesquieu. However, the separation of powers did not necessarily mean an equal division of powers. As indicated earlier, whereas all states advocated a separation of powers in theory, in practice, the legislature was almost always supreme.

The first two plans of government suggested at the Convention were patterned on the model of many state governments. If adopted, the continued predominance of the legislative branch on the national level would have been assured.

The Virginia Plan, submitted by Governor Edmund Randolph of Virginia, proposed two houses of the legislature, a lower house chosen by the electorate and an upper house chosen by the lower house from candidates nominated by the state legislatures. A national executive, chosen by the legislature, was to have the authority to execute the laws and "enjoy the executive rights vested in Congress by the Confederation." The veto power was vested not in the executive but in a Council of Revision composed of members of the executive and judicial branches.[5]

The second plan, proposed by Charles Pinckney of South Carolina, provided for a stronger executive and a bicameral legislature.[6] As in the Virginia Plan, the upper house was to be chosen by the lower house and the lower house by popular election. The most interesting aspect of the Pinckney Plan was the division of powers between the executive and legislative branches. Article VI gave the legislature the power to appoint the treasurer and the Senate the sole and exclusive power to declare war, make treaties, and appoint ambassadors and judges. As in many state constitutions, the legislature's power was limited by a Bill of Rights that included such items as freedom of the press and by a provision that prevented federal regulation of commerce unless favorably approved by two-thirds of the members. Although Pinckney was probably the most vehement advocate of a strong executive, his vision of the executive was far more limited than that which finally emerged.

BICAMERAL REPRESENTATION

The first main topic of discussion at the Constitutional Convention was, not surprisingly, the legislative branch, since that was the branch with which most members identified. The resolution for a bicameral legislature passed without dissent, because a two-house legislature was the accepted form in every state except Pennsylvania, Vermont, and Georgia. Only Benjamin Franklin, an avowed advocate of unicameral legislatures, proposed a one-house Congress. Arguing that two houses were so unwieldy as to prevent effective and prompt congressional action, Franklin set forth his criticism of a bicameral legislature in a well-known parable:

Has not the famous political fable of the snake with two heads and one body some useful instruction in it? She was going to a brook to drink, and on her way, was to pass through a hedge, a twig of which opposed her direct course;

one head chose to go on the right side of the hedge, the other on the left; so that time was spent in the contest, and before the decision was completed, the poor snake died of thirst.[7]

However, most members viewed bicameralism as a vital check on a too-powerful legislature; with two houses, one would counteract the other.

The main controversy in establishing a bicameral legislature involved the means for selecting the members of each house. In every Congress since the First Continental Congress the states had enjoyed equal representation, regardless of property or population. Moreover, there was equal representation of large and small states in the Constitutional Convention. Small states like Delaware refused to give up the equality they enjoyed under the existing federal schemes. Thus, the members of the Convention cleverly forged the "Great Compromise," whereby equal representation prevailed in the Senate and representation by population prevailed in the House of Representatives. The framers of the Constitution anticipated that the House of Representatives would probably have more clout than the Senate:

> Notwithstanding the equal authority which will subsist between the two houses on all legislative subjects, except the originating of money bills, it cannot be doubted that the House, composed of the greater number of members, when supported by the more powerful states, and speaking the known and determined sense of a majority of the people, will have no small advantage in a question depending on the comparative firmness of the two houses.[8]

To avoid the problem, which existed in many colonies, of changing populations, a census was to be taken every ten years to ensure that there was no more than one representative for every 30,000 persons in each legislative district, and the composition of the legislature was to be adjusted according to the new population counts.[9] Although the formula for counting slaves encountered intense controversy, the principle of population-based representation was nevertheless viewed as a cornerstone for the legitimacy of the House of Representatives. Pennsylvania delegate James Wilson believed, for example, that the "federal pyramid" should be given "as broad a base as possible"[10] to allow the legislature to play a vigorous federal role. Most members of the Convention agreed that the strength of the lower house would be derived from the continued ability of the representatives to accurately reflect the "interests and circumstances" of their constituents. Interestingly, the responsibility for creating congressional districts was left to the state legislatures, which were also responsible for conducting the elections. However, the Congress retained the responsibility for judging election results.

THE SENATE

The method of selection of the upper chamber, the Senate, was more controversial and reflected the very special role the Senate was expected to play. Some proposed that the second branch of the National Legislature (as the Senate was often referred to during the constitutional debates) should be chosen by the first branch from persons nominated by the state legislatures. This scheme was derived from the Randolph plan and was similar to the method of selection in some states. Only three states, Massachusetts, Virginia, and South Carolina, voted for this means of selection. Other delegates, like James Wilson, insisted that the Senate should be independent of both the lower branch of Congress and the state legislatures. Still others made the proposal, which prevailed, that each state should get an equal vote in the second branch and that the senators should be chosen by the state legislatures. The three main arguments in favor of this compromise included: senators chosen by state legislatures would be of a higher grade than those chosen by the electorate at large; legislative selection would provide an incentive for individual state legislatures to support the national government and thereby preserve harmony between the two levels of government; a different mode of representation between the House and Senate would better balance the legislative power between the two branches. This compromise—that state legislatures would appoint senators—was instantly accepted by the public. The state legislatures had elected the members of the Continental Congress, the delegates to the Congress of the Confederation, and the members of the Constitutional Convention. The linkage made good political sense.

Although similar in concept to the upper chamber of some state legislatures, the Senate, as created by the Constitutional Convention, had no exact parallel in any of the thirteen states. The main purpose of the Senate (derived from the Latin word *senex*, meaning "old man" or "adviser") was to check the excesses of the popularly elected lower chamber. As James Madison said: "The use of the Senate is to consist in its proceeding with more coolness, with more system, and with more wisdom than the popular branch."[11] George Washington analogized its role to that of a saucer into which legislation from the lower chamber, like hot tea, would be cooled.

In creating the Senate, the authors of the Constitution were probably somewhat ambivalent about its relationship to the House of Representatives. During the colonial period, the "upper" chamber performed judicial and executive as well as legislative functions. Viewed as the arm of the royal governor—and not elected directly by the populace—the upper chamber was quickly demoted in stature after the Revolution. Although in some state legislatures it was given roughly equivalent powers to the popular assembly, in others it was actually subordinated.[12] For example, in Virginia, all laws were originated in the House of Delegates and approved or rejected by the Senate. In only a very few state legislatures did the "upper" chamber retain any of the special powers.

Despite the trend in the states to elevate the importance of popular assemblies, many authors of the Constitution, well versed in ancient history, hoped the Senate would not be subordinate. The Senate was intended to function as a Council of Elders,[13] which would bring wisdom and precision to the activities of an unruly lower branch. A senator was to serve six years, a House member for two years, and the minimum age required for Senate membership was 30, whereas the minimum age for those in the House was 25. Moreover, the selection process itself was intended to result in a wiser, more seasoned body. In the earliest years of the Congress, between 1789 and 1809, 78 percent of the laws originated in the House; the Senate merely revised them. Other members of the Convention believed that the Senate should serve primarily in an advisory capacity to the president, as the upper chamber had in many colonial legislatures.

Despite its similarity to the upper chambers of some states, the Senate was designed to fulfill a unique role in the federal constitutional scheme by sharing certain powers with the executive branch. This blurring of the powers between the branches was common in many state governments, where the legislatures chose the judges, the justices of the peace, the officers of the government, and usually even the governor. The authors of the *Federalist Papers* had castigated these state practices as concentrating too much power in the hands of the legislature.[14] Nonetheless, the prevailing sentiment in the Convention was that the national legislature should not forfeit all its responsibility for judicial nominations, appointments of high-level executives, selection of ambassadors, and the formulation of treaties.

The desire to retain some legislative responsibility for high-level executive appointments can be explained by the delicate, but close, relationship between the Congress of the Confederation and those officials who carried out executive functions under the Articles of Confederation. As discussed in the preceding chapter, the Continental Congress and its successor under the Articles of Confederation established quasi-independent committees staffed by experts to carry out the executive functions of the United States. The heads of these committees were named by Congress, reported to Congress, and were exclusively accountable to Congress. Thus, during the Convention, there was understandably some reluctance to forfeit all the ties between the legislature and the executive department heads.

The Senate provided the link between the Congress and the executive branch. The Constitutional Convention gave the power to nominate public officials to the president but required that the Senate approve the nomination by majority vote. As Gouverneur Morris of New York said: "As the President was to nominate, there would be responsibility, and as the Senate was to concur, there would be security."[15]

The power to "advise and consent" to high-level appointments became important from two perspectives. First, it allows the Senate to influence the policies of an incoming department head. And second, it has provided the senators with valuable patronage in the home state and thus has acted as a means of linking the federal and state party systems.[16]

The "advise and consent" powers have been used gingerly, for the Senate is loathe to deny the choice of a president, unless fraud or corruption is apparent. Nonetheless, the threat of humiliating a president by refusing to confirm a nominee, on occasion, has been wielded effectively. For example, in 1981, President Ronald Reagan nominated Ernest Lefever to be assistant secretary of state for human rights. His nomination was particularly startling in view of his comments against an aggressive consideration of human rights matters in relation to foreign policy. When Lefever failed to get enough votes for approval by even the Foreign Relations Committee and it seemed unlikely that he could command a majority of votes on the Senate floor, his name was withdrawn. However, the Lefever controversy is the exception, not the rule.

The delegates to the Convention wanted the legislature to play a role in the area of judicial nominations. In many state legislatures, as noted before, the judges were selected by the popular assembly. Madison was inclined to give the nomination not to the popularly elected lower house but to the Senate, which was "sufficiently stable and independent to follow their deliberate judgments."[17] His proposal that the Senate make judicial appointments was adopted by the Committee of the Whole without dissent. However, in the full Convention, Gouverneur Morris objected on the grounds that the Senate was too cumbersome a body and that the power to try judges on impeachment charges and the power to appoint should not reside in the same body. Thus the members reached a compromise: judges would be appointed by the president with the advice and consent of the Senate. Under this compromise the selection of judges would always be, at least in part, a political process, which guaranteed that the political values of the nominees would reflect a rough consensus of national political values.

Finally, the members of the Convention were not ready to relinquish the powerful role the Congress of the Confederation had played in foreign policy. The Senate was given the power to block all presidential nominations for ambassadors with its "advise and consent" authority. Moreover, it was given great powers to reject presidential treaties. The initial resolution, which was reported out of the Committee of Detail, included a provision that the Senate of the United States have the *exclusive* role in the formulation of treaties. This resolution provoked instant controversy for two reasons. Some members believed that the power to make treaties should be the exclusive domain of the president, whereas others believed that the importance of treaty ratification was sufficient to require the agreement of both houses; still others, like James Madison, believed that peace treaties should require a simple majority. Madison's reasoning was curious and insightful. If a treaty was made too difficult to ratify, a president who derived too much importance from war would be tempted to impede a treaty of peace.[18] Under the final compromise, treaty ratification required the approval of two-thirds of those senators "present," not two-thirds of all senators. In practice, this procedural requirement has been significant, for, as will be shown in later chapters, obtaining attendance of two-thirds of the entire body on the Senate floor would indeed have been a major obstacle.

Critics of the Constitution argued that the sharing of so many powers by the Senate and the president would diminish the ability of the legislative branch to provide an effective check on executive activities.[19]

THE HOUSE OF REPRESENTATIVES

In contrast to the uncertain and tenuous role of the Senate, the House of Representatives—referred to as the first branch rather than the lower house—was firmly rooted in colonial experience and widely viewed as the most effective check on the powers of the executive branch. Indeed, a major controversy concerned whether a representative should have a one- or two-year term. Most state legislators were elected annually, and a popular axiom of the time warned that "where annual elections end, tyranny begins." Although the authors of the *Federalist Papers* defended biennial elections, they nonetheless agreed on the need for a short term: "As it is essential to liberty that the government in general should have a common interest with the people; so it is particularly essential that the branch of it under consideration, should have an immediate dependence on, and an intimate sympathy with, the people."[20]

The House of Representatives was given one major power not possessed by the Senate: the power of taxation.[21] Under the Constitution, the House of Representatives possesses the exclusive power to initiate bills of revenue, although the Senate retains the right to amend such bills. The power to initiate revenue bills was placed in the House because the members of the Convention thought it unfair to give the smaller, less wealthy states an equal role in taxation. It was critical, they believed, for the elected representatives of the populace to control the power of the purse and thereby curb abuses by the executive: "This power over the purse may, in fact, be regarded as the most complete and effectual weapon with which any Constitution can arm the immediate representatives of the people for obtaining a redress of every grievance, and for carrying into effect every just and salutary measure."[22]

Hardly any provision of the Constitution received such frequent and protracted debate as the Senate's role in the origination of money bills. Originally, the Convention provided that the House alone would have the power to originate revenue bills and to appropriate money. Moreover, many delegates urged that the Senate not be given the right to amend appropriation and money bills. This hesitancy about giving the power of the purse to the Senate, which was not directly elected, is understandable. Few had forgotten the rallying cry of the Revolution: No taxation without representation. Some members of the Convention felt so strongly about congressional power over the purse that they suggested that the Congress, not the president, appoint the treasurer. The final compromise allowed the Senate to amend money bills and placed no limitations on the Senate's rights to originate appropriations bills, although subsequent practice has created the tradition of initiating all appropriation bills in the House.

A LIMITED GOVERNMENT

The members of the Constitutional Convention did not want to rely exclusively on the abstract theory of checks and balances to ensure that the power of the federal government remained limited. The members of the Convention wanted the powers of the new federal government to be enumerated carefully, especially those of the Congress. Article I, Section 8 of the Constitution enumerates eighteen powers entrusted to the legislature. Interestingly, almost half these clauses refer to the role of the Congress in conducting national defense. Section 8 provides that Congress shall have the power to provide for the common defense; to declare war; to make rules concerning captures on land and water; to raise and support armies; to provide and maintain a navy; to make rules for the regulation of the land and naval forces; to provide for calling forth the militia; to execute the laws of the union and repel invasions; to suppress insurrections; to provide for organizing armies and disciplining the militia. In light of the successful role of the Continental Congress in conducting the Revolution, the emphasis on the defense powers of Congress is not surprising. Although the chief executive was made commander in chief of the army and navy, it was clear that the Convention intended Congress to play a key role in defense policies. Even Charles Pinckney, the most vigorous advocate of a strong executive branch, said that he was afraid to give the president the power of peace and war for that would "create a monarchy of the worst kind."[23]

Among many other explicit powers given to the Congress but not to the Congress of the Confederation was the power to initiate constitutional amendments by a two-thirds vote of all members. Once adopted, constitutional amendments must be ratified by three-quarters of the state legislatures. Congress could regulate both foreign trade and interstate commerce. Most important, it was delegated the authority to establish an "inferior" federal judiciary. The Constitution provided only for the establishment of the Supreme Court. Because power to create lower courts involved defining their jurisdiction, the Congress was awarded a powerful tool, indeed. In the early years of the Republic, the federal court system under Supreme Court Chief Justice John Marshall became the most important advocate and supporter of an activist federal government. Perhaps most significant, under the Constitution Congress could make all laws "which shall be necessary and proper for carrying into execution its enumerated powers." An expansive interpretation of this clause by a Federalist Supreme Court—coupled with an enthusiastic acceptance of this mandate by the Congress—has enabled the Congress to expand its powers into many spheres never before anticipated. Indeed, Woodrow Wilson interpreted this legislative prerogative as one of the many reasons for the ultimate dominance of the federal legislature over the state governments.

In recent years, many members of Congress and some judges have come to believe that a limitation is necessary on the expansion of the federal government into the sovereignty of the states. In the *National League of Cities* v. *Usery* case, [24] Justice William Rehnquist held that the Tenth Amendment, which provides that all powers not included in the Constitution shall be reserved to the states, restrains the intrusion of the federal government into certain traditional state functions—in this case, setting minimum salaries for certain state employees. Some legal scholars believe that this case is unique and will not be applied generally. However, the new "states' rights" momentum has found strong advocates in President Reagan and the Republican chairman of the Senate Judiciary Committee, Strom Thurmond, who has publicly stated his belief in the need to revitalize the Tenth Amendment. Indeed, a reading of the *Federalist Papers* cogently demonstrates that the framers of the Constitution intended that the strength of the state sovereignties was to be the best check against an overly intrusive federal government. [25]

The Constitution also gave Congress certain housekeeping and disciplinary functions. It was to adopt its own rules and to discipline its own members. Whereas the states retained the right to draw up congressional districts, the Congress had the power to judge election results. The right to remove the president or members of the judiciary was firmly invested in the Congress. The House could initiate removal proceedings through the power of impeachment, whereas the Senate was entrusted with conducting the trial.

Finally, it should be pointed out that the authors of the Constitution were careful to list explicitly the limitations on the power of Congress throughout Article 1 and the rest of the Constitution. However, even with these limitations, the states were not comfortable. They insisted on certain protections—freedom of speech, freedom of the press, the right against self-incrimination, which were highly valued in state constitutions. These protections were specifically enumerated in a Bill of Rights, ratified in 1791. Thus the genesis of the first ten amendments to the Constitution highlights the prevailing belief that the federal government should be limited to protect individual liberties.

Despite the many limitations and checks on the legislature, the Congress still predominates over the other branches. Although the president has the veto power, the legislature can override his veto by a two-thirds vote. Although the courts can judge an act of Congress unconstitutional, Congress can initiate a constitutional amendment. The Congress was given the exclusive power of declaring war, rejecting treaties, and confirming ambassadorial nominations. The Congress was given almost unlimited powers to control the executive branch through its power of the purse and its ability to reject high-level executive appointments. Finally, although the Tenth Amendment sought to protect the sovereignty of state legislatures, the supremacy clause, which provides that federal legislation supersedes conflicting state requirements, the vast power to regulate interstate commerce, and the "necessary and proper clause" quickly enabled the federal legislature to relegate the states to a subordinate role. In short, with the exception of certain individual rights carefully protected in the Bill of Rights and certain other places in the Constitution, the Congress could control almost everything.

THE FIRST FEDERAL CONGRESS

The Constitution contained the grand design of the new government of the United States, but, like an architect's drawing, it needed the skills of those experienced in translating plans into actual structures.

Even before ratification by nine states had made the Constitution the law of the land, those who favored a stronger national government began to publicize the importance of choosing senators and congressmen friendly to the new system. The first federal elections were therefore crucial to the success of the Constitution, for legislators opposed to its principles could destroy the new plan as effectively as if they had blocked its ratification, either by limiting the power of the central government through extensive legislation or, worse still, by calling for another convention. Seven of the states chose their representatives through a districting system that ensured a specific constituency, while four states chose their representatives at large. (North Carolina did not ratify the Constitution until November 21, 1789, nor Rhode Island until May 29, 1790; neither sent representatives to the opening of the First Federal Congress.)

By the end of March, 1789, all but two congressmen and the senators from New York had been chosen, demonstrating an overwhelming Federalist victory. Two of the twenty-two senators and ten of the fifty-nine congressmen had been opponents of the new system. With the seating of members from Rhode Island and North Carolina, only two more anti-Federalists were added to the House, and one to the Senate. The voters, whatever their views during the bitter struggle over ratification of the Constitution, had decided to give it a fair trial.

The sixty-six men who eventually served in the House during the first Congress were of diverse backgrounds: one-fourth came from wealthy families, one-third of them were lawyers, nearly one-half were college graduates. Most were men whose political training had been acquired during the revolutionary period, with only three having begun political careers before 1770–72; yet their number included four signers of the Declaration of Independence. Despite Madison's early fears expressed to Edmund Randolph that "I see on the lists of Representatives a very scanty proportion who will share in the drudgery of business," most of the men were experienced: all but six had served in their state legislative bodies, and thirty-six had been members of the old Congress. Unlike the First Continental Congress, the First Federal Congress was made up of men who knew each other.

The Constitution had specified that the state legislatures should choose each state's two senators, and the expectation that this branch would be filled with men of wealth, importance, and political experience was fulfilled; the first Senate was composed of a group of men who were older, had more political experience, and were more geographically mobile than their counterparts in the House. All but one had served in their state legislatures, while twenty of the twenty-nine who served in the Senate from 1789 to 1791 had been members of the Confederation Congress. Ten of them had held some sort of office before the beginnings of the revolutionary crisis in 1773; one-third of those who served in the first Senate were undisputed members of the colonial elite.

The task these men faced was formidable; there were skeptics who thought it unlikely that the new Constitution would succeed in governing a population of four million people scattered over an area larger than any European state except Russia. The battery of thirteen guns in New York harbor was fired to signal the end of the Confederation on the evening of March 3, 1789, and the church bells rang out peals of celebration to welcome the new Constitution the morning of March 4, but the Congress itself got off to a slow start that for many was too reminiscent of the dilatory habits of the Confederation Congress. A bad winter had made roads impassable throughout much of the South; the House did not achieve a quorum until April 1, and the Senate not until April 6 when Richard Henry Lee arrived from Virginia. The Senate immediately proceeded to count the electoral votes and declare that George Washington had been elected president, and John Adams vice-president. While they waited for the new executive to arrive, both houses decided on their own organizational rules: in the Senate, the appointment of committees would be by ballot, and each member was given the privilege of introducing legislation; the House left the appointment of committees to the speaker, and decided that bills could be introduced only by special committees, following discussion by the Committee of the Whole. Each house also appointed its own chaplain, and chose its other officers.

In all of these activities they were acting on the basis of the procedures learned through long experience in other legislative bodies, but simultaneously creating new procedures that matched both changed expectations of the enhanced importance of the new national legislature and the framework of the new Constitution. Throughout their deliberations, both houses were conscious of their prerogatives vis-à-vis each other and the executive branch. The Senate attempted from the beginning to assert its superiority over the House. It tried unsuccessfully to force the House to have messages and communications delivered by two congressmen, while senators would send down their communications with their secretary. (In the newly refurbished Federal Hall, the Senate chamber was on the second story, and the House on the first, so the former was quite literally the "Upper House.") Of limited success was the senators' bid to mark their importance by giving themselves higher pay than their congressional counterparts; compromise reduced the pay differential to $1.00 per day, and that only for special sessions. Even that was dropped when the pay act was reenacted in 1796 during the intense antiaristocratic sentiment stirred up by the French Revolution. The Senate followed the precedent of deliberating in secret, behind closed doors, while the House adopted a policy of open debates.

Equally important for the future of the legislature was its establishment of independence from the executive branch. Despite the long experience of congressional government under the Articles of Confederation, and the distrust of governors carried over from the colonial period, the First Congress recognized that George Washington's enormous personal prestige, amounting almost to hero-worship, had the potential to give the president substantial executive power at the expense of legislative authority. The Senate has been ridiculed for its lengthy debates over such procedural issues as titles: John Adams thought that senators should be addressed as "Right Honorable," and the majority of the Senate were willing to address the president as "His Highness, the President of the United States of America." Both of these schemes were thwarted, but they reflect the importance of titles in conveying power and enforcing deference. The House stood fast in its insistence that Washington, as first among equals, needed no more formidable title than "President." But for the Senate, "the exaggerated deference toward the president was designed, at least in part, to ensure that if court politics developed, the senators would have first rank as courtiers. The... insistence on formality... was part of a design by the senators to protect their prerogatives against executive encroachment."[26]

Prerogatives of the Senate were also the central issue in the translation into action of the constitutional power given to that body to "advise and consent." The Senate carefully tried to guard that power against erosion. On Saturday, August 22, 1789, accompanied by his secretary of war, General Henry Knox, Washington came to the Senate to confer with it on some Indian treaties. After several readings of the treaties were disrupted by the noise of carriage traffic outside, the senators refused to vote, and referred the issue to committee rather than discuss it in Washington's presence. "I saw no chance of a fair investigation of the subjects while the President of the United States sat there, with his Secretary of War, to support his opinions and overawe the timid and neutral part of the Senate," recorded William Maclay in his journal. Washington "started up in a violent fret," and eventually agreed to postpone the business until Monday, when "a tedious debate" ensued in the president's presence. The idea that obtaining the Senate's consent was a mere formality was quashed, and Washington's first visit to the Senate was his last, paving the way for the precedent of presidential communications by written message. The Senate did continue to function both in its executive and its legislative capacities. Ever since the First Federal Congress the Senate, recognizing its special executive powers, has directed the Secretary of the Senate to keep a separate Senate Executive Journal, in which its executive activities are recorded. In part, its physical proximity to the House, where communication and cooperation were as easy as walking up and down a flight of stairs, and its distance from the executive department offices, ensured the gradual emphasis on its legislative functions.

The Senate was also given powers of advice and consent over presidential appointments, and engaged in extended debate over whether the power extended to executive removals as well. The issue was raised during debates over the House bills creating the executive departments; four of the five roll call votes in the Senate on the executive department bills were on removal, and in the end the House insistence that the power be reserved to the president carried the day.

The legislative program carried out by the First Congress was designed to implement as quickly as possible the four fundamental aims of the new Constitution: a stronger central government, national economic growth, better foreign relations, and an integration of the diverse states and sections. To accomplish this, the Congress faced seven basic problems: 1) completion of the structure of government by creation of the executive and judicial branches so sketchily laid out in the Constitution; 2) establishment of new agencies under those branches for services not available under the Confederation government, and adaptation of agencies and laws that existed under the Confederation government to the new Constitution; 3) response to the widespread demand for constitutional amendments to secure individual liberties and preserve state autonomy that had emerged during the process of ratification of the Constitution; 4) establishment of commercial rules among the states and between the United States and foreign governments; 5) provision for payment of both the foreign and domestic debt, failure of which had seriously compromised the power of the Confederation government during its last years; 6) decision among such alternative means of raising revenue as impost, direct tax, excise, stamp tax, or a combination of several of these; and 7) creation of a permanent residence for the national government.

In pursuit of this ambitious program, the First Congress considered an impressive amount of legislation. One hundred and forty-two bills were introduced in the House, and twenty-four in the Senate. The House created the executive departments, but it fell to the Senate to establish a federal judiciary provided for in a sketchy Article III of the Constitution. In carrying this legislation from introduction to final publication of enrolled engrossed acts, the First Congress worked out procedures that still govern legislative behavior, from creation of committees of members who became skilled in particular subjects, to establishment of conferences between the houses when disagreement had to be resolved. Even the protocols associated with official signatures at the bottom of each act represented new procedures, and required justification of choices; John Adams, for instance, insisted on affixing his signature with both of his titles, vice-president of the United States and president of the Senate. Under the skillful legislative handling of James Madison in the House and Oliver Ellsworth in the Senate, the flood of proposed amendments to the Constitution, some of which might have seriously hamstrung the ability of the new government to function, were condensed and packaged into a Bill of Rights that guaranteed individual liberties against federal abuse without fundamentally altering the new system.

By the time that the First Congress ended its third session on March 3, 1791, it had created a sound basis for a permanent federal government dominated by an activist legislature. It had made substantial progress in achieving three of its four basic goals: government had been strengthened, economic growth had been made possible by well-devised financial and commercial legislation, and better foreign relations had evolved from the brilliantly conceived Hamiltonian plan to provide for the debt. These accomplishments also led to the emergence of permanent political parties along largely sectional lines. The most conspicuous failure of the First Congress was its inability to reconcile the interests of warring sections, but the establishment of a strong national legislature guaranteed that those sectional differences would be played out for an extended period of time within legal and constitutional battlefields.[27]

FOUR

POLITICS
ON THE HILL

THE CONGRESSIONAL PARTY

The Constitution does not mention political parties. The record is not clear whether their absence was founded on a naïve hope that parties would be unnecessary or a pragmatic judgment that the document would be more easily accepted without mention of such "factional" notions. George Washington himself was opposed to parties, and he was characteristic of a general repugnance to party discipline. In 1816 Andrew Jackson wrote to president-elect James Monroe, "Now is the time to exterminate the monster called party spirit."[1] As early American author James Fenimore Cooper said in *The American Democrat*:

> No freeman, who really loves liberty, and who has a just perception of its dignity, character, action and objects, will ever become a mere party man. He may have his preferences as to measures and may act in concert with those who think with himself, on occasions that require concert, but it will be his earnest endeavor to hold himself a free agent, and most of all to keep his mind untrammelled by the prejudices, frauds and tyranny of factions.[2]

Despite this initial opposition to parties, the First Congress had barely begun when a party system developed.[3] Since that time, it has been the key organizational unit in the legislative process. The party system governs the election of congressional leaders, the allocation of staff and financial resources, the determination of the chairmen of committees and subcommittees, the daily flow of legislative activities, and even the actual seating of the members both in the committee rooms and on the floor. Unlike their counterparts in Europe, American parties were intended not to be ideological in purpose but to be an amalgamation of a wide diversity of viewpoints. That the parties do accomplish this is evidenced by the presence in the Democratic party of members with such diverse views as those of conservative southerner Russell Long of Louisiana and liberal northerner George McGovern of North Dakota, and the presence in the Republican party of such liberals as Senator Charles Mathias of Maryland and such conservatives as Jesse Helms (Republican of North Carolina). Without a party mechanism to force a broad consensus to create broad-based coalitions, Congress would disintegrate into hundreds of different factions.

Historically, the congressional party has experienced dramatic shifts in power and prestige. For the first forty years of the Congress, "King Caucus" reigned supreme not only in establishing the legislative agenda but also in choosing the nominees for president. Subsequent to that period, the congressional caucus generally played a less activist role, although it continued to be a major influence on the allocation of power in the Congress. At certain points, the party has been revived as a mechanism for improving congressional effectiveness. In recent times particularly, Congress has turned to the party caucus as a way to make committee chairmen more accountable to congressional leadership and party membership without hindering the smoothness of the legislative process.

Despite the pervasive and consistent influence of the party in Congress, political scientists have generally ignored or disparaged it—with the exception of the seminal book on this subject by David Truman in 1959, which examined the impact of the party on voting behavior.[4] Today the common wisdom is that the party is in trouble. Political savant David Broder lamented the decline of the overall party system in his widely read book *The Party's Over: The Failure of Politics in America*.[5] As recently as 1980, James David Barber, writing about the national party, commented in *The Pulse of Politics: Electing Presidents in the Media Age* that "the two old national party organizations still exist, but mainly as shells within which the real contest is played."[6] Professor David Mayhew, in *Congress: The Electoral Connection,* went so far as to say that it "does not make sense in understanding Congress to posit parties as analytic units."[7]

All pendulums swing, and concern about the party system is once again on the rise. Most current discussion, however, has focused on the national parties; little attention has been paid to the role of the congressional parties. Chapters 4 and 5 analyze the role of party as an organizational and integrative unit in the Congress by first examining the party caucus as an instrument for forging consensus among representatives of diverse viewpoints. Second, discussion centers around the role of the party leadership in determining the legislative agenda and setting floor strategies. Next, other caucuses in the Congress are described, focusing on those that provide a forum for interests not encompassed adequately by the party caucus. Finally, the relationship of the congressional party to national and local party organizations is examined, along with the need for a stronger party system in Congress. The chapters conclude that better party discipline will enhance the legislative process.

THE CONGRESSIONAL PARTY
VS. LOCAL AND NATIONAL PARTIES

The congressional party has never had a clear relationship with national or local party units. A congressman is a fifth wheel on the party wagon. The national party's primary function is to elect the president. The state party directs its attention to state races. The congressional candidate, in limbo between these two units, gains little support, financial or otherwise, from either. As a congressman once said: "If I had to rely on the party to get elected, I wouldn't be here today."[8]

The relationship between the congressional party and the national party depends to a large extent on whether the congressional elections are considered a priority by the national party committee. A "good" party chairman, at least from the congressional viewpoint, provides funds and other assistance to incumbent party members. Thus, William Brock, himself a former senator from Tennessee, was hailed as an outstanding chairman of the Republican National Committee in the successful 1980 election because of the $30 million provided congressional candidates. Moreover, the national Republican party took the lead in providing significant polling, direct-mail technology, and strategic assistance to local party units and Republican candidates. In superb long-term planning, the Republican party developed an extensive grass-roots fund-raising and get-out-the-vote network, which helped candidates on both state and local levels. Far more than the Democratic party, it sought to integrate the party structure on all governmental levels.

The Democratic party is generally reluctant to divert resources to congressional races. Historically, many Democratic members of Congress have relied on labor unions to provide campaign contributions and person power to fill phone banks, lick envelopes, and stand at polls. The national party prefers to lavish monies on the presidential race and pays little attention to congressional races or to local party organization.

In turn, the congressional Democratic party generally ignores the national party. Little effort is made to carry out the party's national platform or to punish members who do not vote in accordance with it. On only a few occasions have congressional party members been disciplined for refusing to support the national party presidential candidates. When Democratic Congressman John Bell Williams refused to support Lyndon Johnson, he was threatened with loss of his committee seniority by the Democratic caucus. He promptly mooted the threat by switching parties and parlaying his dramatic Republican rebirth into the governorship of Mississippi. A few years later Congressman John Rarick of Louisiana refused to support Hubert Humphrey's presidential candidacy. The Democratic caucus did, in fact, discipline Rarick, by demoting him to the most junior position on the Agriculture Committee. However, because his previous position on the committee had been only two notches higher, the caucus thrust was hardly fatal. Democratic Congressman Phil Gramm was ousted by the Democratic caucus from the Budget Committee in 1983 for leading a Republican budget fight in the previous Congress. An effort was made to take away the Veterans Committee chairmanship from Congressman G. V. (Sonny) Montgomery of Mississippi for similar transgressions, but it failed.

The congressional party's allegiance to the national party varies with the influence of the president who wears the same party label. In the 1930s President Franklin Delano Roosevelt had so put his personal imprimatur on the Democratic party label that anyone running on that label, from congressman to coroner, was subject to White House influence. James Farley, New Deal chairman of the Democratic National Committee, delivered that message to congressional candidates in the political vernacular. When a president is weak, the converse is true. By the time Richard Nixon was ready to resign the presidency, even the most timid Republican congressman had disassociated himself from his party's administration. Jimmy Carter could never apply the kind of pressure that was available to a Lyndon Johnson or a Roosevelt. Although not a party man, Eisenhower had such influence and goodwill in the country that his every wish was viewed as a near command by Republican congressmen. Ronald Reagan did not rely exclusively on his personal charisma; he wooed members of his party not only with the traditional cufflinks but also with agreements to support proposals helpful to a member's home district.

The desire of the party caucus to identify with, and work for, the national party varies largely with whether its candidate is in the White House. In that case, the caucus is responsible for implementing the administration's legislative and policy initiatives. For example, early in the Ninety-seventh Congress, the Senate Republican caucus decided to award top legislative priority not to the divisive social issues sponsored by the moral majority Republicans but to the new Republican president's economic package. This overall strategy was hammered out in the caucus and, with a few exceptions, was followed. Without the caucus, there would have been no means of ironing out differences to allow the members to unify behind the administration's initiatives.

When the nominee of the congressional party is not in the White House, the caucus provides the home base for opposition to the administration. How well it performs this role may well determine the party's chances for regaining the White House in the next election. Because the electorate does not applaud opposition for opposition's sake, the caucus must tread carefully. The effectiveness of party caucus leverage over administration policies depends on its ability to unify its strategy.

The congressional party rarely becomes involved in state party affairs. Originally when state legislatures chose senators, the state party had some leverage in the congressional political arena. However, the direct election of senators has largely eliminated congressional influence in state parties. The two organizations probably come in closest contact at election time when state campaign organizations sometimes supply money and staff to local congressional candidates. In addition, the state party structure is essential after every ten-year census when the state legislatures redraw congressional district lines. However, for the most part, congressional candidates must rely on themselves for campaign funds, campaign organization, and media coverage. On arrival in Washington, a congressman has little or no loyalty to the state organization.

IS A STRONGER PARTY
NEEDED IN CONGRESS?

From the very beginnings of the Congress, national leaders, in both the party and the executive branch, cast longing eyes at British party loyalty. As the First Lord of the Admiralty in Gilbert and Sullivan's *H.M.S. Pinafore* sang: "I always voted at my party's call, / and never thought of thinking for myself at all. / I thought so little, they rewarded me, / by making me the ruler of the Queen's Navy." Under the British system, party loyalty is well rewarded— heresy is not. Indeed, the British party nominating system is geared to producing candidates who will toe the party line. When successful at the polls, the party chooses executive branch ministers from among its own parliamentary members. The British system is characterized by accountability. The members of Parliament are accountable to the party that elected them, and the party is accountable to the electorate for implementing its campaign pledges. In the early days of the Republic, American leaders made a half-hearted attempt to form a ministerial system similar to that in England in which members of the same party in both the executive and legislative branches functioned as a team. Thus, Thomas Jefferson tried to preside over his party's congressional caucus. Likewise, King Caucus designated presidential nominees on the basis of their party loyalty. However, the Constitution forbids members from simultaneously serving in Congress and the executive branch. With the development of the committee system, the evolution of seniority, and the nomination of presidential candidates by national conventions, the caucus became far less powerful. By the time Woodrow Wilson wrote about Congress in 1885, he found party responsibility indistinct and organized party action almost impossible.[9] Wilson advocated (at the time of his writing but not after he became president) control of the administration by Congress so that party responsibility could be exercised in the Congress. He envisioned a system that resembled the pure parliamentary system. His criticisms re-emerge with a predictable degree of constancy. Recently President Jimmy Carter's counsel, Lloyd Cutler, espoused a ministerial system not to provide Congress with power over the president but to provide the president with greater leverage over the legislature.[10]

The binding of the president and the Congress to a single party platform or stringent party discipline, of the sort imposed by the British system, poses difficult questions about the American constitutional system of separation of powers. In the American system, unlike the British system, the executive ministers are not elected from the Parliament. Indeed, this approach was explicitly rejected in the Constitution. Under the American plan, the president's initiatives are screened and evaluated by Congress, not merely rubber-stamped simply because the congressional majority and the president are of the same party. Of course, a congressman gives great weight to the wishes of his party's president, but his constitutional responsibility requires consideration of other factors—the merits of a proposal and its impact on his home district—in voting.

The resistance toward linking national party objectives to congressional party priorities makes the implementation of the president's legislative program difficult. Even President Reagan, who in 1981 did an excellent job in lobbying his economic package, sometimes forgot that Congress was an equal, not a subordinate, branch. When David Stockman, director of the Office of Management and Budget, asked Budget Committee Chairman Peter Domenici, Republican of New Mexico, to rubber-stamp the administration's budget package and thus ignore the different spending proposals adopted in the

Senate, Senator Domenici gave David Stockman a lesson in civics. When a similar tactic was played on the tax bill, Senator Robert Dole, Republican of Kansas, insisted on the senatorial position.

In a two-party system, the coalition that elects a president tends to cross party lines and depend on factors—the candidate's personality—that have little to do with the candidate's political views on the national party platform. Indeed, the president's personal views often differ from those expressed in the national party platform. President Jimmy Carter rejected several planks of the Democratic National Platform when he ran for reelection in 1980. Thus, the election of a president sometimes creates the mirage of a mandate for rapid change when, in actuality, the electoral mood speaks for much slower and smaller change. Academics, after conducting a multitude of polls, will probably argue for years to come the significance of the 1980 elections: Did they signify a mandate to dump Jimmy Carter, a mandate for substantive social change, or simply a political realignment between the Democratic and Republican parties?

Congressional elections generally do not reflect a broad-scale public demand for change. In the House, approximately 90 percent of incumbents are reelected, and seldom achieve reelection by advocating radical change. Because only one third of the senators are up for reelection in any election year, in most circumstances the composition of the Senate does not clearly demonstrate demand for political change. An incumbent is much more apt to emphasize his experience, his seniority, his ability to get along—qualities that are counterindicative to drastic change or to control by a national party leader or platform.

The independence of Congress from national party priorities and pronounced political swings is not without negative side effects. Congress frequently appears to stand in the way of progress, particularly after a president has been elected by a wide margin. Moreover, political blame is difficult to assess, given the different perspectives of Congress and the president; there is a natural tension between the two branches. President Harry Truman complained of the "good for nothing, do-nothing Eightieth Congress" and Henry Cabot Lodge contended that Americans were "thoroughly tired of the stagnation of business and the general inaction of Congress. They are disgusted to see year after year go by and great measures affecting the business and political interests of the country accumulate at the doors of Congress and never reach the stage of action."[11]

But times change and points of view change. Lodge and Woodrow Wilson, both of whom criticized the functioning of Congress in the 1880s, found their views of Congress changed by events and positions after World War I. President Wilson, who had earlier advocated congressional control of the presidency, changed his view drastically when the postwar Senate, led by Senator Lodge, blocked his vision of a world peace maintained through the League of Nations. Senator Lodge, on the other hand, found that the stagnation he had complained about thirty years earlier was not so bad after all.

When a strong bond exists between the congressional party and the national party, both the executive and the legislative branches lose some incentive to check one another's activities, particularly when the congressional majority and the president belong to the same party. The Senate's Republican majority during the first session of the Ninety-seventh Congress was strongly criticized for unthinkingly yielding to the directives of the executive branch. A strong national party system that binds the president and Congress together is incompatible with the healthy tension between the two branches that is envisioned in the "checks and balances" philosophy of the Constitution. Thus the Congress should not be blamed for slowing down the process by which perceived national mandates are implemented: Such a slowdown is precisely what the framers of the Constitution intended. However, the separation of the congressional party from the president and national party priorities does not obviate the need for a stronger congressional party.

Since the 1970s, it has been clear the congressional caucus and leadership, particularly in the House, have more clout to persuade, or coerce, the rank and file to support important legislative packages. Because the evolution of the caucus as a power base has weakened the power of committee chairmen, it has met with great resistance. Nonetheless, without the existence of a cohesive party organization, Congress would best be characterized as warring committee fiefdoms that randomly set legislative priorities. A strong party caucus makes it easier for an individual congressman to subordinate his personal political needs to those of the national interest. It is easier for a congressman to go home to his district after supporting a budget cut favored by a majority of his party than one favored by only a minority of his party.

Although few would advocate the creation of sanctions analogous to those in the British system, it might be appropriate to create additional rewards for those who incur political risks in their efforts to enact the party's priorities. Similarly, penalties might be inflicted on recalcitrant members. Only with a strong congressional party system can Congress effectively temper parochial reelection needs with pressing national responsibilities.

THE PARTY CAUCUS

Each party in each chamber has a "caucus," consisting of all the members elected on that party's label. The Republicans in the House and both parties in the Senate refer to their caucus as a "conference," but the term *caucus* is the common parlance for the party organization in both chambers. The caucus provides the umbrella to unify party members who have vastly differing political perspectives. Such an organization is essential in a governmental system that has only two major parties. On the rare occasions that a third party has emerged in the United States, it has either failed miserably or provided the foundation for a realignment of existing parties.

The party *caucus*—a term derived from the Algonquin Indian word for "adviser"—was used initially by the Federalists (in particular Treasurer Alexander Hamilton) to resolve issues before they reached the floor. It proved to be such an effective liaison between the executive branch and the Congress that President Thomas Jefferson encouraged its growth.[12] Although the Democrats under Jefferson were criticized for using such an "undemocratic" device, Jefferson even presided at some congressional caucuses to make sure his point of view was given full consideration, and it can hardly be doubted that many of his successors would have been delighted to do the same. However, as a result of the aggressive leadership of young Speaker Henry Clay, who used the caucus as an effective tool to enhance his own powers, the party caucus evolved into an organization independent of the presidency. The congressional party caucus not only proved to be the chief adversary of the executive branch but at one point, as the infamous King Caucus, actually controlled the nomination of the president.[13]

Daniel Webster described the effectiveness of the caucus: "It was attended with a severe and efficacious discipline by which those who went astray were to be brought to penitence."[14] The most important role of the caucus was to nominate the president and vice-president. By controlling the nomination, Clay and his fellow "war hawks" were able to influence foreign policy. Thus the caucus, by keeping President James Madison uncertain about his renomination to a second term, pressured the president into recommending a war against the British.[15] As historian Wilfred E. Binkley said in *President and Congress*:

> The Congressional caucus, which had been employed by Jefferson as an
> integrating agency co-ordinating the executive and the legislature, was no longer
> serving the executive for that purpose but was used by congressional leaders for
> that purpose to secure party solidarity in putting programs through Congress.[16]

The caucus flourished until the administration of Andrew Jackson, which marked a new turn in the development of American political institutions. During the period from 1812 to 1828, the two-party system disappeared as the central fact in national politics. Personal, local, and sectional conflicts replaced in importance those former broad differences over public policy.

The party caucus has risen and fallen numerous times since then. With the revolt against tyrannical Speaker Joe Cannon, at the turn of the century, the party caucus system was revived to enforce order in the House, although party discipline prompted by the caucus system was almost as rigid as the discipline delivered by the harsh regime of Speaker Cannon. According to the new caucus rules, a proposal that mustered a two-thirds vote of the caucus went to the floor with the united support of the party membership. Its power enabled President Woodrow Wilson, assisted by Congressman Oscar W. Underwood, floor leader of the Democrats and chairman of the Ways and Means Committee, to expedite passage of his tariff and Federal Reserve Board legislation before World War I. As historian Binkley stated: "So compact was the party organization that without the use of cloture or even a motion to limit debate the bill passed the House without material change and by a large majority."[17]

The caucus also determined committee assignments and developed legislative proposals that were referred to committees not for debate but for their rubber stamp of approval. The caucus instructed committees on what legislation to report, and even the Rules Committee was not immune from the long arm of the caucus. Thus, the demise of the personal tyranny of the speaker led to an equally ironclad tyranny by the party caucus.[18]

But power of the party caucus was again to be short-lived. In the early part of the twentieth century the seniority system was developed to protect members against abuses by the speaker. By virtually guaranteeing the succession of ranking majority members to committee chairmanships, the seniority system gave committee chairmen an independence from party leadership they had never before enjoyed. The party caucus remained limp and ineffective until the Watergate era when it was revived to bring more accountability to congressional institutions. In part, the revival of the caucus in the 1970s resulted from a widespread dissatisfaction with the seniority system, which had placed conservative and ancient congressmen in chairmanships, and, in part, from a widespread desire to organize the Congress against the onslaughts of President Richard Nixon, who, to an unprecedented degree, had attacked legislative prerogatives in every area from the budget to foreign policy.

Revival of the Caucus

A key reform of the 1970s provided that an amendment proposed by a minimum of fifty members and approved by a majority of the caucus must be permitted to reach the floor for consideration. Previously, the Rules Committee, when determining how legislation would be considered on the floor, limited the number and kinds of measures which could be offered as amendments to pending legislation in the manner sought by the chairman of the committee reporting the legislation. For example, if the chairman of the Agriculture Committee opposed an amendment eliminating tobacco subsidies, the Rules Committee would in all likelihood refuse to allow such an amendment under its rule. The new caucus procedure required the consideration of certain amendments even over the objections of the chairman of the Rules Committee and the standing committee. The Rules Committee had to provide in the rule that such amendments would be "in order" for floor consideration.

To protect the caucus procedure from being bypassed by quick moves from substantive committees, a further rule provided that a committee chairman who wanted to obtain a closed rule (barring or limiting amendments to the bill) from the Rules Committee was to give five days' notice of such intention in the *Congressional Record*. During the five-day period, a special caucus could be called to review the rule and "instruct" the Rules Committee Democrats as to any amendments to be allowed. (This procedure permitted the repeal of the oil-depletion allowance. Tax legislation, reported out of the Ways and Means Committee, generally receives a closed rule and cannot, therefore, be amended on the floor. Because of the five-day procedure, the Rules Committee Democrats altered the closed rule sought by the Ways and Means Committee, and thus permitted an amendment repealing the oil-depletion allowance to come up for floor debate.) The oft-sought debate on the Vietnam War was finally achieved when the Democratic caucus instructed the Foreign Affairs Committee to report out a resolution to the floor for debate under another provision of this same caucus procedure. All of this was heady stuff to a Congress that had traditionally accepted the rule of the minority as long as that minority was garbed in the seniority cloaks of committee chairmanships.

However, as with all sudden winds in the political arena, the potency of these caucus procedures was easily diverted and deflected. One of the first deflections came about when a southern conservative Democrat, William V. Chappell, Jr., proposed that all caucus meetings be open to the public. Thus, not only the press would be present to hear the intraparty squabbling about hard issues but the Republicans would be present as well. The argument made by proponents that the open caucus was part of the "government in the sunshine" ideal urged by liberal reformers was hard to answer. The compromise finally worked out required the caucus meetings to be open whenever legislative business (as opposed to internal party business) was being discussed unless the caucus, by a recorded vote, closed the meeting. Consequently, all caucus meetings to "instruct" Rules Committee members were to be open meetings. It became considerably more difficult to persuade marginal Democrats to take strong positions under such tough "partisan" tactics—especially in view of Republican complaints about government by King Caucus. (In the Ninety-seventh Congress the rules were once again changed to close the caucus unless there was a specific vote to open it to the public.)

The influence of the caucus on substantive legislation was further decreased with the revival of the "government-by-quorum" technique. Because a quorum in the caucus is necessary to do substantive business, the opponents of a proposal of substance simply organized a boycott of the caucus. Nothing is easier to organize among busy legislators than a boycott of a proceeding where controversial, vote-costing proposals are to be acted upon. Anyone who had given the required advance notice of (had "noticed-up") a substantive proposal via the fifty-member route described earlier could lay claim to being the first order of business whenever a quorum was present. The leadership frequently had to lean heavily on advocates of such substantive proposals to persuade them to withdraw to allow the caucus to go on to other important party business.

Still another way was found to diminish the influence of the party caucus on substantive matters when the conservatives decided that two could play the liberals' game. "Redneck" proposals were noticed-up to the caucus— proposals seeking to put the caucus on record as opposing busing, favoring prayer in public schools, and otherwise forcing recorded votes in the caucus on the highly emotional social issues that have dominated congressional concern over the last three decades. Even when sufficient votes were available in the caucus to defeat such proposals, the cost was high to marginal members who had to record their views. The controversial caucus votes polarized the party membership and threatened any semblance of party unity for other issues before the House.

All this game-playing about the influence of the caucus on substantive legislation was accompanied by a steady drumbeat of Republican attacks on King Caucus. John Anderson, chairman of the Republican Conference and otherwise a moderate concerning most issues on which his party was beginning to move more to the right, used the Democratic caucus regimen as a foil to keep his own party unified and to denigrate the majority power of the Democrats. With all these countereffects, the decline in the use of caucus procedures is not surprising. Although the procedures still exist in the Democratic caucus rules, their efficacy has declined. As the House of Representatives became more badly split on ideological issues, the caucus lost the legitimacy to use the procedures developed during the post-Watergate era.

The party caucus in the Senate has never been as influential as its counterpart in the House. Historically it has served an organizational function, choosing candidates for president pro tempore, secretary of the Senate, sergeant at arms, party secretaries, and chaplain, and deciding the distribution of committee assignments among the party members. While legislative programs and strategies are discussed, members of the caucus are never bound to follow a determination of the caucus as in the House. The relative impotence of the Senate caucuses reflects the fact that the political party in the Senate was slow to evolve.[19]

The caucus system is still the primary forum in both the Senate and the House for battling out compromises within the party before legislative packages are scheduled for floor debate. To the extent that committees have declined in influence and power has been fragmented and distributed to subcommittees, the caucus provides a critical information-gathering network for the party leadership, an invaluable tool for forging consensus, and an important safety valve within the party to work out internal strife. Because its appendage on the Democratic side, the Steering and Policy Committee, is responsible for commitee assignments and scheduling the legislative agenda, the House party caucus is presently influential.

Integrative Role of the Caucus

Most democratic legislatures have a multi-party system, with each party representing a different ideological perspective. In such a system an activist can associate himself with the party that best reflects his views. He can shop around until he finds a party suited to his political needs and personal passions. If none is available, he can find enough like-minded citizens to start his own party. Not so in a two-party system. Because each party seeks majority status, it must establish an agenda that both ignores some causes and champions others. This consensus approach frustrates the individual who believes that a party should take stands on important controversial issues. A member of Congress, thus, is elected on a party label, or "cue," even though the national platform of that party may be antithetical to the views of the voters who elected him. However dissatisfied an individual candidate may be with the national party, once he is elected he can rest assured that the congressional party is an organizational, not an ideological, unit. Thus, a southern Democratic congressman can speak for, promote, and vote for issues that violate the national party caucus.

The congressional caucus has no analog in England. In the Parliament, there are three distinct political parties (with occasional additional parties emerging in response to national issues). Members of these parties run for office by pledging to implement certain programs if the party succeeds in winning a majority. The parties embody separate and contrasting traditions of an economic, social, and even ideological character. When a party succeeds, its members form the cabinet—the executive branch; the losing party forms the loyal opposition. All members run on the national platform, follow the direction of the party leadership, rely on the national party for office space, staffing, and campaign financing, and are completely dependent on the party for their political futures.[20] The parliamentary party is the national party. There are no distinct local parties.

In this country, on the other hand, party adherents do not so clearly represent opposing political viewpoints. In the Democratic party there are northern liberals and southern conservatives. The Republican party includes liberals who are loyal members of Common Cause and conservatives who belong to the Moral Majority. Each party serves to unify. In particular, the congressional caucus functions primarily to create alliances, agreements, and compromises to form the basis for policy and action. When the caucus is strong and its leadership powerful, the caucus is usually successful in hammering out critical differences behind-the-scenes, providing thereby a powerful front to the opposite party on the floor of the chamber. Without this forum for ironing out differences within the party (a forum that is not always successful), frequent free-for-alls would occur on the floor with each member following his own political conscience and needs.

The Senate and the House caucus structures are quite different. In the Senate the caucus functions primarily as an informal forum for forging consensus, although the party leader has few weapons to enforce party discipline on stray sheep. In the House, on the other hand, where the caucus includes many more members, very elaborate procedures have been devised to define the limits to party responsibility. For a long period of time the caucus had a rule on the books which stipulated that upon approval of a two-thirds vote, a member would be bound by a caucus decision. This rule was substantially watered down, however, so that a member was never actually bound by a caucus decision that contravened his campaign promises. Rather, members were to be bound only on the election of the House leadership and on questions of rules.

Controversy remains, however, over fundamental matters essential to party power and the consequences of failing to go along with the caucus decision. On the opening day of the Ninety-seventh Congress, which convened in 1981, a few Democrats refused to support a procedural vote to determine party ratios in House committees. Some members defected because they objected to the ratios; at least one Democrat failed to follow the caucus decision because historically he had refused to vote for any procedure that would cut off the possibility of amending a measure before the House. The vague punishments meted out hardly diminished the good standing of the defectors in the congressional party. Subsequently, numerous Democrats defected from the party leadership when they supported President Reagan's tax and budget proposals rather than the Democratic alternatives. They risked the possible wrath of the party rather than defy a president who, for the most part, had won by substantial margins in their home districts.

Committees also caucus on a party basis, although the formality and structure varies from committee to committee and from House to Senate. On the House Ways and Means Committee, where major tax and economic matters have always been taken up in full committee rather than subcommittee, Democratic members frequently caucus to gauge majority sentiment for a piece of legislation. On other committees where partisanship is not as marked the use of the caucus device is less frequent. The same holds true for subcommittee proceedings. Because most subcommittees are comparatively small, the need for a formally structured caucus is not as clear. Nevertheless, depending on both the subject matter of the legislation under consideration and the personnel of the subcommittee, party caucuses of subcommittee members are not unusual.

Organization of the Caucus

In most cases the party caucus is the first formal contact between the member-elect and the institution he has just won the right to enter. A few weeks after election, after the congratulatory letters have trickled down to a few, a letter arrives from the chairman of the caucus or conference announcing a meeting of all members prior to commencement of the Congress. The meeting usually takes place before the official swearing-in of new members. The meeting sometimes lasts two or three days, depending on the length of the agenda. For House members-elect, a special travel allowance is provided to permit the new member to fly to Washington with a staff member to start the transition process. The Democratic caucus meets in the "hall," the chamber itself—a perquisite of the long-standing majority party. The Republican caucus meets in the Caucus Room of the Cannon House Office Building.

In either event, the meeting agenda contains a long list of tasks to be accomplished. Nominations are made for the House leadership, a speaker for the majority and floor leaders for both parties. The congressional party leaders—the caucus and conference chairman and other officers—are elected. Maneuvering begins for choice committee assignments. Some committee slots (Ways and Means members and Appropriations subcommittee chairs) require individual election by the caucus. New members (and old) are wooed by those seeking to retain, or to challenge, committee chairmanships. Rules changes, especially those desired to reflect the enhancement, or diminution, of party strength in the last election, are debated. (Much of the controversy over rules changes is incomprehensible to new members.)

But perhaps the matter most confusing to new members is what is *not* on the agenda, for the great issues that divided the national parties in the recently concluded election are not discussed. In the evenings at the watering spas, there may be some talk about the economy, war and peace, liberty and justice, or other more pertinent matters. But the purpose of the organizing caucuses is not to resolve substantive matters but to provide the means by which the congressional parties will succeed in the upcoming session. The impetus for initial party unity usually transcends the sharp divisions within the caucus membership on the national issues.

For members-elect who have served in other legislative bodies, confusion is tempered by their past experience. Almost without exception, the legislative process on the state level involves alignment by party label. The intensity of the party label may vary from legislative body to legislative body, but the pragmatic needs of organization tend to overwhelm the ideological differences among the members of the same party. Those differences are reserved for later exploitation, after the organization of the caucus is completed.

In the Senate the pre-opening sessions are not as formal, in part because two-thirds of the senators have not been involved in the elections. Moreover, unlike the House, the Senate does not adopt new rules every two years. However, when control of the Senate changes from one party to the other, the pre-session caucus is more significant. Thus, following the 1980 election when the Republican party took control of the Senate, the agenda of the Republican conference of the Senate was fuller than usual to discuss the various committee ratios, chairmanships, and rules.

The caucus meets frequently throughout the legislative year. Sometimes the members merely eat lunch together and exchange information. More often, however, the meetings are focused on specific items on the legislative agenda. For example, in 1981 when the administration's budget legislation came to the Senate floor, Minority Leader Robert Byrd quickly called a caucus to determine which amendments the Democrats would offer. Other times, the caucus is used as a mechanism to obtain advice from other members. In 1981 Missouri Senator Thomas Eagleton, the chairman of the Regulatory Reform Task Force of the Democratic caucus, had to decide whether the Democrats should, as a group, co-sponsor the regulatory reform legislation sponsored by Nevada Republican Senator Paul Laxalt. Eagleton went to the caucus for advice, and the Democrats as a party decided to endorse the legislation. The caucus in the Senate exerts influence on each member by peer group pressure only. However, because the caucus meets in private and because there are no caucus procedures, peer group pressure has only limited effect, and the senators tend to follow their own political instincts.

The House caucus is more formal and historically has had more power over individual members. At times, the caucus has been the key to floor passage of legislation. For example, the funds for the war in Vietnam were cut off after the Democratic caucus instructed its committees to that effect. The House Foreign Affairs Committee voted out a resolution to "end the war." The House adopted it and refused to vote any more funds to continue the war.

Caucus Sanctions

The party leadership has few sanctions to implement the decision of the caucus. Although Speaker Sam Rayburn effectively admonished House members "to get along, you go along," that same advice cannot be given as easily by Speaker Tip O'Neill. Rayburn controlled many "goodies" to reward the faithful; O'Neill is not as fortunate. Although a speaker on your side is helpful in seeking advancement, a member knows that advancement can be obtained by other methods. Bella Abzug of New York, never the darling of House leaders, was effective without their blessing. She even managed to command a subcommittee chair. Nevertheless, such emoluments as appointment to preferred committees and foreign travel are within the power of the leadership to give or withhold. Members who too often ignore party issues in their votes frequently find themselves among the unrewarded.

The judgment of peers also serves as an effective deterrent to recalcitrant behavior. Although members are aware of parochial pressures, they often resent a member who never "walks the plank" for the party or its issues. When that same member seeks a committee chairmanship or pushes parochial legislation, his prior lack of support for the party is often used against him. Although few members have been denied advancement to which they were entitled by seniority, it has happened on occasion. Memories are long in Congress, and such peer pressure sometimes serves as a restraint.

Prior to the reform of the 1970s, seniority had allowed individual members to remain independent of their congressional parties. Seniority had limited the sanctions that could be directed against a party defector. His committee assignments were protected by seniority; his advancement to positions of leadership were enhanced, if not guaranteed, by seniority. Party leaders and disciplinarians had little left to threaten the standing of a senior member who left the reservation.

The potential threat of withholding party help at reelection time is limited. The impact of a defection from the party line is minimized because congressional campaign committees tend to organize on geographical levels and because of the normal fraternal concerns party campaign committees have toward fellow members. In addition, campaign committees have a need to be pragmatic. Withholding help from a member of their congressional party might effect the desired discipline but at the cost of the seat. That kind of capital punishment is not likely to be self-inflicted. Finally, the forces that persuade a member to bolt his party on a key issue usually provide effective substitutes for party reelection help. The notorious special-interest political action committees often provide assistance to the congressman who defies his party to support their legislative causes.

Given all these negatives, it is surprising that loyalty to the party is as strong as it is. However, most congressmen shed their labels only when such defection is perceived as necessary to reelection. For most politicians, the political label is a familiar and comfortable security blanket.

Informal Party Groups

Democratic Study Group

Because the party caucus cannot function effectively to represent the ideology of all members, informal groups and caucuses have developed. In the House, the senior and largest group is the Democratic Study Group. Originally organized to counteract the strong leadership control exercised by Speaker Sam Rayburn, it has played different roles at various times since then. At the beginning it was commonly known as McCarthy's Marauders, after Democratic Congressman Eugene McCarthy of Minnesota, whose liberal leadership was suppressed regularly by House seniors. Although the group has steadfastly sought to avoid conflict with the House leadership, its very existence, its potential challenge to the powers that be, causes it to be viewed with suspicion. Nevertheless, it has functioned primarily as a research service supplying information about "liberal" and reform causes as well as all issues before the House. Most members, including many Republicans, have relied on its research facilities.

State and Regional Groups

State delegations and regional caucuses focus congressional attention on concerns of different geographic regions. Most state delegations meet on both a partisan and a bipartisan basis, depending on the issues to be discussed. Because most larger states embrace a good number of differences both between and within parties, the issues usually tend to be parochial—for example, a public works or relief program that benefits the state. Sometimes governors and mayors use the state delegation caucuses to represent their needs in Congress; most frequently such communications occur through the "dean" of the delegation or some other designated leader.

Regional caucuses seek to protect one region of the country against others in the logrolling process. The New England Caucus, for example, sought to make sure that energy programs did not unfairly penalize the users of heating oil in New England. Sometimes these regional concerns persuade members to form renegade groups to joust with their party leadership. In the Ninety-seventh Congress many southern Democrats united to form the "boll weevil" caucus. Many liberal northern Republicans formed the "gypsy moths." Regional caucuses complain when too many federal programs or other goodies are awarded to other parts of the country.

Special-Interest Caucuses

Some caucuses—the Black Caucus, Women's Caucus, Italian Caucus, Jewish Caucus, Steel Caucus, Blue-Collar Caucus, and Arts Caucus—meet regularly and are highly structured, with staff, stationery, and office space. Some are much less than that. The Jewish Caucus denies that it functions as a caucus and points to its non-Jewish members. Some Jewish Caucus members call it the Jewish Noncaucus.

Some groups, like the Steel Caucus, form exclusively around an issue. The Environmental Study Conference has maintained an active agenda and staff on all environmental issues. The Members of Congress for Peace Through Law is perhaps the only bipartisan, bicameral group that continues to function. Originally formed by Senator Joseph Clark of Pennsylvania, it has sought to mobilize congressional opinion and action on military affairs as well as disarmament and foreign affairs.

The Senate seems to find less need for such informal groups, although some do exist. The Wednesday Group has functioned as a caucus for more moderate and urban-oriented Republican senators (as well as Congressmen). The Conservative Coalition and the Republican Policy Committee have represented the other side of Republican party ideology.

FIVE

PARTY LEADERSHIP

he ability of Congress to respond effectively to national problems rests in the strength of its leadership. Strong leadership is particularly important in the House of Representatives where the enormous size of the membership—435 men and women, each with a widely diverse political constituency—necessitates some semblance of a centralized power structure capable of forging coalitions and imposing, sometimes with an iron hand, sometimes with a velvet glove, order and decorum in its proceedings.

Effective leadership is equally necessary in the considerably smaller Senate where each senator is allowed almost unlimited powers to delay and block passage of legislation. Indeed, given the diversity and size of the membership in the two houses, that any major piece of controversial legislation succeeds in passing both houses must, at least in part, be attributed to the skills of the congressional leadership. The constitutional requirement of a majority vote in both houses to pass legislation hardly explains the machinations necessary to usher a bill successfully through the legislative labyrinth. Without leadership, mere support for a bill by a majority of the congressional rank and file would be virtually meaningless.

As would be expected from the different sizes and constituencies of the House and Senate, the style, powers, and formation of the leadership are quite different as well. Designated by the Constitution as the presiding officer, the House speaker wields significant procedural powers and has extensive staff resources. His constitutional counterpart, the president of the Senate, an office filled by the vice-president, on the other hand, is a ceremonial figurehead with few powers except his constitutionally mandated power to cast the deciding vote in the event of a tie vote. The real powers of the Senate reside in the majority leader and the minority leader, who are elected by their respective party organizations. Unlike the speaker, the majority and minority leaders possess few procedural powers and must control floor proceedings through their powers of persuasion, their superior knowledge of the rules, and their ability to muster consensus within the party on legislation.

But despite the significant differences of the House and Senate leadership, one important characteristic is common to both: Their strength is derived from the coherence of the party membership and the degree to which the members of each party identify their own legislative priorities with the agenda set by the party leadership. Otherwise, the congressional leader is a general without soldiers.

LEADERSHIP IN THE HOUSE

The Speaker

The office of speaker of the House of Representatives is the second most powerful in the land. Although he stands behind the vice-president in terms of succession to the presidency, his powers as a constitutionally established leader of the House of Representatives far surpass those of the vice-president in his role either as president of the Senate or as theoretical second-in-command in the executive branch.

Joint sessions of Congress highlight the special role of the speaker as a constitutional officer and as third in succession to the highest office in the land. Joint sessions are almost always held in the House chamber. When the president delivers his State of the Union message or addresses the Congress on other occasions, the speaker calls the House into session, whereupon the doorkeeper announces that the Senate is at the door and desires admittance. The speaker answers, "You will admit the Senate of the United States," and the senators enter as a body. The vice-president, in his role as president of the Senate, mounts the rostrum to sit beside the speaker, but the speaker continues to preside. He successively directs the admission of the cabinet officers, the Supreme Court (dressed in their black robes), the diplomatic corps, and finally the president of the United States. He presents the president (or other dignitary who is present to address a joint session) and adjourns the session when it is completed. Although mostly pageantry, the contrast in roles between the speaker and the vice-president offers a measure of the importance of the speaker to the legislative scheme.

The manner of selecting the speaker at the beginning of each Congress is also indicative of the importance of his job. In actuality, the speaker is chosen behind the scenes by the majority party caucus, and the minority leader is chosen in the same manner by the minority party. Thus, the outcome of the vote of the membership of the House of Representatives is a foregone conclusion. With the rarest of exceptions, the new House members support the choice of their caucus, however close or hard fought the race for the post may have been in the caucus. Yet, since 1839, at the beginning of every Congress, even before the members are sworn in, the speaker has been chosen by a 90-minute-long roll-call vote, each member-elect proclaiming his party's choice.[1] It is a legislative pageant that plays an important symbolic role in legitimizing the extensive powers delegated to the speaker—powers greater than those exercised by any other official in the Congress. When the roll call is completed, the defeated candidate of the minority party (who thereupon becomes the minority leader) hands over the gavel to the victor and makes a plea to the members of both parties to join in cooperation to achieve bipartisan goals. Finally, the speaker takes the gavel, accepts the responsibility of his office and ushers in the new House by swearing in all the members.

The ritualistic commencement of House business emphasizes several important limitations on the authority of the speaker. First, his ability to lead the House depends largely on his ability to maintain party cohesion or, when that fails, to forge coalitions with some members of the minority party. Second, just as he appeals to minority-party members for the votes necessary to create a majority for the passage of legislation, so too he must be aware of members who stray from his own camp. Finally, the speaker holds his position only as long as his party is in power. Unfair treatment of the party out of power is likely to reap its just deserts when the political pendulum swings.

The office of speaker dates back to colonial legislatures. During the prerevolutionary period, the "speakers" became popular spokesmen for rights of the colonies.[2] However, despite the popularity of the speaker in the colonial period, there was no analogous role in the Congress of the Confederation because the authors of the Articles of Confederation had an excessive fear of concentrating too much power in the hands of one person. Therefore, the powers of the leader of the Congress (called the president of the Congress) were strictly limited, and the number of terms he could serve successively were carefully circumscribed. In the early years of the House of Representatives, members continued to be reluctant to give the speaker too much power. Viewed as an impartial arbiter of disputes in the House, the speaker accordingly became in the words of historian George B. Galloway a "mere figurehead."[3] Actual legislative leadership and control were possessed by the floor leaders, who were handpicked by the president as his "lieutenants."

In the British Parliament, the speaker of the House of Commons was known originally as the "king's man" and served as the majority leader of the party in power. However, by the end of the eighteenth century, the speaker of the House of Commons had evolved into an impartial, almost judgelike figure. He wore a wig and gown and, although elected by the Commons, upon election he gave up all political affiliations. He was required to leave the House of Commons after resigning his position as speaker. By 1839, while the role of the speaker was becoming increasingly partisan in America, the British speaker had evolved in the opposite direction.

Many symbols surrounding the House and the speaker are direct carryovers from the British system. After King John finally yielded to the lords at Runnymede and agreed to a stronger Parliament, fights to control parliamentary proceedings were stormy. When efforts to cut back on the king's requests for funds were made, the speaker, as the king's man, carried back tales to the king about the identity of the budget-cutters. Because this made the price of fiscal responsibility very high—perhaps a stay in the Tower of London—Parliament devised an evasive tactic. When any bill before the Parliament was to be amended, the king's man, the speaker, was directed to leave the chair and the chamber. He took his mace, the symbol of his authority from the king, and left. The members of Parliament then selected one of their own to preside over the House until the amendments and their debate were concluded. The speaker was then summoned to return (mace and all) to preside over the final passage of the king's budget.

To this day, when the House is in full session the speaker presides and the mace (a black pole adorned with silver) stands in its holder to his right, as the symbol of authority. When the House commences its amending activity on a bill, a member moves that the "House resolve itself into the Committee of the Whole House on the State of the Union" to consider the proposed bill. When that motion is adopted, the speaker leaves the chair, appointing another member to preside over the session. The mace is removed from its holder and put upon the ground. When the amending process has been completed, the floor manager for the particular bill moves that the "Committee do now rise," and the speaker is summoned to return. When he does, the mace is returned to its holder, the chairman of the Committee of the Whole reports

The sergeant-at-arms carrying the mace,
the speaker's symbol of authority, into the House.

to the speaker as to whether any amendments were adopted, and the House proceeds to final passage of the bill. Although only symbolic, the ritual reminds legislators that the affairs of state are well protected from the dominance of a single individual.

In retrospect, it is difficult to understand why the American speaker became so identified with the party structure, whereas his English counterpart was required to eschew all party affiliation. Perhaps the answer lies in the need to establish a formal structure and role for the party leadership in the Congress to serve as a check on the executive branch—roles that in England, with its parliamentary system, have no parallel.

Another possible answer lies in the creative and aggressive leadership of the man who first gave the speakership the prestige and esteem that it enjoys today: Henry Clay, who, at the age of 34, ended the era of executive supremacy over the affairs of the legislature. Clay developed two main tools for countering executive power. First, he encouraged the establishment of additional standing committees and the development of expertise in the drafting and consideration of legislation. Previously, congressmen had relied on information provided by the executive departments to develop policy initiatives. Thus, during Clay's leadership, the number of standing committees increased from ten to twenty-eight.[4] Second, as mentioned earlier, Clay promoted and nurtured the development of the party caucus, which provided an important means for reaching legislative decisions and enforcing party discipline.

Speaker as Czar

Throughout the nineteenth century, the House leadership experimented with different procedures to cope with the rapidly increasing size of its membership. With the decline of the party caucus under Andrew Jackson, who used the veto and popular opinion to reassert the power of the president, an effective means for disciplining members and promoting efficient and expeditious passage of legislation was lacking. To fill the vacuum left by the declining party structure, over the course of the nineteenth century the speaker accumulated greater and greater powers. The speaker obtained the power to choose not only committee chairmen but also committee membership. In 1858 he began to chair the powerful Committee on Rules, which served, as it does today, as a "traffic cop" to regulate the flow of legislation on the floor.

Speaker Thomas B. Reed, elected in 1889, probably did more than any one else to buttress the powers of the House leadership. At the time, the major procedural barrier facing the House was the "disappearing quorum." By this technique, a minority of the House could thwart any legislative effort by refusing to answer "present," thereby preventing the quorum necessary to conduct business. Reed, through procedural legerdemain, ordered the clerk to record those present who refused to be counted as part of the quorum. This procedural maneuver was met with curses, threats, and even physical assaults by the Democrats who, as the minority, used the "disappearing quorum" to thwart Republican initiatives. Nonetheless, an appeal on the procedural point was tabled and a new procedural precedent was established.[5] Indeed, the problem of defining a "quorum" was so serious that a challenge to legislation, based on the absence of a quorum, actually reached the Supreme Court, which upheld the Reed position.[6] Reed also pioneered efforts to stop dilatory motions by using the procedural power of the speaker. For example, additional limitations were placed on an individual member's ability to debate. In short, Reed spent his time in office creating the necessary procedural tools and precedents for effectuating his belief that the "object of a parliamentary body is action and not the stoppage of action."[7]

Reed's successor, Joseph G. "Uncle Joe" Cannon (also known by his enemies as the "czar" or "Foul-mouth" Cannon), increased the powers of the speaker to a point never known before in the history of the House of Representatives. With these powers he stopped legislation that he did not support even though it was supported by a majority of his party and by the president. By consistently thwarting the will of the majority of his party, he provoked the rank-and-file membership of the House to revolt.

Cannon's source of power was his appointment and control of committee chairmanships and membership. In awarding chairmanships Cannon demanded, and usually obtained, the fealty of a sixth of the House. His grip on the committee system was so extensive that many committees actually sought his approval before drafting legislation. Chairmanships were critical because they provided the only financial resources available to members. Chairmen alone had offices provided at public expense. Representatives who were not chairmen had to pay the rent for desk space from their personal incomes. Furthermore, chairmen received free stationery from the House, extra money for staff, and special floor privileges for the conduct of House business. As chairman of the Rules Committee, Cannon's power was almost complete, for he could prevent any legislation from coming to a floor vote. In addition, by appointing the members of the influential Ways and Means Committee, he controlled the power of the purse and the ability to raise revenue.

In the beginning, Cannon used his powers in a positive way to help the new president of his party, Theodore Roosevelt. The two men made a good team; they both believed in the necessity of strong leadership to keep the nation on the correct path. Theodore Roosevelt was the first president in modern times to use his office as a "bully pulpit" to enact legislation that he believed was in the public interest. He believed that a "good executive under present conditions of American life must take a very active interest in getting the right kind of legislation."[8] Before creating his liaison with Cannon, Roosevelt's relationships with Congress were strikingly poor, because he failed to consult with congressional leaders before taking executive action. The Congress, accustomed to weak presidents who did not initiate legislative action, worked to stymie his efforts. At one point, Roosevelt nominated a commission on country life and subsequently asked Congress for an appropriation. Congress not only refused the appropriation but also passed legislation prohibiting the appointment of any future commissions without specific congressional authorization. Congress also passed a resolution forcing the president to file a copy of every executive order, followed by a citation of law, and even established a commission of experts to evaluate the president's acts.

Thus, at a time when the tensions between a strong executive and a strong legislative branch threatened any progressive action, the liaison between the president and a strong speaker, both of the same party, seemed ideal.

Revolt Against Cannonism

At first Roosevelt sounded out every serious recommendation with Cannon before sending it to Congress and learned from Cannon how to use the congressional bargaining process to achieve his ends. But the honeymoon was short-lived, and Cannon and Roosevelt started to work at loggerheads on substantive policy. Roosevelt, able to muster a majority of the Congress behind his progressive policies, provoked a revolt against Cannon, which substantially weakened the power of the speaker for future generations. Of the many changes the insurgents managed to obtain in the following congresses, the most prominent was the "Calendar Wednesday" rule, permitting a committee chairman to call up a bill reported out of his committee for floor consideration even without the approval of the speaker or the Rules Committee.

In 1909, during the Taft administration, the speaker was denied chairmanship of the Rules Committee and deprived of the privilege of naming the powerful Committee on Committees, which determined committee membership.[9] The speaker was thus stripped of his exclusive power to make committee assignments. Instead, at the commencement of each Congress, the members of each committee and the chairmen were elected by the party caucuses and confirmed by the whole House. Finally, with the decline of the speaker, the party caucus reemerged in a short-lived burst of energy. However, the seniority system, which reached full bloom in the 1920s, ensured that for more than fifty years the congressional committees would be the real sources of power in Congress.

Revival of the Speaker

During the 1960s and 1970s congressmen with seniority held the powerful positions of committee chairmen. As increasing numbers of liberal and younger rank-and-file congressmen were elected to office, the demand grew to replace older chairmen with younger members, or at least to limit their influence. Liberals turned to the speaker as the counterpoint to the conservative committee seniors. Numerous measures during this period, in particular the Legislative Reorganization Act of 1970, enhanced the office of the speaker. Under the short-lived "21-day rule," the speaker was given the power to permit a committee chairman to bring a bill to the House floor if the Rules Committee failed to act within a 21-day time period. Most important, the Democratic party caucus was revived as an instrument for forcing committee chairmen to abide by the wishes of the congressional rank and file.

The caucus, turning to the speaker as an ally, created a new Democratic Steering and Policy Committee to assist him in developing party and legislative priorities. The membership of the Steering and Policy Committee was designed to reflect the geographical make-up of the Democratic majority. Although the country was divided into "zones" for the purpose of electing almost half of the committee, the speaker retained substantial input into the committee's membership. The elected leadership of the House—the speaker, the majority leader, and the Democratic caucus chairman—and several of the key committee chairmen were voting members of the committee by reason of their office. In addition, the speaker was allowed to designate six members of the committee. Thus, the committee was crafted to give the speaker operating control. By and large, that is the way it worked out.

Finally, the caucus beefed up the speaker's power over appointments to the committees. Prior to 1974, the Democratic members of the Ways and Means Committee had served as the Committee on Committees, which appointed freshman congressmen to committee slots. This function was switched to the Steering and Policy Committee under the auspices of the speaker. The speaker was then entrusted with the power to nominate the Democratic members of the Rules Committee subject to caucus ratification. Thus, the Rules Committee once again became an important ally of the party leadership.

Despite the increased formal powers of the speaker in the 1970s and 1980s—the greatest since "Uncle Joe" Cannon—his real power remains carefully circumscribed by the growth and increasing autonomy of the subcommittees and by his ability to put together a winning coalition on the floor. Successive legislative defeats can devastate his continued ability to achieve important policy objectives with the support of fellow party members. On the first day of the Ninety-seventh Congress in January 1981 new Minority Leader Robert Michel highlighted this limitation by inviting Democrats who disagreed with the liberal philosophy of the speaker to join with Republicans in enacting a conservative agenda. Michel knew that a coalition of conservative Democrats and Republicans could succeed on substantive issues and thereby threaten the continued effectiveness of the House majority leadership.

Control of the House depends on procedural cooperation from the minority leader and his minions. Although House procedures usually allow a majority of the members to work their will, the minority can delay and harass to a substantial degree. A single member can ensnarl the House procedurally and impede progress. An individual member can become irritated over matters that occurred either on the floor or even in committee. By making persistent quorum calls, demanding votes on every matter that comes before the House, no matter how trivial, and otherwise using the procedural safeguards designed to prevent surprise or steamrolling, a member can stall the House business. At such times the speaker needs his prestige, his persuasive powers, and all the individual and party support he can muster to get the House back on the track. Sometimes these House versions of "filibusters" can last for days or weeks. Only a speaker who understands both his power and its limitations can mend the rifts.

To the extent that the speaker wields his instruments of power and thus contravenes majority House sentiment, he jeopardizes his own ability to continue in a leadership position. The history of the last century of House leadership illustrates a constant redistribution of party power between the speaker, the caucus, and the committee chairs. The ebbs and flows of power between these bases of power usually result from a dissonance between those in power and the desires of the House rank and file. Therefore, it is critically important for a speaker to have a solid power base and to maintain this base by keeping his finger constantly on the pulse of the House.

The Education of a Speaker

Not since the remarkable career of young, brash Henry Clay has a member of the House of Representatives become the speaker in his first term. Indeed, in the twentieth century, all speakers have had between 15 and 34 years of service before attaining the speaker's chair. There is a predictable career path for the speaker. First, a promising young congressman is chosen as whip by the speaker and majority leader. If he shows promise as a whip, he becomes the prime candidate for majority leader. Finally, he ascends to the position of speaker. Only rarely is this ineluctable progression challenged.

In the early 1970s young Arizona Congressman Morris Udall, who represented the new reform faction of the Democratic party, challenged the more traditional, conservative choice of the leadership for the position of majority leader. The story of his attempt to short-cut the mandatory career ladder best describes the traditions and norms that have developed to groom a speaker.

Congressman Mo Udall arrived in Congress in 1961. He tried successfully to get assigned to the House Interior Committee because of an upcoming water project important to Arizona. His other assignment was the Post Office Committee. Udall achieved notoriety and respect not from his committee responsibilities but from his active role in the liberal Democratic Study Group. Udall described his own legislative initiatives and his power base in the House:

> Udall wrote critically in national publications of the seniority system, of loose and deceptive campaign laws, of unsupervised lobbyists, of general congressional anemia and harmful fuddyduddyisms. He knew he might forfeit the smiles of elders, but for all the institutional chill there was a counterwarming: young House liberals looked more and more to Udall as their natural spokesman, and perhaps here he saw his first private visions of power.[10]

In 1968, after only eight years in the House, Udall decided to challenge Speaker John McCormack:

> Udall sent out an eight-page, single-spaced letter to House Democrats. For all its diplomatic language, it could not have brightened the old Speaker's New Year. Should he win—Udall wrote—he would step aside to allow a second election permitting Congressmen more freely to vote their hearts once the giant had been slain. There was much of personal conviction in it, the demands of the times, and other high-minded soundings. Old John McCormack may not have bothered to read it all, and if he did, it likely registered as superfluous information or as the ravings of an organizational madman: how does an old man of seventy-seven, who has campaigned funeral trains, understand a young one who pledges to surrender the spoils unused?
>
> Old John McCormack had risen through the ranks, where you were loyal to the block captain past his death. As with all instinctive partisans or doctrinaires, he abhorred deviation or fratricide. He had learned as a young and disadvantaged South Boston Irishman that lesson of tribal truth common to all who must fight group oppression or exclusion: solidarity above all. He was a natural product of ward politics, a poor boy who had left school in the eighth grade to sustain a widowed mother by working for $4 weekly in a law office; at night, he "read law" to prepare for the bar exam. As with so many ambitious South Boston products who had no opportunity to become priests or prizefighters, he made the earliest possible connection with the Democratic party. You did not need to be Harvard or rich to thrive in The Organization—merely loyal, persistent, and a little lucky. The old man could no more comprehend Mo Udall's "symbolic"

candidacy than an orangutan would be capable of grasping the concept of infinity.

Mo Udall went to the Democratic caucus in January of 1969 counting on a respectable eighty-one votes, the number he interpreted as honorably pledged. The secret ballot, however, went against him a thumping 178 to 58. This did not prevent maybe a hundred statesmen from later seeking out Udall to whisper that they had stubbornly stayed hitched.[11]

In 1970 Udall decided to take another stab at running for a leadership position. Speaker McCormack had decided to step down, and Congressman Carl Albert (Oklahoma), the majority leader, was next in line. Udall decided to mount a challenge for the majority leader position against front-runner Hale Boggs of Louisiana, who had served nine years as the House whip. Other potential contenders were eighteen-year veteran Tip O'Neill, a liberal from Cambridge who had once served as speaker of the Massachusetts Great and General Court; Dan Rostenkowski of Illinois, chairman of the Democratic caucus and a member of the Ways and Means Committee; and finally James O'Hara, labor's choice from Michigan. The press was extremely important in the legislative battle for majority leader:

Washington's pols may enthusiastically revile The Goddamned Press, but few ignore it. Columnists are probably more influential than is good for either themselves or the country. They are read, particularly if they appear in the *Washington Post* or *New York Times*, and politicians gossip like fishwives on what they say. Udall fretted that Boggs was "winning the battle of the columnists."[12]

But despite his trepidations, the Washington newspapers, a week before the poll, clearly had Udall winning the fight.

However, Boggs' long years as the whip came to his assistance against Udall:

Not for nothing had Boggs sat all those years at power's right hand. He had watched tough-talking freshmen come and go, had seen the revolutionaries of three decades turn uncertain and humble on first encountering the trappings of power. He knew freshmen to be new kids on the block, a bit fearful of the bully, and he knew that something universally human in them silently cried out for acceptance: new breed or no, they were politicians. Experience assured Boggs that these new revolutionaries, too, would accommodate to the basic realities. In time they might cause all the trouble they now promised, but initially they would require a period of adjustment, time to rally themselves, and Boggs knew he would be dealing with them at their most vulnerable.

The morning following their victories in November, all Democratic freshmen received nice telegrams from Hale Boggs. Knowing there were houses to rent, schools to consult, curiosities to satisfy, Boggs warmly welcomed the new kids to town and offered to open doors. He wrung their hands and put them at ease with harmless questions about themselves. He buzzed staffers, ordering them to relieve this rookie or that of some nagging Washington worry. The freshmen sat in the deep soft chairs, and every time Hale Boggs pushed a button, another small miracle happened; this guy knew his way around.

Eventually Boggs might inquire the freshmen's committee desire. Naturally, everybody had a vital one. Perhaps Boggs here said a word on the difficulty of freshmen attaining their primary selections—regretfully, of course—quickly coupled with observations on the importance of committee assignments to the congressional career. Then he would surely let it slip that as a member of Ways and Means—"the committee-on-committees, you know"—he was fortunately situated to help. And then the cake's icing: introductions to three or four Boggs friends on Ways and Means, including, of course, the all-important chairman, Wilbur Mills. Only later would the friendly pressures be applied: debts called in by way of firming up prior understandings.

Udall could provide some of the same services, and occasionally did. He did not, however, have the natural advantages—the prestige of internal office, the trappings, the crucial committee connections. He could not risk introducing people to Old John McCormack, nor presume ceremonial claims on Carl Albert's time as easily as the Whip might. And these things, too, Hale Boggs knew.[13]

Ultimately, Boggs beat Udall, on the second ballot, 140 to 88. Undaunted, Udall decided to run for whip but was dissuaded by strong pressure from the leadership. Thus, in a two-year period, Udall, a young maverick, was trounced every time he tried to buck the established leadership ladder. He concluded:

The leadership ladder bit—tradition, promotion, seniority—was stronger medicine than I originally thought. This House apparently just insists on people getting in line, serving time. Boggs knew this, and exploited the sentiment very effectively. He worked his ass off, and he used all his tools. In the south, the Boggs people put the heat on recalcitrants through lobbyists for various industries: oil, tobacco, textiles, and so on. They snatched six or eight votes from me there. He played the freshmen like a virtuoso: he could pass out more goodies than I. The big-city boys came to him through a combination of his contacts with mayors and other politicians I didn't know externally, and through such guys as Rostenkowski and Carey and a few of the old deans. Boggs had people all over Washington—lawyers and lobbyists and bureaucrats—dating back to the New Deal, and almost all of them knew somebody to pressure for him.

The remaining bitterness over my McCormack race surprised me. I thought I'd conducted myself like a gentleman, and so I guess people just hated the idea. At a critical juncture somebody brought word that Tip O'Neill had said he couldn't buy me under any circumstance. I said, "*Goddammit*, I've got a lot to learn." I remember trading funny stories with Tip O'Neill, and once we had a marvelous time on a trip. It's easy to translate such personal experiences into potential support—easy to forget that Tip O'Neill's shared friendly moments with others and for longer. I knew that Ken Gray of Illinois had been sore at me over a Post Office bill I had handled—he thought it encroached on his subcommittee's territory—but I assumed that old difference settled long ago. Then, late in the campaign, I heard he was still talking about it.[14]

From the perspective of a young liberal with a relatively brief term of service in the House of Representatives, like Mo Udall, the process of selecting the House leadership is frustrating and seems likely to ensure a leadership that will be unrepresentative of the changing political consensus in the House. In a sense this frustration is well founded. Certainly Speaker McCormack could not possibly have represented the class of the Ninety-fourth Congress elected in the Watergate era. Nonetheless, this education of the leadership has its merits. In an institution where the ability to lead depends strongly on a fine balance between short-run and long-run political needs, leaders need a finely honed sense of how to accomplish legislative goals; how to obstruct legislation supported by a majority of the members but damaging to Congress as an institution; and how to use the "carrots" and the "sticks" of leadership most effectively.

Party Responsibilities

The speaker's first responsibility in each Congress is to work out committee assignments for his party with the help of the Steering and Policy Committee, assigning each freshman congressman to the committee most likely to satisfy his particular needs. Thus, a congressman from Iowa is likely to obtain a slot on the Agriculture Committee; one from Massachusetts, a position on the Committee on Banking, Finance and Urban Affairs; and one from Arizona, a position on the Interior Committee with jurisdiction over water projects.

The speaker dominates the Steering and Policy Committee. Usually, the new member seeking a particular committee assignment persuades his zone members on the Steering and Policy Committee to nominate him for that committee, although technically any member of the Steering and Policy Committee can make nominations. The zone members do enough horse-trading to get their nominees on the committees of their choice, with obvious and notable exceptions.

Everyone wants to sit on some committees, and others are as popular as the Black Hole of Calcutta. In the first category are the "exclusive," elite committees—Ways and Means, Rules, and Appropriations—which traditionally have been reserved for members of the House who have served lengthy terms, who have safe seats, and who have "proven" themselves worthy of the assignments. They are called exclusive committees because generally service on any one of them precludes the member from assignment to any other standing committee. In recent years, however, the need for a safe seat has become less important. Abner Mikva, a co-author of this book (sometimes called "Landslide" because of his narrow margins of victory), was appointed to the Ways and Means Committee in the tumultuous Ninety-fourth Congress. In the 1980 election, three members of Ways and Means, including the chairman, lost their seats. In previous days, such "electorate heresy" was unthinkable.

At the other end of the current spectrum is the Judiciary Committee, which has suffered in recent years from a lack of eager applicants. In the Ninety-seventh Congress, Speaker O'Neill tried to fill the spots left by Congressman Robert Drinan and Congresswoman Elizabeth Holtzman, two liberals, with congressmen who were not afraid to tackle the thorny issues of school prayer, abortion, and busing. He found several liberal congressmen who were willing to serve on the committee only if they could also serve on committees that would better help their constituents. Under the Democratic caucus rules of the previous Congress, assignment to two "major committees" was prohibited. To rectify this problem, the speaker proposed, and lobbied in the caucus, rules changes to permit the congressmen to sit on Judiciary plus another committee, in effect demoting Judiciary from a major committee status. Thus, to obtain a specific substantive result—encouraging willing, young Democrats to sit on the Judiciary Committee—the rules of the caucus underwent basic change.

Another critical function of the speaker at the beginning of every Congress is to get House approval of the committee ratios of the respective numbers of the members of the majority and minority parties. Although the ratios are not determined with mathematical precision, they are usually roughly equivalent to the percentage of Democrats and Republicans in the House. However, on occasion, to obtain substantive results, the speaker can play "hard ball." In the Ninety-seventh Congress the Democrats recognized that an important part of President Reagan's economic package would involve tax cuts. Thus, it was critically important for the Democratic party in the House to maintain firm control over the Ways and Means Committee, particularly as the Senate

Finance Committee was controlled by the Republicans. Although the ratio of Democrats to Republicans in the House was roughly five to three, the Democratic caucus, at the urging of the speaker, assigned the Ways and Means Committee a ratio of two to one. (The Republican lawsuit challenging this ratio had no effect on the speaker's decision.)

Traditionally, the speaker negotiates with the minority leader on committee ratios for the non-exclusive committees, frequently giving or taking a deviation from the percentage in order to accommodate a particular member or need. When the Democratic caucus "instructs" the speaker, however, he can rightly claim that he has no discretion for any negotiation. Members of the majority party frequently demand more than a proportionate share of the membership on certain key committees to protect party positions on floor actions. The practice—and the argument about it—are neither new nor restricted to Congress. State legislatures frequently insist on "stacking" key committees when the party balance is close in the legislative body. The alternative to obtaining comfortable pluralities on key committees is to impose a loyalty test on all who ask to serve on such a committee. Whenever either party has a substantial working and ideological majority, the party ratio argument tends to disappear. When the ratio in the House is close, the argument is renewed.

Perhaps the most difficult of the speaker's jobs is to put out "fires" within his own party. When two powerful members fight over the jurisdiction of committees or subcommittees, he must step in to forge a compromise to prevent dangerous rifts in the committee structure.

Although the House Rules seek to be specific on the jurisdiction of committees, many a bill provokes a jurisdictional dispute. The first energy bill that was proposed by President Jimmy Carter fell within the jurisdiction of five separate committees. To alleviate the concerns of turf-minded chairmen, the speaker proposed a separate Energy Committee to synthesize and amalgamate the work of the separate committees after they had dealt with those parts of the energy bill within their normal jurisdictions. The procedure was a short-term success. When a subsequent proposal was made to establish a standing Energy Committee to avoid such overlaps, it was roundly defeated. In addition, a procedure for "sequential referral" is available, whereby a bill goes from one committee to another to avoid any usurpation of jurisdiction. That procedure also has enjoyed very modest success.

Although the speaker appoints the members of the Rules Committee, subject to caucus ratification, he does not control the daily workings of that committee. He frequently must "lobby" bills through the Rules Committee when the subject matter is particularly controversial or an anathema to some committee members. As indicated earlier, the 1976 tax bill contained a substantial repeal of the oil-depletion allowance. The Democratic caucus had instructed the Rules Committee to grant a rule which would make that amendment "in order" on the floor. Neither the House Rules nor the caucus rules specifically covered a situation in which the Rules Committee failed to obey the caucus mandate. Speaker Carl Albert spent many hours phoning the Democratic members of the Rules Committee to persuade them not to provoke that kind of confrontation with the caucus. In the end, he prevailed.

Although the speaker traditionally does not vote on measures before the House, he is hardly the neutral arbiter epitomized by his British counterpart. The speaker in America votes to break a tie and whenever his vote is symbolically important to the way the House votes on a matter. Frequently he is on the floor on close votes, seeking either by speech or action to twist arms on his side of the aisle for those marginal votes that spell the difference between carrying an issue and losing it. Because the House almost always votes electronically, there is a fifteen-minute period after the voting starts before the final result is tabulated and announced. During that period the speaker is frequently seen in the hall of the House, cajoling, persuading, or leaning. Sometimes, both to emphasize the importance of a vote to the party and to summon all his loyalists to the floor, the speaker delivers the concluding speech on a particular measure. Usually a quorum is called prior to the speaker's peroration, to make sure he has a full House and to give the whip organization an extra opportunity and extra time to corral and count up the votes necessary to carry the issue. On all the important issues of the day, the speaker is hardly a dispassionate neutral.

Moreover, he is responsible for disciplining and coaching freshman congressmen. A particularly poignant example: A liberal freshman from Massachusetts decided to vote against the leadership's choice for chairman of the Subcommittee on Housing and Community Development in the committee caucus at the start of the Ninety-seventh Congress. Somewhat a "hotshot" in his state legislature, he let everyone know his dissatisfaction with the speaker's choice. When the speaker asked the freshman for whom he intended to vote and the freshman indicated he would vote against the leadership's choice, the speaker said, "You *are* going to vote for him." The new member, not realizing he was getting an order rather than a question, started giving the reasons for his position when he was interrupted with a repetition of the same command in harsher tones. Rather then defy authority within his first few days in the House, he voted for the subcommittee chairman. Rebellion against the speaker may not reap instant penalties, but frequent rebellion certainly makes favors from the leadership—choice committee assignments, high-profile roles in House business, or attractive "junket invitations"—more difficult to come by. Moreover, because of the speaker's influence on the distribution of campaign funds from the House Democratic Campaign Committee and because his help in local elections is frequently desired, provoking his ire except on major issues is less than wise.

The speaker is responsible for setting legislative priorities. The Democratic caucus established the Democratic Steering and Policy Committee to aid the speaker in examining legislative initiatives and in screening and evaluating legislation proposed by the president, the Senate, and House committees. In only rare examples—for example, the energy bill of the Ninety-fifth Congress—are the resources of the Policy Committee used aggressively to impact strongly on legislation. The energy bill was the lynchpin of Carter's program to resolve our energy crisis. Since the bill adversely affected so many powerful special interests, the Policy Committee engaged in a major lobbying effort. More frequently, the Policy Committee decides how the House leadership should treat legislation. What kind of "rule" should it get? Should it be placed on the suspension or unanimous consent calendar? Should the speaker urge the chairman to bury or expedite the legislation? The Policy Committee also attempts to hammer out compromises within the House and with the Senate to make the legislation palatable to the speaker and his constituencies.

The passage of the Regulatory Flexibility Act of 1980,[15] legislation proposed by Senator John Culver of Iowa to reduce the impact of government regulations on small business, illustrates the behind-the-scenes role of the Policy Committee. The speaker, who has exclusive control over expediting House legislation under suspension procedures, has enormous leverage over legislation sent over by the Senate. To ensure the speaker's support for the regulatory bill, the Culver staff and the speaker's Policy Committee staff hammered out a compromise bill in a late-night marathon session prior to passage of the bill in the Senate. The bill passed the Senate, and with the speaker's endorsement, easily passed the House under suspension of the rules. The speaker's enormous procedural powers enabled him to gain behind-the-scenes amendments to the legislation and thus permitted the supporters of the legislation to get a quick legislative victory.

As the party leader, the speaker plays an important role as the liaison between the president and the House. President Lyndon Johnson recognized the value of cementing an extremely close relationship with the speaker. Johnson told the following anecdote to illustrate the lesson, which taught him the value of always keeping the speaker informed:

> I was standing in the back of the House behind the rail as Speaker Sam Rayburn listened to the House clerk read an important new administration message President Roosevelt had just sent to the Hill. Several dozen Democrats were gathered around him. As he finished, a unanimous chorus of complaints rushed forth: "Why, that message is terrible, Mr. Sam—we can't pass that. . . . That

last suggestion is awful. . . . Why in the world did you let the President send one up like that? . . . Why didn't you warn us?"

Speaker Rayburn listened to all the criticisms and then responded softly: "We'll just have to look at it more carefully. That's all I can say now, fellows. We'll have to look at it more carefully." The crowd scattered. Mr. Sam and I were left alone in the back. I could see that something was wrong. "If only," he said. "the President would let me know ahead of time when these controversial messages are coming up. I could pave the way for him. I could create a base of support. I could be better prepared for criticism. I could get much better acceptance in the long run. But I never know when the damned messages are coming. This last one surprised me as much as it did all of them." He shook his head sadly and walked slowly away.

I could see that his pride was hurt. So was the President's prestige and the administration's program. I never forgot that lesson.[16]

Not all presidents take the important step of "stroking" the House leadership. President Jimmy Carter came to Washington proud of his outsider status, that "didn't owe anything" to anyone. But neither did anyone owe anything to him. Unlike Lyndon Johnson, who had extensive experience in the House and Senate, President Carter knew little or nothing about the Hill. Rather than making overtures to the speaker of his party, he alienated him and thereby endangered his own legislative priorities. Indeed, hostilities between the president's staff and the speaker became so intense that Speaker O'Neill referred to the president's chief of staff, Hamilton Jordon, as "Hannibal Jerkin." An early dispute arose when the speaker, a few days before the 1976 Inauguration, called to ask for additional tickets for the events— hardly an unheard-of request in Washington folkways. Jordon, still fresh from Georgia customs and with the anti-Washington rhetoric of the campaign still ringing in his ears, was less than forthcoming. Afterward, this snub, which received much media coverage, was cited as the reason for some of the president's early defeats on the Hill. One of the cloakroom wags suggested that there be a second Inaugural so that "Hannibal" could make amends. As a result of the general ill will that developed in the early months of the Carter administration, the president gained a reputation throughout the country as being ineffective with Congress—a reputation that haunted his entire term in office. Ironically, Speaker O'Neill became President Carter's best ally on the Hill. On more than one occasion O'Neill used up "chits" to gain support for the president's programs. No similar closeness ever developed between O'Neill and Jordon, however.

The speaker leads the "loyal opposition" when his party is not in the White

House. After the Reagan sweep of 1980, which led to a Republican-dominated Senate, the speaker of the House then became the highest Democratic office holder. As such he was in a unique position to spearhead party initiatives and determine the future direction of his party. It is not surprising that President Reagan went out of his way to "court" the speaker. However, the speaker all too soon recognized his limited ability to forge a majority coalition when many members of his own party agreed more with the president's ideology than with that of the more liberal party leadership. As O'Neill said, "We are the opposition; he is the President of the United States. He is the leader of this nation."[17] As a result of his 1980 electoral victory, his powerful use of the media, and the disorientation of the Democrats, Reagan managed to bring enough Democrats into his camp to win three decisive battles against the speaker in the first six months of 1981. The damage to his prestige was so great that rumors circulated that the speaker would step down before the 1982 election. However, the speaker's power revived, in the second session, after the presidential honeymoon[18] was over. Nonetheless, even though he is the leader of the "loyal opposition," the speaker's power to provide a foil to the president derives largely from his ability to win on the floor.

Institutional Role of the Speaker

The speaker has a constitutional obligation to ensure the orderly functioning of the House. He is entrusted, therefore, with determining all procedural questions with the aid of a parliamentarian. Although they are nonpartisan, parliamentarians work at the pleasure of the speaker[19] and can help him achieve substantive results by supplying precedents to support his actions. Appeals from procedural decisions are almost never successful. When an appeal is taken from a ruling of the speaker, the majority party is expected to treat the issue as a party issue. Frequently, even the minority leadership supports the speaker's ruling, recognizing that there is no way to maintain order in a body as unruly and as large as the House without an acknowledged authority in the chair. In the Senate, however, such appeals are both successful and frequent.

Although not as autocratic as those possessed by Speakers Reed and Cannon at the turn of the century, the powers of the speaker are sufficient to pass important, or block undesirable, legislation. His powers include the authority to recognize members wishing to speak on the floor of the full House; to plot the course and timing of legislative consideration; to decide the referral of legislation; to rule on parliamentary procedure; to appoint conference committees; to expedite legislation through the use of the unanimous consent and suspension procedures; to set the legislative agenda; to influence the decisions of the Rules Committee through his authority to choose its members; to exercise great leverage over committee assignments; to utilize the superior resources of the Steering and Policy Committee; and to enlist the aid of the majority leader and the whip organization.

A speaker's skill as a negotiator is his most valuable asset. As political scientist Charles O. Jones pointed out: "Ultimately each representative, even the freshman, has some bargaining power (at minimum—his vote). It is on the basis of bargaining that the 'middle-man' thesis of congressional leadership has been developed. Rightly or wrongly, House leaders must attend to their majorities."[20] To forge a majority consensus, the speaker must be both ubiquitous and always accessible to the members of his party. Congressman Clem Miller described the role of Speaker Sam Rayburn in the early 1960s:

> The Speaker, through whom all of this consent must be filtered, is immediately and continuously available. As he leaves the dais, he will be stopped in the Speaker's Lobby by four or five persons. He stands solid, and square, clamping down hard on a cigarette with his teeth, then rolling it along between his lips. Or he may sit on one of the overstuffed mohair couches beaming and smiling, giving a nod to everyone who may pass by.... Endless delegations come to tell the Speaker their stories. An appointment is arranged by telephone. Singly, in twos or threes or more, the Speaker will see us all when we feel the need. A matter of national significance, a matter of personality, a matter of individual trouble—the Speaker listens, friendly and attentively. He has heard it so many times. But this attention is riveted out of deference to the close-knit feeling for the House and its members, great and small. Attentiveness, a precious political commodity because of its rarity, is one means he employs to cement the bonds. For the Speaker is not only the outward and visible symbol of the House, but he is its inward guardian and counsellor.[21]

Despite his role as "guardian and counsellor," the speaker must yield to the realities of majoritarian politics. When it is clear to a speaker that a majority of the House disagrees with his position, he is wise to temper his position. There are limits to party loyalty. One Congressional observer described Speaker Tip O'Neill's intense frustration at the decline of party loyalty:

> Whatever the cause—the devolution of the powers of the Speaker, an antipathy to Rayburn-like arm twisting, the decline of Democratic party funds for candidates, the noncoattails of President Carter—this lack of party cohesion in the face of Republican solidarity has consternated Tip O'Neill. "What the hell is going on here?" he bellowed when he was told that up to 100 Democrats would be voting against a consumer protection agency bill. "They're all independent now. Voters aren't as loyal to the Democratic or Republican ticket anymore. People are not awed by the President or me either."[22]

Legislative defeats substantially impair the speaker's legitimacy and his ability to bargain with the rank and file. The plan to establish the Energy Mobilization Board, a major plank of President Carter's energy program, was designed to "cut red tape" that stood in the way of building priority energy projects. When the board was proposed on a sultry summer evening by President Carter in his "malaise" speech of 1980, the whole White House staff geared up for its passage. Although the Democratic leadership mustered its resources to support the bill, it was opposed by the liberal wing of the party, which was led by old-timers like Congressman Morris Udall of Arizona and young mavericks like Edward Markey of the speaker's own Massachusetts delegation. The legislation passed both the Senate and the House and differences were ironed out in conference. After the conference report passed the Senate overwhelmingly, it was sent to the House for its concurrence. In an almost unprecedented move, the liberal Democrats joined with the conservative Republicans to defeat the legislation—a sharp blow to the leadership.

Speakers are reluctant to "punish" party members for disobedience, for such reprimands may cause future problems in forging a majority. For example, Sam Rayburn refused to discipline a leader of the then conservative wing of the party, Mississippi Congressman William Colmer, second-ranking member on the Rules Committee, when he refused to support President John F. Kennedy because Rayburn feared an irreparable breach with the southern wing[23] of the Democratic party. Similar motivations may have persuaded Speaker O'Neill to refrain from inflicting severe punishment on the Democratic renegades, or "boll weevils," from the South and West who facilitated the passage of the Reagan economic plan.

The Speaker as a House Member

Like the other 434 members of the House, the speaker must seek reelection every two years. Although no speaker has ever failed to be reelected in the twentieth century, he nevertheless risks defeat, like any other House member, if he neglects the interests of his constituents. As a member of the House, he is forced to be sensitive to a changing political climate. During the period of intense student protest over the war in Vietnam, Speaker John McCormack took time out of his busy schedule to meet with a delegation of students from his home district in Boston. Although he clearly did not agree with their opposition to the war in Vietnam ("I was proud to fight in the First World War"), he did send follow-up letters to each student with whom he met.

In one of his campaigns, Tip O'Neill was confronted with an opponent who constantly referred to "Trip" O'Neill as one of the great junketeers in the Congress. The speaker was highly indignant at the charge and complained about the low road his opponent was taking. Observers noticed, however, that O'Neill's subsequent travels were somewhat curtailed. Perhaps the most obvious response to a constituency occurred as O'Neill moved from being a supporter of the war in Vietnam to being a neutral and then a critic. Massachusetts O'Neill-watchers insisted that his vocal Harvard constituency had more than a little to do with his reassessment of the Asian war and his support for it. In the controversial fight over the reauthorization of the Federal Trade Commission (FTC) in the Ninety-sixth Congress, Speaker O'Neill sided with a Massachusetts funeral-home director in supporting an amendment that would strip the FTC of its authority to regulate funeral homes.

The value to a district of having the speaker of the House as its congressman virtually guarantees reelection. That Massachusetts has had two speakers in recent history has ensured the continued expenditure of military funds in the state, even though economics and national needs might have indicated that those expenditures were not necessary. However, when the speaker is the leader of the opposition party, he can sometimes hurt the home district. At a time when President Reagan was helping industries, like the auto industry, combat foreign competition, he applied his "free trade" philosophy to the quota on imports of cheap shoes from places like Korea, thereby hurting a key industry in Massachusetts. The urging of the Massachusetts delegation to retain the quota had no effect. That Speaker O'Neill and both Massachusetts senators were vocal opponents of the president's platform was obviously a factor.

Majority Leader

Next in line of succession, the majority leader, ostensibly elected by the party caucus, is sometimes preselected by the speaker. Because the succession from majority leader to speaker has been almost automatic, much of the majority leader's power is derived from the expectation that he will ascend to that powerful position.

Originally handpicked by the president as his personal floor lieutenant, the majority leader, not the speaker, wielded the real power on the floor of the House. The speaker was largely ignored until the rise of Henry Clay, who made the speaker's office an effective counterpoint to the presidency: The predominance of the speaker obviated the need for a floor leader, and until 1899 no such position existed. The chairman of the Ways and Means Committee served as floor majority leader until 1919 when the floor leadership became a separate position.

Today the majority leader wields considerable influence, in the main because he is heir-apparent to the office of speaker—that is, if the majority party continues in power. Thus, his incentive is great to ensure the sensitivity of the majority party to the ever-changing political climate. The main role of a House majority leader is to persuade party members to vote the party line. Majority Leader James Wright of Texas stated that the "majority leadership has become primarily a hunting license to persuade."[24] Wright, cognizant of the limits of his position, never asked members to violate promises to constituents but did expect party loyalty in the absence of such pledges. As Wright said: "This lack of arm-twisting pays off in the long run, because when I do come to them on a crucial vote and they know I need it, they're generally good about giving in to me."[25] The majority leader, as party spokesman, campaigns for other House members and thereby assures support for his reelection in the party caucus. For example, despite his reputation for being conservative, Wright won the support of liberal Congresswoman Barbara Mikulski of Maryland by campaigning for her in the Baltimore business community: "Congressman Wright was very helpful to me last summer in breaking the ice with the Baltimore business community . . . and I was there when Wright needed me."[26] That vote counted when Wright won the leadership position in 1976 by a one-vote margin, 148 to 147.

In practice, the majority leader greases the wheels for the party's legislative program. He schedules legislation, presides over procedural debates in the absence of the speaker, ensures that committee chairmen report bills deemed important to the party, and helps the speaker establish legislative priorities. He also works closely with the whip organization to determine support for legislation and to coax votes when necessary.

With a forceful speaker, the majority leader clearly plays a subordinate role. Speaker Sam Rayburn felt strongly that the majority leader should be seen and not heard. His oft-expressed and much-followed opinion was: "You either run the House from up here [the speaker's rostrum] or down there on the floor. You can't have it both ways." As a result of that opinion, speakers tend to seek out less than the strongest member to assume the role of majority leader. Many observers believed that both John McCormack of Massachusetts and Carl Albert of Oklahoma were encouraged to be majority leaders by speakers who wanted to ensure that the House would be run "from up here." Even though Speaker O'Neill proclaimed neutrality in the Burton–Bolling–Wright majority leader race of 1976, some observers felt he breathed a sigh of relief when neither Phillip Burton of California nor Richard Bolling of Missouri won the race because of their strong personalities.

When party majorities are weak, the majority leader is often a critical element in cementing dissonant party factions. For example, in the Ninety-seventh Congress, the speaker, coming out of the traditional "bread and butter" wing of the Democratic party, relied heavily on Jim Wright, a conservative and a southerner, to put his "finger in the dam" of a disintegrating Democratic majority. He was the critical link between the conservative Democrats and the more liberal House leadership. To cement the liberal and conservative wings of the Democratic party, Wright—to his later regret—facilitated the appointment of certain conservatives to the Budget and the Ways and Means committees. (These boll weevil Democrats then provided critical floor votes for President Reagan's budget and tax measures.) The majority leader probably played a far more important role in the first session of the Ninety-seventh Congress than ever before.[27]

The majority leader, whatever his personal influence, still derives his powers largely from the expectation that he will one day be speaker.

Minority Leader

The House minority leader plays a difficult and frustrating role. The minority cannot control the legislative agenda, either at the committee level or on the floor. The main clout of the minority leadership lies in its power to obstruct, which is more pronounced in the Senate than in the House. However, a minority leader who represents a substantive majority has enormous leverage even though he lacks a party majority. This leverage is particularly powerful when the minority leader and the president are of the same party. Through devices like discharge petitions and other parliamentary maneuvers, the minority leadership often undermines the legislative agenda of the majority party.

Gerald Ford, as minority leader in the Ninety-second Congress, used his post to seek impeachment of Supreme Court Justice William O. Douglas for alleged unethical conduct. Many House members believed that Ford's loyal and dogged efforts against Justice Douglas, although unsuccessful, created a strong sense of gratitude in President Nixon. Ford's subsequent nomination to the vice-presidential vacancy caused by Spiro Agnew's resignation may attest to that fact. In any event, Douglas and the Democratic majority had to deal seriously with the attack, as the protagonist had an important forum as the minority leader of the White House party.

Under the present rules of the Republican Conference, the minority leader has a strong voice in committee assignments; he establishes the whip organization, which provides him with a communication network for minority strategy; he provides a liaison with a president of his own party; he coordinates party strategy on the floor; and most important, he bolsters the morale of members frustrated at being ignored by the majority party.

The Whip Organization

The whip organization in the House was formalized at the end of the nineteenth century as a device of speakers to buttress their legislative prerogatives. The position of "whip" originated in about 1770 in the Parliament to enforce party discipline in the House of Commons. Its name comes from the popular British fox hunts, in which one hunter, "the whipper-in," kept the dogs in line.[28] Unlike the parliamentary whip who possesses innumerable carrots and sticks to enforce party loyalty, the House majority whip has virtually no disciplinary authority. Like the majority leader, his clout is derived from the speaker. The main purpose of the House whip organization is not coercion or even persuasion; rather, it is to collect and disseminate information and to ensure the presence on the House floor of necessary members when a key vote is taken.

Although conventional wisdom puts the whip on the succession ladder, Tip O'Neill was the last whip to climb that ladder. His whip, Congressman John McFall of California, was defeated by Wright when he tried to make the leap forward to majority leader. Indiana Congressman John Brademas, who served as Wright's whip, was defeated at the polls in 1980. Previous whips have also failed, and an analysis of that job suggests that it has neither the power nor the purpose to ensure institutional success. The minority whip, on the one hand, has been treated as the heir-apparent to the office of minority leader during recent congresses. Congressmen Robert Michel of Illinois, John Rhodes of Arizona, and Charles Halleck of Indiana all moved from whip to minority leader.

The case of Indiana Congressman John Brademas, the majority whip during two recent congresses, illustrates the problems faced by the whip. When he assumed the position of whip, Brademas, a Rhodes scholar and a senior member of the House, lost some of the influence he had gained in the academic community as a result of his being on the House Education and Labor Committee. To prepare for roll-call votes, he positioned himself at the door through which most Democrats entered the chamber and held his thumb up or down to indicate the leadership's desires on the pending vote. Despite valiant and innovative efforts to inform and lead the House with numerous other activities, some of Brademas' irreverent colleagues insisted on calling him "Thumbs." As political scientist Nelson W. Polsby states:

> The purpose of the party whip system is not so much to lead as to discover whether leadership in any given area is possible or can be effective. The whips monitor floor attendance and provide a few routine informational services to Members in exchange for which Members are obliged to be pleasant—though not necessarily informative—when asked how they are disposed toward legislation.[29]

The whip organization consists of the chief whip and many assistant whips. Because the chief whip usually reflects the sentiments of the party leadership, there is some incentive to heed his call. Both the Republican and Democratic whip organizations maintain fairly detailed voting records so that the whips can, in political scientist Randall Ripley's words, "berate the goats and praise the sheep when the occasion demands."[30] When the party is a loose coalition of disparate groups without much central allegiance, as in Democratic party tradition, the role of the whip is largely informational. When the degree of consensus is high, however (e.g., after the Franklin Delano Roosevelt landslide of 1932, after John F. Kennedy's assassination in 1963, and after Reagan's victory in 1981), the role of the whip to keep the few stray dogs in line grows easier.

Prestige Committee Chairmen and the Party Caucus

The men who chair the three "prestige" committees in the House—the Rules, the Ways and Means, and the Appropriations committees—play key roles in the leadership structure. Mere membership on these committees elevates a member above his peers, because his selection signifies a vote of confidence in his leadership abilities, party loyalty, and effectiveness. The members of the Rules Committee, handpicked by the speaker, are particularly important because they are responsible for determining the House's legislative agenda and the fate of most major legislation.

The Ways and Means Committee chairman is also extremely important in the party hierarchy. Originally, the Ways and Means chairman served as the floor leader, and committee members served as the Committee on Committees, which was responsible for committee assignments. The power of Ways and Means is largely derived from the House's constitutional responsibility for originating revenue bills and thereby controlling the power of the purse. The Ways and Means chairman also derives considerable influence from the other legislative responsibilities the committee has acquired, largely through the efforts of empire-builder Arkansas Congressman Wilbur Mills. Even though the committee no longer controls committee assignments for Democratic members, it still has jurisdiction over all social security programs, most welfare programs, international trade bills, health programs, and any programs involving earmarked funds (highway programs, airport construction programs, etc.).

Finally, the chairman of the Appropriations Committee has enormous power as the person who controls the monies available to all the agencies in the federal government. The prestige of the Ways and Means and Appropriations committees has declined in recent years, a result, in part, of the new budget process (see chapters 11 and 12), which transferred some of the powers previously held by these committees to the Budget Committee.

By tradition and perception, membership on the prestige committees remains a token of leadership interest and respect. Experience gained on these committees constitutes "spring training" for those promising stars who might make their way to the big leagues. By the time they become chairmen of these committees, they are presumed to be leaders who not only control their own committees but have wide influence throughout the House. Although seniority sometimes elevates a short-hitter to chairman, these chairmen usually are, in fact, heavy sluggers: Wilbur Mills of Ways and Means, Texas Congressman George Mahon of Appropriations, Judge Howard Smith of Rules, and Missouri Congressman Richard Bolling, the 1982 chairman of Rules.

The chairman of the majority caucus is also a member of the leadership. With the reemergence of the caucus as a forum for setting party policy and implementing legislative goals, the caucus chairmanship has again become paramount. Although dominated by the speaker, the chairman of the caucus historically has been a spokesman for reform. During his tenure as chairman of the caucus, Dan Rostenkowski of Illinois appointed the committee chaired by Julia Butler Hansen of Washington to propose reforms of the seniority system. Phillip Burton of California, a key member of the Hansen committee, could implement and expand on many of the committee's reforms when he was elected chairman of the caucus in 1975. He was succeeded by Tom Foley of Washington, who went on to become whip in the Ninety-seventh Congress, and by Gillis Long, a "national" Democrat from Louisiana. At least since 1975, the caucus chairman has sought to be the spokesman and special pleader for the newer members and others who have no forum of their own. The chairman of the Republican Conference, unlike his Democratic counterpart, has not been bathed in the national limelight. Although John Anderson of Illinois, who held the post for many years until his unsuccessful run for the presidency in 1980, was an influential member of the House, his influence stemmed from his legislative and oratorical talents, not his party post.

LEADERSHIP IN THE SENATE

President of the Senate

The Constitution provides that the vice-president of the United States shall fill the position of the president of the Senate and that he shall vote only when the senators are evenly divided.[31] The Senate is directed to choose its other officers and to appoint a "president pro tempore" to serve in the absence of the vice-president.[32] Other than these few directives, the Constitution provides no guidance as to the congressional role of the vice-president. Alexander Hamilton explained the rationale behind the decision to award the Senate leadership to the vice-president:

> It has been alleged, that it would have been preferable to have authorized the Senate to elect out of their own body an officer answering that description. But two considerations seem to justify the ideas of the convention in this respect. One is, that to secure at all times the possibility of a definite resolution of the body, it is necessary that the President should have only a casting vote. And to take the Senator of any State from his seat as Senator, to place him in that of President of the Senate would be to exchange, in regard to the State from which he came, a constant for a contingent vote. The other consideration is, that as the Vice President may occasionally become a substitute for the President, in the supreme executive magistracy, all the reasons which recommend the mode of election prescribed for the one, apply with great if not with equal force to the manner of appointing the other.[33]

Neither the Constitution nor the *Federalist Papers* indicate whether the primary role of the vice-president was intended to be legislative or executive. His role was without parallel in earlier national and state legislatures. Originally it was hoped that the vice-president would serve as an important liaison between the two branches, especially as the Senate and the executive branch shared certain responsibilities, for example, confirmation of judicial and high level executive officers and ratification of treaties. Indeed, this was precisely the role that John Adams, the first vice-president, believed the president of the Senate should play. John Adams became an activist in the Senate, providing advice to the new president, George Washington, on the strategies he should take in the Senate. He also presided over most sessions of the Senate, deciding procedural questions and taking aggressive stances on pending legislation.

The vice-president's constitutional role was at that time commonly seen as predominantly legislative. Indeed, in 1797, when asked if he wanted to play a formal role in the administration, Vice-President Thomas Jefferson replied: "I consider my office as Constitutionally confined to legislative functions and could not take any part whatever in executive consultations, even were it proposed."[34]

Under the original constitutional scheme, the vice-president was the runner-up for the presidency.[35] Thus, as a member of the same party that controlled the Senate but of a different party than that of the president, he obtained a forum for advancing his political views. However, as a member of a minority party of the Senate, he was an outcast. Because of his ambiguous and uncertain role as president of the Senate and as he was not a member of the Senate, he was afforded virtually no procedural powers, powers of appointment, or prestige as a Senate leader. As historian George Haynes said:

> From the beginning the Senate has shown a determination to hold within narrow limits the powers to be exercised by a presiding officer not of its own choosing nor responsible to its majority. The "President of the Senate" is never to be allowed to forget that "the Senate is a self-governing body." [Citation omitted.] Many illustrations of this vigilant jealousy might be cited.[36]

The Standing Rules of the Senate give the president of the Senate no role except the constitutionally mandated right to cast the deciding vote in the event of a tie.[37] In the absence of the vice-president, the Senate is required to choose a president "pro tempore." These rules further specify that the president pro tempore may delegate to other senators the authority and "duties of the chair."

Today the vice-president rarely, if ever, is seen in the chambers of the Senate. The vice-president's ornate office, which is located off the even more ornate lobby where senators mingle with staff and lobbyists, is mostly frequented by the White House liaison staff and favored outside lobbyists.

Even the president pro tempore, elected by the majority of the Senate, is rarely visible after initiating the morning business. Although technically third in the line of succession to the presidency, the president pro tem is mainly a titular position. The person actually presiding changes with virtually every legislative debate. All the senators in the majority party take turns as presiding officers, with junior senators bearing the major time responsibility for the chair. As a leader of the majority party, the president pro tem (South Carolina Senator Strom Thurmond in the Ninety-seventh Congress) would rarely, if ever, designate a senator in the minority party as the presiding officer because of his power to rule on procedural questions. In the main, the presiding officer is a bored onlooker to a drama between the majority and minority leaders. Many senators actually do office work, like answering letters, while sitting on the dais. Therefore, the post of president of the Senate is parallel to the post of speaker in theory only; in reality, the president of the Senate is an emperor without clothes. The true power in the Senate is wielded by the majority leader—an office that is never discussed in the Constitution.

Majority Leader

Career Track

The majority leader is the leader of the Senate to the extent that anyone is. Because each of the 100 senators considers himself equal to anyone else, the Senate resists delegating to any one member the power to be "more equal than the rest." The Senate, with its smaller numbers, longer terms, and statewide electorates, tends to promote more independence among its members than does the House. Because of its relaxed rules and procedures, it is a very difficult body "to lead."

As national figures, senators are rather stubborn about accepting direction from anybody. The ongoing national debate about changing the electoral college method of selecting the president prompted a proposal in the Senate in the last century whereby the Senate would choose the president from among its membership. The speaker of the House, snorted in ridicule, suggesting that such a solution would result in perpetual stalemate: "They will just take ballot after ballot, with every Senator getting one vote."

As part of this tradition of individualism, senators often accord one another great deference and courtesy. The Senate is often referred to as a "Gentlemen's Club." Although this tradition of courtesy is less pronounced today, a breach in the etiquette is viewed as dangerous to the effective functioning of the Senate, which relies to a considerable extent on goodwill to conduct legislative business. Throughout the history of the Senate, few women have sought access to the gentlemen's club. In the Ninety-seventh Congress, there were two, Republican Nancy Kassebaum of Kansas and Republican Paula Hawkins of Florida, neither of whom was elected to succeed deceased husbands, the usual route for women senators.

The posts of majority and minority leaders did not become official political positions in the Senate until approximately 1920.[38]

Today, the majority leader serves many of the same functions as the speaker. As the leader of the majority party, he serves as a liaison between the president and the Senate on matters of policy, particularly when they are members of the same party. Moreover, the majority leader coordinates the activities of the Senate with those of the House. Finally, although he has fewer procedural powers than has the speaker, the majority leader, through his greater information, leverage, resources, and floor know-how, has considerable control over the scheduling of legislation and coordination of party strategy.

The majority leader is chosen by a majority of the caucus of the majority party. The apprenticeship is usually service as party whip, whose duties allow him to accumulate extensive knowledge concerning the lives, values, and goals of each senator in his party. In a legislative entity where procedural clout is minimal, information becomes the main ingredient of power. After starting out as an elected whip, the youngest in history, Lyndon Johnson was promoted to minority leader. Historian Doris Kearns Goodwin described his quest for power:

Democratic Senator Mike Mansfield (Montana),
majority leader 1961–1977, conferring with
Republican Senator Everett Dirksen (Illinois),
minority leader 1959–1969.

Johnson had become Minority Leader without the slightest illusion about the relationship between his formal position and the actual authority—both the process and the men—that govern the conduct of the Senate. After all, he was, as we have seen, a man who believed that success in any institution depended upon the most detailed possible knowledge of the way things worked—how and why some objectives were achieved, and others defeated, which individuals exercised the greatest authority, and what were the sources and limits of that authority. In the Senate as elsewhere, he pursued such knowledge with unremitting, almost obsessed persistence—through his own observation and from the experienced and powerful men to whom he gained access. The information was synthesized by a mind gifted with an almost shocking capacity to comprehend the structure of an institution, to become aware of the process through which it operated and to sense the vulnerabilities of that process. . . .

Johnson reassured himself that open coercion was not a practical possibility in the quest for Senate leadership; his instrument would be the power of persuasion. By providing others with services and desired resources, he would establish superiority over them; by providing benefits that would serve the political and personal interests of others, he would attain power. Yet the line between persuasion and coercion is thin and ambiguously drawn; the receipt of regular rewards from a benefactor who will also be the source of future benefits can create a dependency close to coercive power, because the ability to bestow also implies the authority to discontinue or refuse as a sign of disapproval or as a punishment.[39]

The use of knowledge to obtain power also proved to be a successful strategy almost twenty years later when West Virginia Senator Robert C. Byrd defeated Massachusetts Senator and Majority Whip Edward Kennedy for the position of Senate whip in 1971. In 1969 Kennedy had been handpicked for whip by Majority Leader Mike Mansfield. Representing the liberal insurgents and preferring to focus on policy matters, Kennedy failed to attend to the mundane, earthy details of catering to 100 "prima donnas." Byrd, on the other hand, like Lyndon Johnson, took meticulous care in learning intimate details about each senator. He remembered to send them anniversary notes; he telephoned the airport to hold a plane for a fellow colleague; he attempted to reschedule votes to accommodate a senator's time schedule. As one senator stated: "Bobby Byrd was proud to be an errand boy."[40] Byrd defeated Kennedy in the Democratic Conference by a surprise upset of 31 to 24. From the whip position, Byrd rose to be majority leader.

The majority leader is the chief spokesman for his party in the Senate. Styles of leadership vary tremendously. Majority Leader Lyndon Johnson aggressively spearheaded the party's activities without giving much leeway or responsibility to other senators. Thus, he controlled committee assignments, appointed the chair of the Senate campaign committees (thereby controlling political funds), and gave only token responsibilities to the formal entities within the party: the Democratic Conference, the Democratic Steering Committee, and the Democratic Policy Committee. From 1953 to 1958, only five party conferences were held. The Policy Committee, despite its name, did little more than formally ratify the scheduling of decisions made by Johnson, although the diversity of the membership occasionally helped Johnson identify the best strategy for floor action. The Steering Committee, which formally had the power to make committee assignments, usually rubber-stamped Johnson's decisions.[41]

Mike Mansfield, on the other hand, used the party organization to reach decisions rather than to ratify them. The Policy Committee met more frequently under Mansfield and played a key role in scheduling legislation. Operating on a consensus-building model, Mansfield usually delegated to the principal proponents and opponents of legislation within the Policy Committee the task of working out disagreements within the party before full Senate action. Under Mansfield, the Steering Committee regained its power over committee assignments.[42]

Robert Byrd represented a third model of party leadership. As majority leader, Byrd was more than willing to devote most of his energies to processing legislation desired by members of his party. Known as a "traffic cop" and the "man who makes the trains run on time," Byrd viewed his main responsibility as ensuring the orderly scheduling of legislation desired by members of his conference. He also used the caucus to smooth differences between party members.

As majority leader, Byrd occasionally tried to encourage the conference to act as a party in sponsoring policy recommendations. For example, shortly before the 1980 election, he proposed an Economic Task Force to deal with Republican proposals for across-the-board tax cuts. Byrd acted in an institutional sense to protect the credibility of Democratic senators in the eyes of the American public, thereby divorcing the congressional party from the faltering Carter administration.

In general, however, the majority leader takes a passive approach to policy formulation, because of the reluctance in the Senate, unabated to this day, to yield to the leadership any individual prerogatives enjoyed by each senator.

Procedural Powers

The majority leader has few procedural powers to buttress his authority. Unlike the speaker of the House, the leader has no Rules Committee to dictate the order, priority, and manner in which legislation is to be considered.* Moreover, it is the parliamentarian, not the majority leader, who determines the action to be taken on bills and resolves points of order. A challenge to his ruling involves a floor vote. Because, as mentioned earlier, many acting presidents pro tempore are freshman senators who have little familiarity with Senate rules, the parliamentarian controls the daily flow of legislative business by advising the chair on the order of business. Theoretically, the parliamentarian has no party affiliation and must counsel all senators and Senate staffs alike. Thus, if the minority wants to filibuster a bill and the majority wants to break the filibuster, the parliamentarian is under an obligation to provide procedural advice to both sides of the aisle. As one may suspect, in practice this impartiality does not always work. The parliamentarian has an obligation to respond to all inquiries, but often staffs and senators do not know the correct procedural questions to ask. If the parliamentarian agrees with the position taken by a senator, he tends to propose procedural solutions that will obtain the desired results. But, as consumer advocate Ralph Nader said, "Indications are that he does not dispense information equally: some Senators must ask very specific questions to get a usable response, while others may ask very open-ended questions."[43] In practice, parliamentarians tend to identify with the majority party. Thus, when Murray Zweben "retired" after the Republicans gained control in 1980 and his assistant Robert Dove took over, the Democrats felt they had lost a valuable ally.

Although the majority leader cannot rule on procedural issues, he does possess a few key procedural powers. First, he controls floor scheduling. Most business in the Senate proceeds under suspension of the rules. As Robert Byrd once explained, if the rules were actually followed, the Senate would get bogged down in "messy" procedural complications.[44] Instead, most activities of the Senate are conducted under unanimous consent agreements. These agreements serve the same function as the rules reported by the Rules Committee in the House. They control the scheduling of legislation, the extent of the debate on a measure, and the referral of legislation.

The majority and minority leaders are responsible for forging unanimous consent agreements. As point men for their respective parties, the majority and minority leaders exercise tremendous leverage over the flow of legislation.

---

*The Senate Rules Committe is the counterpart of the House Administration Committee and acts as the budgetary and space allocator for Senate committees and members. It also reviews and maintains the standing rules. However, because the Senate, as an ongoing body, does not go through the biennial ritual of reexamining the standing rules, the Senate Rules Committee exercises none of the significant authority of its House counterpart. Moreover, legislation in the Senate does not require a "rule" prior to being scheduled for floor action.

The majority leader also is responsible for the interpretation of unanimous consent agreements. As the co-author of the agreement, he controls to a large degree the implementation of the agreement on the floor, including the formal responsibility of determining which senators on his side will debate the legislation and how much time they will have. Although the chairman of the committee responsible for the legislation takes the primary role as the floor manager, the majority leader plays a critical role in resolving controversies within the party over the progress of the legislative agenda.

When the unanimous consent system breaks down on controversial pieces of legislation, the majority leader is accorded first recognition in floor debates and is thus able to move legislation even without a unanimous consent agreement. Although he cannot prevent obstructionist tactics like a filibuster by opponents of the bill, the majority leader can, through a motion to adjourn, end the "legislative day" and thus provide time to consider new legislative tactics. Because most members of his party will vote with him on procedural votes, the ability of the majority leader to limit the scope of the agenda, even without unanimous consent, gives him substantial power. With a better knowledge of procedure and an effective whip operation, the majority leader often outsmarts the opposition.

Despite his procedural leverage, a majority leader's powers are circumscribed by his ability to put together a majority coalition on the floor. In the spring of 1981 Majority Leader Howard Baker, flushed with his recent victories on President Reagan's economic package, decided to teach the Democrats a lesson. Once again the Department of Justice authorization bill was the lightning rod. The Democratic caucus, attempting to take the lead in the fight against violent crime, impetuously approved an anti-crime package forged by three Democratic senators. Senator Strom Thurmond, who hoped to be Mr. Anti-crime for the Republican party and the new chairman of the Judiciary Committee, was furious.

Majority Leader Howard Baker devised a strategy to stymie the Democrats. Prior to the Democratic crime package, Senator Jesse Helms had introduced his usual anti-busing amendment to prohibit the Civil Rights Division of the Justice Department from using federal funds to seek busing as a remedy to school segregation. Republican Lowell Weicker of Connecticut began a filibuster against a vote on the busing proposals, thereby bogging down the entire bill. Baker's solution would kill two birds with one stone. He introduced a cloture petition to limit debate on not only the busing filibuster but also on the whole DOJ bill, which would also preclude the Democrats from effectively offering their anti-crime package. However, a bipartisan group of senators defeated this and subsequent cloture petitions and delayed reconsideration of the DOJ bill for six months. This defeat not only put a blemish on Baker's reputation as a politically savvy majority leader but also proved to be a harbinger of the problems the Republican leadership would have in maintaining internal party harmony on divisive social issues.

Minority Leader

Because of the importance of unanimous consent agreements in the Senate, the minority leader, elected by his party caucus, has more significant influence over the activities of the Senate than does his counterpart in the House. In addition to providing the procedural foil to the majority party, the minority leader has internal responsibilities within the party to harmonize diverse elements and thus create a compact, unified, coherent party strategy. Howard Baker, as minority leader prior to the take-over of the Senate by the Republicans, jeopardized his leadership status by supporting the Panama Canal treaty, a position that antagonized the members of the New Right. The minority leader must be sensitive to the demands of the centrist powers of the party. After the Reagan victory, for example, the new Democratic minority leader, Robert Byrd, was pressured by the moderate Senate Democrats who believed that the liberal wing of the Democratic party had shifted it too far to the left. Byrd was castigated, for example, for permitting the long, fruitless debate on the controversial fair-housing legislation during the lame-duck session of the Congress after the November 4 landslide. The legislation went down to embarrassing defeat and was viewed as the Democratic "swan song." During the early days of the Ninety-seventh Congress, Byrd accommodated the moderates in the party by establishing a task force on regulatory reform, a task force on Democratic alternative strategies, and a task force on the economy. As members of the task forces, middle-of-the-road Democrats used them to influence party policy.

Perhaps the most important role of the Senate minority leader is to minimize conflict within the party. During the fights over the Reagan budget cuts in the spring of 1981, Senator Byrd attempted to create consensus behind certain amendments. However, Democratic rhetoric and strategies failed to sway Republicans, and amendment after amendment went down to shattering defeat. As it became increasingly clear that Democratic unity would not lead to victory, the incentives for cohesion decreased, and individual Democrats increasingly went their own way to score political points. During the debate over the Reagan three-year tax cut, this lack of internal consensus became crystal clear to all observers, and Minority Leader Byrd became virtually ineffective in creating coalitions. The alternative tax proposals of several Democratic senators each received fewer than 25 votes. Senator Byrd retained his influence on only procedural votes that involved institutional concerns about the operations of the budget process—hardly the substantive meat to revitalize Democratic morale or ideology.

The minority leader has very few weapons at his disposal. He can threaten to withhold coveted committee assignments or hold back floor action on particular legislation as a means to force recalcitrant senators to vote the party line. But, for the most part, he must rely on persuasion. In short, as venerable Republican Senator Everett Dirksen pointed out, it is much harder being minority leader than majority leader. Often it is no more than being a cheerleader for a losing team.[45]

The Whip Organization

The whip systems of both the Democratic and Republican parties in the Senate are less elaborate than those in the House. The chief whips are elected by the party membership and may in turn choose deputy whips, each responsible for certain designated members. With far fewer members, it is much less difficult to gather information about members' positions. Moreover, because most measures are handled under unanimous consent agreements, the need for votes on a moment's notice is less. In general, the whip function is informational and rarely coercive. Every Senate office receives a "whip notice" of the Senate's legislative agenda and the terms of unanimous consent agreements. Unlike the majority and minority leaders, the "stars" of the Senate pageantry, the whips are virtually mute. Another, indeed important, function of the whip position is as a training ground for prospective majority leaders. Johnson, Mansfield, and Byrd all began as whips.

SIX

COMMITTEES— CREATURES OF CONVENIENCE

ithout committees, Congress would be a reactive institution unable to fulfill its constitutional mandate to oversee the executive branch. In addition, committees provide Congress with the expertise, skill, and organizational structure necessary to allow it to cope with the increasingly complex and technical questions in both the domestic and international arenas of the twentieth century. Each committee is responsible for exploring and resolving problems in a major policy area—agriculture, energy, the environment, the judiciary, taxation, banking, to name only a few—a delegation of responsibility that provides a relatively efficient and effective allocation of congressional resources.

In his description of the origins of power in modern social and economic organizations, social scientist Max Weber said power comes from knowledge, and "technical knowledge...by itself, is sufficient to ensure...a position of extraordinary power."[1] Without the existence of the specialized committee system, Congress would be an organization of dilettantes unable to respond intelligently to national problems. It would be forced to surrender its co-equal position in the formulation and promulgation of law to the executive branch with its vastly superior resources of manpower, money, and information-gathering technology.

But the very system essential to promoting congressional leverage over policy formation is also the nemesis of an effective, politically responsive Congress. As they developed in this century, committees often function as feuding, jealous fiefdoms, which by rule, tradition, and generally accepted norm have virtually unlimited power to control the outcome of legislation within their bailiwicks. Thus a committee chairman sometimes bottles up legislation even though it is widely supported by a majority of congressmen. Introduction of legislation that is not supported by a committee chairman or at least by a powerful committee member of the majority party is, to use a common expression on the Hill, like dropping a rock to the bottom of a very deep ocean. It will never again emerge.

Certain recent developments have placed some constraints on committee power. For example, through the newly enacted budget process, policy outcomes can be achieved without the acquiescence of the committees that have jurisdiction over the policy area. But, on the whole, committees, particularly in the House, retain strong institutionally recognized power to obstruct legislation, even when that legislation is desired by the party leadership, the executive branch, and the majority of the American people. This inordinate power is deleterious to the esteem and legitimacy of Congress because it allows a systematized distortion of congressional goals and prevents Congress from responding to newly emerging political consensus. Thus committees remain somewhat immune to changes in public opinion (as long as the party majority remains in power).

Chapters 6 and 7 examine the committee system from several perspectives. First, they trace the evolution of congressional committees and in particular focus on the reforms of the 1970s that made the system more vulnerable to public pressure. Second, they briefly describe the various protean forms of committees. Unlike the popular perception, there is not just one kind of congressional committee. There are many: the Committee of the Whole, the select committees, the joint committees, the conference committees, the ad hoc investigative committees, and last but not least, the standing committees.

It is the next chapter that concentrates on standing committees, the major organizational units in both the Senate and the House of Representatives. It describes in detail the three primary functions of the standing committees: to provide the Congress with expertise, to provide a forum for reelection, and to encourage such institutionally important values and skills as party loyalty and procedural savoir-faire. Attention also is paid to the subcommittee's relationship to the full committee and to the full committee's role within the overall congressional structure.

That the committee structure is vital to the effective functioning of Congress as a co-equal branch of government is not in dispute. However, Congress is constantly challenged by the necessity to temper the parochial concerns of the committees with the needs of the nation. The procedural tools and political strength of the congressional leadership and the party caucuses are used to continuously pressure the committees to respond to national and party objectives.

HISTORY OF THE COMMITTEE SYSTEM

In the early days of the Republic, Congress had no permanent committees. The First Congress, which convened in 1789, did not feel the need for its own committee experts. It was content to continue the practice established under the Articles of Confederation of relying on executive departments to work out the technical details of legislation. Not surprisingly, Federalist presidents discouraged the formation of committees, which were regarded as dangerous rivals to the executive branch.[2] Indeed, the Ways and Means Committee established by the House of Representatives in 1789 to handle revenue and appropriation bills was abolished temporarily due to pressure applied by Federalist Treasurer Alexander Hamilton.

Congress soon recognized, however, that executive departments were inadequate, and both the House and the Senate turned to ad hoc select committees to draft legislation. In the House of Representatives, legislation was first debated conceptually in the Committee of the Whole House on the State of the Union. Named after its predecessor in Parliament,[3] the Committee of the Whole had been a viable structure in the Continental Congress as well as in most state legislatures. As a subunit of the House, presided over by a person other than the speaker, it provided a manageable working group to thresh out legislative compromise. After broad agreement had been reached on the principles involved, a select committee was named to draft the legislation and report back to the Committee of the Whole. Usually the select committee was composed of members who favored the legislation. By the Third Congress, in 1793, well over 350 select committees had been formed in the House of Representatives.

Recognizing the importance of the committee system, the House speaker quickly sought control of committee membership. In 1790 the speaker obtained the power to appoint select committees unless otherwise directed by the House. In 1794 the House empowered the speaker to name the chairman of the Committee of the Whole. In 1809, during the Eleventh Congress, the powers of the speaker were enhanced even further when he was awarded the privilege of designating committee chairmen.[4]

ASCENDANCY OF THE COMMITTEE SYSTEM

The expansion of the federal government throughout the nineteenth century was accompanied by an increasing reliance on permanent, or standing, committees to formulate policy initiatives and to oversee the activities of the executive branch. Between 1809 and 1829 in the House of Representatives, standing committees emerged as the principal forums for the initial consideration of legislation. The standing committees, which tripled in number during that time period, gradually replaced the ad hoc select committees.

By the end of the century, the standing committees had become virtually autonomous. Woodrow Wilson, in *Congressional Government*, poignantly (and a bit melodramatically) described committees as "seigniories,"[5] which made life and death decisions about every piece of legislation. He pointed out that committees were not controlled by any strong party mechanism, and, consequently, were somewhat immune to the sentiments of the majority of the House:

> The [House] legislates in its Committee-Rooms; not by the determinations of majorities, but by the resolutions of specifically commissioned minorities; so that it is not far from the truth to say that Congress in session is Congress on public exhibition whilst Congress in its Committee Rooms is Congress at work.[6]

The growth of the committee system throughout the nineteenth century was necessitated, in part, by the changed nature of the congressional membership. In the early days of Congress the turnover in congressional membership was high, with frequent resignations and low rates of reelection. By the turn of the century, however, the incumbency rate had greatly increased, for most members sought reelection. In addition, just as a longtime member of any organization expects rewards and additional prestige, a longtime member of the Congress expected to obtain "tenure" in his committee position and eventually, by virtue of his seniority, the position of committee chairman. And thus the seniority system evolved. It is safe to say that few labor union contracts create such vested rights in career promotion as does the congressional seniority system.

Because the only threat to committee tenure was defeat at the polls, membership on a committee of stature became a powerful tool. After the rebellion against "Czar" Cannon in 1909-10, committee autonomy was complete. When the speaker was stripped of his power of appointment, he lost much of his ability to penalize members who did not adhere to the party line.

For a brief time party committee members were required to support a measure whenever it received a two-thirds vote of the party caucus. The caucus instructed committees regarding the legislation to be considered and the bills to be reported. However, the renaissance of the caucus was short-lived, attaining the height of its influence under the administration of Woodrow Wilson. Throughout the first half of the twentieth century, committees reigned supreme. As autonomous bodies, many committees became the legislative equivalent of Britain's "rotten boroughs"—they were incapable of responding to public sentiment and prevented the centralization of authority in Congress.*

ATTACK ON THE COMMITTEE SYSTEM

In dealing with the national crisis of the 1930s, the aggressive presidency of Franklin Delano Roosevelt contrasted sharply with the ineptitude of a lethargic Congress. The effectiveness of the committee system and its ability to reflect the will of the congressional majority became subject to debate. After World War II Congress made a concerted effort to modernize its organizational machinery. The number of standing committees in both the House and the Senate was cut in half. New procedures were imposed to enhance the responsiveness of committee decision making and to curb the arbitrary powers of chairmen. The Legislative Reorganization Act of 1946 established specific days for committee meetings, instructed committees for the first time to keep records of votes, required the presence of a quorum of a majority of the committee members to conduct business, and mandated open public hearings (but not open bill-drafting sessions, which are called "mark-ups").[7]

In what may be the most significant reform measure, each standing committee was authorized to appoint four professional and six clerical staff members. The Congressional Research Service, the research arm of the Library of Congress, was established. The additional staff and research facilities allowed committees to effectively check an aggressive and informed executive branch.

A prolonged struggle to decrease the inordinate power of the committees commenced with an attack on the Rules Committee during Sam Rayburn's tenure as speaker. The Rules Committee has always been the most powerful House committee—because it determines whether, how, and when a bill is to be considered on the floor. Until the reforms of the 1970s, the chairman of the Rules Committee had almost invincible authority to decide the fate of all legislation. Because the Rules Committee chairman ascended to his throne through seniority, he often was unrepresentative of the rank-and-file House

---

*An election district that has many fewer inhabitants than other election districts with the same voting power. "Rotten boroughs" were common in nineteenth-century England.

membership and unaccountable to anyone—neither the party leadership, the president, nor the majority of the House.

Throughout the period commencing in 1948 and ending with John F. Kennedy's presidency in the early 1960s, the Rules Committee was controlled by a conservative coalition of four Republicans and three southern Democrats. The iron grip of the Rules Committee over legislation was so strong that Rules Committee Chairman Howard W. Smith of Virginia managed to kill civil-rights legislation supported by President Kennedy by vacationing for a long period of time on his Virginia farm.[8] In 1961, to counter the power of the Rules Committee, Speaker Rayburn persuaded the Democratic caucus "to pack" the committee, expanding its membership from twelve to fifteen, which created an eight to seven majority for the leadership. In addition, in 1964 Congress continued its effort to curb the Rules Committee by establishing a rule that, although short-lived, authorized a committee chairman to bring a bill reported favorably by his committee to the House floor if the Rules Committee failed to act within twenty-one calendar days.

Efforts to reform the committee system were not limited to the Rules Committee. Because of the firmly entrenched seniority system, committee chairmen in the mid-1960s and early 1970s were unrepresentative of the majority party. Most major committees in the House of Representatives and the Senate were chaired by southern conservatives who tended to have high reelection rates, whereas the more recently elected rank-and-file membership of both chambers became more and more liberal. For example, a chairman of the powerful Senate Judiciary Committee, conservative Mississippi Senator James O. Eastland successfully killed most of the civil-rights bills,[9] much to the chagrin of the liberal rank-and-file committee members. On the House side the difference between the ideologies of the octogenarian House chairmen of various committees and the rebellious newly elected anti-Vietnam representatives was even more stark. The dissonance between those in power and the majority of the Congress led to major institutional reforms, which would alter the balance of power for decades to come.

Between 1970 and 1976 reform after reform swept through the Congress. The Legislative Reorganization Act of 1970 required written committee rules to thwart the arbitrary abuse of power by committee chairmen and the public announcement of roll-call votes taken in closed sessions.[10] To provide an independent means for evaluating committee recommendations prior to floor action, the Act required committee reports to be available three days before floor consideration.[11] The "sunshine" reforms required all committees and subcommittees to open bill-drafting sessions and other business sessions to the public unless the majority of the committee voted to the contrary in open session.[12]

The first open mark-up (bill-drafting) session in the House occurred when a Judiciary subcommittee, chaired by Congressman Robert Kastenmeier of Wisconsin, persuaded the chairman of the full committee to authorize the open session. Amid great trepidations and despite the special preparation of wearing blue shirts for television cameras, the first great open American mark-up was a bust. Aside from a few staffers, the committee room was empty. The bill, which involved a technical matter, clearly lacked sex appeal.

However, the sunshine reforms made a substantial difference in the way things are done. Even the late-night sessions of the Ways and Means Committee are well attended. A member who tries to put through special legislation for a particular lobbyist is more than likely to be exposed by the press in attendance, regardless of the hour. At a late-night committee mark-up a retroactive tax provision was offered as an amendment to a tax bill. Typical of tax provisions, it was utterly confusing to most members. However, reporter Albert Hunt of the *Wall Street Journal* spotted a lobbyist-lawyer in the crowd who seemed to be taking special interest in the amendment. By interviewing the lobbyist and doing some gumshoeing on his own, Hunt discovered that the amendment would bestow large benefits on a single taxpayer, a taxpayer who had contributed generously to the campaign funds of many committee members. Even though the provision passed handily in committee, the subsequent public disclosure of the facts prompted the Rules Committee to allow a separate vote on the amendment on the floor, where it was overwhelmingly defeated.

Critics of the open mark-up point out that without open mark-up the lobbyist would not have been in the committee room in the first place.* How the absence or presence of lobbyists during mark-ups affects the communication of the members is more difficult to explain. However, the presence of lobbyists does impact on the deliberative process. Despite the critics, open mark-ups in both the Senate and the House have become a matter of course.

In 1975 the House/Senate conference committee meetings were also opened. Earlier a new House member, Montana Democrat Max Baucus, now a senator, tried to attend a conference on an appropriations bill. He was told politely to leave, especially as he was neither a member of the committee nor the conference committee on the bill in question. Baucus's crusade to open conference committee meetings lasted most of his first term. After the House had agreed to his reform proposals, the House leadership pressured the Senate to adopt the reform as well. Although quite a few exceptions to open conferences are

---

*Certainly the framers of the Constitution were not advocates of sunshine in government— the public was barred from the Constitutional Convention.

An early cartoon illustrating the theory of
the "secrecy and silence" of executive sessions
of the Senate and the reality of "leaks."

allowed, most conferences are held in the sunshine. (Of course, "in the sunshine" is quite a euphemism for the dingy backrooms in which conferences usually are held. Frequently the rooms are far too small to accommodate the legions of lobbyists and staff who want to attend. The conference rooms burst at the seams with sweating, cigar-smoking congressmen and straining, cramped staff—with most lobbyists left outside to fret.)

In the House of Representatives committee reforms were spearheaded by the party caucus (prodded by the Democratic Study Group), which had commissioned numerous studies on reform by such advocates as Congressman Richard Bolling of Missouri. It is not surprising, then, that the caucus gave itself some new powers, including one that further curbed the Rules Committee. The reform measure provides that the Rules Committee must allow an amendment to be considered on the floor whenever an amendment is proposed by fifty members and approved by a majority of the caucus. In addition to further curbing the Rules Committee, this reform, authored by Congressman Phillip Burton of California, was directed at the Ways and Means Committee, which generally did not permit amendments to tax bills on the floor. (It still is customary for Ways and Means bills to come to the floor under a "closed" rule, which does not permit amendments.) The caucus also created a new Democratic Steering and Policy Committee to assist the speaker in developing party and legislative priorities.

Another long-time vestige of committee autonomy was eliminated when the caucus voted to deny the automatic guarantee of succession to committee chairmanship via seniority. Instead, each chairman is elected by secret ballot. This reform was used in 1974, after the Watergate scandal, when the new Democratic freshmen outnumbered the old-timers by 2 to 1. Three Democratic committee chairmen—Wright Patman of Texas of the Banking, Currency and Housing Committee, Edward Hebert of Louisiana of the Armed Services Committee, and W. R. Poage of Texas of the Agriculture Committee—were ousted for various reasons in the Ninety-fourth Congress. The message was clear. Committee chairmanships were no longer secure: To continue as chairmen, congressmen would have to respond to the sentiments of the party majority.

With the demise of the power of the committee, the subcommittees came into their own. Originally, committee chairman controlled subcommittee budgets, chairmanships, membership, and jurisdiction. In the 1970s House Democrats provided, by rule, many limitations on the chairman's powers over the subcommittees. In 1971 the caucus provided that a Democratic committee member could chair only one subcommittee. In the subcommittee "Bill of Rights" adopted in 1973, the Democratic caucus provided that a caucus of the majority party committee members should select subcommittee chairmen,

TABLE 6–1
NUMBER OF CONGRESSIONAL
SUBCOMMITTEES

	House	Senate
1945	106	68
1968	139	104
1974	133	156
1981	130	101

establish subcommittee jurisdictions, provide adequate subcommittee budgets, and ensure a major subcommittee assignment to each member.[13] Committee chairmen were required to refer legislation to the appropriate subcommittee within two weeks after referral to the full committee. Finally, all subcommittee chairmen and ranking minority members were each entitled to one staff person.

In 1975 the Democratic caucus voted to "spread the action," by limiting the number of positions of power to be held by any one member and by requiring the full committee chairmen to delegate much of their power. All full standing committees having more than twenty members were required to establish at least four subcommittees[14] and each member could serve on only two subcommittees. Finally, to ensure a subcommittee assignment of choice, the reform specified that each committee member could choose his first subcommittee position before any member selected a second subcommittee assignment.[15]

In the Senate the prestige of subcommittees witnessed a parallel rise. In 1953 Majority Leader Lyndon B. Johnson initiated efforts to guarantee every senator, regardless of seniority, at least one major committee assignment. Similar rules were then adopted in the 1970s to ensure each senator the opportunity to chair and serve on important subcommittees. Rule XXV of the Senate Rules carefully delineates restrictions on subcommittee membership. Each senator may serve on only three subcommittees of the major standing committees. A committee chairman can chair only one subcommittee. A committee member can chair only one subcommittee in any committee. But these requirements are not immutable.

Each committee handles its subcommittees differently. In the Judiciary Committee, for example, under the chairmanship of Mississippi Senator James O. Eastland, the subcommittees became virtually autonomous entities with strong staffs. The full committee served as a clearinghouse for the legislation processed by the subcommittees. In other committees, like Agriculture, Banking, and Foreign Affairs, the full committee has always played the dominant role. The committee chairman and, to a lesser extent, the ranking minority member control the subcommittees, the legislative agenda, and the staff.

Each senator in the majority party becomes chairman of a subcommittee in his first year in office. From this vantage point, he develops his own forum to attract national attention and establish a power base. On the Judiciary Committee, for example, subcommittees are devised to accommodate the interests of freshmen senators. In 1979 Chairman Edward Kennedy established the Subcommittee on the Limitations on Contractual Authority for freshman Democrat Max Baucus of Montana; in 1981, the new Republican Chairman Strom Thurmond eliminated that subcommittee and reestablished the Subcommittee on Juvenile Justice for former District Attorney Arlen Specter, the new Republican senator from Pennsylvania. Subcommittees provide the opportunity for junior members to shine in the national limelight. Timely stroking is effective; happy newcomers are supportive newcomers.

The rise of the subcommittee has contributed to the decentralization of power. A senior senator, on watching a subcommittee chairman of the House Banking, Finance and Urban Affairs Committee kill legislation providing economic aid to cities, stated: "I can't believe that that little unknown chairman whom no one has ever heard of before can stop this legislation which the President and the whole Senate want." The power of the subcommittee has reached new heights, indeed.

The new budget procedures, instituted by the Congressional Budget and Impoundment Control Act of 1974, have also diminished the power of congressional committees. The Budget Act requires Congress to set spending ceilings for every government program. According to a schedule established by the 1974 Act, the Budget Committee proposes a First Concurrent Budget Resolution, recommending target amounts for each program. Subsequently, the authorizing and the Appropriations committees report their legislation to the floor. A discrepancy between the amount committees authorize for spending and the budget ceilings results in reconciliation legislation, which forces the committees to rethink and reduce their projected allocations. Congress is thus forced to treat the budget as a whole, rather than as the fragmented bits and pieces characteristic of congressional budget making prior to 1974.

Theoretically, the Budget Act was not to tamper with a committee's existing jurisdiction: the Agriculture Committee was to continue to determine the fate of dairy price supports; the Commerce Committee was to continue to determine the programs of the Consumer Product Safety Commission; and the Judiciary Committee was to continue to evaluate Justice Department programs. However, the Budget Committee has to a large extent usurped these jurisdictions. The conflict between the Budget Committee and other standing committees is well illustrated by the struggle over the Reagan budget cuts early in the Ninety-seventh Congress. Under the Reagan economic plan, a series of budget cuts that curtailed or eliminated many major governmental programs was proposed by David Stockman, director of the Office of Management and Budget. Among the programs to be axed were the Juvenile Justice programs in the Justice Department; funds for mental health centers (to be replaced by block grants); the FTC Bureau of Competition; and 30 percent of the budget of the Consumer Product Safety Commission. Because the standing committees responsible for those programs have no jurisdiction over the budget resolution reported out of the Budget Committee, their capacity to protect their programs was greatly diminished. True, the standing committees can ignore the budget instructions and fight ceiling decisions with floor amendments. For example, the threat of a bipartisan effort of both the Commerce and Judiciary committees to preserve the FTC's Bureau of Competition forced Stockman to back down; the funding level of the Bureau of Competition was cut only 10 percent. Nonetheless, the Budget Committee has significant leverage to influence the future of legislative programs.

COMMITTEE OF THE WHOLE

The largest and oldest congressional committee is the Committee of the Whole House on the State of the Union. Originating in the Parliament, the Committee of the Whole, as it is called, was the working nucleus of the Continental Congress, early state legislatures, and the Constitutional Convention. Because its original purpose was to handle revenue and appropriation matters, the speaker, or king's representative, was barred from the working sessions of the committee to allow freer debate. Today the committee has a mandatory quorum of 100 congressmen, and its chairman is appointed by the speaker.[16]

Most legislation is debated in the Committee of the Whole before coming to the House for a vote. With few exceptions, the Rules Committee proposes a rule for a bill which must be approved by the entire House before debate can proceed on the bill itself under the terms contained in the rule.

The rule generally specifies that the Committee of the Whole House on the State of the Union will consider a measure first in general debate. Subsequently, amendments (either limited or unlimited, depending on the rule granted) will be considered under the five-minute rule. The five-minute rule allows any member to speak for five minutes on any amendment offered in the Committee of the Whole. Indeed, it permits members to say almost anything at all pertinent to the measure under consideration. Members frequently "move to strike the last word" of an amendment, which is a parliamentary device indicating that at that time they merely want to talk about, rather than specifically support or oppose, the amendment under debate. When the Committee of the Whole has concluded its consideration of the legislation, it reports the bill and amendments, if any, to the full House with recommendations for or against passage.

SELECT COMMITTEES

The select committees propose recommendations in certain policy areas but generally do not have the authority to report legislation for floor consideration.

Committee membership is valuable for it provides opportunities to woo special-interest groups and to establish a reputation as a leader in an important policy area. Democratic Senator Lawton Chiles of Florida used his position on the Select Committee on Aging to make political points on social security with his elderly constituents in Florida.

Assignments to select committees are "extras," that is, supplements to assignments on the more important committees. Furthermore, membership often is accompanied by staff and financial resources. In the Senate the members are chosen by caucuses;[17] in the House the members are appointed by the speaker—often as a reward for party loyalty.[18]

Select committees, which are usually created by resolution, sometimes meet stiff opposition from standing committee chairmen who fear the select committee will impinge on his turf. The prime mover in the creation of the select committee is usually designated as its chairman. Thus, Congressman Claude Pepper of Florida became chairman of the Select Committee on the Aging not only because of his premier status as a House octogenarian but because he pushed the idea of the select committee through the House.

The Senate Select Committee on Ethics has been in recent years the most important such committee and also the most unpopular. Whereas senators compete with one another to get on the "apple pie and motherhood" committees—small business and the elderly—they shy away from judging their Senate brethren on ethical violations. Much arm twisting is required to persuade members to agree to such an assignment. During the Ninety-sixth Congress, the Ethics Committee was chaired by Senator Howell Heflin, a former judge on the Alabama Supreme Court (indeed, he is still frequently referred to as Judge Heflin). His judicial experience was welcomed by both sides of the aisle in the committee's deliberation of Senator Harrison Williams, who had been convicted by the U.S. District Court in New York in an Abscam trial, of taking a bribe from an Arab sheik in return for certain favors. When he lost the chairmanship in the Ninety-seventh Congress to Malcolm Wallop, a conservative Republican from Wyoming, Judge Heflin nevertheless remained a symbol of judicial nonpartisanship. It is noteworthy that on the House side the Standards of Official Conduct Committee was given the increased stature of a standing committee.

JOINT COMMITTEES

The joint committees of House and Senate members are usually designed to handle activities common to both. Joint committees generally have their own staff, and the chairmanship alternates between the House and the Senate. Joint committees rarely deal with substantive issues. For example, the Legislative Reorganization Act of 1970 established the Joint Committee on Congressional Operations, the Joint Committee on Printing, and the Joint Committee on the Library.

The Joint Economic Committee and the Joint Committee on Taxation have legislative functions. Although they have independent staffs and subcommittees to research and prepare reports they cannot report out specific legislation. The staff of the bipartisan Joint Committee on Taxation is composed of a well-respected cadre of taxation experts. Their independent expertise on the activities of the standing Ways and Means and Finance committees is available to all members. During the tax-cut fight in the spring of 1981, some staff of the Joint Committee on Taxation provided representatives and senators with the necessary fodder to challenge the president's tax plan and to demonstrate (through charts and statistics) that the tax-cut package benefited favored groups disproportionately. The unique success of the Joint Committee on Taxation has been due in all likelihood to the special skills of a former staff director, the late Lawrence Woodworth. Because he enjoyed the confidence of committee members from both the House and the Senate, he was able to operate in a much wider area than most joint committee staffers. When Dr. Woodworth left the committee to go to the Treasury, the influence of the Joint Committee staff waned somewhat. But the Joint Committee continues to fulfill its unique bicameral function.

CONFERENCE COMMITTEES

A conference committee is established on an ad hoc basis by the House and Senate leadership to hammer out differences between legislation passed by the two houses so that the same bill can be passed by both houses and be subsequently submitted to the president as the Constitution requires.[19] The role of conference committees is discussed in detail in chapter 10.

INVESTIGATING COMMITTEES

Congress often establishes committees to investigate a particular subject. The first official congressional investigating committee was established by the House in 1792 to determine the reasons for the atrocious defeat of General St. Clair by a group of Indians in the Ohio region. Since then, investigating committees have influenced major events in American history, most often looking over the shoulder of an irritated president who would prefer to operate without the congressional spotlight. During the Civil War a committee investigating the conduct of the war, composed chiefly of radical anti-slavery Republicans, questioned everyone and everything, from General George McClellan about his southern strategies to fraud in government contracting. Carl Sandburg described the committee:

> Nothing less than genius shone and coruscated from some facets of this Committee. They were to help Lincoln, and more often to interfere with him for a long time. They sniffed out waste and corruption; they cleared away stenches; they muddled, accused men wrongly, roused fear and suspicion, and left ranklings. They wrangled and bombinated; they played with the glory and despair of democracy.[20]

In recent wars Congress has continued to use its investigatory powers to maintain leverage over foreign and military policy. Senator Harry Truman chaired the Preparedness Committee during World War II and Senator William Fulbright conducted numerous investigations on the conduct of the Vietnam War.

Beginning in World War I, Congress took a renewed interest in the expression of political views. In 1919 the Senate investigation of "the brewing industry and German propaganda" was expanded to include "any efforts being made to propagate in this country the principles of any party exercising authority in Russia and to include the overthrow of the government of this country or all governments by force or by the destruction of life or property, or the general desecration of industry."[21] Thus began investigations into un-American activities. In 1930 the Fish committee (Hamilton Fish of New York) was set up as a special House committee to investigate Communist activities in the United States. Its successor the Special Committee on Un-American Activities was established in 1934 under Chairman John W. McCormack, a Massachusetts Democrat, and another committee, chaired by Texas Democrat Martin Dies, was established to investigate Communist infiltration of labor unions. The Senate developed two committees to expose Communist plots: the Internal Security Subcommittee of the Senate Judiciary Committee in 1951 and the Senate Permanent Investigations Subcommittee of the Govern-

mental Affairs Committee, chaired by Wisconsin Republican Joseph Mc-
Carthy, who used it as his soapbox from 1951–54. The hearings focused on
Communists in the State Department, which McCarthy dubbed the "politburo
in residence," and the defense establishment.

In 1953–54 the subcommittee undertook 445 preliminary hearings and
157 investigations, 17 of which were made public. McCarthy's downfall came
when he clashed swords with the Pentagon. The conflict between the upper
echelons of the Army and McCarthy took place every day for thirty-five
days on television before 20 million Americans. The hearings dealt with
McCarthy's charges that the Army used pressure to terminate the investigations of alleged Communists in the Army and with countercharges that McCarthy
had secured preferential treatment for former subcommittee consultant Private
G. David Schine.[22] The drama of the hearings and the confrontation grabbed
the attention of the entire American public, which waited with rapt concern
to learn the outcome. The Army won. The select committee to study censure
charges recommended censure of McCarthy.

To understand Congress as an institution, the Army-McCarthy hearings
are important from a couple of perspectives. First, McCarthy clearly demonstrated the power that Congress could exercise over the executive branch
by combining its investigative authority with an effective use of the media.
Second, in highlighting the clash between individual liberties and congressional prerogatives, the hearings promoted the establishment of better protections for individuals testifying before Congress. The House, for example,
instituted its own reforms to ensure fair play for witnesses. Each witness now
has a right to counsel. If the committee decides evidence may be incriminating,
such evidence is received in executive session and the person in jeopardy
may appear as a witness and subpoena additional witnesses as well. Furthermore, no incriminating testimony may be released without the consent of
the committee, and a witness must get a transcript of his testimony.[23]

The un-American activities committees in both the House and the Senate
were abolished or reduced in stature during the 1970s reforms. However, in
1981 Senator Strom Thurmond, the new chairman of the Senate Judiciary
Committee, reconstituted the Internal Security Subcommittee (under the name
Security and Terrorism), directing it to concentrate on international terrorism.

In recent times the most famous investigating committee, the Senate
Watergate committee, or the Senate Select Committee on Presidential Campaign Activities, was established after the 1972 presidential election and
dissolved in 1974. Chaired by Senator Sam Ervin of North Carolina, the
Watergate committee, convened in the elegant Senate Caucus Room, focused
public attention on the Watergate scandal and set in motion the House im-

Republican Senator Joseph McCarthy (Wisconsin) challenges Democratic Senator Millard Tydings (Maryland) in the Foreign Relations Committee.

peachment proceedings of the president. The importance of the Watergate committee lies not in its somewhat inconclusive report, which recommended several reforms concerning campaign finance, but in the impetus it provided to the disclosure of Nixon's transgressions, including the tapes of White House meetings, which led to his ultimate disgrace. As a forum for disclosing unconstitutional activities in the executive branch, the Congress had proved itself.

Seven years later in the so-called Billy-Gate scandal, a Senate investigating subcommittee looked into the alleged activities of Billy Carter, the president's brother, in dealing with the Libyan government and lobbyists for the Libyan government. Although the investigation lacked the impact of Watergate, it did affect the president's subsequent relations with the electorate.

COMMISSIONS AND AD HOC COMMITTEES

Commissions, composed of both public officials and private citizens, are established by statute to review a certain subject and recommend governmental action.

The Brown Commission, created in the Eighty-ninth Congress to recommend a new criminal code to the Congress, included members of both houses, several federal judges, and several private sector lawyers and academicians. Although the commission labored long and well, a new criminal code has yet to be adopted.

In the early 1970s the Obey Commission was created to review staff allowances and other operating expenses of the House and House members. The Obey report improved the accounting methods used by the House, eliminated some of the "outside income" loopholes used by some members, and generally provided more open and truthful bookkeeping as to the way the House is run.

Occasionally "internal" ad hoc study committees are created. In the 1960s two committees, one chaired by Congresswoman Julia Hansen of Washington and the other chaired by Congressman Richard Bolling of Missouri, were established to propose procedural reforms in the House. On the Senate side, Adlai Stevenson of Illinois chaired a group to study committee jurisdiction and numbers of staff required. Although many committee reports rest on dusty shelves in the Library of Congress, some have resulted in significant reform.

SEVEN

COMMITTEES—
THE STANDING COMMITTEES

The standing committee is the main organizational unit in the Congress. It is responsible for legislation, agency oversight, and nominations. In the Senate, there are sixteen standing committees, and in the House, there are twenty-two (see Appendix). Each standing committee establishes its own rules of procedure and legislative agenda. Unlike the other kinds of committee discussed in an earlier chapter, it is permanently provided for by the House or Senate rules which define its jurisdiction.

Jurisdiction of the standing committees, established by the rules of each chamber, often lacks rhyme or reason. The jurisdiction of similarly named House and Senate committees is frequently different; many committees have overlapping jurisdiction. For example, a plethora of House committees is dealing with various problems in the energy field. Congressman John Dingell of Michigan tried to alleviate, or at least disguise, the problem by changing the name of his committee from the Interstate and Foreign Commerce Committee to the Energy and Commerce Committee. Without eliminating the overlapping jurisdictions of several other committees, the name change was more cosmetic than substantive. Consequently, the difficulties in passing a comprehensive energy bill were not resolved.

141

It is incongruous that both the House and the Senate host a standing committee on veterans affairs but only a select committee on aging. It is equally incongruous that a standing committee deals with the District of Columbia, but all territories and commonwealths are reviewed, if at all, by a subcommittee of the Interior Committee. The anachronisms of the committee system serve only to increase the difficulties inherent in the legislative process—and to protect some power of senior congressional members.

Reorganization plans generally meet with the opposition of senior members who have the power to prevent the loss of committee turf.

ROLE OF THE STANDING COMMITTEE

Committees as Experts

Standing committees provide Congress with the expertise necessary to deal with national problems. Most House and Senate members choose to work on a particular committee as a way to affect national policy. To become experts, they frequently hire staff experienced in the committee's policy area.

To take the lead in policy innovation, expertise is critical. As one study pointed out, the fragmented and decentralized policy-making structure of Congress facilitates, rather than inhibits, policy information.[1] For example, in the Senate Health Care Subcommittee, staffed by doctors and health-care professionals, Chairman Edward Kennedy developed comprehensive health-care legislation and focused national attention on the need for a national comprehensive health-care program. Although this legislation was not passed, it stimulated important debate and prompted other senators and the executive branch to focus on the area. Likewise, Maine Senator Edmund Muskie, through his expertise in, and dedication to, environmental issues, was able to develop a program to deal with national water pollution.

Without expertise, a committee could not effectively oversee the executive branch agency within its jurisdiction. For example, the House Government Operation Committee, chaired by Congressman Ben Rosenthal of New York, conducted in-depth hearings on the functioning of the Securities and Exchange Commission and the way the Commission handled foreign investment in American industry.

Because of the committee system, executive branch initiatives can be evaluated and criticized. As one longtime professional staff member pointed out, committees sometimes change elements of a presidential package to let the president know that they are "in the driver's seat." Without committee expertise, Congress would most certainly play a role subordinate to the better staffed executive branch. The importance of committees in checking the president is ably demonstrated by the role of the Foreign Affairs committees in ultimately criticizing government Vietnam policies in the 1970s.

Because of committee expertise, most presidential legislative packages are not rubber-stamped, not even when the Congress is controlled by the president's own party. Often the president, bound by internal bureaucratic infighting in the executive branch, is unable to present legislation with popular appeal; in such cases the Congress can and does often propose innovative ideas to change the legislation. For example, Senator Robert Dole of Kansas took the lead in 1981 in presenting indexing legislation to provide relief to taxpayers from the tax rate increases generated by inflation. Since the Treasury Department opposed the bill, the president could not act; Senator Dole had no such restraints.[2]

Institutional Role of Committees

The committee system allows Congress to function. Without a clearly defined separation of responsibilities, Congress could not process the hundreds of bills, resolutions, and nominations that it considers every year; nor could it adequately oversee the executive branch. Each committee oversees a specific function in the executive branch. For example, the Judiciary Committees oversee the Justice Department, and the Labor Committees oversee the Department of Health and Human Services. Some committees, like the Commerce Committee, are composed of numerous subcommittees, each responsible for a particular agency. To effectively watchdog more than 100 federal agencies, specialized committees are the only answer.

In addition, committees provide on-the-job training for new members. In the smaller, friendlier, less formal confines of a committee room, a member can begin to understand the legislative process, parliamentary procedures, and collegial niceties. Even the peculiar style of addressing other members (never by name but always as "the Gentleman or Gentlewoman" from the particular state) is best learned in committee.

Finally, committees block ill-advised, inadequate legislation. In 1979, more than 8,456 pieces of legislation were dropped into the hopper. Most of these bills were referred to committee. Before legislation hits the floor for debate, committee experts criticize it, revise it, and fully explore the merits of the proposal. In addition, committees prevent extremely controversial legislation from reaching the floor when the majority party is trying to achieve other priorities. During the first month of the Ninety-seventh Congress, the clear priority for the Reagan administration and the Republican party was the enactment of budget cuts and tax legislation. Although the Republicans had come to power in the Senate with the enthusiastic support of the Moral Majority, it was clear that Judiciary Chairman Strom Thurmond and Constitution Subcommittee Chairman Orrin Hatch would resist efforts to report out controversial constitutional amendments that would distract the resources, efforts, and media attention from the high priorities of the majority party.

Certain committees in the House of Representatives—the Ways and Means Committee, the Appropriations Committee, and especially the Rules Committee—were established as institutional "traffic cops." Usually, the members chosen for service on these committees are intelligent party loyalists from somewhat stable constituencies. Known as the "Speaker's Committee" because the speaker personally chooses the members to serve (with caucus ratification), the Rules Committee, in particular, plays the critical institutional role of blocking legislation that would thwart the priorities of the majority party or that would hurt the ability of Congress to operate as an institution. For example, in both the Ninety-fifth and Ninety-sixth Congress the Rules Committee persistently refused to report out "sunset" legislation, legislation that would require every standing committee to reauthorize periodically all legislative programs because it would create an unreasonably heavy workload. The refusal of the Rules Committee to report out high-profile sunset legislation strongly indicates that the House leadership viewed it as unwise. Thus in many ways all committees, and in particular the Rules Committee, provide, in Professor David Mayhew's words, "institutional maintenance."[3]

Reelection Role of Committees

Committee membership helps congressional members to get reelected. Not surprisingly, members of the Agriculture Committee tend to come from farming states. Members of Banking and Housing committees come from urban areas. Members of the labor committees tend to care intensely about labor issues, from either a pro-union or pro-management perspective. Congressmen choose to join one committee rather than another to help the constituencies that elected them to office. Indeed, it is in the self-interest of the party leadership to ensure membership on a committee that will facilitate reelection.

In addition, membership on a committee affecting powerful interest groups is also a key to raising campaign funds from political action committees (PACs) that desire results from the committee. Commerce Committee members received considerable sums from the PACs of the airlines and the Teamsters Union, which are reliant on legislation in that committee. The use of committee membership to gain reelection has been criticized by many political scientists as benefitting the agency, the regulated entities, and the congressional members but not the American people.[4] These so-called iron triangles and subgovernments have been castigated as contributing to inefficient and inequitable government. In a sense, the criticisms are true. As one staff member on the Agriculture Committee candidly admitted: "Let's face it, our job is to protect the farmers." However, from the other perspective, the assignment to committees of members who care about, know about, and want to expend their energies to help a certain segment of society makes good organizational sense. Why put a congressman from Brooklyn, New York, on the Wheat, Soybeans, and Feed Grain Subcommittee? When Congresswoman Shirley Chisholm of Brooklyn was assigned to the Agriculture Committee in her first term, she complained that her congressional district did not even have the "tree" that grew in Brooklyn. The parochial interests of committees are tempered in floor debate where amendments dealing with other segments of the country are added. For example, farmers are forced to take urban needs into account in comprehensive farm legislation by robust floor debate and subsequent floor amendments.

Committees also serve electoral needs by providing a forum. The committee is a soapbox upon which senators and congressmen can grandstand and receive media coverage. Through hearings, committee members become nationally known. A hearing without media coverage is a hearing without committee members—almost. In a dry, noncontroversial hearing, the committee room resembles a vast tomb. The committee chair presides with one staff member at his side; a witness testifies in a low, droning, monotonous style. The presence of more than one senator or congressman is rare.

On the other hand, where television cameras whirr, senators in blue shirts are present. A hearing is viewed as a success when it is covered on the six o'clock news. Missouri Senator Thomas Eagleton once dryly commented on the presence of a number of senators to hear a businessman testify on the costs of regulation: "I'd like to note for the record that I've never seen so many senators show up for a hearing where there are no television cameras." When hearings are targeted at the interests of their home states, senators make concerted efforts to get local coverage. For example, Utah Senator Orrin Hatch held hearings on a charter to make the ski patrol a federal corporation, a trivial piece of legislation. It was covered by all the Utah television stations.

STRUCTURE OF THE STANDING COMMITTEE

The Party

The congressional committee is a party-oriented entity. In the committee room the members sit by party. The chairman sits in the middle of a crescent-shaped table next to the ranking minority member. The members of the majority sit in declining order of seniority, next to the chairman, and the members of the minority party arrange themselves similarly on the other side of the crescent. Subcommittees organize themselves in a similar fashion. The chairman and the ranking minority member serve as the key spokesmen for their respective parties. The majority party gets two-thirds of the budget; the minority gets one-third. The chairman and the ranking member have the authority to distribute budget shares to their respective party members. In addition, the majority and minority leadership controls the room assignments and has considerable leverage over committee assignments.

Most important, the chairman and ranking minority member control the flow of legislative activity. In the Senate, legislation is generally not placed on the committee agenda unless it has been cleared with the ranking minority member. As for sensitive nominations, FBI and intelligence data are often available to only the chairman and the ranking member. The committee leadership has the largest staff and the capacity, therefore, to develop expertise on each legislative initiative. By monopolizing the information necessary for legislative activity, the ranking majority and minority members have considerable power.

The committee staffs in the House are not quite as partisan as those in the Senate. In part, because of their smaller numbers and, in part, because the members of the committees play a more active role in the legislative process, the staffers tend to be more bipartisan. Although selection may be on a partisan basis, the staffers are not expected to respond on a partisan basis. Obviously, a staff member acts at his peril if he forgets who appointed him in the first place, but most subcommittee staffers and many full committee staffers come to view their work on an institutional basis.

The ratio of majority and minority members in the committee determines the ability of the minority party to block or initiate legislation. In 1981 in the House of Representatives, for example, Speaker O'Neill provoked great ire among the Republicans when he insisted on a 2-to-1 ratio on the Ways and Means Committee, whereas the overall membership in the House was 5 to 3. The need for ratios larger than the partisan split in the legislative body stems from the obvious concern that some members will defect from the party line on individual issues before the committee. The defenders of large ratios argue that the majority status of the particular party obligates it to churn out legislation in keeping with the party's principles and mandate. Without a provision to compensate for possible defections, some kind of blood oath would be needed from each committee member before he or she is allowed to serve. Blood oaths are hardly reliable. In 1981 House Majority Leader Jim Wright obtained a position on the Budget Committee for conservative Democrat Philip Gramm in exchange for his promise to support the party position on budget cuts. Democrats came to rue the day Gramm was given that important committee assignment, since Gramm provided the key votes for Republican programs. So much for blood oaths.

Ratios are not quite as important in the Senate because committees are smaller and because each senator has a much greater capacity to block and influence legislation.

The rules of the committee are usually party oriented. In the Senate Judiciary Committee, for example, the majority has the exclusive power to initiate hearings on legislation or nominations, but the minority has the right, by tradition, to hold an additional day of hearings with minority witnesses. By Senate rule the minority has the right to file dissenting views to any report issued by the majority. Also, the right of filibuster is as valued in Senate committee rooms as it is on the Senate floor. Debate in the exec can be cut off in some committees only if it is supported by at least one minority member.

Alignments, friendships, and allegiances in a committee revolve around the party. When a party is in the minority, party unity is particularly important, of course, because leverage is obtained by voting en bloc. It is not uncommon for the ranking minority member to organize a boycott of an executive session to prevent the quorum necessary to enact business. The minority often exhibits an underdog "give-em-hell" attitude reminiscent of the French Resistance. Republican Senators Jacob Javits from New York and Charles Mathias from Maryland often voted with the Democrats and were thus often regarded by Republican peers as "traitors" or "turncoats." Likewise, on the Democratic side, certain southern and western senators tended to vote with the Republican party, thus incurring the wrath of their more liberal Democratic colleagues.

Party discipline is a constant factor in committee operation, especially on important bills. A chairman, whether of a subcommittee or of a full committee, often convenes a caucus of the committee members of his party to discuss important legislative matters before they are put to vote in the committee. In the caucus, the leader obtains an accurate count on the votes, sounds out the various points of a view among the members, and forges a consensus. Sometimes a chairman finds it more convenient to forge a coalition with some or all of the minority committee members. If he does it too often or does it contrary to important party positions, he is usually reminded, either by the leadership or by the dissenting members of his committee, that the votes of the minority did not give him his chairmanship. A committee chairman and a ranking minority member display their displeasure with errant committee members in a variety of ways: they are awarded smaller budgets, their subcommittees are eliminated, legislation is not referred to their subcommittees, they are not recognized at committee meetings, the rooms they request are not available, and so on. Although political science literature is quick to point out the decreasing power of the party, it must be recognized that in the committee room the party structure, although not omnipotent, still prevails.

Subcommittee Membership

During the first month of every new Congress, committee members are assigned to subcommittees and subcommittee jurisdiction is defined. The assignment process acts as a harbinger of the committee agenda for the coming Congress and indicates the substantive direction legislation is likely to take. For example, the fate of automobile airbag legislation opposed by the automobile industry was sealed at the beginning of the Ninety-seventh Congress, when Congressman John D. Dingell, as chairman of the Committee on Energy and Commerce, eliminated the subcommittee to have been headed up by New York Congressman James Scheuer, who favored such legislation. Similarly, the appointment of Michigan Congressman John Conyers as chairman of the Criminal Justice Subcommittee was a fair indicator that the overhaul of the criminal code would again be moribund in the House, as Congressman Conyers was a known opponent of code reform.

In choosing House subcommittee chairmen, seniority is not as compelling a factor as it is at the full committee level. Maryland Congressman Mike Barnes successfully opposed an incumbent subcommittee chairman of the House Foreign Affairs Committee. Liberal California Congressman Henry A. Waxman defeated a popular and senior member of the Energy and Commerce Committee for the important Health Subcommittee chairmanship in the Ninety-sixth Congress. In some committees, like the House Appropriations Committee, seniority is still used as the rigid measure for choosing subcommittee chairmen. They tend to be the exception.

On the Senate side, the choice of Nevada Republican Paul Laxalt, a close friend of the newly elected president, to chair the Regulatory Reform Subcommittee of the Senate Judiciary Committee indicated the high priority given by the Judiciary Committee to comprehensive regulatory reform legislation.

Jockeying for subcommittee assignments is not at all uncommon. In the Ninety-seventh Congress, for example, Democrats were far from eager to serve on the Constitutional Law subcommittees of the House and Senate Judiciary committees, which would consider the constitutional prayer, balanced budget, busing, affirmative action, and antiabortion constitutional amendments. Many Democratic arms of both House and Senate committee members were twisted before members were willing to accept such a "hot" subcommittee assignment.

On the other hand, the Senate Regulatory Reform subcommittee was oversubscribed. (After the Reagan landslide, everyone wanted a "piece of the action" in "getting government off the back of the people.") Originally, the membership of the committee was 4 to 2. The two minority members were Vermont Senator Patrick Leahy, who had just won reelection, and Minority Leader Robert Byrd, who chose the subcommittee as his first and only choice. Senator Edward Kennedy, who had a long history in the deregulatory area, asked to be added as a third minority member. However, Arizona Senator Dennis DeConcini, who wanted to be identified with regulatory reforms, for 1982 reelection purposes, had been lobbying Senator Paul Laxalt behind the scenes for appointment to the subcommittee. Senator DeConcini urged that the subcommittee be reconstituted as a 6-to-4 subcommittee (large compared with most Senate subcommittees), with Kennedy and DeConcini being the two extra minority members. At that point, liberal Ohio Senator Howard Metzenbaum stated that he did not favor DeConcini's appointment because his usually conservative vote would undermine the ability of the Democrats to make the bill more liberal. Senator Leahy, who would be ranking minority member of the subcommittee, agreed with Metzenbaum's sentiments. When Metzenbaum announced that as he was more senior than DeConcini, he would "bump" DeConcini from his position if a 6-to-4 committee was created, the Republicans backed away from the 6-to-4 alternative. The staff of Senator Thurmond said that under no circumstances could Metzenbaum join the subcommittee. The subcommittee membership remained 4 to 2.

On the Republican side of the aisle the jockeying was similar. Senator Mathias had long been treated as a pariah by the Republicans for his liberal voting record. In 1981, he paid dearly for his recalcitrance. Thurmond abolished the Antitrust Subcommittee rather than let Mathias chair it. The Criminal Law Subcommittee, which Mathias chaired, was stripped of most of its jurisdiction; instead, Senator Thurmond kept important criminal legislation at full committee. Most important, Mathias, the second-ranking majority member of the Judiciary Committee, received approximately the same staff and subcommittee budget that he had as a minority member!

Sometimes the wishes of the members are easier to accommodate. When the reform measures of the Ninety-fourth Congress forced the House Ways and Means Committee to reorganize into subcommittees, the Trade Subcommittee was born. Not only was its jurisdiction—foreign trade—interesting but considerable foreign travel would most likely be necessary. Because opportunities for travel had been rare with Wilbur Mills at the helm, Ways and Means members flocked to the Trade Subcommittee to take advantage of the new bonanza. The membership of the subcommittee was finally increased to nineteen, far and away the largest. More cynical members suggested that the name be changed to the Trade and Travel Subcommittee.

Committee vs. Committee

The institutional interests of the committee are different from those of the entire legislative body. Most notable, the committee is interested in turf protection and turf accumulation. In their squabbles over major legislative packages, committees seeking jurisdiction often create bitter divisions within the majority party.

Numerous procedural devices have been adopted to effect compromise in jurisdictional battles. The most notable is on the Senate side, where, because of the procedure, the turf fights tend to be more bitter. The initial referral decision, which is made by the parliamentarian, can be challenged by a motion on the floor. In the House, because the speaker is the final arbiter of referral, the behind-the-scenes power plays are seldom aired publicly.

Most committees do not passively await the decision of the speaker or the parliamentarian on jurisdiction. They hold hearings to establish expertise in the area; they write reports; they lobby the parliamentarian; they work out deals between chairmen in the cloakroom. They draft legislation expressly with referral in mind.

As chairman of the Subcommittee on Antitrust, Senator Kennedy held numerous hearings on the anti-competitive effects of trucking regulations imposed by the Interstate Commerce Commission. The asserted basis for his hearings was the antitrust jurisdiction of the Judiciary Committee, as the trucking industry operated under an exemption from coverage of some antitrust prohibitions. When he decided to introduce legislation, he argued that the bill should be referred to the Judiciary Committee, jointly with the Commerce Committee, because of the antitrust immunities. The parliamentarian agreed with the Kennedy position. However, Howard Cannon, chairman of the powerful Commerce Committee, which had jurisdiction over the ICC, disagreed. He argued that his committee had substantive authority over the ICC and threatened to challenge the parliamentarian's decision on a floor vote. The jurisdiction decision was critical. Kennedy was viewed with distrust by the Teamsters Union and the trucking industry because he wanted to eliminate trucking regulation. Senator Robert Byrd, fearful that an open floor fight would further damage an already fragmented party, held a closed Democratic caucus meeting to hammer out the differences. When it was apparent that Kennedy did not have enough votes to prevail, he agreed to compromise, giving the Commerce Committee primary jurisdiction with sequential referral to the Judiciary Committee.

Health legislation is the most pervasive case of overlapping jurisdiction in the House. During his empire-building days, Wilbur Mills claimed jurisdiction over the legislation because it resembled social security, over which Ways and Means had jurisdiction. When Mills and the Ways and Means Committee had their wings clipped, the Rules Committee awarded jurisdiction over health legislation to both Ways and Means and Interstate and Foreign Commerce (now called Energy and Commerce). The divided jurisdiction and responsibility explains, in part, the difficulties in obtaining the passage of health legislation in the House. Each bill has to be sequentially referred to the second committee before it can come to the floor. Thus, President Carter's efforts to obtain passage of a hospital cost containment program came to naught, because the opposition had two opportunities to shoot it down. When opponents failed to defeat the bill in the Commerce Committee, they simply doubled their efforts and were successful in killing it in Ways and Means.

Sequential referral, a system whereby a bill is referred to more than one committee in a sequence designated by the leadership, has not worked out too well. First, getting two or more committees to schedule a single piece of legislation is both difficult and time-consuming. Most legislation that is sequentially referred gets sidetracked along the way. Second, it is difficult to confine the various committees to their respective jurisdictions when the bill finally comes before them. The House Ways and Means Committee has insisted on getting sequential referral of all bills in which trust funds, such as the highway fund, are used to fund the particular program involved. Persuading the Ways and Means Committee to keep hands off the substantive programs involved has been exceedingly difficult.

Although committee battles rarely escalate to a bitter division of parties or provoke floor confrontations, nonetheless such battles are waged behind the scenes, for committees carefully protect their turf and jealously guard against intrusions. Lobbyists have a vested stake in preventing strange committees from grabbing their programs; the members of those alien territories have not been carefully cultivated with PAC contributions and do not have long experience with the nuances of the program's development. Committee fights are primarily motivated by neither partisan concerns nor concerns about substantive legislation. Rather they turn on bipartisan committee loyalty. Republican Senator Strom Thurmond and Democrat Senator Edward Kennedy of Judiciary will join sides against Robert Packwood and Howard Cannon of Commerce because committee turf transcends party label and ideology. Because of the divisive nature of such battles, every effort is made to compromise early on.

Committee Bills on the Floor

Strong bipartisan support for a bill in committee augurs well for its chance of passage intact on the floor—without ravaging amendments. When a Senate committee reports out legislation with few or no dissenting votes, the likelihood of floor passage is great. Generally, the committee chairman serves as the floor manager in both the Senate and the House to ward off undesirable amendments. When he is joined by his ranking minority member, it becomes very difficult for any other senator or House member to separate the committee ranks.

In shepherding legislation through the House, committee chairmen are responsible for getting favorable rules from the Rules Committee. Without strong committee leadership and a committee consensus, the Rules Committee can kill a bill by not granting a rule or by granting a rule other than the one desired by the chairman. The Rules Committee, on occasion, will thwart the desires of the committee chairman when the party leadership demands it.

A junior committee member rarely challenges his party's leadership on the committee. The penalties are too great: loss of staff, loss of budget, loss of peer group respect. Nonetheless, maverick actions can and do take place. For example, in 1981 Vermont Senator Patrick Leahy, a junior Democrat on the Agriculture Committee, challenged the Reagan nomination for the head of the national forests. Although the nomination was opposed by the environmental community, it was supported in committee by the committee's chairman, Jesse Helms, and Dee Huddleston of Kentucky, ranking minority member. Senator Leahy calculated that the political benefits from mounting this challenge (given the strength of the environmental community in Vermont) outweighed the congressional risks. Leahy's insurgency was doomed to fail, however, in face of bipartisan support for the nominee.

Many committees pride themselves in standing together on the floor for the compromise product reported out. For example, Democrats and Republicans on the Senate Finance Committee and House Ways and Means Committee will generally stand together to oppose amendments. When, however, because of intense ideological opposition, the bill barely squeaks through the committee, there is rough sailing ahead. In 1979 the Senate Judiciary Committee reported out by a one-vote margin extremely controversial legislation to provide additional antitrust remedies. The bill was opposed bitterly by the Chamber of Commerce, the Business Round Table, and the Republican committee members. Because it was so divisive, the legislation was never brought up for floor action. On the other hand, the nomination of Stephen Breyer (chief counsel of the Senate Judiciary Committee in 1980) to the First Circuit Court of Appeals received unanimous support from both the Democrats and the Republicans on the Senate Judiciary Committee. Consequently, the minority and the majority party worked in unison to bring cloture to a filibuster attempt by a small number of senators. Breyer was confirmed in a lame-duck session after the election—a highly unusual occurrence.

Because a small group of senators can kill any legislation, a large degree of Democratic and Republican committee cohesion is essential to floor passage of legislation. Of course, committee cohesion becomes less important as party cohesion increases. In the budget and tax battles at the beginning of the Ninety-seventh Congress, the Republican leadership was able to maintain such a high degree of party loyalty that the sharp division along party lines of the Senate Budget Committee was not critical.

Coalitions in the House take on a different cast. Because the committees are larger and more diverse, a solid committee bloc on any bill is difficult to maintain. Even when ranking minority members are in accord with the legislation, some committee member may well object and offer amendments or opposition. Once committee consensus is achieved, the House itself is likely to get into the act.

Ideological coalitions, however, are more prevalent in the House than in the Senate. On many issues, conservative southern Democrats are more likely to vote with conservative Republicans than with their own party. On closely fought legislation, the coalition of southern Democrats and conservative Republicans has constituted a majority for some years. In addition to the southern Democrats, the Democrats from the rural, suburban, and western areas tend to be more independent of party leadership, at least on some issues. Other areas of parochialism also produce coalitions, for example, the New England delegation's efforts to cooperate on issues affecting water. The House leadership peels off some members from one or the other group to pass any legislation. Some Carter administration proposals passed the House by one- or two-vote margins only because Speaker O'Neill twisted some arms of the more conservative Democrats.

The House committee structure is more powerful because all legislation must be processed through subcommittee, committee, and the Rules Committee. If the chair of any one of these three entities opposes legislation, it is virtually impossible for it to pass. Because discharge petitions are rarely successful, and nongermane amendments not permitted, the legislation of a minority member has virtually no chance of passage unless the member has enough muscle to overturn a rule on the floor or unless he or she can persuade a chair to report the legislation.

In the Senate, any senator can introduce any legislation he wants by way of nongermane amendments. When Senator Jesse Helms introduced legislation to cut off jurisdiction of the federal courts to hear cases involving prayer in public schools, he offered his prayer proposal as an amendment to the Department of Education appropriations bill. Arkansas Senator Dale Bumpers introduced a major regulatory reform amendment to the unrelated Federal Courts Improvements Acts. When senators propose amendments to unrelated legislation there is relatively little the committee chair can do except argue against it on the floor.

Committees, like any institution, act to protect, and expand, their own turf. Parochial committee concerns are tempered continuously by the desires of the congressional majority and of the Congress itself as an institution responsible for forging national consensus. House and Senate leaders are confronted with a two-edged sword: They must encourage committee members to initiate and develop legislation dealing with serious problems and at the same time limit the power of committees to allow the will of the majority to prevail. Every time a Howard Smith blocks nationally demanded civil-rights legislation through the power of his office, the whole Congress, indeed the nation, suffers. Consequently, congressional leaders and party caucuses put continual pressure on the committees to be responsive to the party's needs and desires. Some reforms in the 1970s destroyed the immunity enjoyed by committee chairmen. That House committee chairmen are elected in party caucus by secret ballot ensures that committee chairmen cannot continually thwart the programs of the party. The future role of the party caucus can be enhanced, however, by its identification of congressional party priorities. Such a procedure would increase the accountability of committees and allow their expertise to be focused on the gut work of thrashing out the details to achieve consensus.

EIGHT

THE PEOPLE WHO WORK
ON THE HILL

The presidential election in 1980 was interpreted by some as a national mandate to reevaluate the role and the functions of the federal government. With that mandate President Reagan assailed governmental regulation, drastically cut back liberal "big government" spending programs, and redistributed power from the federal government to the states. His attacks were leveled at the anonymous, unelected, nameless, faceless bureaucrats in the executive branch who have the power to make decisions controlling the daily lives and activities of virtually every citizen and business—or so the rhetoric goes. As criticisms of executive branch bureaucracy escalated, the corollary question arose with respect to Hill staff. To what extent do the "elected" representatives really make decisions? To what extent are major policy outcomes influenced by staff?

In the legislative branch, the criticism of Hill staff is truly a Washington, D.C., phenomenon. Unlike presidential advisers, who become media stars on the seven o'clock news every night, Hill staff receive virtually no attention. Few people ever hear of Ari Weiss who, before he had reached the age of 30, became executive director of the House Democratic Policy and Steering Committee, which controls the Democratic party's legislative agenda under Speaker Tip O'Neill. No one would recognize the name of Bobby Shapiro, who was the head of the staff of the Joint Committee on Taxation. The mention of a staff member by name in the media is rare because most congressional members strongly oppose public recognition of their staff. Therefore, the concern about the size and power of Hill staff must be placed into perspective. At least until now, this malaise has been concentrated in the hearts and minds of Washington insiders and a few political scientists. Congress is not yet on the verge of a crisis because of the prominent role of its staff in the legislative process.

With that perspective in mind, it is important to recognize that there are some responsible critiques of the role of the Hill staff. Michael Malbin, the author of *Unelected Representatives* and a Fellow at the American Enterprise Institute, presents a compelling criticism. Conceding that large staffs may be essential, Malbin nevertheless concludes that the deliberative capacity of the Congress has been undermined by their assumption of duties and responsibilities previously performed by congressmen.

This chapter evaluates the role of the Hill staff. Its thesis is that aggressive, entrepreneurial staff do not detract from the effectiveness of the congressional process but enhance it. Without the resources and expertise provided by staff, Congress could not possibly oversee the executive branch, initiate legislation, or serve constituents.

The chapter has three main parts. First, it provides a historical perspective on the growth of Hill staff. Second, it describes the various categories of staff: the personal staff; the committee staff; the leadership staff; the staff in the various "arms of Congress." Finally, it expands on the Malbin thesis and responds to it.

HISTORICAL PERSPECTIVE

Early representatives were willing and eager to become personally involved in the nitty-gritty details of daily legislative activities. John Adams complained of the Continental Congress: "The business of the Congress is tedious beyond expression. This assembly is like no other that ever existed. Every man upon every question must show his oratory, his criticism and his political abilities."[1] Historians discuss the detailed deliberations between members of the Congress over every bill and every resolution. In the Second Continental Congress, Thomas Jefferson of Virginia and Pennsylvania's John Dickinson had lengthy disputes over the wording of the "Declaration and Necessity for Taking up Arms."[2] And Jefferson, who reluctantly agreed to write the Declaration of Independence, worked mornings and evenings drafting and redrafting different versions of that soon-to-be famous document. At the Philadelphia Convention of 1789, delegates debated throughout the day, at dinner, and late into the evening at taverns over the provisions of the Constitution. Details of the provisions were hammered out in ad hoc working groups. James Madison recorded, in painstaking detail, the colloquies of the constitutional debates.[3] Delegates strove to surpass one another in the elegance of their speech and rhetoric. Without the high degree of personal involvement in the constitutional deliberations, it is doubtful that the fragile compromise behind the adoption of the Constitution would have been possible.

Thus, our earliest congresses consisted of men who drafted their own legislation, wrote their own speeches, answered letters in their own hand, and personally negotiated their own compromises. They concentrated on a broad spectrum of issues, from the most sweeping discussion of the origins of democracy to the most tedious, mundane problems of equipping an army.

In contrast, the members of Congress today remain aloof and distant from most details of daily legislative activity. Instead, they focus their energies on the "big picture"—the problems and controversies—and on getting reelected. They choose a legislative arena in which to participate and delegate to staff the responsibility of developing initiatives and expertise in that area. They may appear at hearings, vote in committee, give speeches on the floor, and cast a "yea" or "nay" in floor debates, but virtually all the planning, drafting, and legwork is done by staff. Rare is the member who, like Thomas Jefferson, toils the night away drafting his own speeches or who, like the authors of the Constitution, negotiates provisions of legislation late into the evening at local pubs.

Hill staff today control, to a remarkable extent, the daily activities not only of the Congress but of most congressmen. More often than not, staff write the speeches and statements delivered by members; draft the legislation; negotiate with other staff over legislative compromises; establish the format for hearings; write legislative history; and influence the congressional agenda. In essence, staff members perform most of the functions previously performed by the congressmen themselves.

The prominent role of Hill staff evolved over a period of two hundred years. Congress has always looked to staff for aid in the performance of constitutional responsibilities. Under the Articles of Confederation, the Congress hired staff to perform some of the necessary daily executive functions of the new Republic.[4] At first, after the adoption of the Constitution, the Congress looked to the executive branch staff as if it were its own to provide expertise about the technical details of legislation.[5] Soon, however, the Congress recognized the need for its own independent expertise to ensure the continued sovereignty of the legislative branch. And thus the standing committee system was initiated. By the middle of the nineteenth century, Congress passed special resolutions every session to ensure adequate staff assistance for the committees.[6] In 1856 the House Ways and Means Committee and the Senate Finance Committee received regular appropriations for full-time clerks, and by the turn of the century clerical staff was provided for all standing committees and for each congressman.[7] However, despite the gradual evolution of an in-house congressional staff, no major changes in the number or quality of staff took place until after World War II when Congress improved its internal management in order to provide a more effective check on the activities of an increasingly dominant executive branch. Under the Legislative Reorganization Act of 1946, each committee was allowed to hire four professional staff members and six clerical members. Thus, the total number of staff allowed for committees under the 1946 act was 340, not including the staffs of the appropriations committees.

The Changed Role of Staff

The 1946 act officially recognized the need for a professional—as opposed to a clerical—staff. However, the development of a professional cadre of staff was not completed until more than twenty years later, with the passage of the Legislative Reorganization Act of 1970. By that time the size of committee staffs, both professional and clerical, in both houses had more than tripled. Because committee staffs were generally available only to chairmen, the minority was at a great substantive disadvantage in pursuing its policies. When the minority demanded its own committee staff, the Congress expanded the size of the professional committee staff from four to six, allocating at least one-third of the money to the minority. The size of committee staffs continued to increase in the 1970s, but in the House the one-third requirement was deleted in 1975. Instead, the House provides one professional staff member to the chairman and the ranking minority member of each subcommittee.[8]

In addition to retaining the one-third requirement, the Senate went one step further. In 1975 the Senate adopted a resolution that guaranteed to each senator a personal committee staff member at a top professional staff salary for each major committee assignment—in addition to his personal staff. This access to professional staff has contributed to the autonomy of each senator from the committee and party leadership. With loyal professional staff members, a senator can obtain expertise and advice from a person whose allegiance is clearly established. In the House, with a few exceptions, individual congressmen are not entitled to staff for each committee assignment; instead, they must rely on information and advice from staff members whose primary loyalties are to the chairman or ranking minority member. Thus, less senior congressmen frequently complain that the committee staff are not responsive enough to their needs.[9]

Recently elected congressmen complain they are hard pressed for legislative staff resources. Because most house members are "limited" to eighteen office employees, the legislative responsibilities are often divided between one or two legislative assistants. Younger congressmen, afflicted with reelection fear (a fear that begins the moment they enter office), devote far greater staff resources to casework, correspondence, and district office than do their Senate counterparts who have a luxurious six years to gear up for the next election.

As the size of the Hill staffs has grown, the guilt associated with it has also increased. Members are usually squeamish about revealing the cost of these staffs to the taxpayer. For many years the infamous "clerk-hiring" allowance was perpetrated. Calculated in 1945 dollars, the record on paper indicated a salary of $3,150.00 when in actuality the sum was $11,523.04. Such practices were abandoned in 1971 when staff allowances were listed in real dollars.

In 1982 the total staff allowance for a House member was $336,384. The limit on the earnings of an individual employee was $50,112.50. The amounts for senators vary, depending on the population of the senator's state. Senate clerk-hire allowances range from $592,608 for a senator representing a state with a population of less than 2 million to $1,190,724 for a senator representing a state with a population of 21 million or more. Complementing the staff are the unpaid interns and volunteers who descend on Washington, mostly during the summer. Some colleges give academic credit for time spent in such internships, and many interns stay as long as a year. House members also use their clerk-hire or office allowances to staff various groups, such as the Democratic Study Group, the Environmental Study Group, and Members of Congress for Peace through Law. These groups provide research and other legislative needs in the areas of concern for which they were formed.

Need for Professional Staff

The development of a cadre of professional committee and personal staff has been a mixed blessing. Few, if any, congressmen are willing to turn back the clock to the days when staff consisted of a clerk or two. Common wisdom on the Hill indicates that the more staff one has, the more powerful one becomes. With sufficient staff, a congressman is able to become involved in many more subject areas, to influence policy outcomes of legislation outside his committee expertise, and to perform more effectively as an ombudsman for his constituents in his home district. For a committee chair, the power arising from large committee staffs cannot be overemphasized. On assuming the chairmanship of the Senate Judiciary Committee, Senator Edward Kennedy gained control of approximately sixty-five staff members. With this staff, his personal staff, and the staff of the Health Subcommittee of the Labor and Human Resources Committee, Kennedy put together a "shadow government" capable of expertly critiquing virtually every function of the Carter administration. Almost every senator seeks, in a way that is not feasible for most House members, similarly to develop staff expertise in the major policy areas of the executive branch. Thus, from an institutional perspective, a lively Hill staff enables the Congress to function effectively and aggressively as a check on the executive branch and to be an innovative force in affecting and developing national policy.

The importance of having a competent staff is widely recognized. Senator Strom Thurmond (Democrat of South Carolina) was well known for his antagonism to large congressional staffs. When he became chairman of the Judiciary Committee in 1981, he promised to cut the staff by 25 percent. Boasting publicly about the quality of his staff, he pointed proudly to his chief counsel, a dean at the University of South Carolina Law School. Committee chairmen recruit graduates of the best law and graduate schools and rely on staff to identify legislative areas that will reap the greatest political awards. Freshmen, in particular, need excellent staff with "Hill experience" to teach them Hill procedures, how to deal effectively, and even how to get the best office space.

Criticism of Staff Role

Despite the clear institutional and personal need for a strong and intelligent congressional staff, queasiness about its prominence continues to escalate. Some senators and congressmen feel imprisoned by their staff. In 1975 Senator Ernest Hollings, a South Carolina Democrat, said on the floor of the Senate:

> There are many Senators who feel that all they are doing is running around and responding to the staff. My staff fighting your staff, your staff competing with mine. It is sad. . . . Everybody is working for the staff, staff, staff; staff; driving you nutty. In fact they have hearings for me all of this week. Now it is how many nutty whiz kids you get on the staff to get you magazine articles and get you headlines and get all of these other things done.[10]

And Democratic Senator Herman Talmadge of Georgia said:

> The Senator from Georgia knows that when you get more staff and more clerks they spend most of their time thinking up bills, resolutions, amendments. They write speeches for Senators, and they come in here on the floor with Senators. Unanimous consents are obtained for so-and-so to sit. He is there prodding, telling the Senator how to spend more money.[11]

Anecdotes about over-reliance on the congressional staff are legion. On one embarrassing occasion New Mexico Senator Joseph Montoya, who had total confidence in his staff, read to an audience the press release of his speech, rather than the speech itself, including the press aide's final line: "Senator Montoya assured his audience, who gave him a standing ovation, that he was on their side." Secretary of State Haig got off to a rocky start at his confirmation hearing before the Senate Foreign Relations Committee when he was heard to mutter that the question Senator Pell was propounding to him had probably been written by Claiborne Pell's staff. Congressman John Fary of Illinois, first elected to fill a vacancy resulting from the death of his predecessor, told an inquirer that he intended to retain his predecessor's legislative assistant: "He's real good in getting my remarks printed in the Congressional Record." The public image of Hill staff, not particularly flattering, was recently depicted in *The Seduction of Joe Tynan*, a movie about a fictitious senator on the Judiciary Committee. The senator's staff was young, aggressive, obnoxious, sycophantic, and insensitive, reflecting a public perception that young kids still "wet behind the ears" are too often the authors of public policy.

The growth in Hill staff is another concern. At the beginning of the Ninety-seventh Congress Democratic Senator William Proxmire from Wisconsin introduced a resolution calling for a cap on the growth of Hill staff.[12] Between 1965 and 1975, the committee staffs doubled (see Table 8-1). However, when viewed in the context of the commensurate growth in the executive branch, such rapid growth is not quite so startling. For example, in the same time period the size of the White House staff also doubled. Likewise, the federal budget outlays almost tripled, and the size of the regulatory establishment roughly quadrupled, with more regulatory agencies being established during that period than at any other time in our history. The explosion of new national policies and concerns explains some of the growth of congressional staff.

The increased size of congressional staff is actually of less concern than the increased power of Hill staff. Members of Congress, particularly senators, openly acknowledge that much horse-trading in legislation is done by staff. Senator Abraham Ribicoff, as chairman of the Governmental Affairs Committee in the Ninety-sixth Congress, routinely and publicly directed the "committee staff to work it out." In the Senate Energy Committee's consideration of President Carter's legislation on the proposed Energy Mobilization Board, which was to expedite the construction of energy projects, the energy committee staff testified day after day in open session before the committee on the meaning of the various provisions. It was an exhilarating experience for Jim Pugash, a recently graduated Harvard law student who had never practiced

TABLE 8-1

COMMITTEE STAFFS IN THE HOUSE AND THE SENATE, 1891-1981

Year	No. of Employees in House	No. of Employees in Senate
1891	62	41
1914	105	198
1930	112	163
1935	122	172
1947	167	232
1950	246	300
1955	329	386
1960	440	470
1965	571	509
1970	702	635
1971	729	711
1972	817	844
1973	878	873
1974	1,107	948
1975	1,433	1,277
1976	1,680	1,201
1977	1,776	1,028
1978	1,844	1,151
1979	1,959	1,098
1980	1,917	1,101
1981	1,843	1,022

SOURCES: 1891-1935: HARRISON W. FOX AND SUSAN W. HAMMOND, *CONGRESSIONAL STAFFS: THE INVISIBLE FORCE IN AMERICAN LAWMAKING* (NEW YORK: FREE PRESS, 1977), P. 171; 1947-1978: JUDY SCHNEIDER, *CONGRESSIONAL STAFFING: 1947-1978* (WASHINGTON, D.C.: CONGRESSIONAL RESEARCH SERVICE, AUGUST 24, 1979); THOMAS E. MANN. NORMAN J. ORNSTEIN, MICHAEL J. MALBIN, AND JOHN F. BIBBY, *VITAL STATISTICS ON CONGRESS, 1982* (WASHINGTON, D.C.: AMERICAN ENTERPRISE INSTITUTE, 1982). SCHNEIDER'S FIGURES ARE FOR THE STATUTORY AND THE INVESTIGATIVE STAFFS OF STANDING COMMITTEES ONLY. THEY DO NOT INCLUDE SELECT COMMITTEE STAFFS, WHICH VARIED BETWEEN 31 AND 238 IN THE HOUSE AND 62 AND 172 IN THE SENATE DURING THE 1970S.

law, to find himself, in open committee session, recommending legislative alternatives to the president's proposed legislation. Increasingly, members of Congress have delegated to secretaries and assistants the authority to sign their names. As a result of delegating responsibility, important correspondence is signed and legislation is co-sponsored, frequently without the real assent or foreknowledge of the member. Because members read little mail, frequent gaffes occur. One Senate staff member sent a scathing letter to Carla Hills, President Ford's Housing and Urban Development secretary, without informing his member, who was understandably irritated when he received an irate phone call from Hills.

Staff members are essential to negotiations in Senate floor fights. Often senators seek out committee staff experts, sitting nearby on leather couches lining the chamber, to ascertain the feasibility of their legislative proposals. Remarkably, Senate staff members have presided at committee hearings in the absence of a senator and have asked questions of committee witnesses.

The role of House staff is less prominent because they are fewer in number and because the norm of specialization is greater: House members are willing to immerse themselves more deeply in the nitty-gritty of legislation. When one House member, appropriately deferential, went to a senator's office to discuss a matter, he was surprised to find two Senate committee staff members present. "What's the matter, don't you trust me?" the House member asked. "No, no, it's not that at all," replied the senator. "It's just that I am so swamped, that I don't know anything about what you want to talk to me about, and I won't remember anything we agree upon unless I have the staff present." The presence of the staff required the legislators to be more circumspect in their comments, the whole conference was stilted, and the give-and-take necessary to find a middle ground between the various legislative positions just did not take place.

The working sessions of the commission to recommend a new criminal code, under former Governor Pat Brown of California, were ill attended by the three Senate members. Claiming prior commitments, they designated a staffer to attend and bespeak their concerns. As their representative, the staffer compromised and bargained on various controversies. When the three errant senators repudiated many agreements the staffer had made, the commission was forced to retreat on certain key issues, an embarrassing position for all participants, to say nothing of the lost time.

The differential level of involvement between House and Senate members leads often to an imbalance, favoring the House, during conference committee meetings, for House members are frequently better informed on the details of legislation. However, even in the House, the committee staffs play a critical role in forging legislation.

The Kinds of Staff

In the outside world, the people who work "on the Hill" are often lumped together into one amorphous, undifferentiated group. Yet there are four major kinds of Hill staffers. The first category includes the staffer who works in a member's personal office and whose main goal is the reelection and promotion of "the boss." In the second category is the committee staffer, who technically works for the committee but who more realistically works for a member or sometimes for a party within the committee. This staffer's work is more substantive and generally involves the development of policy in major areas of national concern, for example, agriculture, foreign affairs, banking. In the third category there is the leadership staff, a small group of professionals who are responsible for ensuring that the party leadership understands and controls the daily activities of the Congress. The fourth category includes those who work in one of the four support agencies—the Congressional Budget Office, the General Accounting Office, the Office of Technology Assistance, and the Congressional Research Service—which were established as "arms of Congress" to help both sides of the aisle evaluate policy and legislation. In addition, the fourth category includes the Senate and House legislative counsel, who are not technically part of any agency, but who provide essential technical drafting services on a nonpartisan basis for legislation and amendments.

PERSONAL STAFFS

Every member's personal office is essentially a political operation. Its key function is to reelect "the boss," to deal with his local and national constituencies, and to ensure his place in history. Most personal offices are separated into two divisions: the Washington and the district offices. The former is responsible for legislative activities, and the latter for political visibility and effectiveness with the electorate. Personal staffs focus their daily activities around the needs and whims of the member. In most offices, when the member is in town, his staff also are in town; if he does not leave the office for lunch, neither does the staff. When he is in a bad mood, the office is on edge; when he is happy, the office glows. Every ounce of power possessed by a staff member in the personal office derives from the member. The derivative nature of power is more pronounced on the personal staff than on committee staffs where expertise and professional reputation give staffers independent powers of persuasion. Because of the reliance on the member for power, "access" to the boss becomes imperative. Thus, the most important ingredient and index of power is prompt and frequent access to the member.

Administrative Assistant

Even the titles used by Hill staffers denote their far-reaching and integral influence on the legislative process. Each member has an administrative assistant, or AA, who usually is the alter ego of the member. He or she (many AA's are women, as distinct from other professional posts on the Hill) usually manages the staff; supervises the scheduling and allocation of the member's time between Washington and home (as well as the use of his time in Washington); decides who will have access to the member; tries to ameliorate the tension between family demands and public demands; supervises office accounts and expenditures; and usually reviews anything of importance that is being mailed under the member's imprimatur. Often the AA was the campaign manager for the congressman in the previous election. Occasionally, the AA is a close personal friend of the congressman or senator. In addition to controlling access to the senator, the AA determines which staff members are invited to meetings, recommends salary hikes and promotions, and hires and fires the staff. The AA also controls the perquisites of the office. For example, the AA decides which staff members get parking spots and allocates office space. Not all offices give AA's such autocratic powers, and every office varies in regard to staff members' relationships with the member. Nonetheless, to the extent that they control office resources and access, AA's have substantial influence over office policy.

Legislative Assistant

By nature, the legislative assistant, or LA, is a generalist. Often a chief LA is supported by two or three general LA's. Because of the broad scope of issues he or she is expected to cover, the LA is usually, but not always, a lawyer. Generally, the substantive areas are divided into three main categories: economics, domestic "soft" issues (like health care and education), and foreign policy. Sometimes committee staff are borrowed to help the personal office handle substantive concerns. The LA's main function is to follow floor activity and track committee action of interest to his member. Every week the party whip sends at least one notice to each office, describing the expected legislative activities on the floor.

Once legislation is scheduled for floor action the LA goes into action. In a brief period of time he must understand the main provisions of the legislation, determine the positions of the various interest groups and contact the party leadership on any amendments that will be raised. Equally important is a clear understanding of the impact of the legislation and amendments on the home district. Thus, an LA must be a legislative Sherlock Holmes who can ferret out the rhymes and reasons of legislation. When the member goes to the floor to vote on legislation, he is thus prepared with the total picture.

Many members use "idiot cards," which include the number of the bill coming up, an analysis of the subject matter, a brief description of possible amendments, a list of the principal groups supporting or opposing the bill or any of the amendments, and a reminder to the member on how he intended to vote on the various proposals. When a roll-call vote is ordered, members hurry onto the floor, consult their cards, and talk to their party whips and other bellwethers (in the House they look at the electronic scoreboard to see how other members are voting). To an outsider, the entire process seems a helter-skelter admission of inadequacy. The immediacy and urgency of the voting itself belies the exhaustive and frequently agonizing work that the LA's and their members have invested in preparing for the vote. It also belies the influence of the lobbying effort that has been invested in many substantive bills and amendments that are finally considered on the floor of either chamber.

The floor consideration of dairy price legislation in the Senate in 1981 illustrates the legislative responsibilities of a Hill staff member. In 1981 the Reagan administration decided to challenge the omnipotent dairy industry as part of its economic program by proposing legislation to suspend a semiannual dairy price support increase. As the dairy industry was the only agricultural industry to have a semiannual increase, Reagan predicted that the elimination of the April 1 scheduled increase would not only win a symbolic victory against "special interests" but also save $147 million in fiscal year 1981. The dairy industry, recognizing that it would probably lose the battle if it attacked the budget cuts frontally, decided to use a more devious tactic. It proposed an amendment to the dairy price support legislation to put a 50 percent quota on the import of casein, a little-known milk protein not generally produced here, which is used in the production of imitation dairy products like imitation cheeses and coffee creamers. This amendment would serve two purposes. First, it would slow down the legislation because it was strongly opposed by other business groups—like General Mills, General Foods, and Pillsbury— who relied on casein for everything from frozen pizza to baby formula. Second, because it was unlikely that the casein amendment would be adopted in the House, the legislation would have to go to conference between the two houses. Consequently, time would be the industry's ally, for it was unlikely that the legislation would pass by April 1, the date on which the second price increase would go into effect.

Every LA responsible for this issue was instantly inundated with hundreds of letters, phone calls, and telegrams from lobbyists on both sides of the casein issue. Dairy farmers were contacted by the Washington lobby and asked to phone their legislators. Indeed, representatives from major companies flew into town to "visit" with their representatives.

Sometimes the trickiest aspect of an LA's job is to learn the party politics of a piece of legislation. In the floor fight over the dairy legislation, the Democrats, newly in the minority, decided at the last minute to use the casein amendment as a litmus test of party loyalty and as a symbol to the new majority leader that the Democrats could act in a cohesive fashion to block important Republican initiatives. At the party caucus before the vote on casein—staff is generally excluded from the caucus—the Democrats agreed to vote against the procedural motion of Majority Leader Howard Baker to table the casein amendment. Thus, the merits of the amendment became incidental to the show of party solidarity. Even liberal senators who would normally vote against any amendment supported by the dairy industry were persuaded to vote with the party on the procedural motion. Democratic Whip Alan Cranston and Minority Leader Robert Byrd hovered at the well to assure Democratic members that their votes were needed for the good of the party. (The well of the House and Senate is the front and center of the chamber.) Some senators even changed their initial vote after a strong arm-twist by the party leadership and assurance that they could vote on the merits on the subsequent substantive vote. Only two senators, Bill Bradley and Daniel Patrick Moynihan, strayed from the flock. The strategy of party cohesion on procedural votes is not new, particularly for a minority party. In previous congresses, such liberal Republican senators as Jacob Javits of New York and Charles Mathias of Maryland were known to reaffirm their party loyalty on procedural motions while preserving their substantive position on the underlying legislation.

By using this party tactic, the Democrats, in their first stand of the Ninety-seventh Congress, managed to defeat Majority Leader Howard Baker's tabling motion 53 to 47. Chagrined, Baker instantly recessed the Senate, thereby postponing the vote on the merits of the bill until he could get "his ducks in line." Although Baker ultimately prevailed on the substantive vote, the Democrats had made their point.

To advise his member correctly, as the dairy legislation illustrates, the LA cannot merely read a committee report or listen to a few lobbyists. Rather he or she must be in constant contact with the party leadership, the committee staff, lobbyists from both sides of the issue, and the office politicos who can best judge the impact of the vote on the member's reelection.

The difficulties of following legislation are far more pronounced in the Senate than in the House. In the House, every piece of legislation is governed by a "rule" which generally determines whether an amendment will be debated in the Committee of the Whole. Transcripts of Rules Committee hearings in which amendments are discussed are usually available. There are few surprises.

An LA can inform his congressman in a variety of ways about floor politics. He can put a floor memo "in the bag" for the member to read overnight or before the vote. More frequently, however, the staff member walks to the floor with the member or waits for him in the lobby outside the chamber. In the Senate, the LA's line up in the front of the elevators next to the Senate chambers to be in position to notify members of an impending vote when the first bell rings. The senator, by filing a form, can gain access to the chamber for a staff member to allow him or her to follow political maneuvers firsthand when the senator leaves to attend to other business. Strict rules now apply limiting the number of staff members per senator and per committee allowed on the floor. But this was not always so. Until 1970, an unlimited number of staff were allowed on the Senate floor and to line the walls of the Senate chamber. During the battle over confirmation of Judge G. Harold Carswell to the Supreme Court, staff flocked to the Senate chamber to watch the roll call. Upon his defeat (51 to 45), the staff let out a cheer, which greatly infuriated Vice-President Spiro Agnew, then presiding as president of the Senate. Soon thereafter, the Senate leadership established a complicated bureaucracy to govern staff access to the floor. In the House, the LA follows floor votes by watching a closed-circuit television screen; in the Senate, only a "squawk box" follows the daily proceedings. Staff is usually available at the party hot line, cloakroom, and leadership offices to answer telephones and keep LA's informed of floor events. However, without comparison, the best way to find out what is going on is the time-consuming firsthand monitoring of the congressional floor and lobby.

The LA's opportunities for any substantive, strong floor role in legislation are rare. Passivity converts to activity only when the senator or congressman proposes an amendment. When the member poses a floor challenge to legislation, the LA is responsible for putting together the coalitions necessary to make the amendment successful. He or she polls the other offices to determine what the vote count is likely to be, works with lobby groups, and writes lengthy briefing books and floor statements for the senator or congressman to use in discussing the legislation. Most important, the LA obtains co-sponsors for his member's amendment; advises the member on which congressmen to phone and which to approach on the floor to lobby for votes; and recommends procedural strategy. Freshmen members often lose amendments when their staff do not understand the procedures well enough to control the floor. Under the rules of the Senate, for example, legislation can be amended in only two degrees. A staff member who understands that procedural requirement can protect his amendment from assault by drafting the legislation as a second-degree amendment. Thus, when Jesse Helms proposed his anti-busing amendment to the Department of Justice authorization bill, he welcomed the second-degree amendment of Senator Bennett Johnston of Louisiana, which expanded the anti-busing strictures. (An amendment is called "second degree" when it seeks to amend a pending amendment to a bill. Amendments in the "third-degree" are not permitted.) Johnston's second-degree amendment short-circuited any efforts by moderates to ameliorate the Helms amendment. The staff who are experts at the rules of procedure can tie the Senate in knots.

Finally, LA's perform many important political functions for their members. They write speeches to be delivered at the local chamber of commerce, meet with constituents who visit Washington, and usually handle the issues section of the reelection campaign. Because of the ready availability of a substantive policy staff, members seeking reelection have a distinct advantage over challengers. The use of staff on issues that "look good" back home— from writing position papers to compiling selective voting records—is a built-in plus for all incumbents.

Press Aide

Most personal offices today include a press secretary or press aide.[13] In 1979, only three senators did not list a press secretary on their office payroll and many senators have as many as three press secretaries. The press secretary association in the Senate has grown from a handful of members in 1960 to well over one hundred. Less eager to rely on press secretaries, the House did not establish a Republican and a Democratic press secretary association until 1976. Even committees sometimes hire press aides. The Congress has responded to this growth in the reliance on press secretaries and the media by opening various press galleries. Following the establishment of press galleries in 1957, Congress more recently opened a radio gallery, a TV gallery, a periodical gallery, and a photographers' gallery for each house.

The press secretary's main concern is to get good press coverage for the congressman. Consequently, he encourages everyone in the office to look for opportunities to get the congressman on television. When a member is chairman of a committee or a subcommittee, television and newspaper coverage is obtained simply by holding a hearing on a timely matter. Moreover, press releases on the legislative activities of a senator are almost always published by local press eager to get information on their representative's activities. If a press secretary's contacts are good, he can "plant" editorials in the newspaper to support his member's legislation.

The Congress provides each member with the most advanced media technology to promote his cause or himself. A good press secretary trains his member in the use of a TelePrompTer so that television speeches flow smoothly. He maximizes the member's opportunities for television interviews. Just above

Archibald Cox, a well-known law professor,
holding a press conference after President Nixon
fired him as Watergate Special Prosecutor.

the floor the press gallery contains a studio for television statements and interviews on pending legislation. Members stand in line to use the studios, particularly on controversial votes.

Use of the press to advance legislative ideas is particularly necessary when they conflict with the agenda of the executive branch, which has instant access to the media. Without the media, members of Congress would find it difficult to explain legislation to constituents, get credit for initiatives, and build public support. That coverage also advances the individual member is a political reality. Many sponsors of important legislation prepare press releases for their co-sponsors, leaving appropriate blanks for the co-sponsor to fill in for local use. Sent by the co-sponsors to their local papers and other media, the release suggests to local people that their congressman or senator courageously took the initiative on the important issue of the day, even though his main involvement was to co-sign the bill before it was put into the hopper. Most larger newspapers and stations will use their press release prose, of course, primarily to monitor the events and people described in the press releases, but some smaller journals and stations use the releases verbatim. This, in part, accounts for the dichotomy between the reputation of a legislator in Washington and his image back home, where his constituents are convinced that their congressman is a legislator to be reckoned with. A good press secretary is worth many votes.

The press secretary often prepares the newsletters sent to constituents and screens requests for interviews with the congressman. To obtain national recognition in the media for his congressman or senator, the press secretary must cultivate contacts in the national press and spread the message that his boss is thought of as the "lead person" on important legislation or as one of the "young leaders" in the party. Often the party leadership helps a younger member get press attention. For example, on occasion Speaker O'Neill has invited a congressman to a press interview and introduced him as an expert.

The Mail Room

Several other essential members are on the congressional team, although their relationship to the legislative process is one more remote. The legislative correspondents process the flood of correspondence that swamps every congressional office. An average size senatorial office receives 2,000 to 3,000 letters each week. No Senate office gets less than 700 letters a week. Senator Moynihan of New York receives a weekly average of 8,000 constituent letters. [14] Most offices now have sophisticated computer equipment to print out "robos" (automatically typed letters that appear to be personal responses). An average senator has five letter processors, which operate as part of a sophisticated Senate correspondence management system that allows the mailing of 2,500 personalized letters per week. Some experts estimate that approximately one million targeted letters a month are sent by Senate offices to constituents having certain characteristics. When a senator gives a speech on small business, the computer ferrets out all the small business people who have written to him and sends them a copy of the speech. Computers, targeting, and the congressional franking system have all contributed to a vast increase in the amount of congressional mail. And the importance of an efficient mail operation in reelecting a congressman is not overlooked. Some congressmen personally scrutinize and read all mail and insist on a 24-hour turn-around for letters.

Schedulers and Caseworkers

Another key position in most offices is the scheduler, who collects and sorts all the requests for the member's presence and participation, a role not without power. Sometimes the functions are performed by two schedulers, one for the district and one for the Washington office. Because he can choose not to bring an invitation to a member's attention, a scheduler has a strong initial veto power over the member's time.

Caseworkers, the final major component of the personal office, take care of the constituents back home. Usually at least one member of the Washington staff handles legislation affecting the home state. However, the home state is a responsibility for all staff members. One survey of Senate staff indicated that nearly nine out of ten professionals handle at least once a week such constituent projects as sewage systems, urban renewal, water systems, dams, roads, airports, health grants, and educational assistance.[15] In Senate offices, the intensity of commitment to state problems invariably increases in the last two years of the six-year term. In House offices, it is a continuing priority. The importance of helping the state obtain a new project cannot be overemphasized. Some citizens of Keokuk, Iowa, voted for former Senator John Culver—one of the few towns to do so in his 1980 campaign—because they believed he was responsible for their new bridge over the Mississippi River. And in most states the rivalry between representatives as to which member can get more credit for major federal grants is constant.

The District Office

In recent years the number of district and state offices has increased dramatically. One Library of Congress study indicates that between 1970 and 1978 the number of district employees of House members increased from

1,035 to 2,317. In 1972 congressmen devoted 22.5 percent of personal staff to district offices and 36.1 percent in 1980.[16] Richard Fenno, in his book *Home Style*, also reports that congressmen and senators are spending more time at home.[17] The district office has two main objectives: to help constituents with their individual problems and to provide high visibility for the congressman in the district. Each time a congressman is successful in dealing with a constituent's problem—in helping to locate a missing social security check or in helping a local business deal with a regulatory agency—he enhances his prospects for reelection, for the happiness of one contented constituent "ripples" throughout the neighborhood.

Some district offices arrange for members to visit post offices or other meeting places on weekends in different district locations to deal with constituent problems and at the same time maintain a high profile in the district and the media. The office also plants "op ed" articles on local issues by the congressmen in local newspapers. Finally, the district office schedules speeches and sessions with local constituents on a regular basis. In essence, from the moment a member is elected, the district office is a low-key campaign organization dedicated to reelection.

Staff Life

From one perspective, personal staff jobs are truly exciting. They provide an opportunity to influence national policy and to be part of the national debate. A strong camaraderie develops, particularly among staff of the same party. The atmosphere is similar to that of a college campus. Staff "hang out" at the "plastic palace," the Dirksen Cafeteria, in the Senate basement. The work year, like the school year, allows for summer, Christmas, and spring vacations. The hours are long, but much of the day is spent in meetings and sessions with constituents, lobbyists, and other staff discussing the "big issues" of the day. Although some measures restrict the participation of staff in political campaigns, in reality staff play an integral role in every reelection fight, spending "vacations" in the home district and writing speeches that just happen to be used on the road.

On the other hand, staff jobs have their downside. Salaries are completely discretionary with the member. Civil rights laws do not protect congressional employees; the only legal safeguards are the minimal ones afforded by the Constitution. There is no civil service, and consequently, no job protection. Working conditions are abominable—crowded offices, poor lighting, and high noise levels. Women traditionally have not held high positions in congressional offices, and blacks and other minorities have fared even worse. Iris

Mitgang, the leader of the National Women's Political Caucus, testified before the Senate Committee on Labor and Human Resources in January, 1981, about the employment practices of Congress (dubbed "The Last Plantation"): "Instead of standing as a shining example of equal opportunity and employment equity, Congress is symbolic of the obstacles and barriers to fair employment for women. To combine the House and the Senate, the average female salary was 71 cents for every one dollar earned by men."[18] Political parties are not a factor in the wage disparity. Only 9 percent of the administrative assistants are women, and in the Senate only 15 percent of the women were in policy-making positions.

Staff work long hours, give Congress the best years of their lives, and can lose their jobs in twenty-four hours if the congressman does not win reelection or if he develops a "firing" fit toward the staff. The problems with becoming too identified as a Hill staffer were highlighted after the presidential election of 1980 when most of the Senate Democratic committee staffs were fired because of the shift in party power. Although the Senate provided a transition salary subsidy for employees who could not find new jobs immediately, the Washington unemployment lines remained filled for a long time by former Hill staffers who had lost their ability to transfer to other jobs. Thus, although the professional staff likes to think of itself as a well-established entity, with a vested interest in developing expertise in the congressional institution, the reality is that most professional staff people plan on staying only a few years. If they are wise, they leave of their own accord. As with congressmen, the other two ways of leaving the Hill are far less pleasant.

COMMITTEE STAFFS

Every committee is a world unto itself. Unlike the personal legislative staffer who gets a panoramic view of the activities of the Senate or House, a committee staffer peers at the legislative process through only one small window. Only rarely, for example, does a Judiciary Committee staff member have the opportunity of working with an agriculture staffer. However, what a committee staff member lacks in scope of perspective, he gains in depth. A committee staffer, particularly if he works for the chairman of a committee or a subcommittee, is able to concentrate most of his efforts, talents, and attention on certain narrow policy issues and thereby gain an expertise that makes him invaluable to the Congress.

Committee staffs function as specialized law firms at the disposal of the Congress. When a committee staff member drafts and works on legislation that becomes enacted into law, the expertise thus gained facilitates his entrée into the executive branch or the private sector. After a long period of service as a top staff aide for Senator Warren Magnuson of Washington on the Senate Commerce Committee, Michael Pertschuk became chairman of the Federal Trade Commission, which came under the Commerce Committee's jurisdiction. His expertise in administrative law paved the way for his confirmation and transition.

Because they are viewed as "more substantive" and "less political," jobs on committee staffs are more prestigious than those on personal staffs. Lawyers populate majority committee staffs and are responsible for setting up hearings, drafting legislation and amendments, writing committee reports, establishing the priorities of the committee, setting the agenda, and mapping out floor strategy for legislation reported out of committee. The obstructionist role of minority staff members is more passive, for it is much easier to "kill" legislation than it is to pass it. Because the minority party cannot initiate hearings, it threatens to prevent a quorum or to filibuster to ensure cooperation of the majority in addressing at least some of its legislative priorities. The minority staff, therefore, act as facilitators, persuaders, and, when all else fails, obstructionists.

Because the effective functioning of the Congress depends on the committee system, committee staffs have grown faster than any other kind of congressional staff. House committee staffs vary in size from the Energy and Commerce Committee with 149 slots in 1978 to the Public Works Committee with 25. In the Senate the Judiciary Committee ranked first with more than 200 staff members in the Ninety-sixth Congress, compared with the Veterans Affairs Committee with 24. Committee staff slots are allocated between majority and minority parties, and the leadership of each party allocates staff funds to the various committee members. A 1970 House reform allows each subcommittee chair to designate some of his own professionals, a privilege previously retained by the chair of the full committee. To the outside world, professional staff positions are generally regarded as better "plums" than personal staff positions. However, in terms of the needs of the senator or congressman, the personal staff is usually more important because of their deep involvement in his reelection. The committee staff is a more visible part of the Washington network.

LEADERSHIP STAFFS

An often overlooked congressional staff is the leadership staff. On the House side, the speaker controls the Democratic Steering and Policy Committee staff, and the minority has its own staff. On the Senate side, the majority

TABLE 8–2
NUMBERS OF LEADERSHIPS STAFF MEMBERS, 1982

	House	Senate
Speaker	25	
Majority Leader	17	14
Majority Whip	17	5
Minority Leader	17	7
Minority Whip	17	3
Total	93	29

NOTE: STAFF OF THE VICE-PRESIDENT IS NOT INCLUDED.
SOURCE: COMPILED BY THE LIBRARY OF CONGRESS

and minority leaders have separate staffs. The most striking aspect of the leadership staffs is their small size. (See Table 8–2).

Leadership staffs in both houses are smaller than those of most committees. According to the Congressional Research Service, in 1978 the staffs of the Senate leaders numbered twenty-two; the staff of the smallest Senate committee, the Veterans Affairs Committee, numbered twenty-four. On the House side, in the same year, the combined staffs of the majority and minority leaders were smaller than the staffs of fourteen of the twenty-three committees.

The comparatively tiny size of the leadership staffs explains, perhaps, the inability of the party leadership to rein in committees and set meaningful policy priorities. In the speaker's office, the staff serves primarily to screen and process. They are utility infielders who deal with political crises originating in committees. For example, the speaker's staff reviews requests to "fast-track" legislation, that is, to place legislation on the suspension calendar, a power that rests exclusively with the speaker, and thus enable legislation to circumvent the cumbersome Rules Committee. To do this, the staff quickly checks the committee staff, the lobby groups, and the Senate side to determine the ramifications of fast-tracking a particular bill. Likewise, because the speaker works closely with the Rules Committee, the speaker's staff is intimately involved in determining the rule to be applied to a particular bill or whether to bottle it up in committee. Thus the leadership staff, except on the rarest of occasions, sees legislation at the end of the tortuous and lengthy legislative process after most of the deals have been "cut" in committee and the interest groups have aligned themselves. With the meager resources available to it, the speaker's office can barely keep up with the job of facilitating, blocking, or processing the myriad of legislative measures that arise.

On the Senate side, the staff resources of the majority leader are meager in contrast to those available to each committee chair. To exacerbate the

No. 15   May 18, 1981

DEMOCRATIC LEGISLATIVE BULLETIN

Democratic Policy Committee
Robert C. Byrd, Chairman

H.R. 3132, CASH DISCOUNT ACT

CALENDAR NO.: 78

FLOOR ACTION: Not yet scheduled. Democratic floor manager—Senator Williams; Republican floor manager—Senator Garn.

BACKGROUND: H.R. 3132 is identical to H.R. 31 as passed the House on February 24, 1981 (by a vote of 372 to 4), and by the Senate on March 12, 1981 (by voice vote). However, it does not contain a nongermane Helms amendment, agreed to by voice vote on the Senate floor, which permits the nomination of a Surgeon General who may be more than 64 years of age. H.R. 31 was sent to conference on April 29, but the conferees were unable to reach agreement on this provision.

On May 4, 1981, H.R. 3132 passed the House by a record vote of 296 to 43 and was placed on the Senate calendar on May 6.

SUMMARY: Removes the current 5 percent limit on discounts that a merchant may offer customers as an inducement to pay for an item by cash or a means other than open end credit or credit card and repeals all Federal Reserve Board regulations governing these types of transactions; defines the term "regular price" as the higher or credit price which must always be the price listed on the tag or posted;

Extends for 3 years, until February 27, 1984, the current ban which prohibits a merchant from imposing a surcharge on customers who use a credit card to make their purchases; requires the Federal Reserve Board to prepare a study on the effect of charge card transactions upon card issuers, merchants, and consumers and to submit a report of its findings to the Banking Committees within two years; and....

RELATED VOTES (1981):
Cash Discounts—Credit Surcharge Ban Extension (H.R. 31)
28 Proxmire-Glenn amendment: Strikes 3-year extension of ban on credit card surcharges. (41-56)

On every major piece of legislation, the leadership staff of each party prepares this bulletin which is distributed to every member of the caucus.

disparity in staffing, the majority leader, unlike the speaker, does not have any procedural powers—the power of referral or the power to place legislation on the suspension calendar. Without procedural clout or sufficient staff, the Senate majority leader is little able to influence Senate policy. The major clout of the Senate leadership is derived, of necessity, from within the party and depends on its ability to muster sufficient peer group pressure to coerce straying sheep to return to the fold. Occasionally, to bolster certain substantive perspectives, the leader creates task forces on certain issues. By controlling the membership of task forces, he controls the substantive outcome. However, the staffing of a task force depends on the resources of the senators appointed to serve on it.

To influence the outcome of legislation, the staff sends out feelers to staff of every senator, indicating that the leadership wants the membership to vote the party line on a particular bill. With special floor privileges, the leadership staff is either in the cloakroom or on the floor itself during Senate action. Many senators rely on the leadership staff for information on the procedural status of a vote or on the schedule for the day. The Senate leaders, unlike the speaker, have committee assignments, which the staff must also handle. (Most frequently the leader serves on committees in absentia.) On rare occasions, the leadership staff becomes involved in substantive legislative matters. In the battle over President Reagan's budget cuts, for example, the staff spent weeks compiling data on the impact of the budget cuts and formulating recommendations for the Democratic caucus. Unlike committee staff, the leadership staff is usually permitted to attend caucus meetings.

In striking contrast to committee staffs, which exercise such pervasive influence over the committee agenda, legislation, and priorities, the leadership staff—because of its small number and limited responsibility—is relatively ineffective. Institutionally, if size of staff does indeed mean power, the lack of staff must indicate the lack of power. The paucity of staffing for the party leadership in comparison to committee leadership reflects quite cogently the power distribution between committees and parties in both chambers.

SUPPORT AGENCIES

General Accounting Office

Of the four main congressional support agencies established by Congress to provide technical expertise to members of Congress, the oldest is the General Accounting Office (GAO), which was established by the Budget and Accounting Act of 1921 to strengthen congressional control over the public purse. Prior to this act, effective fiscal oversight of the executive branch was impossible because the budgetary estimates of each agency for the upcoming fiscal year were sent to the congressional committee responsible on an individual basis. In 1921 Congress reconstituted the budget system, directing the president to prepare and transmit to Congress one annual comprehensive budget. To help the president, the Bureau of the Budget was established. To ensure the continuance of its co-equal role in the budget process, Congress established the General Accounting Office. Originally designed to provide budget analysis for the Congress, audit federal programs and expenditures, and expose unauthorized spending, the GAO in recent years has expanded to include legislative recommendations for eliminating waste in federal programs. According to the GAO, the number of times it has testified before Congress increased by a factor of five between 1966 and 1980. In the last five years alone the number of reports increased by 66 percent,[19] and the number of staff increased over the decade by almost a quarter.[20]

The GAO willingly serves as the congressional gadfly on the executive branch. Congress often asks the GAO to audit a federal program and recommend improvements in its implementation. Just as major corporations use consultants to legitimize their policy decisions, so too do congressional committees turn to the GAO to justify committee recommendations, recommendations that frequently have important political ramifications. For example, when the MX missile system was under heavy attack in Congress, the GAO issued a report criticizing as "incomplete and misleading" the environmental impact statement issued by the Air Force for its proposed MX missile system in Nevada and Utah. The GAO report fueled bipartisan opposition to the MX in the House Interior Subcommittee and received national media coverage.[21] The GAO reports also refute administration statistics. For example, when President Carter claimed that the amount of federal paperwork decreased during his administration, his critics pointed with glee to a GAO study documenting the opposite. During the gas deregulation fight, the GAO study on the costs of deregulation focused congressional debate on the impact of deregulation on American households.[22]

The GAO considers the political impact a study might have in deciding which subjects to study and preserves its bipartisan support by avoiding no-win issues. Critics point, for example, to the GAO's refusal to tackle inefficiencies in defense procurement. Instead, the GAO contracted out these reports to consultants. Some reports never get written. When a study to make a political point is considered and the GAO concludes that the study will have the opposite outcome, the GAO usually recommends behind-the-scenes to let the report die aborning. A freshman member once requested a GAO study to demonstrate the effectiveness of various gun-control statutes to rebut the lobby's claims that the laws were not, and could not be, effective in stopping street crime. Rather than get into that political thicket, the GAO representative paid a personal call and explained the politics of gun control to the freshman member. The report could still be written, he said, but it would be filled with caveats and wherefores. The member got the message.

Because it has maintained a reputation as a neutral bipartisan support agency, the GAO is entrusted with many controversial tasks. For example, the GAO plays a central role in the enforcement of the Impoundment Control Act of 1974.[23] Passed in response to Nixon's cavalier and frequent decisions to impound funds appropriated by Congress for important social programs, the Impoundment Act of 1974 requires legislative approval of presidential recommendations to "rescind" appropriated monies or "defer" their expenditure until another fiscal year. Under this act, the comptroller general of the General Accounting Office must report to the Congress on executive compliance with impoundment controls. He is required to inform Congress when the president fails to report an impoundment and when an action is improperly classified and is also empowered to bring suit to enforce impoundment controls. The GAO's responsibilities under this act have been enormous. The office has evaluated more than 600 proposed presidential rescissions and deferrals and responded to hundreds of complaints by legislators about alleged executive abuses.

Because of the enormous scope and flexibility of executive fiscal actions, the discovery of an impoundment is not always immediate. Indeed, the GAO has been criticized for taking too passive a role in investigating executive activities. In *Congress and Money*, Allen Schick, a budget specialist at the Library of Congress, wrote:

> Moreover, GAO has adopted a reactive posture toward executive branch impoundments. Rather than initiating investigations, it gets involved only after the President has filed an impoundment report or a third party has complained about executive action. This procedure does not always protect congressional interests. Thus when President Carter decided to terminate the B-1 bomber, he ordered the cancellation of construction contracts three weeks before notifying Congres. Although Congress could have disapproved the rescission proposal and compelled the Defense Department to resume work on the airplane, reopening the program would have entailed considerable costs.[24]

The GAO is also required to perform some congressional housekeeping tasks. For example, it audits the accounts of congressionally chartered organizations, like the American Red Cross and the National Ski Patrol. For a short period of time it was responsible for monitoring the paperwork requirements of independent agencies, like the Securities and Exchange Commission, which the Congress was reluctant to put under the control of the Office of Management and Budget. To its credit, the GAO proved to be as strong a critic of itself as it is of the executive branch when it proclaimed publicly its abysmal failure to control the paperwork of these independent agencies. This candid appraisal led in 1980 to the transfer of the paperwork control function from the GAO to the OMB, with certain procedural safeguards to protect the autonomy of the independent agencies.[25]

In sum, the GAO plays a critical function in the Congress. Through its reports on government waste, fraud, and inefficiency, it provides the information necessary to allow the Congress to wield its budgetary knife effectively and intelligently. More important, perhaps, members of Congress do not have to rely exclusively on the executive branch and special-interest groups to supply expertise and information.

Congressional Research Service

The Congressional Research Service (CRS), the second oldest congressional support agency, serves as an indispensable appendage of every personal office. On a moment's notice, it provides that one statistic a member needs immediately, as well as esoteric information in response to constituent requests. Employing computer technologies, the CRS is capable of on-the-spot legislative research. Upon staff request, it analyzes Supreme Court cases, proofreads committee reports, critiques legislation, recommends amendments, and provides an index of newspaper articles on virtually any issue. The productivity of the employed clerk-hires of most House congressional offices is substantially increased by their access to the more than 800 staff members at CRS.[26] The only task the CRS religiously refuses to perform is historical analysis of a campaign opponent.

CRS, originally called the Legislative Reference Service, was established by the Legislative Reorganization Act of 1946 to provide Congress with modernized decision-making technology and information resources. Until 1970, the 332 CRS employees performed largely bibliographical and research tasks. In 1970 the second Legislative Reorganization Act expanded the service and provided the resources to analyze and evaluate legislative proposals. Between 1970 and 1979, the CRS staff almost tripled, growing from 332 to 847. With its increased resources and budget, the CRS became more than a machine to grind out quick research. It has developed into a congressional think-tank and now attracts nationally known experts to its staff.

Like the GAO, the CRS issues reports that are often politically generated, politically cited, and politically exploited. For example, to demonstrate a dramatic increase in violent crime, a committee staff person will request the Congressional Research Service to compile a report from FBI and Department of Justice crime-rate statistics. To criticize agricultural subsidies, a staff member need only ask CRS to generate a chart illustrating the percentage of crop subsidies distributed to wealthy farmers. Although reports and memoranda are carefully screened and scrutinized by the internal controls of the CRS, a committee staff person working closely with a knowledgeable CRS staffer can orchestrate a report that will be helpful in providing a political point. Technically, the CRS functions as a bipartisan staff; "leaking" information to one congressional staff member about a request for information from another is not tolerated. Nonetheless, CRS staff members do have substantive biases; by selectively providing access to information, they can be influential in affecting certain substantive outcomes.

The CRS has been timid about inserting itself into the open political arena, but it does, on occasion, have an impact on political strategy. During the fight on the 1981 tax bill, the Senate Republican leadership wanted to act on the Reagan economic package before the House acted on its own tax bill. The Senate was not overly concerned about the constitutional requirement of Article I, which stipulates that the House of Representatives must initiate revenue bills, for the Senate had frequently circumvented this requirement by amending minor House taxation measures with major Senate proposals. And in 1981 Senator Robert Dole was content to amend a minor tariff measure with the administration legislation. However, Dole's strategy had to be scuttled when a CRS report, prepared over the weekend at the request of the Democratic leadership, cast doubt on whether tariff legislation was a revenue bill for purposes of Article I. The pressure on the House Ways and Means Committee, which was struggling to forge a compromise bill, was alleviated when the Senate Republican leadership acknowledged that it would have to substitute its bill for the House legislation after it was eventually sent to the Senate. Although but a minor skirmish in the overall battle, this episode illustrates how a neutral, scholarly body can influence the direction of political events.

The availability of the CRS to members of Congress has been critical in chipping away at the information monopolies possessed by committee chairmen. Before the CRS expansion, every congressman relied on committee staff of the Agriculture Committee and lobby groups to evaluate the impact of dairy price supports. Because most LA's are generalists and because in-house congressional library resources are few, most members lacked the informational tools and neutral advice necessary to evaluate agricultural legislation. The expansion of the CRS destroyed this information monopoly, for the CRS provides in-depth legislative history, newspaper clippings, and staff critiques to any member of Congress. However, having a better informed Congress can create difficulties. With 535 better informed congressmen, responsible decision-making by the party leadership becomes more difficult.

Congressional Budget Office

With increased national concern over the exploding federal budget, the Congressional Budget Office, originally led by Alice Rivlin, a Brookings Institution economist, has been in the center of most of the significant legislative battles of recent congresses. Established by the Congressional Budget and Impoundment Control Act of 1974, CBO was assigned three statutory functions: budgetary assistance, economic analysis, and policy analysis. The structure of CBO resulted from a legislative compromise between those who wanted the newly formed House and Senate Budget committees to have exclusive control over budget information, and, therefore, great power and leverage over the budget process, and those who wanted the CBO to be responsible to all members of Congress, thereby ensuring a wide distribution of budgetary power. Consequently, the CBO has many taskmasters. Its priorities are: first, to assist the House and Senate Budget Committee staffs; second, to work with the Appropriation and Revenue committees; third, to help "to the extent practicable" the authorizing committees; and fourth, to help members gain access to budgetary information.[27] In its first three years of operation, the CBO had roughly 218 staff members,[28] a figure that did not increase significantly because some committee chairmen feared that the power of the budget process was beyond bounds, and because some old guard conservatives worried that Rivlin had turned the CBO into a left-wing think-tank.

Perhaps the most striking characteristic of the CBO is its analytic independence. Rivlin consistently maintained that the role of the CBO was not to work for the Budget Committee staffs but to work for the entire Congress. More important, Rivlin categorically refused to let the CBO become a mere bookkeeper, insisting, instead, that it maintain an independent role as budget analyst: "CBO does not make recommendations on matters of policy; rather, we analyze options, their cost to the federal government, and their impact on the national economy and the budget."[29]

However, despite her public reluctance to describe the CBO as a policy adviser, Rivlin's impact was more substantive, as Allen Schick described:

Rivlin saw CBO as a change agent for Congress—not for any particular change (she admirably upheld CBO's claim of neutrality in the face of disbelief by some members of Congress) but for the proposition that Congress should search for more efficient and effective alternatives to its current programs. The bias for change is inherent in policy analysis. The analysis intervenes in order to change policy outcomes; the budget maker puts a high value on stability and order.[30]

Because the CBO does, in fact, spearhead policy changes, it can be distinguished from the CRS and the GAO, which respond in a much more reactive way to congressional initiatives.

Originally established as a congressional counter-agency to OMB, the role of the CBO was justified by the budget battles in the Ninety-seventh Congress. The need for independent congressional expertise in budgeting was never more obvious. In the earliest months of the Ninety-seventh Congress, President Reagan proposed far-reaching, unprecedented budget slashes in domestic programs, choosing guns over butter. With a bravado that infuriated Republican congressmen, Dr. Rivlin issued an alternative to the president's much heralded budget, an alternative that attained the desired level of cuts without focusing primarily on the social programs targeted by OMB Director David Stockman.[31] The CBO staff went even further than the CBO report, criticizing (sub rosa, for sympathetic congressional staff members) the data and numbers used by the OMB and even recommending budget alternatives that were not contained in the official CBO report. As budget specialists, the CBO staff provided interpretations of the OMB budget figures that related them to their ultimate consequences. Upon request, the CBO described the impact of the budget cuts on any member's home district and suggested alternatives that would be less damaging to a program.

In addition to budget analysis, the CBO forecasts economic projections for the Congress. Early in the Ninety-seventh Congress the CBO announced that the Reagan administration had underestimated its projected deficit for fiscal year 1982 by $22 billion and predicted that the budget would be unbalanced by $49 billion in 1984. Reagan was furious at the CBO for attacking his economic projections at a critical time in the legislative battle over the budget. The *Washington Post*, under the banner headline "CBO Analysis to Show Administration Falling Short of Budget Goals," described the president's reaction:

> But Reagan's first instinct was to fire back. He labeled the CBO forecasts
> "phony." Later, after consulting his top advisers, the President decided to be
> more conciliatory. He said he had chosen the wrong word. What he meant was
> that the numbers contradicting his were incorrect.[32]

Rivlin's projections received national media attention and provoked heated debate in the House and Senate committees. Although the House Ways and

Means Committee chose the administration's estimates, the CBO clearly provided the necessary fodder for opposition cannon.

In addition to economic and budgetary analysis requirements, which are tied to the yearly budgetary system, the CBO also analyzes the budgetary impact of new authorizations. According to House and Senate rules, all legislation reported out of committee containing new authorizations must be analyzed by the CBO. The CBO impact report is included in the committee report. A significant impact can influence the terms of legislative debate. Often the budgetary impact statement is negotiated in advance by the committee staff and the CBO staff, the former usually arguing to decrease the CBO budget figures. Lucky is the legislation stamped "no budgetary impact."

Office of Technology Assessment

The smallest and least well-known congressional support agency, the Office of Technology Assessment (OTA), was spawned by sputnik. During the 1960s, Congress became concerned with its inability to analyze the complex technological questions essential to enacting responsible legislation. In the Technology Assessment Act of 1972, Congress recognized the necessity of understanding, "to the fullest extent possible, the consequences of technological applications" in making public policy determinations.[33] The OTA is a bipartisan panel of ten House and Senate members with the chairmanship alternating between chambers. In 1978 the professional staff numbered between 80 and 90 (with a total staff of 164).

The OTA prepares long-term studies on policy problems. Its reports include studies on U.S. industrial competition in the international markets of steel, electronics, and automobiles and a study on "Technological Innovation and Health, Safety and Environmental Regulations." Most study areas are extremely technical and targeted at a small audience of experts. Occasionally, the reports are timely, for example, the study on American competitiveness in international industries, which came at a time when American industry was worried about foreign imports. However, most OTA reports are relegated to dusty shelves, never to be heard of again.

Unlike the GAO, which ferrets out waste and fraud, or the CBO, which aggressively espouses certain policy preferences, or the CRS, which is essential to every Hill office, the OTA suffers from relative obscurity. Michael Malbin, in his book *Unelected Representatives*, describes the OTA malaise: "OTA has had difficulties defining a distinct mission for itself and for a time was in danger of becoming almost like personalized professional committee staff aides for OTA's congressional board members. The latter difficulty may have eased somewhat, but not the former."[34]

Legislative Counsel

Both the House and the Senate possess an Office of Legislative Counsel to assist in drafting legislation and amendments. (These offices are distinct from the Legal Counsel who represent the House and the Senate in legal disputes.) In 1978 the House Legislative Counsel included 47 members, the Senate, 22. Although not technically congressional support agencies, the professional legal staffs nonetheless provide a critical service in drafting and redrafting legislation in the statutory jargon appropriate to the United States Code. Trained to think about legislation as law, the lawyers of the Legislative Counsel examine whether proposed legislation conflicts with the United States Code and remember to include details, such as the date when the legislation goes into effect, that most staffers tend to forget. The Legislative Counsel representatives sit in at committee mark-ups and at conference sessions.

The Legislative Counsel is non-partisan. All communications are held in confidence. A staff member of "Leg Counsel" is often in the anomalous position of writing legislation for the Democrats and amendments for the Republicans or vice versa.

DO HILL STAFFS WIELD
TOO MUCH INFLUENCE?

In *Unelected Representatives*,[35] Michael S. Malbin classified committee staffs into three categories. First, he described the passive, bipartisan staff, which serves as neutral expert. Typified by the Joint Committee on Taxation, the passive staff limits (at least theoretically) its role to evaluating proposed legislation and suggesting alternatives to achieve the same substantive goal. The second kind of staff is the purely technical staff, which provides the figures and data necessary to develop legislation, such as the staff of the Armed Services Committee. Finally, there is the entrepreneurial staff, which aggressively asserts a committee's legislative priorities, tries to grab jurisdiction from other committees, and dominates policy formation. Malbin classifies the staffs of most standing committees as entrepreneurial, and it is with respect to this kind of committee staff that Malbin addresses most of his attention.

Malbin asks a basic question: Does an entrepreneurial committee staff conflict with the needs of the legislative institution as a whole? On balance, Malbin answers that question in the affirmative. Although he concedes that large staffs may be essential for Congress's effort to keep track of the bureaucracy,[36] he criticizes highly personalized staffs who devote their loyalty to individual members, not to Congress as an institution and not to the leadership. In a chapter pointedly entitled "Congressional Staffs and the Future of Representative Government," Malbin reluctantly concedes the importance of staff, especially given the heavy congressional workload:

> If we take Congress' workloads as given and focus on negotiations, we see that the staffs, acting as surrogate for their "bosses," do as creditable a job of representing their interests as any attorney would for a client in a parallel situation outside Congress. With loyal surrogate lawyers carrying out their wishes, the members are able to follow more issues than they could if they had to attend all meetings personally. Institutionally, this means that both the members as individuals and Congress as a whole are able to manage a heavier workload with the staffs than would be possible without them. To some extent, therefore, the staffs seem to help Congress do its work.

> But, as we have seen, the surrogate-lawyers are generally expected to be more than just passive representatives of their clients: they are also expected to go out and drum up new business. The increased use of personalized, entrepreneurial staffs has helped Congress retain its position as a key initiator of federal policy, despite the growing power of the executive branch. The relationship between this use of entrepreneurial staff and Congress' power seems almost obvious. Most other national legislatures depend on their cabinets for almost all policy initiatives. Congress is not so passive today, thanks largely to its staff.

> The system of individualized staff control seems also to be responsible for much of the oversight that gets accomplished outside of the General Accounting Office. Having a substantial number of staff people with appropriate investigative authority seems a necessary condition for congressional oversight of the executive branch and the independent regulatory commissions. . . . Thus, the movement away from a system of collegial non-partisan committee staffing to a more personalized one has been associated with an increase in congressional oversight activities, largely because a personalized system lets chairmen have activist staff entrepreneurs, and chairmen who use entrepreneurial staffs tend to be more interested in maintaining their independence from the executive branch.[37]

After conceding the weighty advantages afforded by an "entrepreneurial" staff, Malbin proceeds to give the "gloomier" side,[38] arguing that the overuse of staff destroys legislative deliberation:

> For a process of legislative deliberation to function reasonably well, at least three distinct requirements must be satisfied. The members need accurate information, they need time to think about that information, and they need to talk to each other about the factual, political, and moral implications of the policies they are considering. The new use of staff undercuts each of these.[39]

Malbin launches three arguments against the use of "entrepreneurial staff." First, he argues that such a staff provides distorted or "partial" information.[40] Because the entrepreneurial staff generates an increase in the number of hearings and amendments, Malbin argues that each legislator becomes so overextended that he cannot personally become involved in legislative decision making.[41] Finally, Malbin points out that legislative deliberation has been replaced by "staff negotiations."[42] Malbin concludes that a nonpartisan, neutral staff serves Congress better than does the entrepreneurial staff because it does not inject itself into policy making. By restoring the deliberative function to the members themselves, Congress will better serve the national interest because the members will then concentrate on only those issues of most importance to their constituencies. It is only because of the existence of a legislative staff, he argues, that members have the resources to spread themselves so broadly over so many issues and to distance themselves from the logrolling so important to forging a national consensus in a nation as diverse as the United States.

Malbin has a point. The examples are legion of the excessive powers and authority exerted by staff. After the passage of the Regulatory Flexibility Act of 1980, which reduced the impact of regulations on small business, one staff member said no senator had read the legislation—and he was right. Furthermore, in a related piece of legislation, the staffs of the Governmental Affairs and Judiciary committees were entrusted by their respective leaders to hammer out a compromise; the subsequent product is another example of legislation not by committee, but by staff. More often than not, committee staffs write committee reports, which are never read by any committee member, but nonetheless become critical legislative history. Some committee staffs have extracted policy promises from nominees, both judicial and executive, by threatening to slow down the confirmation process. Likewise, staff members threaten to "kill" a bill unless it is modified to meet their member's alleged concerns, even on issues to which members are not committed or did not even know about. With a good poker face, staff members—through promises, threats, and cajoling—often accomplish policy objectives without the member's awareness. Frequently, a Senate staff member places a "hold" on legislation without the member's advance knowledge. And finally, many members vote on amendments after a thirty-second briefing or a three-line memo from the staff. Of course, the power of a staff varies with the different management style of different members. Some members delegate tremendous authority to their staffs; others use staff in a very limited, controlled fashion.

Despite the problems of an entrepreneurial staff, so well articulated by Malbin, the benefits of an aggressive, personalized staff exceed the costs both from the perspective of the member and the Congress as an institution. As Malbin himself would concede, without an aggressive staff it is unlikely that Congress would be able to maintain its role as an assertive policy initiator and vigorous overseer of the executive branch. Although Malbin cites the *Federalist Papers* to support his thesis that staff impedes the deliberative process, the most fundamental thesis of the *Federalist Papers* militates toward the opposite result:

> But the great security against a gradual concentration of the several powers in the same department, consists in giving to those who administer each department the necessary constitutional means and personal motives to resist encroachments of the others. . . . Ambition must be made to counter ambition. The interest of the man must be connected with the constitutional rights of the place.[43]

Without staff, the ambitions of each member, each committee, and the Congress as a whole would not be well served, and the ambitions of the legislative branch could not possibly counter the equally strident ambitions of a much better staffed executive branch. Thus, the doctrine of checks and balances would not work without an aggressive staff.

Moreover, the Malbin thesis is a bit overstated. Members do participate to a large degree in deliberations on the major issues that affect their local and national constituencies. Anyone who has spent a large amount of time on the floor, in party caucuses, and in committee mark-ups realizes that the issues aired publicly represent a distillation of all the issues upon which the staff failed to forge consensus. Therefore, the members themselves work out the big policy differences, whether through compromise or floor votes. As the clerk reads the endless quorum calls during a legislative fight in the Senate, clusters of senators huddle in a corner trying to work out the details of an amendment. Sometimes staff members are there to help, but the decisions are made by the elected representatives. In the Democratic party caucus over Reagan's budget reductions, the fights were often acerbic, but the members themselves—not the staff who were barred from the room—worked out the compromise on amendments that was acceptable to all: school lunch funds would be fought for, legal services would not. Even in the committee, where an entrepreneurial staff can exercise the most clout, the members themselves must resolve the major controversies on issues of enough concern to generate public attention. The staff may have considerable leverage over marginal issues, but it does not extend to the major concerns of constituents. The arm-twisting and peer-group pressure necessary to enact any piece of controversial legislation remains the prerogative of the members—much as some staff would like to think otherwise. Consequently, leaving the details of legislation to the staff is not harmful but rational, sane, and effective, for then the members are free to "wheel and deal" on the big issues.

A closing thought: An overly aggressive entrepreneurial committee staff can be harmful from one institutional viewpoint. It places inordinate power in the hands of committees at the expense of a more centralized policy coordination by the party leadership. It is hardly surprising that the role of the leadership in both the House and the Senate is so minimal in developing coordinated strategies and policies when one considers that the party leadership has a smaller staff than that possessed by even the smallest committee. Perhaps a staff of experts loyal to the party leadership and more aggressive on behalf of the party would enable Congress to act more efficiently, promptly, and effectively in sorting out legislative priorities. The problem of party strength and coordination is particularly acute when the party affiliation of the leadership differs from that of the president. With a more centralized, party-oriented staff to complement, not supplant, committee staffs, it is possible that the Congress could serve as a more effective counterpoint to the president.

NINE

RITES OF PASSAGE I

"Laws are like sausages.
It is better not to know how they are made."

he process of enacting legislation is indeed complex and much criticized. Throughout the history of the Congress, critics have complained of the special interests that influence, and sometimes corrupt, the legislative process. In 1912 President Woodrow Wilson remarked: "The Government of the United States at present is a foster-child of the special interests."[1] Today this concern has intensified[2] as political action committees (PACs) magnify the power of special interests in election battles and therefore in Congress.

Other critics of the legislative process claim that Congress is too slow and unresponsive to rapidly changing political needs. They point with frustration to the various hoops through which legislation must jump before enactment and decry the barriers erected by the congressional power structure to block popular pieces of legislation. They complain about the seniority system, which immunizes committees from changing political winds, and point with derision at such congressional procedures as the filibuster, which permit minorities to slow down and even kill legislation. Their perspective, that Congress follows an antiquated, archaic legislative process, which cannot respond rapidly to imperative national desires, is not without merit.

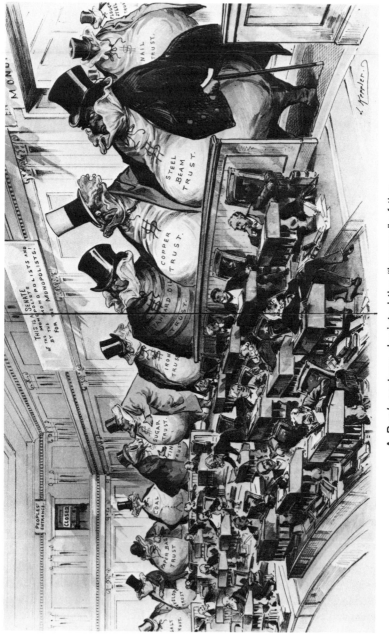

A *Puck* cartoon depicted the "bosses" of the Senate, who represented special interests.

Still another criticism arrives at the opposite conclusion: Congress is irresponsible in that it can, with lightning speed and in defiance of predictability, pass amendments on the floor without adequate consideration of their long-range ramifications. This attack is most often—and accurately—launched against the Senate, which, because of the absence of rules on germaneness or advance notice, can adopt amendments of sweeping dimensions with a legislative legerdemain that leaves observers breathless.

Finally, critics complain that Congress, by its own ineptitude and lack of energy, has relegated itself to the back seat in the legislative process, doomed to follow the cues of the executive branch. Some members of Congress even adhere to the tenet: "The President proposes; the Congress disposes." As Joseph Califano, former special assistant to President Johnson and health, education, and welfare secretary under President Carter, said:

> The Congress is presently the separate but unequal branch of the federal government... [and] responsibility for its separate but unequal status rests largely with the Congress itself. The Congress is dependent upon the executive branch for most of its information, with an occasional and too often superficial assist from outside experts. Congress has ignored the revolution in analytical technology.... The stark fact is that neither Congress nor any of its committees has the consistent capability—without almost total reliance on the informational and analytical resources of the executive branch—of developing coherent, large-scale federal programs.

> From this vantage point, Congress is no longer the author of legislation but merely rubber-stamps the directives of the executors. This criticism seems particularly accurate when the majority of the Congress and the President are of the same party.[3]

Like most criticisms, there is some degree of truth here and some insight. Congress is sometimes too responsive to political pressure and sometimes not responsive enough. It has acted both too slowly and too precipitously. It has followed the president too meekly and on other occasions obstreperously thwarted his will.

The heart of the matter lies in the challenge of being both "responsive" and "responsible." The quest to reconcile these two competing goals helps to explain the complex, labyrinthine process to which most legislation is exposed. The history of congressional procedure is, in large part, the quest of Congress to be both responsive to changing political consensus and responsible in deliberation on the nation's needs.

This chapter describes the seven-stage legislative cycle. Each stage in the legislative process marks an important decision-point in its development.

Throughout the history of a piece of legislation, its contents are affected by changing political forces. Long after a bill has been enacted, the electoral process continues to govern the extent to which legislation is enforced by the executive branch, the interpretation given to it by judges, and the level of funding and attention it receives from Congress in the budgetary and oversight process. The legislative cycle is dynamic—it never ends. Thus, although the chapter focuses primarily on the congressional process, it also briefly examines the impact of the executive and judicial branches on the development of legislation.

STAGE ONE—
LEGISLATION BEFORE INTRODUCTION

Introduction of a Bill

Nothing could be simpler than the physical act of "introducing" a piece of legislation into the legislative arena. A senator or congressman merely walks to the chamber floor and drops a document called a "bill" into the "hopper." Indeed, on the Senate side, it is not necessary that the senator himself perform this task; he simply signs the legislation in his office and sends it to the floor. The hopper is a removable box attached to the side of the clerk's desk. When the House or the Senate is in session, bills can be introduced. Any piece of paper properly placed in the hopper becomes a bill. Thousands of bills are introduced each year. In the Ninety-sixth Congress 12,583 bills were introduced (but only 977 enacted). A bill is sometimes handwritten by a member acting on the spur of the moment, sometimes the handiwork of expert drafters employed by the government or the private sector. Sometimes, a member seeks to disclaim some of the authorship by indicating that the bill is being introduced "by request," although the identity of the requester is usually not revealed in the bill itself.

The disincentives to introducing legislation are few. Because most legislation never passes, no stigma is attached to the introduction of legislation that dies a natural death. Occasionally, of course, legislation comes back to haunt a political career. For example, during the 1980 presidential campaign, liberal candidate John Anderson suffered some embarrassment when the press discovered that he had introduced, in his early political career as a congressman from Illinois, a constitutional amendment to require the president and certain other constitutional officers to be Christian. Nonetheless, in most situations, the introduction of legislation carries little responsibility and provides an important symbolic vehicle that allows a member to show his constituent that he cares about an issue.

Origin of Legislation and the Role of Lobbyists

The Member as Originator
The substance of a piece of legislation is sometimes, but not always, generated by the congressman who introduces it. A message from an aggrieved constituent or a problem reported in a newspaper often prompts a congressman to instruct his staff to draft legislation to rectify the problem. For example, a high school student once complained to a congressman that there were federal "concentration camps" near his home. Dubious of the validity of these claims, the congressman instructed a staff member to look into the allegation; upon discovering that there were indeed such camps, the congressman launched a successful effort to eliminate the camps. The camps had been "authorized" in 1950 as contingent detention facilities for "dissidents"; while never put in operation, the existence of these camps was chilling. Other legislation stems from personal commitments and campaign pledges. North Carolina Republican Senator John East, newly elected with the aid of the Moral Majority on an anti-abortion platform, felt so personally committed to fight for federal legislation to prohibit abortions that he antagonized even the Republican leadership by his single-minded pursuit of the passage of his "Human Life Legislation" early in the Ninety-seventh Congress.[4]

Occasionally, legislation is generated not by the member, but by his staff or interested experts.[5] Professor Robert Eisner, chairman of Northwestern University's Economics Department, was a strong supporter of job credits in the tax code. He provided the idea and the supporting data to the coauthor for introduction and approval by the Ways and Means Committee and, ultimately, the Congress.

Special-Interest Groups
If successful in persuading a member to introduce their legislation, special-interest groups labor long in doing the legwork in lobbying the bill and preparing materials for its passage. "Special-interest" legislation is of critical importance. In the First Amendment to the Constitution, which guarantees the right to "petition the government for a redress of grievances," the founders recognized that affected constituents are those most likely to propose legislation that will respond to real, not theoretical, problems. Many members adhere to the principle "If it ain't broke, don't fix it." Lobbyists are most likely to know what is broken. Thus, although lobbyists are often castigated, they provide an important source of information available to staff and members.

Of the many different kinds of interest groups, one, the public-interest group, spawned in the post-Vietnam, -Watergate era, lobbies for reforms in behalf of large segments of the population who are not represented members of a specific group. Common Cause, for example, has been instrumental in achieving "good government" reforms of the conflict-of-interest and campaign finance laws. Public-interest groups—the American Civil Liberties Union, the Consumer Federation of America, Congress Watch, Common Cause, and the environmental groups—rely primarily on grass-roots fund raising to run their operations. Because of limited financial resources, they exert pressure on the legislative process primarily through their access to the media, which can whip up public support for a proposal with nationwide editorials and news coverage.[6]

Business is a major source of legislative initiatives. Understandably, each industry works to protect its own interest. Unlike the public-interest community, business has the financial clout through PACs to make a quite substantial impact on the legislative process. One company, for example, the largest timber cutting company in America, gave lavishly in the 1980 campaign to candidates in its home state of Oregon and in the presidential race; subsequently, its general counsel was nominated to be the assistant secretary of agriculture in charge of the national forests. It is not surprising that the American Telephone & Telegraph Company contributed largely to those key members of the Commerce Committee who would be examining legislation to deregulate the communications industry. (Hedging its bets in 1980, AT&T supplied campaign funds to all the major presidential candidates.[7]) The 23 PACs sponsored by AT&T in the 1980 elections spent and collected more than twice as much money as did the PACs of any other U.S. corporation.

Labor unions also play an active role in the lobbying process. The originator of PAC campaign finance, labor has always gone to the Hill to get protective legislation. In addition to funding, labor provides workers and grass-roots support during election fights to pro-labor and liberal candidates, who consequently hesitate to lock horns with the labor establishment.

The organizations of local and state officials have strong stakes in the outcome of legislation. Fully one-third of all expenditures outside of defense and social security in 1980 took the form of grants-in-aid to state and local governments.[8] States, cities, towns, counties, public school systems, labor unions of public employees, all have jumped into the legislative arena with proposals and suggestions to enhance their share of the federal financial pie. The National League of Cities and Towns woos congressmen and senators to increase revenue sharing and to enact programs dealing with the plight of the cities and other urban problems that vitally affect local resources.

Not all legislation inspired by special interests is concerned with new programs or additional protection. Many federal programs are not permanent but are terminated at a specific time. The termination point usually prompts major legislative battles between groups who hope to extend the legislation and those who hope to seize the opportunity to kill or modify it. In the Ninety-seventh Congress, the historic Voting Rights Act was due to terminate.[9] Hispanic and black groups, who viewed the act as the most effective vehicle for ensuring their continued voting rights, grew concerned when the new chairman of the Senate Judiciary Committee announced that he did not favor extension of this legislation. The administration hemmed and hawed over the bill. The groups concerned, led by respected Congressman Don Edwards, put together a large coalition of ethnic and civil rights groups to fight for an extension of the legislation. Likewise, termination of a two-year federal statute promoting the use of credit cards prompted a major battle by major credit card companies, led by the American Express Company, to extend this legislation. Although Senator William Proxmire of Wisconsin led a valiant effort to prevent the extension, he could get only 41 votes in the Senate.[10]

The President as Chief Lobbyist

Although the administration and the administrative agencies are theoretically precluded from lobbying on the Hill, they are, in fact, a major force in the initiation of considerable legislation. Because the president can play an aggressive role in initiating legislation, some scholars refer to him as the "Chief Legislator."[11] Most presidents, ruefully pointing to their low batting average in getting their proposals through Congress, deny that title. However, the president has at his disposal more resources to pressure the Congress than the most wealthy lobbyist. In the first 100 days of his administration, President Reagan took a personal interest in lobbying for his major legislative initiatives. With breakfasts, lunches, phone calls, and modest but nevertheless coveted mementos of presidential attention, he successfully pressured members of both houses and both parties to support his economic program. His enhanced popularity in the country, following the attempted assassination, made it even more difficult for individual members to resist the president's blandishments, particularly after he personally agreed not to campaign against anyone who backed his proposals.

Often a president sends legislative "packages" to the Hill. Such a package is frequently preceded by a presidential message to Congress and to the country, explaining the crisis that occasions the president's concern. President Carter sought to have Congress address the energy crisis through such a package and approach. First Carter told the country on national television that the energy crisis was the "moral equivalent of war." Then, in a speech before Congress he outlined his far-reaching proposals, including the establishment of the separate Department of Energy. He then requested the speaker and others to introduce the specific bills that would effect the program he had outlined. Despite Carter's perceived difficulties with Congress, most of the proposals were adopted in the form that Carter sought. Only the tax proposals deviated substantially from the president's requests. Several committee chairmen, although disagreeing with Carter's specifics, nevertheless introduced his proposals "by request," a not uncommon occurrence, especially when the president is of the same party as the chairmen.

Although the president, as head of the executive branch, uses the Office of Management and Budget to keep the agencies in line, many agencies find ways to press their own perspectives and needs on Capitol Hill. This is particularly true of the "independent" agencies, which are not subject to so tight a degree of presidential supervision. Cabinet officers are free to play separate roles on the Hill, but a secretary who leaves the presidential line does so at his peril. Joseph Califano was well known and regarded on the Hill during the Carter administration because of his prior experience in government and on the Hill during the Lyndon Johnson administration. Although Carter and Califano both proclaimed interest in passing health-care legislation, their approaches were sufficiently different to cause tension. Califano let the world know that he opposed the creation of a Department of Education, which was President Carter's pet proposal. Largely as a result of his independence, Califano was unceremoniously fired midway through his term.

Most federal officials make their own deals with Hill leaders, but they are not quite so blatant in their efforts to obstruct administration initiatives. The problem of controlling the agencies in their contact with the Hill is particularly acute after a changeover of administrations, because many holdovers from the previous administration cannot be fired for one reason or another. Hill staffers who have good contacts in the bureaucracy can undermine administration incentives by obtaining information to which they could not otherwise have access.

When the party affiliation of the congressional majority party and the White House differs, any pretense of cooperation usually vanishes pretty quickly. In the Ninety-seventh Congress, Speaker Tip O'Neill pledged cooperation in the most general terms, but it was soon clear that on key issues, like the membership of the Ways and Means Committee, the budget-cut priorities, the tax program, and the future of social security, the Democrats would not follow the lead of the president. The president, when working with members of his own party, obviously must encourage and facilitate discussion between Congress and the executive branch. However, when party affiliation is not shared, the president can use strategies that plant dissension among the opposing party. Open warfare is often pronounced. Because of his access to the media and his extensive array of "carrots" and "sticks," a president is often effective in lobbying for administration packages, even over the opposition of leading members of the Congress, whether in the opposition or his own party.

Legislating in Crisis

Much legislation is inspired by crisis. When the citizens of Love Canal in New York State suffered from exposure to the toxic waste deposited by chemical companies, they became a national media attention-getter. The introduction of Superfund legislation, which provided federal monies to clean up toxic waste dumps, was immediate and its passage came with almost unprecedented speed. When the Chrysler Corporation threatened to go bankrupt and thus create massive unemployment, legislation was promptly introduced and passed to provide loan guarantees to Chrysler. In short, when the emergency is sufficiently critical and the public outcry is sufficiently loud, congressional reaction is usually swift.

Constituent-Oriented Legislation

Many members sponsor legislation to benefit local industry and constituents. Legislation for the benefit of aircraft manufacturers, railroads, the automobile industry—all have local champions who seek to persuade their colleagues that what is good for the sponsor's parochial concerns is also good for the whole country. Every year holiday resolutions are introduced to please special groups and their commercial promoters. In addition to the weighty matters of the moment, the prestigious Senate Judiciary Committee considers such important legislation as National Mime Week, National Jogging Day, and National Grandparents Day (which pleases grandparents, grandchildren, and greeting card manufacturers with equal delight).

Congressmen introduce private relief bills to take care of egregious problems faced by an individual constituency. Because the military is legally immune from lawsuit, legislation was introduced to compensate a family for the loss of a son who drowned when he was forced by the army to cross a lake even though the army knew he did not know how to swim.

The doctrine of sovereign immunity protects the government from lawsuit except in instances expressly stated in the Constitution and subsequent laws. Congress has created some generic exceptions to this doctrine, the most important of which is the Federal Tort Claims Act. This particular act allows citizens to sue the government if they are injured by any federal vehicle, be it a mail truck or a low-flying military plane. In addition to generic legislation, Congress has the power, frequently exercised, to allow a specific claim, such as that of the soldier's family. The House and Senate Judiciary committees usually maintain separate subcommittees to process these claims. The views of the appropriate federal agency are sought to determine the worthiness of the claim and the appropriate payment. Because subsequent claims are usually brought on the same basis, the precedent being set is of some concern. If the subcommittee disallows the claim, it becomes an uphill struggle for the claimant to get the claim allowed. The claim always takes the form of a "private" bill, introduced by a member to provide for the "relief" of the claimant by name.

Numerous private immigration bills are introduced each year. In past congresses, the mere introduction of such a bill allowed the immigrant to stay in the United States while the bill was pending, even though immigration authorities were seeking to deport the individual involved. To stay in the country indefinitely, an immigrant needed only one friendly congressman. However, in 1969 the House changed its rule; mere introduction of a bill no longer provided a stay. The Senate continues to operate under the old system, although senators are more wary of introducing such bills. (The Abscam cases were planned, in part, around phony Arab sheiks who were seeking the intervention of members of Congress to help them stay in the United States.)

Congressmen introduce legislation to benefit their areas, like authorization for a dam or an amendment to provide monies for a public park. After trying for many years, Senator Paul Douglas of Illinois finally succeeded in passing a bill to establish the Dunes National Lakeshore. His task was particularly onerous because the land he sought to protect was in Indiana. Although the lakeshore was used primarily by people from Illinois for recreational purposes, traditional congressional wisdom dictated that the wishes of the Indiana delegation would prevail on anything that looked like parochial legislation. Although Douglas argued assiduously that the dunes area was a "national treasure," it was not until he received help from Indiana legislators and the backing of President John Kennedy that the bill passed. (In one of his dune speeches, Douglas said that when he was first elected to the Senate he wanted to save the world; now as retirement time approached, he was willing to settle for saving the dunes. He barely made it.)

Legislation Initiated by "the Other" Chamber

Numerous pieces of legislation are sent from the House to the Senate and vice versa. Often, particularly when legislation is sponsored by the administration, identical bills are introduced in both the Senate and the House. However, legislation that passes one chamber is not guaranteed to pass the other. The comprehensive revision of the federal criminal code that passed in the Senate in the Ninety-fifth Congress never had a fighting chance in the House. Although sunset legislation succeeded in obtaining Senate passage, it had less appeal in the House. Conversely, legislation providing for the public financing of congressional campaigns and general reforms of the election laws passed the House only to be lobbied to death in the Senate. The Constitution provides that "all bills for raising Revenue" shall originate in the House, but that the Senate may amend such bills. The Senate Finance Committee has long sought ways to circumvent that restriction and has sometimes used the power of amendment to take bills making small changes in revenue laws and to convert them into major tax proposals in the Senate, an effort that is always greeted with indignation and outrage in the House Ways and Means Committee. Sometimes movement in one house will set the other chamber into action.

It is difficult to believe that the country's founders envisioned the full impact of bicameralism. The interplay between the House and the Senate, which are totally separate and, for all practical purposes, equal in power— but are completely dependent on each other to pass any legislation or otherwise perform their functions—defies description by even the most avid Hill-watchers. Jealousy, suspicion, condescension, distrust, petulance, are only some of the angry emotions expressed by the members of one body toward the members of the other, especially when their committees share a legislative jurisdiction, or when they come from the same state. Yet they cannot succeed in any endeavor unless they cooperate.

Perhaps the most astonishing aspect of the two-chamber Congress is the lack of communication between the two bodies; indeed, it is practically a miracle that any legislation passes, given the differences in the perspectives, the constituencies, and the procedures. Previous reference was made to the variety of groups within each chamber that work on various projects and exchange information. However, no such groups operate bicamerally, with the possible exception of the Members of Congress for Peace Through Law, which was most active during the Vietnam War. Although state delegations in each chamber meet occasionally on a bipartisan basis, they seldom meet on a bicameral basis. (The House members never refer to the Senate by name; it is always called "the other body.")

Instead, lobby groups (including the administration) act as lines of communication between the two bodies. Staff find out more from lobbyists about activities on "the other side" than they do from picking up the phone and calling counterparts on the other committee. Occasionally, however, particularly with legislation concerning a geographical region or a specific district, senators and congressmen from the same state join forces to work for its passage.

Pre-introduction Strategy

The strategy for introducing a bill is all-important, for it sometimes determines its fate. Several key decisions have to be made. Is the legislation symbolic, with no intention of passage? If so, such factors as who will co-sponsor the bill and its potential for media coverage may not be significant. However, in most cases, even if the bill does not have a "snowball's chance in hell," consideration of such factors is essential if the legislation is to get the maximum political mileage.

Co-sponsorship Politics

Who co-sponsors a bill is vital to its passage. Legislation co-sponsored by a committee chairman and the ranking minority member has a good chance of passage. In the Ninety-sixth and Ninety-seventh Congress, both Senator Edward Kennedy and Senator Strom Thurmond supported the criminal code package, thus ensuring that it would at least be reported out of committee— a major hurdle. Similarly, in the Ninety-seventh Congress, Nevada Senator Paul Laxalt, a conservative Republican, who chaired the Regulatory Reform Subcommittee, met at length with Vermont Senator Pat Leahy, a liberal Democrat and the ranking minority member of that subcommittee, to ensure that Senator Leahy's concerns were met—*before* introduction of legislation. Leahy's co-sponsorship was guaranteed to smother any major opposition to the regulatory reform package.

The co-sponsorship game can be played by persons who are not members of the committee to which the legislation will be referred. As a result of the 1980 trucking deregulation legislation, numerous truckers, including the American Trucking Association, were concerned about the loss of value of their operating trucking rights. They wanted legislation that would provide a tax write-off for the loss of these rights. The legislation, although referred to the Finance Committee, was co-sponsored by the chairman and ranking minority member of the Commerce Committee, which has jurisdiction over the trucking industry. Their co-sponsorship gave the bill clout in the Finance Committee, which it could not otherwise have had, and it was eventually enacted as part of the comprehensive tax legislation of 1981.

An absence of co-sponsors may indicate either that the bill is entirely symbolic, and will not be pressed by the member, or that the bill is a controversial hot potato. But the reverse is not necessarily true. Having numerous co-sponsors does not guarantee easy sailing. Maine Senator Edmund Muskie's sunset legislation in the Ninety-sixth Congress had seventy-seven co-sponsors but was never reported out of committee. In the House, the legislative veto proposal (symbolically numbered H.R. 1776), sponsored by Georgia Congressman Eliott H. Levitas, routinely mustered a majority of the House as co-sponsors but for years did not reach a floor vote because of leadership opposition.

Media Trumpets

The introduction of a bill sometimes involves "packaging" worthy of Madison Avenue. After the chief sponsor has marshaled his co-sponsors, he announces a press conference to which all the co-sponsors are invited, along with any interest groups that will lend credence to the legislative effort. Amid props, charts, graphics, and perhaps a witness to tell the press why the proposed legislation is so desperately needed and why the sponsors are a credit to their profession, the trumpets, symbolically, blare. A physical package is often delivered to each co-sponsor—a copy of the bill itself, a summary of the salient provisions of the bill for popular consumption, and a press release that describes the bill in purple prose but leaves the sponsor's name blank. (As mentioned earlier, in *district* politics, each co-sponsor is expected to pretend that the legislation is solely his idea.)

Shortly after the press conference, to put information about the new bill in the *Congressional Record*, the chief sponsor will speak about the bill on the floor, either during the Morning Hour in the Senate, the one-minute speech time in the House, or as a Special Order (when he and his co-sponsors can talk at length after the legislative business is done on any one day). Reprints of the *Record* are mailed to the home folks. Publication in the *Record* also provides the sponsors with an opportunity to invite additional sponsorship and interest from their colleagues.

The last piece of the package may be a "Dear Colleague" letter, which announces the bill to all or to a selected group of colleagues and invites co-sponsorship.

Wooing Special Interests

Gathering interest-group support for legislation is another critical step in the pre-introduction phase. Endorsements of legislation from major groups do not drop like manna from the heavens. Alterations are often made in the legislation before introduction to accommodate the wishes of a support group. For example, the one-page Voting Rights Act of 1981 required weeks of work by the staffs of the House and the Senate Judiciary committees to accommodate all the Hispanic, black, and civil rights groups. The introduction of any crime legislation necessitates discussions with both civil liberties groups and the law-enforcement organizations prior to introduction in order to eliminate any unnecessary battles.

In short, the politically astute strategy is to minimize conflict and define lines of agreement before the introduction of a bill, particularly when such legislation has clearly anticipated opponents and proponents. The necessary coalitions are much more difficult to forge after introduction. In the Ninety-sixth Congress, Republican Senator Richard Schweiker of Pennsylvania and Democratic Senator Harrison Williams of New Jersey introduced a bill to rewrite the Occupational Safety and Health legislation. Although Williams as chairman of the Labor and Human Resources Committee had been a longtime friend of labor, he was bitterly denounced by his labor constituents for giving this legislation credibility. He had not done the political homework necessary to minimize the outcry from those constituents vital to the enactment of the legislation. The polarization on the bill was so severe that it was never reported out of committee.

Drafting Legislation

The drafting of the legislation, a mundane, boring, but necessary pre-introduction step, is sometimes done by professional law firms or by lobby organizations. Occasionally, a staff member tries his or her hand at writing the legislation. Often the administration provides legislative language. Probably the best two resources available are the Legislative Counsel's office and the Congressional Research Service (CRS).

Poorly drafted legislation frequently causes problems. In 1979 Senator Dale Bumpers of Arkansas introduced a technical amendment to reform the standards of judicial review of agency regulations in the Administrative Procedure Act. Although the legislation made non-lawyers' eyes glaze over, it had far-reaching ramifications for the legal community. Inaccurate and imprecise as initially drafted, it was subject to criticism from all quarters. After considerable revision by the American Bar Association and some of the best administrative law professors in the country, the legislation was refined to withstand technical criticism and could then be criticized on its merits. (The Senate does not always stop to read; when Senator Bumpers originally introduced his proposal in the Ninety-sixth Congress, it passed the Senate by a 2-to-1 margin, warts and all. Its passage was perhaps aided by Bumpers' proclamation: "You're either for regulatory reform and with me, or against regulatory reform and against me.")

Bills as Symbols

Many bills represent ideas whose time has not yet come. The purpose of introducing them is to begin the process of building a national consensus that will gradually militate toward passage of the bill. When Senator Kennedy introduced his health-care bill yet again in the Ninety-sixth Congress, no one seriously thought that it had a chance of passage. President Carter wanted his own phased-in version of health care and Russell Long, chairman of the Finance Committee, wanted coverage for only catastrophic illness. (Indeed, the bill was never reported out of the subcommittee.) Nonetheless, just as Medicaid took almost twenty years to pass, supporters of health-care legislation recognized that a serious effort had been made to focus national attention on the need for a comprehensive approach to the health-care crisis. In similar fashion, Representative Bella Abzug used her ability with the press to gain national attention for women's issues.

Similarly, Moral Majority Republicans effectively use the media to highlight their legislative initiatives. Senator Jesse Helms was not afraid to use the press to spotlight views on busing, school prayer, and abortion. Hearings are often used to flag an issue for the media's attention. Senator Orrin Hatch, a Republican from Utah, scheduled hearings to consider the problem of sexual harassment in the workplace. The press loved seeing Phyllis Schlafly, the nemesis of the feminist community, testify in front of whirring cameras that harassment was not a problem for "the virtuous woman."[12] The use of proposed legislation as a vehicle to spark national attention gives great power to those who can use it most effectively.

Jurisdiction

Committee Referral

The final and perhaps most important step in the pre-introduction phase is to ensure referral of the legislation to the committee that will be most likely to pass it. As stated in Chapter 7, the importance of jurisdiction, at both the committee and subcommittee level, cannot be overstated.

The terms of referral are critical. Legislation may be referred to one committee or to two or more committees jointly, or sequentially, that is, to one committee after another. Legislation referred to two committees can be killed by either committee. Consequently, in advance of introduction, sponsors of legislation subject to joint or sequential referral insist that the terms of referral specify a defined period of time within which the second committee is to report out its version of the legislation. Sequential jurisdiction often ensures a legislative fight. In the Ninety-sixth Congress both the Senate Select Committee on Intelligence and the Judiciary Committee had jurisdiction over legislation to outlaw the publication of the names of CIA employees regardless of the source of those names or the intent of the publication. Obviously, the perspective of the committee entrusted with protection of intelligence activities was different from that of the Judiciary Committee, which is concerned with upholding the rights set forth in the First Amendment. The bill did not pass. However, in the Ninety-seventh Congress the legislation reemerged and passed, with the perspective of the Intelligence Committee prevailing over that of the Judiciary Committee.

In the Senate referral decisions are announced by the presiding officer but actually determined by the parliamentarian. Referrals must receive unanimous consent and generally do. To challenge a referral ruling, a senator appeals the ruling of the chair and thus a floor fight ensues. But this is rare. Usually the majority and minority leaders, together with staff, hammer out a compromise over jurisdiction before a bill is introduced.

In the House the speaker has the final word on referral. The jockeying is of a different nature. Consultations with the parliamentarian and other staff in the speaker's office ensure against an unfavorable and unexpected referral. Because many overlapping jurisdictions occur among House committees, the speaker can justify sequential referral to two or more committees. The added roadblock of an extra committee to screen a bill frequently portends the death of the bill.

Advance consultation with the parliamentarian sometimes provides helpful advice for a bill's sponsor. Variations of the legislation to repeal the "federal concentration camps" law had failed when the bills were referred to the House Un-American Activities Committee, an unfriendly forum for such bills. After consultations with the parliamentarian, the sponsor revised the bill to assure its assignment to the House Judiciary Committee. When the Judiciary Committee acted favorably and reported the bill to the floor, the chairman of the Un-American Activities Committee could only complain petulantly that his turf had been invaded. But the mischief was done and the bill passed.

Subcommittee Referral

As a bill can be referred to a friendly or unfriendly committee, so also can its fate be sealed by the subcommittee to which it is referred. Subcommittee referral is often determined before the introduction of a bill. The decision by Judiciary Committee Chairman Peter Rodino to refer revision of the criminal code to the subcommittee chaired by Michigan Congressman John Conyers, Jr., boded ill for any comprehensive rewrite of the code in the Ninety-seventh Congress, for Conyers was a known opponent of the legislation. In the previous Congress the code legislation, referred to a friendlier subcommittee chaired by Massachusetts Congressman Father Robert Drinan, had come close to passage. In the Ninety-seventh Congress the Senate Republican leadership signaled its displeasure when it referred legislative veto legislation to a subcommittee chaired by Iowa Senator Charles Grassley, a freshman, instead of to the subcommittee of Senator Paul Laxalt, a more senior member. The administration, which did not support the legislation, had sent a request for burial.

A Senate chairman often keeps legislation he supports at full committee to keep a firm rein on its course. This practice has no parallel in the House where subcommittee jurisdiction is hallowed and protected by the Subcommittee Bill of Rights adopted in the 1970s. The House Ways and Means Committee, which adopted the subcommittee structure in the mid-1970s under pressure from House reformers, took a page from the Senate book and decided to keep all major tax bills at full committee for action. As there was no existing subcommittee turf to be protected, the committee members agreed, for at full committee they could all be in on all the action rather than restricted to the particular area of a subcommittee.

Timing

Bills introduced early in the first session of Congress have a chance, at least, of passage. Every Congress has two sessions, each lasting a year. The first session begins in the January immediately following the November election. Bills are numbered, usually in the order of introduction. Congressmen jockey to get symbolic numbers, particularly numbers like S.1 or H.R. 1776. A bill that has not passed by the end of a Congress is dead. It must be reintroduced in the new Congress and the entire legislative rigmarole begins again. Although each bill technically has two whole years for passage, in reality the number of actual legislative days is much smaller. In addition to a month's recess in non-election years and week-long recesses throughout each session, most congresses recess the month before an election to let the members campaign. "Lame duck" congresses are not always convened. Given all the dilatory tactics available to a bill's opponents, even two years is a short time in which to obtain passage. To become law, most bills run the legislative gauntlet in more than one Congress.

In sum, the physical act of introducing legislation is simple, and the costs of introducing a bill that is not intended to pass are negligible. However, to introduce legislation intended to become law is a painstaking task demanding a detailed, sophisticated knowledge of the House and the Senate, the relevant interest groups, the right people in the media, the experts to ensure good bill drafting, and a parliamentarian and a party leader of friendly persuasion. The path of legislation is precarious; without the proper foresight, the chances for a bill-signing ceremony at the White House are minimal.

STAGE TWO—COMMITTEES: SUBCOMMITTEE, FULL COMMITTEE, RULES COMMITTEE

Role of the Subcommittee

As a professor at Princeton University, Woodrow Wilson lamented the omnipotence of congressional committees and described the plight of most legislation as doomed to pass over the "bridge of sighs" into the committee domain, never to be heard from again.[13] True of the committee in Wilson's day, in the last quarter of the twentieth century that description accurately reflects the power of the subcommittee. As subcommittees began to multiply in the 1970s, reforms were passed in both houses to ensure a fair distribution of subcommittee chairmanships and membership. The House passed a Subcommittee Bill of Rights to prevent the authority of subcommittee chairmen from overreaching that of full committee chairmen.

The decentralization of power in the Congress has played havoc with the legislative process. It inhibits coordination and goal-setting by the party leadership. Each subcommittee chair has a vested interest in ensuring that his legislation passes and that competing legislation dies. An inactive subcommittee with no legislative successes is not an asset in reelection campaigns; nor does it identify a member as an "effective" legislator.

Thus, a subcommittee moves instinctively toward action—not inaction—regardless of the wishes of the full committee chairman or the party leadership to place the issue on the congressional back burner.

A subcommittee chairmanship in the Senate comes as a matter of course to a freshman member of the majority party. In the House, however, subcommittee chairmanships come only with seniority. Because they include staff appointments not otherwise available and because they elevate a House member above his peers, House subcommittee chairmanships are more prestigious. The incentive for subcommittee action is particularly great on the House side, because without subcommittee successes, a chairman has few other opportunities to forge a successful legislative record. But incentive can sometimes backfire. Democratic Congressman George Danielson of California, chairman of the House Subcommittee on Administrative Law and Government Relations, was intensely anxious to get *his* regulatory reform bill through the Congress. To insist that the legislation be accorded top priority, he convened a meeting of the House leadership early in the Ninety-seventh Congress. His overzealousness was not well received however. His legislation was not awarded top priority.

In addition to the procedural protections provided by the Subcommittee Bill of Rights, subcommittee expertise in arcane areas further protects their status. Consider the House of Representatives Agriculture Committee, which includes subcommittees for soybeans, cotton, wheat, and forests. Although each member wants to make his own determination on broad policy issues, like the grain embargo, that involve deep emotions and engender strong political constituencies, most members are willing to defer a decision regarding soybeans to a subcommittee that has developed an expertise in soybeans.

Life or Death by Referral

The power of the full committee chairman is usually sufficient to influence the agenda of the subcommittee. A bill is referred to a particular subcommittee for a particular reason. In some cases, the chairman of the full committee wants to kill a bill but avoid the "heat" for its demise. To placate the legislation's proponents, a few perfunctory subcommittee hearings may be scheduled. Often, the legislation simply dies. Most minority bills are doomed to this fate. In the Senate such bills are frequently resurrected as floor amendments. In the House such resurrection is possible only when the Rules Committee provides a rule permitting amendments which are deemed germane to the bill under consideration.

To expedite passage of a bill, however, a committee chairman may retain it at the full committee level. In the Senate, chairmen of full committees tend to be more cavalier in the referral of legislation to subcommittees. A chair who has a strong interest in a bill often refuses to refer it to subcommittee even when the subcommittee has clear jurisdiction. As the new chairman of the Senate Judiciary Committee, Strom Thurmond insisted on keeping the death penalty and the criminal code legislation at full committee. Senator William Roth of Delaware, chairman of the Governmental Affairs Committee, refused to refer his regulatory reform legislation to the appropriate subcommittee even though its chairman, Senator Charles Percy, favored the bill. Depriving a subcommittee of rightful jurisdiction carries some risk, however, and a chairman does not take such action if antagonizing a powerful committee member might result. Senator Williams, for example, did not claim jurisdiction of health-care issues, which rightfully belonged to the subcommittee.

A second reason to refer a bill to subcommittee is to nurture and develop it. Once a subcommittee chair decides to support legislation, the subcommittee stage can be the most important in the whole legislative cycle. Unlike a judicial proceeding, in which both sides of a case have an equal opportunity to present their positions, a subcommittee hearing can be rigged and stacked to present only one viewpoint. A subcommittee chairman has complete control over the witness list. The minority has the right to ask questions, and often the subcommittee chair will permit the minority to hold one day of its own hearings or at least allow minority witnesses to testify.

During hearings on anti-abortion legislation,[14] Senator John East of North Carolina refused to accommodate the demands of the ranking minority member of his subcommittee, Montana Senator Max Baucus. The witness list was so stacked with witnesses friendly to the legislation that even certain anti-abortion senators felt queasy. When the media went for Senator East's jugular, many anti-abortionists feared that their movement had been injured by the bad press.

A subcommittee chair usually permits both opponents and proponents to present their viewpoints fully. The length of the scheduled hearings is a fairly clear signal as to a chairman's desire to move or to kill a piece of legislation. Senator Birch Bayh, longtime chairman of the Constitution Subcommittee, scheduled hearing after hearing, thus managing to kill considerable legislation.

Senator Paul Laxalt, on the other hand, as the new chairman of the Regulatory Reform Subcommittee, in an effort to pass his regulatory reform legislation in the first session, was eager to limit hearings to one day. (He failed to expedite passage; the legislation did not pass the Senate until midway through the second session in March 1981.)

Subcommittee Hearings

At both the full and subcommittee level, hearings are seldom a paragon of spontaneity. They are carefully mapped out and scripted in advance. Under the Senate rules, each witness submits his testimony one day in advance of the hearing to allow the members attending the hearing to know the witness's viewpoint. The staff usually prepares an opening statement, which the chair either reads or submits for the record. Each senator or congressman attending the session may make a statement, in order of party seniority. However, for hearings that are neither controversial nor exciting, the chairman is frequently the only member present. Absent members submit statements, which are recorded in the hearing documents as if the members had been present.

Each witness testifies, in turn, usually by reading a statement with a monotony guaranteed to have soporific effects on all observers. Indeed, to curtail verbose witnesses, a system of multicolored lights is sometimes used to warn a speaker that his time is limited. Following the witness's statement, each member, once again in order of seniority, questions the witness. The questions and answers often proceed according to a well-prepared plan. Many witnesses are savvy enough to call in advance to ask the staff what the questions are likely to be. Mike Pertschuk, the former chairman of the Federal Trade Commission and staff director of the Commerce Committee under Senator Warren Magnuson of Washington, often called the staff, not only to find out the questions, but to plant them. Of course, careful planning some-times backfires.[15]

When an important policy proposal is being considered, top White House representatives usually lead off the hearings, either pro or con. In part, such appearances are media events, with the chairman and the witness—usually a cabinet secretary—posing for press photographs before the hearings start and all the committee members assuming the appropriate television image. In addition, however, the status of the White House participant signals the administration's order of priority for the legislation in question. The higher the level of the official sent to testify, the higher the priority of the bill. Whereas the specifics of the White House position are studied in detail by the staff, the general approach of the president to the measure under consideration is of more interest to committee members.

Sometimes glamorous witnesses are invited to testify, not because of their expertise, but because the media follows in their wake. For example, John Denver sang his testimony on an environmental measure while strumming his guitar.

The subcommittee hearing may be the only forum for witnesses to testify on a bill. Additional full committee hearings are held only when the chairman wants some credit for the legislation.[16] At some point hearing transcripts are published in a bound volume by the U.S. Government Printing Office. Unlike judicial transcripts, however, hearing accounts are edited. Statements and questions and answers are frequently completely edited by staff members. Although they do not represent a verbatim account of the actual give-and-take, the hearings are nonetheless useful research tools for interest groups, the courts, and the administration of the act by officials in the executive branch. In addition, the published account preserves for future congresses— legislation rarely passes the first time it is introduced—a record of earlier proceedings.

Most witnesses attend hearings at their own request. Indeed, considerable behind-the-scenes jockeying often goes on to determine which groups will be allowed to testify. Etiquette demands formal requests from special-interest groups. Opponents may be politely rejected by the chairman or, more often than not, by staff members anxious to showcase their boss's views.

However, special-interest groups sophisticated in the ways of the Hill are cognizant of other access routes: contact with minority subcommittee members or with other members of the full committee; a public or semi-public appeal to the chairman's fairness; an appeal to the congressional leadership. It is difficult to preclude a major and well-respected interest group, like the American Bar Association or the U.S. Chamber of Commerce, from testifying.

Witnesses frequently argue over the order in which they will testify. Ralph Nader has refused to go on a panel with other witnesses and often insists on going first. An elaborate etiquette of witness order involves such questions as: Should a federal judge or a cabinet secretary testify first? Should the chairman of the Council of Economic Advisors testify before the director of the Food and Drug Administration? To maximize his opportunity for media coverage as well as the value of his comments, a witness strives to be placed early on the agenda. The last witnesses in a three-hour hearing are indeed fortunate to find even one committee member still present. And when a hearing runs exceedingly late, the gavel may be turned over to a staff member.

Both the full committee and the subcommittee have the authority to subpoena a witness to testify or to present documents.[17] As with a court subpoena, failure to comply can be penalized with such contempt penalties as fines or imprisonment.[18] The subpoena is usually used in investigative oversight hearings; it is seldom used in a hearing to examine the merits of legislation.

After subcommittee hearings are held, the subcommittee may meet to "mark the bill up" by passing amendments, and report it to full committee. Because subcommittee and full committee "mark-ups" are similar, they will be discussed together in the next section.

Mark-ups

Prior to the reforms of the 1970s, the chairman announced at the conclusion of the hearings that the committee would retire into "executive session" to consider the matters in question. Only staff and committee members were present at these executive sessions, and the exchanges and horse-trading were free and easy.

This comfortable way of proceeding was ended when the rules of both houses were changed to require all such sessions to be open to the public (and the lobbyists and the press) unless the committee, under limited circumstances, voted to close the session. Such "sunshine" reforms are still a matter of controversy, with senior members referring wistfully to the "good old days" when the committee really wrote the bill. Critics of the open sessions complain that legislation is currently written in negotiations prior to the public mark-ups, with the mark-ups merely serving to confirm decisions previously reached.

The first main hurdle to overcome in commencing the mark-up or the exec is to obtain a quorum. In the Senate, the lobbying, begging, pleading, and strategizing to obtain a quorum are hard to believe. A minority that desires to block legislation simply boycotts the exec, thereby forcing the majority to obtain attendance from all its members. To reach a quorum, the busy schedules of the members must be synchronized. A chairman frequently sits alone in a mark-up, with staff members milling around, until one by one the other members gradually drift in. To implement a boycott, the minority members designate a watchdog, or spy, to let them know when the majority finally has its quorum. At that point, the minority files in, ready to do battle. As soon as a majority member leaves, the minority too marches out. No quorum, no proceedings.

Alternative methods for reporting out legislation are available for noncontroversial legislation. In the Senate, by unanimous consent of the members, legislation is "polled out," reported out by written ballot or telephone. Another approach is the "rolling quorum," which permits legislation to be reported out as long as a quorum appeared at some time during a mark-up. Technically insufficient, the rolling quorum is used to report out inconsequential bills and noncontroversial nominees. House subcommittees frequently adopt rules to accommodate the difficulty of obtaining and keeping a quorum. Consideration of the proposed new criminal code involved many, many days of mark-up sessions. The subcommittee adopted a rule, which became known as the "Drinan quorum rule," that allowed the mark-up to proceed as long as Chairman Drinan and at least one other member were present. Necessity often bends the rules of Congress.

It is best to report out legislation in as short a time period as possible. If too many amendments are offered, the quorum is frequently lost. Moreover, an exec that runs too late in the day requires unanimous Senate consent to continue (except execs of the Appropriations and Budget committees). Similarly, in the House only the Ways and Means, the Appropriations, and the Rules committees are allowed to sit while the House is in session. Other committees must obtain unanimous consent to sit during such periods, and such consent is usually only given for hearing proceedings, not mark-ups. (Committee rooms are available near the House chamber for the three committees that are allowed to sit while the House is in session. Because space in the Capitol is very limited, the rooms are small. Consequently, committee meetings held in such rooms are complicated by the "size dynamic." Consideration of a controversial measure is further aggravated by the crowds of lobbyists, media people, and citizens that line the Capitol walls waiting to get in to see the action. The patience of members and the duration of meetings held under such conditions are equally short.)

Execs and mark-ups, like hearings, follow carefully designed agendas. Of course, the best laid plans sometimes go astray. Extremely close votes create dramatic cliff-hangers—dramatic for everyone present but annoying to the chairman who prefers to maintain complete control. On the House side, because of the controversial nature of most tax, social security, and welfare proposals and because of efforts to keep a balance on the committee, the Ways and Means Committee has developed—since Wilbur Mills lost his chairmanship in 1975—a tradition of "enthusiastically" endorsing bills for floor action by a 19 to 18 vote. On the Senate side, split committees are common when major social and economic interests are at stake. In the 1980 debate over the legislation to give consumers and small businesses the right to bring certain antitrust suits, the swing vote was Republican Senator Charles Mathias of Maryland, who was undecided until the exact moment of voting. He had been coaxed, cajoled, and threatened by major business constituents. In addition, his vote could affect his upcoming reelection. The myriads of lobbyists swarming around the exec held their collective breath, as did the staff, which had worked for weeks on the legislation. Finally, Mathias, who had been warned by the business community that a wrong vote would have an adverse impact on his PAC contributions,[19] voted for the consumer interest. The bill never was scheduled for floor debate and never became law. Mathias was reelected, presumably without the aid of his PAC contributions. But in

Democratic Senator Edward Kennedy (Massachusetts)
participating in a Labor Committee mark-up.

the next Congress Mathias was appropriately "penalized" for his transgression by the new chairman, Strom Thurmond, who eliminated the Antitrust Subcommittee rather than let Mathias chair it.

A bill may be filibustered to death in the exec. In some committees limits are placed on the amount of time a senator can speak. Rules sometimes specify that a majority vote, including at least one vote of a minority member, can cut off debate. Limiting debate, however, does not limit the numbers of amendments that can be introduced, and the procedural maneuvering in an exec is as complicated as that on the floor. In the House, because the Rules Committee does not act to limit debate in committee, members are allowed to debate infinite numbers of amendments. Debates are ended only when the chair musters a majority to move the previous question on the bill and report it out.

The true talents of a chairman are most evident in a mark-up. The ability to gavel, to channel debate, and to cut off debate before it can disrupt the "flow" of the bill is a valuable talent. The chairman is careful to preserve the coalition necessary to approve the bill. The members are given enough leeway to "do their thing" but not enough to wreck the bill. The ploys a chairman uses during this delicate operation are many: He can urge a member to offer his proposal as a floor amendment (and say at the same time, "But let's not mess up this bill with a lot of extraneous amendments, no matter how worthy they may be") or as a separate bill. He may remind the member that "the train is going to leave the station" with or without the recalcitrant member aboard. He may promise other goodies down the line. When the going gets rough, the chairman sometimes recesses the committee and calls a majority party caucus. However, a knowledge of the rules and a blunderbuss personality are usually sufficient to usher through a piece of legislation, assuming it has the votes and the quorum.

The Committee Report

Legislation cannot be scheduled for floor action until the chamber has had three calendar days to consider the committee report (subject to waiver by unanimous consent). Sometimes the report is prepared by the subcommittee and adopted by the full committee. The report is most often drafted by the staff, occasionally by lobbyists or the administration. The minority files dissenting or separate views, published in the report. The time for filing minority views is short. However, the failure to file minority views in the report does not preclude dissent through floor debate, which is always available. Dissenting views usually forecast the opening shots of the upcoming floor battle. If properly prepared, they set the terms of the engagement and the specifics on which the dissenters intend to wage their effort to defeat or amend the bill.

Each report, by rule, must contain certain items: the actual wording of the bill, showing by the use of italics and brackets the precise changes occasioned by the bill in existing law (called "Ramseyering a bill," originally proposed by Congressman Christian Ramseyer of Iowa); a summary of the alterations of existing law; the impact of the legislation on the budget and federal regulations; a full discussion of the merits of the legislation; and a recording of the roll-call vote. The report, however, is relatively insignificant for purposes of floor action. At best, it serves to educate the legislative assistants of non-committee members. However, its public relations value is considerable. Because the report is generally written by proponents of the legislation, neither the problems nor the opposition's viewpoint is highlighted. The problems are sometimes described in minority reports, but these are not always written.

The committee report also serves an important judicial purpose. Courts frequently rely on it to discern the intent of Congress. As such, its language becomes a critical guide to interpreting broad, ambiguous legislative language.

Staff members use the language in a report as a significant bargaining tool. An interest group is sometimes content to get its language into the report, knowing that somewhere down the line it can point to the language in a court challenge or in an agency proceeding. Because report language is so callously used to assuage important members and interest groups, it often contains conflicting statements or statements that are as vague as the legislation itself. To get a true understanding of the controversial aspects of legislation, transcripts of the debate at the exec or mark-up and the floor debate are far more useful. Rare is the report that is read by a congressman or a senator or that has actually persuaded someone to support legislation.

The Rules Committee

After being reported out of the standing committee, legislation on the House side goes through another legislative hurdle—the Rules Committee—before it is ready for floor debate. The Rules Committee functions as a "traffic cop" to expedite legislation supported by the leadership. Conversely, legislation opposed by the leadership is frequently caught in a "traffic jam."

A "rule" on a bill sets the conditions under which a measure is to be considered. It determines the admissibility of amendments and the terms of debate. Although attempts to reject rules are frequently made, they are seldom successful. In 1981, for example, one of the bloodiest battles of the Ninety-seventh Congress involved the rule for the president's budget package. The Democratic leadership, acting through the Rules Committee, obtained a rule to permit separate votes on the various budget cuts. Because many cuts focused on specific popular programs, the leadership felt that the "divide and conquer" tactic had a better chance of preserving programs dear to the Democratic heart. The Republicans, however, were not asleep at the wheel. Recognizing the strategy, they overturned the rule, 217 to 210, and passed a substitute. This vote on the rule was the key vote on the entire legislation.

On the Senate side, the rules for the passage of legislation are negotiated by the majority and minority leaders and approved by unanimous consent. The procedure is much less democratic in the House, where the chairman of the Rules Committee, acting with the speaker's approval, determines the terms of passage.

A rule on a bill is a privileged resolution adopted by the Rules Committee for a particular bill. (A privileged resolution or matter can be called up for floor consideration at any time, taking precedence over other business.) The resolution recites

1. that the bill is to be considered in the Committee of the Whole House (although sometimes the rule calls for debate and action in the House itself).
2. that a certain amount of general debate is allowed, divided equally between the majority floor manager and the designated ranking minority committee member.
3. that following the general debate, the bill is open for amendment under the five-minute rule, either without any restriction except germaneness, or with such amendments restricted to those kinds spelled out by the Rules Committee; the bill can also be totally "closed," meaning that no amendments are allowed.
4. that one motion to recommit the bill to the committee is allowed, whereby the most ranking minority member of the committee opposed to the bill is to offer the motion and control the limited debate on the motion (sometimes the motion to recommit is spelled out in the rule; sometimes it is subsequently written by the minority member).

The resolution proposing the rule is debatable in the House, usually with thirty minutes allowed to each side. After the debate, a vote is taken on the previous question to close debate on the resolution, and if it is defeated, the rule can be amended. This seldom occurs, and when it does occur, the bill managers frequently pull the rule and the bill altogether rather than allow the rule to be amended in a harmful way. When the rule resolution is approved, the bill's manager moves to go into the Committee of the Whole, where debate commences.

Historically, the Rules Committee has been, as described by Professor David Mayhew, the mechanism for "institutional maintenance."[20] It denies poorly conceived bills access to the floor. By requiring the chairman of the responsible committee to testify on behalf of the legislation and by permitting him to be questioned, the Rules Committee ensures a presentation of the bill in its entirety. Because the political and substantive problems of the legislation are flagged early, proponents and opponents of the legislation are able to devise effective floor strategies. The prestigious committees, like Ways and Means, generally receive better treatment than those with less clout. With rare exceptions, the Ways and Means Committee requests—and obtains—a closed rule, that is, a rule that does not permit amendments.

The reasons advanced for a closed rule are many. In the case of tax legislation, Ways and Means members argue that a tax bill cannot be suitably altered by floor amendments because of the complexity of the tax code (that argument does not usually deter the Senate, however). A closed rule is sometimes sought "to package" certain proposals, thus forcing the House to vote all or nothing. A popular bill, with less popular provisions "locked in" under the closed rule, can carry the unpopular rider or riders to passage.

However, the Rules Committee is also used to thwart the will of the majority. In a classic case, which is recited in most texts on Congress, Rules Committee Chairman Howard Smith of Virginia blocked civil rights legislation on many occasions by refusing to convene Rules Committee meetings for that purpose. In 1961 Speaker Sam Rayburn diminished the power of the Rules Committee by successfully persuading the House to increase the size of the committee with congressmen loyal to the leadership.[21] As a result of the antics of chairmen like Smith, the House changed the rules to allow the leadership to select the members of the Rules Committee. Since the early 1960s, then, speakers have had considerable leverage over Rules Committee members, although loyalty to the speaker is often altered by changes in seniority and the leadership.

The Rules Committee is circumvented only with difficulty. The strategy of defeating a rule in the full House is rarely successful. The party caucus sometimes demands a rule change or at least pressures the Rules Committee leadership to change a rule, as in the oil depletion case previously described. A discharge petition—such as the petition adopted in 1910 during the revolt against Speaker Cannon—is sometimes used to pry legislation from the committee and send it directly to the floor. A discharge petition, as its name implies, discharges any committee, including the Rules Committee, from further jurisdiction or consideration of a particular bill. It can be filed thirty days (seven days for the Rules Committee) after the bill has been introduced and assigned to committee. Filed with the clerk, the petition remains at the clerk's desk for the entire session of Congress unless it is withdrawn by the filer or until it receives the required 218 signatures to occasion the discharge. When sufficient signatures have been obtained, it is placed on the Discharge Calendar where it is privileged business,[22] and the sponsor of the bill can call it up in the House for specific consideration. The discharge petition may not be copied or removed from the clerk's desk, even by the person filing it, and the signatures are not to be made public until the total number of necessary signatures are received. Any House member can surreptitiously note the names appearing on the petition. Even constitutional amendments are subject to the discharge petition, although the House is somewhat uneasy about considering a constitutional amendment without committee hearings and subject to only brief debate. But it has been done; as recently as 1982, when the House considered (and rejected) a constitutional amendment on the balanced budget.

Finally, the Rules Committee can be circumvented by the Calendar Wednesday procedure. Adopted in 1909, also to combat the dictatorial powers of Speaker Joe Cannon, the procedure is rarely used. It permits standing committees, in alphabetical order, to call up measures on Wednesday that have been reported out but are being held in the Rules Committee. The Calendar Wednesday procedure may be dispensed with by unanimous consent or by a two-thirds vote of the House, and unanimous consent is routinely mumbled through.[23]

Considered one of the three prestigious House committees, the Rules Committee usually reports out no legislation of its own. Its power derives from its ability to shape or obstruct legislation and from the closeness of its chairman and members to the leadership. However, the Rules Committee can introduce rules for bills not yet reported by standing committees. The power of "extraction," based on an 1895 precedent, has rarely been invoked in the past three decades. It was used in 1972 when the Committee on Education and Labor refused to report out a dock strike measure. Although Speaker Albert opposed the rule, which was in effect a bill, the proposal was adopted by the House, 203 to 170.[24]

The Rules Committee also is responsible for promulgating the standing rules of the House. Although most work on the standing rules is done at the beginning of each Congress, sometimes rule changes are considered during a Congress. The Rules Committee reports such rule changes, which are voted on by the House as if at the beginning of a session.

TEN

RITES OF PASSAGE II

STAGE THREE—
FLOOR ACTION

Floor Dynamics

The most historically significant and exciting moments of the Congress occur not in committee rooms but on the chamber floor. Here is where Daniel Webster gained national notoriety for his oratory; here is where Congressman John Anderson of Illinois was able to develop a national reputation and following. Although most controversies in the Senate are well orchestrated in advance, the filibuster, or the surprise procedural move, or the unpredictable roll-call vote still sends ripples of excitement throughout the Capitol.

Of course, drama is the exception, not the rule. On most occasions, visitors to the Capitol are disappointed to see one man drone on and on, with maybe two other members wandering aimlessly around the floor. Nonetheless, even at its most boring moments, the cadence, rhythm, and flow of congressional proceedings represent the culmination of years of tradition and experimentation with the best procedures to accommodate the often conflicting demands of individualization and "institutional maintenance."

The drama in the House is less intense now that roll-call votes are electronically computed on a large board at the front of the chamber. The change-over to electronic roll calls did more than simply shorten the time required to record a roll call. Because the votes are posted on the board, members voting later can see how the bellwethers are voting before they cast their own votes. Thus, another ploy has been added to the congressional bag of influence. Influential legislators record their votes early in an effort to persuade their colleagues to vote likewise. The leadership can see at a glance who has not voted or who has left the party line and exercise its influence accordingly. Members who have voted "wrong" or who have not yet made up their minds are subject to considerable arm-twisting by the leadership during the fifteen-minute period allocated to the roll call (in most instances). Indeed, with the advent of television coverage, Speaker O'Neill decreed that the cameras had to remain focused on the scoreboard during every roll call so as not to exhibit the arm-twisting and logrolling to the television audience.

The electronic roll call has freed the members from constant attendance on the House floor. In past days, members hovered on or near the floor when any important legislation was being considered because a teller vote might be called and completed before a member could get from his office to the floor. (A "teller vote" is a procedure under which members point to the member-teller who has been designated to stand at the end of the aisle and count either the yeas or the nays. While no record is kept of who votes which way, the teller vote is binding.) With fifteen-minute voting periods virtually certain, members attend to other business and still arrive in time to cast their vote on any amendment or other motion. Indeed, most members carry "beepers" to notify them of pending votes. (The beepers, which also allow members to stay in touch with their offices, are included in the standard office equipment available to all members.)

The dynamics of the floor are a mystery to the public. Ever since the televising of the McCarthy and the Kefauver hearings of the 1950s and in particular the Watergate hearings of the 1970s, the public has become more cognizant of the committee aspect of congressional work. And the media have increasingly covered committee mark-ups. Only recently, however, has the House permitted cable television coverage, and the Senate has stubbornly resisted even that intrusion (although Senate Majority Leader Howard Baker has fought for TV coverage of the Senate floor debates).

A highly specialized press corps covers the Congress from a balcony overlooking each chamber. Press rooms behind the balcony contain television equipment for interviews. The balconies fill up with the press when a debate becomes acerbic or when a roll call is pending. Occasionally a reporter sends a message to the chamber requesting a televised comment from a senator or a congressman about an amendment or the party's legislative strategy. However, because the press is separated from the real wheeling and dealing, reporters are unable to visually convey the point of a debate. In an era in which the power of the media lies in television, floor events are reported in only written form. Thus, unlike the White House, which is totally oriented to the use of television to gain public support for presidential positions, Congress as an institution has yet to hop on the television bandwagon to achieve the same purpose. Although congressmen use television to advertise their candidacy, some are reluctant to display themselves in unedited action. As Max Kampelman, former aide to Hubert Humphrey, said of the press coverage of Congress, "The benefits . . . are individual and not institutional."[1]

So, the major legislative floor battles continue to be fought, in the last quarter of the twentieth century, still untelevised. In the early days of the twentieth century, as Woodrow Wilson pointed out, most congressional work was accomplished at the committee level. With the decline of committees, floor procedures in both houses assumed renewed importance.

Floor Action in the Senate

Schedules

Although the rules require most legislation to be scheduled for floor consideration in the order they are placed on the calander,[2] most scheduling takes place through unanimous consent.[3]

Proponents strive to get their legislation scheduled on the unanimous consent calendar. However, this honor is usually reserved for bills establishing such events as National Religious Heritage Week and minor noncontroversial private relief or immigration bills. Occasionally, the calendar includes legislation sufficiently compromised beforehand to eliminate all significant objection. In the Ninety-sixth Congress, Senator John Culver of Iowa managed to get his Regulatory Flexibility Act,[4] involving regulatory relief for small businesses, on the unanimous consent calendar because the two chief special-interest groups concerned with the legislation, the small business lobbyists and the labor unions, had reached a compromise.

Often noncontroversial, dry, and technical legislation, which would normally sail through unscathed, is not placed on the unanimous consent calendar because a senator wants to attach a germane—or even nongermane—floor amendment to it. One senator, of course, can block a unanimous consent vote. The proposed Federal Courts Improvement bill of 1980,[5] which was designed to reorganize the judiciary, was a prime candidate for the unanimous

A session on the floor of the Senate in 1850.

consent calendar. But Senator Dale Bumpers of Arkansas voted against unanimous consent because he wanted to attach to the bill his long-pending amendment providing stricter judicial review of agency regulations. His amendment passed by a 2-to-1 margin, but it also effectively killed legislation that otherwise had no opponents.

Unanimous Consent Agreements

A unanimous consent agreement is simply a contract between the Democrats and the Republicans to limit the amount of time for floor consideration of a bill and the timing of amendments.

The majority and minority leaders are responsible for scheduling and forging unanimous consent agreements. To block unanimous consent, a senator places a "hold" on legislation—that is, the senator wants a floor debate and a roll-call vote on the bill. A hold is often placed on a bill not because a senator has substantive problems with the bill, but because he plans to attach a nongermane amendment to the bill. Other times a hold is placed on legislation by a senator to even the score with another senator by tying up his legislative priorities. Early in the Ninety-seventh Congress Senator Jesse Helms attached an amendment to a banking bill to increase the maximum age limitation of the surgeon general. After passing the Senate unnoticed, the amendment was detected by the House. Had his tactic been successful, Helms would have avoided a floor fight for his choice for that position, a vehement anti-abortion foe. Subsequently, Minority Leader Byrd, at the request of numerous Democratic senators, placed a hold on every bill carrying Helms' name and every bill reported out of the Agriculture Committee, which was chaired by Helms. Ultimately, Helms' candidate was approved anyway.

The placement of a hold early in a session is not an insurmountable obstacle. It is simply a signal that a floor debate might be necessary. A senator cannot maintain a hold indefinitely, and at some point he must lift it or mount a floor challenge. A majority leader can bring a hold bill to a vote at any time, thereby forcing the senator to enter into a time agreement or filibuster. Late in the session, when many senators are eager to have their legislation enacted, a hold can be the death-knell for a bill, especially when time pressures make it likely that the only legislation to go through is unanimous consent legislation or short-time agreements. At that point, the hold becomes an ominous weapon. In exchange for lifting a hold, a senator often gets concessions he could not win in a floor vote. Moreover, because a hold is confidential, the placer of the hold does not get much political heat, if any, for killing the bill. Before the 1980 presidential election, the Republican leadership decided to kill the Carter administration's Paperwork Reduction bill of 1980,[6] sponsored by

Democratic Senator Lawton Chiles of Florida. The Republicans were unwilling to give Jimmy Carter a victory that would enable him, during the election recess, to argue that he had fulfilled his campaign pledge of reducing paperwork. A Republican tag team went to work. First, a hold was placed by Senator Barry Goldwater, then by Senator James McClure. Each time a hold was lifted (under pressure from the business community, which wanted the bill), another hold was placed. The bill could not be moved; however, after the election, the incentive to kill the bill no longer existed. The hold silently disappeared and the bill glided through.

President Reagan's first initiative of his new economic package in the Ninety-seventh Congress concerned dairy legislation.[7] The Democrats originally refused to give the majority leadership a time agreement and proposed innumerable amendments, many of which were opposed by the administration. One amendment tried to reduce the import of a milk protein, casein, into the country; another declared that Soviet caviar could no longer be imported; another resolved that the grain embargo against the Soviet Union should end. When everything failed to thwart the onward surge of this legislation, the Democrats finally agreed to a time agreement on the last amendment, which was concerned with hoof-and-mouth disease (some called it the foot-in-mouth amendment):

ORDER FOR CONSIDERATION OF S. 509 AT 3:30 P.M. AND
FOR A VOTE THEREON AT 4 P.M. TOMORROW

Mr. BAKER. Mr. President, notwithstanding those special orders, I ask unanimous consent that the Senate return to the consideration of this measure, S. 509, at 3:30 p.m. on tomorrow and that the Senate proceed to a final vote on this bill at 4 p.m.; and that no other amendment be in order except one amendment, which may be offered by the distinguished Senator from Montana (Mr. Melcher), dealing with hoof-and-mouth disease; and that paragraph 4 of rule XII be waived.[8]

Time agreements are usually far more detailed and complex; they describe each amendment, the time allocated to each, and the time to be given to the entire piece of legislation. The floor manager for the majority is usually the committee chairman, and the minority floor manager is usually the ranking minority member of the proponent of a major amendment. Each floor manager is allotted a specific amount of time, which he "yields" to other senators who desire to speak. Any number of proponents and opponents can speak as long as neither side exceeds the time allocated for the amendment. When that cap is reached, time can be borrowed from time allocated for general debate on underlying legislation.

Although the rules and terms of unanimous consent agreements are quite rigid, the etiquette of the "Gentlemen's Club" accommodates the reasonable request of any senator to speak. Breaches of this etiquette are rare and evoke strong reaction.

During the budget fight in the Ninety-seventh Congress over President Reagan's budget cuts, North Carolina Senator Jesse Helms proposed an amendment to cut $100 million out of the social-service block-grant funds; the sole purpose of the amendment was to deny the Legal Services Corporation funding through block grants. The unanimous consent agreement stated that first Senator Helms would speak, then several other senators, and finally Senator Edward Kennedy. Senator Helms, realizing he did not have the votes to win his amendment and feeling pressure from the majority leadership, decided to withdraw his amendment. He waited to withdraw it, however, until it was Senator Kennedy's turn to speak. Kennedy stood up and angrily demanded his right to speak. Numerous Republican leaders huddled around Helms, trying unsuccessfully to dissuade him from short-circuiting Kennedy; they later then apologized to Kennedy for the breach of etiquette, which only brought additional tension to an already bristling partisan atmosphere.

The Roll Call

After an amendment has been debated according to the terms of a unanimous consent agreement, a roll-call vote is taken (unless the senators consent unanimously to a voice vote). The single buzzer signaling the roll call is like the ringing of Pavlov's bell. (One tourist, watching the Senate floor from the gallery, asked the guard if the buzzing meant that "one of them has escaped.") Suddenly, instead of a mere handful of senators, all of whom were directly involved in the preceding business, the Senate floor is filled with senators who have to record their votes. A senator can vote "yea," "nay," or "present." Unlike committee votes, in which proxy votes are acceptable, the senators must be physically present on the Senate floor to cast a vote that counts.

Occasionally a senator "pairs" his vote with that of an absent senator who would have voted the opposite way, a procedure that allows the absent senator to go on record on a proposition. The paired votes are not tallied in the record vote. The pairing procedure sometimes determines the ultimate fate of legislation. During the debate in the Ninety-seventh Congress over the anti-busing amendment to the Department of Justice Authorization bill, numerous cloture petitions were filed to terminate the filibuster by Republican Senator Lowell Weicker of Connecticut. To obtain cloture, sixty votes must be cast for the cloture petition—a mere three-fifths of those present and voting is not sufficient. The anti-busing advocates had fifty-nine votes when Senator Claiborne Pell, a Democrat from Rhode Island who disliked filibusters, indicated he would vote for cloture. A supporter of the filibuster took him aside on the floor and they formed a "live" pair. Thus, the supporter could go on record against cloture and Pell could go on record for it. Of course, by pairing his vote, Pell failed to provide the sixtieth yea vote, and the cloture petition failed.

After a vote, a member on the prevailing side usually moves to reconsider and the motion is rejected by being tabled. An example of this procedure involving a defeated amendment by Senator Hatch of Utah to the Legal Services Corporation legislation in 1981 follows:

The PRESIDING OFFICER. Is all time yielded back?

Mr. DOMENICI. Mr. President, I yield back any remaining time I have.

Mr. HOLLINGS. I yield back the remainder of my time.

The PRESIDING OFFICER. All time having been yielded back, the question is on agreeing to the amendment of the Senator from Utah.

On this question, the yeas and nays have been ordered, and the clerk will call the roll.

The assistant legislative clerk called the roll.

Mr. STEVENS. I announce that the Senator from Virginia (Mr. WARNER) is necessarily absent.

Mr. CRANSTON. I announce that the Senator from Nevada (Mr. CANNON), the Senator from Florida (Mr. CHILES), and the Senator from New Jersey (Mr. WILLIAMS) are necessarily absent.

The PRESIDING OFFICER (Mr. QUAYLE). Is there any other Senator wishing to vote?

The result was announced—yeas 24, nays 72, as follows:

[Rollcall Vote No. 91 Leg.]

YEAS—24

Armstrong	Grassley	McClure
Byrd, Harry F., Jr.	Hatch	Nickles
Cochran	Hawkins	Proxmire
D'Amato	Hayakawa	Simpson
Denton	Helms	Stennis
East	Humphrey	Symms
Garn	Jepsen	Thurmond
Goldwater	Lugar	Zorinsky

NAYS—72

Abdnor	Ford	Mitchell
Andrews	Glenn	Moynihan
Baker	Gorton	Murkowski
Baucus	Hart	Nunn
Bentsen	Hatfield	Packwood
Biden	Heflin	Pell
Boren	Heinz	Percy
Boschwitz	Hollings	Pressler
Bradley	Huddleston	Pryor
Bumpers	Inouye	Quayle
Burdick	Jackson	Randolph
Byrd, Robert C.	Johnston	Riegle
Chafee	Kassebaum	Roth
Cohen	Kasten	Rudman
Cranston	Kennedy	Sarbanes
Danforth	Laxalt	Sasser
DeConcini	Leahy	Schmitt
Dixon	Levin	Specter
Dodd	Long	Stafford
Dole	Mathias	Stevens
Domenici	Matsunaga	Tower
Durenberger	Mattingly	Tsongas
Eagleton	Melcher	Wallop
Exon	Metzenbaum	Weicker

NOT VOTING—4

Cannon	Warner	Williams
Chiles		

So, Mr. HATCH's amendment (UP No. 72) was rejected.

Mr. HOLLINGS. Mr. President, I move to reconsider the vote by which the amendment was rejected.

Mr. KENNEDY. I move to lay that motion on the table.[10]

This ritualistic motion to reconsider is used to circumvent the Senate rule that permits any senator who voted for the legislation to move to reconsider the bill within two days of the vote for passage.[11] Occasionally, an opponent will vote "yea" on the legislation to obtain the right to move to reconsider later on.

During the fight over the Omnibus Reconciliation bill of 1981, Republican Senator Ted Stevens of Alaska used this tactic successfully. Although he opposed an amendment on Medicaid, he voted "yea," and the amendment passed the first time it was proposed. However, by eloquently moving to reconsider, he persuaded several senators to switch their votes and thereby accomplished his original goal.

The two-day period is usually insignificant. In a close battle, however, a delay sometimes permits the losing side to gather more support. Moreover, at the end of the session, failure to move to reconsider simultaneously with adoption of the legislation may delay the bill long enough to prevent enactment.

Filibuster

Of the myriad of devices available to kill legislation, the most famous is the filibuster.

Each senator has the right to stand on his feet and debate legislation for as long as he wants until the Senate votes to limit debate. He loses this right if he sits down or walks off the floor without unanimous consent. The use of the filibuster has long symbolized the overwhelming pride in individualism that so characterizes the Senate. It is no coincidence that the word *filibuster* derives from the Dutch word *vrijbuiter*, meaning "pirate," "one who plunders freely," and from the French and Spanish words meaning "freebooter." As originally used, without any procedural constraints, the one-man filibuster literally brought the activities of the Senate to a halt.

At the turn of the century the filibuster was successfully used to thwart measures of great popular demand. Senator Robert M. LaFollette, Sr., of Wisconsin became a legend in his own time. Fortified with eggnogs, he held the floor eighteen hours and twenty-three minutes—through twenty-nine quorum calls and three roll calls. One contemporary claims that LaFollette rejected one of the eggnogs as drugged, and indeed, it turned out to contain ptomaine poison.[12]

When Woodrow Wilson's Armed Neutrality bill was filibustered, and killed, by only eleven senators, he was furious. The days of unlimited filibuster were about to end. Wilson called the Senate into a special session to pass its first cloture rule, Rule 22, which provides that a cloture vote of two-thirds of the senators present and voting will end debate. The cloture motion required submission by sixteen senators and a two-day waiting period prior to the vote. Debate was limited to one hour for each senator. After approval of the cloture motion, each senator was allowed one hour of debate. In addition, no new amendments could be offered, except by unanimous consent, and nongermane amendments were out of order. However, even these reforms proved ineffective. In 1935 Senator Huey P. Long, a Democrat from Louisiana—known fondly as the Kingfish—spent fifteen and one-half hours discussing "Southern Potlikker" Turnip Greens. In 1949 the reforms were weakened by requiring support of cloture by two-thirds of the entire Senate membership—instead of just those present. Because of the difficulty of getting a cloture vote under the two-thirds rule, in 1975, at the beginning of the reform-minded Ninety-fourth Congress, the Senate reduced the necessary proportion to three-fifths of the entire Senate, or sixty votes.

The new filibuster rules made it significantly easier to obtain cloture. Between 1960, when frequent use of the filibuster and cloture began, and 1975, of 79 cloture votes, only 18 were successful. However, in 1980 alone there were 9 successful cloture votes.[13]

For years the filibuster was used by conservatives who hoped to block progressive legislation. The plaque on Senator Strom Thurmond's desk commemorates the longest filibuster in the history of the Senate. He spoke for twenty-four hours and eighteen minutes in a round-the-clock session against the 1957 Civil Rights Act. During the 1950s, 60s, and the 70s, liberals disdained the filibuster as a tool of southern conservatives, although they were not too proud to use it during the Nixon administration when they lacked sufficient votes. Liberals used both "extended debate" and full-fledged filibusters on several occasions, for example, to kill controversial Supreme Court nominees and to stop the supersonic transport system (SST). An epic liberal filibuster against the draft law, which tied up the Senate for seven weeks in mid-1971 as anti-war senators tried to force a rapid end to the Vietnam War, marked a watershed in the debate, as Professor Gary Orfield commented:

> This fight brought about a major turning point in the filibuster system, as the philosophic positions of both its supporters and defenders were undermined by strong feelings about one issue. Nine Southern Senators who had consistently supported filibusters on the grounds of freedom of debate and protection of the rights of minorities in the Senate now voted to "gag" the Senate. Suddenly the leaders of the anti-civil rights filibusters arrived at a new understanding of the system. On the other side, some traditional opponents of filibusters like Philip Hart (D. Mich.) now opposed cloture.[14]

To prepare for eventual floor debate on death-penalty legislation, groups like the American Civil Liberties Union began to organize senators and Senate staff for a filibuster early in the Ninety-seventh Congress. Although the filibuster has been widely condemned as an obstructionist tactic, it is still cherished on both sides of the Senate aisle, where the right of the minority party continues to be respected far more than in the House.

Once a filibuster is initiated, the orderly, friendly, courteous Gentlemen's

Club metamorphoses into a den of chaos and havoc. The legislative day often continues around the clock; after a short mandatory waiting period, cloture votes are called as soon as the majority leader thinks he has enough votes. To prevent a filibuster from halting all legislative business, a two-track system has developed that allows a filibuster to block action on one legislative question but not on other questions. Thus, the majority leader moves less controversial legislation forward while the filibuster is postponed. For example, during the filibuster in the Ninety-seventh Congress on an anti-busing amendment, Senate Majority Leader Howard Baker negotiated a unanimous consent agreement that permitted consideration of the tax legislation and the budget conference report by suspension of debate on the busing measure. When consideration of the tax and budget legislation was completed, the Senate returned to the amendment as the pending order of business and the filibuster resumed.

A filibuster can commence at various points in the legislative process. A filibuster can block any amendment. Even a conference report to a bill can be filibustered. In 1980 legislation to protect the rights of the institutionalized[15] infuriated congressional states' rights activists because of the additional power given to the Justice Department to sue on behalf of persons institutionalized unconstitutionally in state and local systems. The cloture petition to stop the filibuster on the passage of the conference report finally passed by a one-vote margin.

Nominations are filibustered. The filibuster over the nomination of Professor Stephen Breyer to the First Circuit Court of Appeals was particularly acerbic. When the Carter administration refused to nominate Harvard Law Professor Archibald Cox of Watergate fame, Senator Edward Kennedy's first choice, Kennedy negotiated an agreement with Senator Strom Thurmond as the ranking minority member of the Judiciary Committee and with the administration to nominate Breyer, the chief counsel of the Judiciary Committee. However, Kennedy's agreement was implemented in the lame-duck session, and Senator Robert Morgan, who had just been defeated as the Democratic senator from North Carolina, decided to vigorously oppose Stephen Breyer, whom he blamed for the defeat of a Morgan judicial nominee. Because Morgan believed that the loss of his judicial nominee was a primary cause for his defeat in the general election to Republican John East, he spent considerable effort in putting together a bipartisan coalition of senators to filibuster the Breyer nomination. To compound the Senate's problems, the Senate Judiciary Committee had reported for floor action a bill amending the anti-discrimination provisions of the housing laws. This set off another filibuster, scheduled prior to the Breyer filibuster. Because both matters came out of the Judiciary Committee, it was relatively easy to forge a coalition to keep the filibusters going. The nomination was saved only because cloture could not be obtained on the housing proposals, and the nomination became the next order of business.

Other Dilatory Tactics

Legislation can be blocked in various other ways. A member can force the most mundane matters to a floor vote. Of all the dilatory tactics, perhaps the most interesting is the use of the quorum call. West Virginia Senator Robert Byrd has described the use of this device:

> Currently, a quorum is "presumed" always to be present and daily business moves forward on schedule in the Senate until and unless the question of a quorum is raised. As soon as the question is raised, however, the Secretary of the Senate is directed to call the roll. Bells ring and buzzers sound, and if the quorum goes "live," Senators emerge from offices, committee rooms, the restaurant, the Senate gymnasium, or wherever, to answer the call. In some instances, a Senator may stay on the Senate floor only long enough to be counted present before he returns to the work with which he was occupied prior to the quorum interruption.

> The question of a quorum may originate for any one of several reasons, and, as a result, can have multiple values and uses. Though usually the question of a quorum is raised by a Senator, the presiding officer may raise it on his own initiative. A Senator in the midst of his speech may call for a quorum count to obtain a larger audience. That might prove risky, however, for if a quorum cannot be raised, his speech could not continue and the declared minority might decide to adjourn, thus losing for him the opportunity to speak that day.

> Or, for one reason or another, another Senator might raise the question of a quorum during a speech, with the speaking Senator's consent, and by unanimous consent, the speaking Senator will retain the floor. But a speaking Senator loses the floor when the suggestion of a quorum is raised, and only when it has been established or the quorum call is called off can it be regained.

> In order to prevent the quorum call from deteriorating into a dilatory tool, subsequent and consecutive quorum calls cannot be suggested if no business has intervened between the calls. Mere debate or continued speech-making does not constitute business in itself, the Senate has ruled on several occasions, but intervening business is not hard to manufacture.[16]

In addition, legislation can be stopped through the use of nongermane amendments. Senators who have been unsuccessful in attaching their amendments in committee are sometimes successful in attaching them as nongermane amendments to legislation that appears to be moving through the Congress. The nongermane amendments can ultimately keep the main legislation from passing.

Party Dynamics

An understanding of party floor dynamics is essential to an understanding of the legislative flow. A major concern of the majority and minority leaders is the protection of the rights of each party member. When a senator has placed a hold on a legislative matter, it is the responsibility of his party leader to protect that hold and prevent any floor scheduling until that member has had adequate notice. On the floor, the leader provides information to the senators, procedural advice, and guidance as to the need for a party vote on an issue.

Although voting the party line is not required on major substantive issues, like abortion, it is frequently expected during procedural votes. It is quite common for the majority to move as a party to table minority amendments. Thus, there may be two votes on the amendment: a procedural vote and, if the procedural vote fails, a substantive vote.

The Congressional Record

The formal account of legislative floor debate is published in the *Congressional Record*. As the most important source of legislative history, the *Record* is used by the courts to decipher the intent of legislation. Unfortunately, despite its significance, the *Congressional Record* is an imperfect source of information, for with embarrassing frequency, the transcript of a day's proceedings is edited beyond recognition.

In a heated debate between Connecticut Senator Abraham Ribicoff and New York Senator Jacob Javits over school desegregation, Ribicoff said: "I don't think you have the guts to face your liberal constituencies who have moved to the suburbs to avoid sending their children to school with blacks." The next day the *Congressional Record* read: "The question is whether Senators have the guts to face their liberal white constituencies who have fled to the suburbs for the sole purpose of avoiding having their sons and daughters go to school with blacks."[17] And in the Ninety-seventh Congress when Senator Ernest Hollings of South Carolina caustically referred to Senator Howard Metzenbaum of Ohio as the senator from "B'nai B'rith" (a Jewish organization), the reference was deleted from the *Congressional Record*.

However, the most notorious failure of the *Congressional Record* is its failure to capture the dynamics of floor debate. Most statements are irrelevant! They are read to empty rooms! Yet the *Record* does not distinguish between statements vital to debate and those wafted on air. Many so-called clarifying colloquies are written by staff members, signed by senators, and submitted. Although statements that actually have been read on the floor are distinguished from unread statements, any statement can be placed in the *Record* as if read by reading the first line of the statement on the floor. When a statement is not read by the member, a small black dot, known as a "bullet," is put before and after the statement in the *Record*. The true intent behind legislation cannot be discerned from the *Record*. Yet it remains the "novel" by which posterity examines logic.

The desire of the House and the Senate to project the spirit of legislative debate has led to a movement to televise floor action. Majority Leader Howard Baker, who led the fight in 1981, said that television would help the Senate "correct the imbalance between the executive and legislative branches that will exist as long as we deny ourselves use of the most powerful communications tool yet devised by man."[18]

Floor Action in the House

In contrast to the madness of the Senate procedures, the House exudes, at least superficially, organization, orderliness, and structure. Four procedures are available for the passage of legislation.

Noncontroversial Legislation

Legislation can be placed on the unanimous consent calendar or the private calendar, which are usually reserved, as in the Senate, for noncontroversial matters or private relief bills. Unlike the Senate, however, where the majority and minority leaders guard the consent calendar, in the House official "objectors" are appointed to the task. The majority and minority leaders announce the appointments at the beginning of each Congress. For example, on March 25, 1981, Majority Leader James Wright announced:

> Mr. WRIGHT. Mr. Speaker, I take this time to announce the official objectors for the Democratic side for the 97th Congress.
>
> For the Consent Calendar, our official representatives will be the gentleman from Alabama (Mr. Flippo); the gentleman from Texas (Mr. Hance); and the gentleman from Maryland (Mr. Dyson).
>
> For the Private Calendar, our official representatives will be the gentleman from Massachusetts (Mr. Boland); the gentleman from Minnesota (Mr. Oberstar); and the gentleman from Pennsylvania (Mr. Ertel).[19]

Similarly, the minority appoints three objectors for the private and consent calendars. Any member on either side can object to the private and consent calendar bills, but the official objectors have the party responsibility for these measures.

The consent calendar is called on the first Monday of every month, with at least three days of advance notice. The sponsors of consent bills notify the objectors at least twenty-four hours in advance to determine the objections, if any. If there are objections, by any member of the House, the legislation is passed over and returned to the consent calendar for the next call. If three or more members object when the bill is called again, the bill is stricken from the consent calendar for the rest of the term.[20]

A similar procedure governs the private calendar. The speaker calls up all private bills on the first Tuesday of each month and may, at his discretion, consider the private calendar on the third Tuesday as well. Private bills are placed on the calendar at least seven days in advance to allow the official objectors to screen them for controversial measures. If two or more members object to a bill on the first Tuesday, it is either sent back to the reporting committee or, at the request of a member, passed over without prejudice. Countless noncontroversial bills that are processed through the consent and private calendars rarely get any public attention.

The Suspension Calendar

The suspension calendar is a legislative shortcut used to fast-track the passage of certain bills. It is a powerful tool wielded by the speaker, who determines which bills are placed on it and when they will be considered. The suspension calendar permits the House, by a two-thirds vote, to suspend its regular procedural rules for any bill. Most important, a bill placed on the suspension calendar bypasses the Rules Committee and goes directly to the floor. Debate is limited to forty minutes, and amendments are not permitted. Bills that fail to gain the necessary two-thirds support may be considered again under regular House procedure assuming a rule can be obtained from the Rules Committee. Although the suspension procedure is used by and large for minor measures, it is sometimes used for major legislation as well.

Sometimes the suspension calendar device is used to circumvent committee chairmen. Often, the suspension calendar is invoked by the substantive committee. When the committee votes to try the suspension route for a bill it has approved, the chairman writes to the speaker requesting placement on the suspension calendar. Usually, but not always, the speaker accommodates this request. In 1976, Democratic Representative Donald Fraser of Minnesota authored a proposal, unanimously approved by the International Relations Committee, to condemn the human rights policies of the South Korean and North Korean governments. Fraser wanted the measure considered under suspension of the rules. Because Speaker Carl Albert considered the bill too controversial,[21] he refused Fraser's request.

When the outcome of a vote is certain and the speaker does not want to force his members to cast a controversial vote, he will sometimes place the matter on the suspension calendar. The use of the suspension calendar remains one of the few powerful tools possessed by the speaker; it can be used by him to aid or to circumvent committee chairmen. It also can be used to avoid embarrassing amendments to a bill.

"Privileged" Legislation

Privileged legislation includes, primarily, "power of the purse" legislation from the Appropriations, Ways and Means, and Budget committees and such other housekeeping committees as the Administration and Rules committees. Selected legislation from these committees can be called up on the floor as soon as a waiting period has been satisfied. The routing of the legislation through the Rules Committee, a requirement imposed on most legislation, is thus dispensed with, as is, frequently, the Committee of the Whole procedure as well.[22]

The Committee of the Whole

Most major legislation proceeds to floor action via the Rules Committee. After a bill has been granted a rule, the majority leadership schedules the adoption of the rule in the full House, which is usually a *pro forma* matter. When the rule passes, a motion is made to resolve the House into the Committee of the Whole (the formal name is the Committee of the Whole House on the State of the Union).

Debate, negotiation, strategy—it all occurs in the Committee of the Whole. Unlike the full House, which demands a quorum of 218, the Committee of the Whole needs only 100 for a quorum, and it is presided over not by the speaker but by his designee, as chairman. The speaker votes only to break a tie, but his presence is accepted and he often participates in the debate.

The proceedings are governed entirely by the rule, which functions in the same way as the Senate's unanimous consent agreement to facilitate debate in an orderly fashion. The rule allocates the total amount of time to be spent on general debate. As in the Senate, the floor managers for the proponents and opponents of the legislation decide which members shall speak in favor of, and against, the legislation. The term *general debate* is indeed a bit of a misnomer. Usually the members simply exchange statements, prepared in advance by the staff, for the benefit of the *Congressional Record*. As in the Senate, the meaning of a bill is often debated in a "colloquy" between congressmen in an attempt to influence legislative history. The colloquies, however, which are often requested by interest groups anticipating judicial review down the line, are unlikely to yield true legislative intent. They are frequently prepared in advance, signed, and submitted to the *Record* for very special purposes without anyone hearing it in the Committee of the Whole. In short, spontaneous, dynamic interchange during general debate is the exception, not the rule.

Legislation receiving an open rule is subject to amendments, and it is under this condition that legitimate debate occurs. Each amendment is subject to the five-minute rule, which allows each member five minutes to explain his amendment, and an equivalent five minutes to each of those who oppose it. Despite the five-minute limitation, amendments can be debated at length by unanimous consent, by the practice of members yielding time to one another, and by a motion to "strike" a word. The motion to strike is used to obtain the floor during the five-minute rule. Literally, the member proposes to amend the bill (or an amendment to the bill) by striking "the last word" of the bill or the "requisite number of words" of the bill. In effect, the motion to strike is the House version of a filibuster. It provides the means by which debate can go on almost indefinitely. The procedure ends when members exhaust their repertoires, or when the floor manager seeks, by vote of the House, to end at a certain time debate on the bill or on any amendment to the bill. When such a motion to end debate is approved, the chairman of the Committee of the Whole records the names of all members standing to seek recognition and divides the remaining time among them. A member might have twenty seconds in which to speak his piece; the debate at that point begins to sound like a tobacco auction. Unlike the requirements in the Senate, each amendment must be germane to the bill and, even more specifically, to the section.[23] Technically, each bill is read section by section and amendments are proposed in order of sections. However, this requirement may be suspended by unanimous consent, and the bill can be opened for amendment anywhere.

Although prior notice to amend is not required, the Legislative Reorganization Act of 1970 provides that amendments printed in the *Congressional Record* at least one day prior to the bill's consideration in the Committee of the Whole are guaranteed ten minutes of floor debate regardless of agreements to terminate discussion or bring the bill to final vote.[24]

The opportunities for delays are infinite. A member can insist that all three readings of a bill that are technically required be made—in full. Amendments can be offered. Recorded votes can be demanded on every amendment. With unanimous consent, members can speak additional minutes on each amendment. As a psychological tactic, a member can move to strike the enacting clause of the bill, a motion that is privileged at all times during the amendment process but in order only once. A successful motion to strike the enacting clause kills the entire bill. Thus, a vote can be forced on legislation early in the debate, although it seldom prevails. In the House, however, dilatory tactics provide only harassment value. Unlike the situation in the Senate, a minority of congressmen cannot delay a vote on legislation indefinitely.

Voting

Votes are cast by computer. A member inserts a personalized card, like a credit card, into one of about forty voting stations throughout the House floor.

Until the reforms of the 1970s, recorded individual votes could not be obtained on amendments offered in the Committee of the Whole, for "tellers" recorded only the aggregate vote. Members voted one way on key amendments and another way on final passage. It was almost impossible to know how an individual member voted on a teller vote, and the vote on an amendment was virtually anonymous. Teller votes are still occasionally used. A congressman who is dissatisfied with the teller vote can ask for a recorded vote at any time before the Committee of the Whole goes on to another amendment. When teller votes were common, the amendment process was treated as virtually anonymous.

With the sunshine movement (and the mechanization of the voting process), however, votes are efficiently recorded not only on final passage but on each amendment that shapes the legislation. The number of recorded votes has increased, and the degree of public accountability has been enhanced. However, a reluctance to take unpopular stands has increased as well, along with "demagogic" amendments that cater to single-interest groups. Thus, an amendment to prohibit legal services from representing homosexuals was clearly defeated by voice vote but passed by a significant margin on a recorded vote. Electronic voting also decreases the negotiating ability of floor managers; members are not together on the floor but can be at any one of forty terminals. Attendance is also decreased for floor debate generally, since members can anticipate the time for voting more specifically.

From time to time the House has debated the advisability of making a recorded vote more difficult to obtain. Under the current rules, a recorded vote is ordered when at least twenty members support a request for a recorded vote. When the amendment lacks that support, the chairman of the Committee of the Whole usually calls a voice vote, in accordance with the wishes of the bill manager. Because the members of the substantive committee are usually on the floor when the bill is being considered, the bill managers control the Committee of the Whole unless and until an organized effort is made to change the bill in ways opposed by the substantive committee. This recalcitrant behavior occurs, for example, on almost every amendment involving congressional pay increases.

Members solemnly deny that they vote for or against matters under pressure from their party leadership, insisting always that their voting behavior is a matter of conscience and statesmanship. Party leaders and committee chairmen similarly deny that they keep books on members who do not cooperate and respond to requests for help. Both sets of denials overstate actual voting behavior. Obviously, some matters are beyond the pale of pressure. A black congressman is not going to vote against a civil rights measure just to satisfy a party leader; a member usually votes nay on a measure to close up a federal installation in his district even if the party leaders urge him to exercise such fiscal restraint. And most party leaders are not so foolish as to request such anti-constituency votes or to hold such voting behavior against the member involved. But most bills, and most amendments, do not involve such cosmic matters; much of the time the member is relatively free from parochial pressures on any individual vote. Although he cannot consistently vote out of character with his district or his reputation in the district (and in the Congress), he can occasionally "give" a vote to the leadership or to a member seeking help on a measure. Voting favors are very much a part of the legislative process; a member who never does any favors will never get any favors. A member identified as a "purist" or "stiff-neck," who does not respond collegially, may find party leaders and other members actively opposing his legislative proposals on a retaliatory basis. He is unlikely to be awarded any advancements or "badges" that come with continued service. The balancing act is difficult for most members; they have to find a happy middle where they are well regarded by their party leaders and colleagues for being willing to "go along" on some matters and still be able to maintain a reputation back home as a "consistent" and "principled" voting member.

A congressman has more difficulties than his Senate counterpart in deciding how to vote on every amendment. The House member has fewer staff, the amendments are often offered without prior notice, and the time to vote is sometimes as short as five minutes. And, unlike the Senate, staff access to the House floor is much more limited. How does a House member decide to vote on the myriad of issues that confront him on a daily basis? First, he is given cards by his staff charting the amendments that have been "noticed" in the *Congressional Record*. Some advance notice about the amendments may come from some House support groups, or the private groups interested in the amendment. Second, he observes the position of his state delegation. Third, he may get some signal ("thumbs up or down") from the party whip at the entrance of the chamber. Finally, he may go with the winning side as the roll call nears the end. However, given the multitude of votes each member must make, most congressmen sheepishly discover at some time in their careers that they voted on opposite sides of the same question.

Final Passage on the House Floor

After all the amendments have been voted on, the Committee of the Whole "rises" and reports back to the full House. The chairman of the Committee of the Whole returns the gavel to the speaker, and, like Cinderella's carriage at midnight, the Committee of the Whole once again becomes the House, and a quorum requires 218 members. Generally, the House gives blanket approval to the amendments of the Committee of the Whole, but, upon demand, a separate vote can be taken on any amendment that was adopted. Amendments defeated in the Committee of the Whole cannot again be offered in the House, but they might be incorporated in the one motion to recommit that is usually allowed under the rule. Any votes on any matters are usually recorded, as the request of any member supported by one-fifth of those present is sufficient to require a recorded vote.

Two pro forma procedures, engrossment and third reading, follow the vote on the amendments. Engrossment simply means that the enrollment clerk must ensure that the bill, as amended, is accurate. Third reading is generally accorded by reading the title. The recommittal motion follows. It is here that an opponent of the legislation—often the ranking minority member of the substantive committee—can offer a privileged motion to return the bill to the committee that reported it. If the recommittal motion is successful, the legislation is actually sent back to committee either to undergo substantial alteration or to die. If the recommittal motion is rejected, a vote is then taken on the whole bill. "The question is on the passage of the bill," the speaker intones. As in the Senate, a supporter of legislation that has just passed raises the pro forma motion to reconsider the legislation; that motion is tabled, and the bill thus cannot be considered later.

The legislation is then sent to the Senate if it has not yet passed there or to the conference committee if it is different from the Senate version. If the House and the Senate bills are identical, the bill is prepared for presidential review.

STAGE FOUR—
THE CONFERENCE COMMITTEE

In many cases the legislation passed in the House is different from the Senate version. Even the most trivial differences between the two versions must be hammered out before the legislation is sent to the president. The differences can be reconciled by "ping-ponging" the legislation between House and Senate until one chamber accepts the other's version; by conducting informal conferences between staff members before legislation passes either house; or by adopting the Senate bill verbatim or vice versa. These informal mechanisms are often facilitated by the executive branch or interested lobbyists. As a last resort the conference committee must be convened.

The conference committee is governed by informal rules. About 10 percent of the legislation enacted into law is hammered out in conference committee.

An effort to persuade both houses to adopt joint House–Senate conference rules failed. Thus, although joint House–Senate rules are not officially binding, they are often voluntarily complied with because of the desire to get legislation through its last congressional hurdle.

The conference committee consists of a varying number of congressmen and senators who meet publicly to thrash out the details of legislation. The House members are chosen by the speaker (usually on the recommendation of the committee chairman and the ranking minority member) and the Senate members are recommended for floor approval by the majority and minority leaders. Thus, the conference committee will usually include the key committee Democrats and Republicans who worked on the legislation. The chairmanship often rotates between the chambers. The leadership is supposed to ensure that a majority of the conferees support their chamber's position. Sometimes, however, conferees are selected by the leadership to attain substantive objectives. For example, in 1981 Speaker O'Neill chose liberal conferees for the conference on President Reagan's tax package specifically because they were unrepresentative of the rank-and-file membership that had supported a more conservative proposal. He also used the selection process to penalize and exclude a "boll weevil" Democrat who had betrayed him during the budget fight.

Considerable jealousy exists between the House and the Senate over the outcome of conference committees. Indeed, one room in the Capitol, EF 100, is set aside largely because of a historical confrontation between the House and Senate Appropriations committees. Early in the twentieth century, each chairman of the two committees refused to allow the conference on an appropriations bill to take place on the other's turf. Government was grinding to a halt as the money to keep it going ran out. The logjam was broken when an ingenious leader hit on the idea of creating a room at the east front of the Capitol that would be considered neutral ground. It is the only meeting room in the Capitol that is not designated by the prefix "H" (for House) or "S" (for Senate) and that contains two sets of voting lights and bells, one for the Senate and one for the House. E-F 100 remains as a monument to the difficulties of bicameralism.

Often conference rooms are deliberately small to crowd out the hordes of lobbyists who hope to pressure the conferees to preserve their hard-fought-for (and paid-for) provisions intact. Many a legislative battle has been lost in a last-minute change in a conference room at midnight. During the battle over the Reagan tax package late on a Friday night in August 1981 the conferees huddled in a tiny room bursting at the seams with staff and lobbyists. As one top Hill staff member said: The goal was to keep out the "pirates." However, the tactic was not too successful. Members of the House have an advantage in these conference committees because they tend to know, better than their counterparts in the Senate, the substance of the legislation. Most House members are active on only a few subcommittees, and, because of fewer staff, they must develop more personal knowledge about the substance of legislation.

Conference committees often become the graveyards of legislative proposals. The tug-of-war between the House and Senate sometimes consumes weeks of haggling. If a member is not represented on a conference committee, his proposal becomes the sacrificial lamb to create a truce. Thus, during the battle over the tax package in 1981, the conferees cavalierly dropped a tax credit for wood-burning stoves that the New England senators had succeeded in passing on the Senate floor as none of the New England senatorial delegation was represented among the conferees. A chairman, forced to accept amendments on the floor, can try to ditch them in the conference.

Sometimes the conference committee never actually meets. When only small differences separate the House and Senate bills, a "paper" conference is often devised, and the members never physically meet. The compromise legislation is worked out completely by staff people from the two houses, who themselves meet only by telephone. Although the conference report is sometimes viewed as a valuable contribution to legislative history, in determining the meaning of controversial parts of legislation, usually it is no more than a staff product with little member input.

The rules of both houses allow a motion to instruct conferees, a device strongly disfavored by committee chairmen but frequently offered by individual members. The motion, if adopted, directs the conferees of that chamber to take a certain position in conference on the bill. It is not binding in any legal sense, but it imposes a moral obligation on the conferees; failure to comply with such instructions sometimes causes difficulty with the conference report when it is later presented to the chamber.

Theoretically, the conference is to consider only matters in the bill that are in disagreement. This limitation is difficult to enforce, and conferees frequently modify matters not in disagreement and occasionally even include new matters. Given the House attitude about germaneness, however, the conferees cannot wander too far from the subject matter. Reference has already been made to the House requirement that all nongermane amendments originating in the Senate and accepted in conference must be voted on separately in the House.

Once a compromise is forged—and in many cases legislation languishes to its death in the conference committee because of inability to compromise— the members of the committee feel committed (except where they voted against the compromise) to return to their respective houses and vocally support and lobby for the legislation. The motion to consider a conference report (which describes in detail the difference between the conference bill and the House and Senate bills) is highly privileged, that is, it can be called up at any time. Moreover, a conference report is immune from amendment in both houses.

Rare and momentous is the occasion in which a conference report is rejected. But it does happen. In addition, in the Senate, a conference report (and even the original motion to appoint conferees) can be filibustered. It took three votes to break the filibuster of the conference report on the Rights of the Institutionalized bill in the Ninety-sixth Congress.

The role of a conference is critical in the overall political strategy for legislation. If legislation must pass within a short time period, opponents will add as many amendments as possible, thereby necessitating a lengthy and complex conference process. This was the tactic used by the dairy industry on President Reagan's legislation to suspend dairy price supports in the Ninety-seventh Congress. Conversely, many legislative supporters do not fight as hard against certain objectionable amendments if they know that the person who proposed the amendment will not be represented in conference. Without representation, the amendment can be easily deleted.

Finally, the president plays a crucial role in the conference process. Once again the FTC Authorization bill provides a useful example. President Carter made it crystal clear that he would veto the legislation if the conference committee retained the most restrictive amendments from the House and Senate bills. To avoid a presidential veto, compromises were made.

Once a conference report is approved by both houses, the papers are delivered to the house that originated the measure. A copy of the final bill is prepared by an enrolling clerk; the enrolled bill is signed by the speaker and presiding officer of the Senate and sent to the president. The enrolling process is usually a matter of form. However, in the last few days of a Congress, a lethargic enrollment may actually kill a bill. Eric Redman, a former legislative aide, explains the drama at the end of a session of trying to make sure that the legislation is properly enrolled and on the president's desk in time to make a pocket veto impossible:

> As it turned out, Vice President Agnew visited Capitol Hill late on the afternoon of December 22, signed S. 4106 (a Public Health Service bill) and the other bills he had compelled to languish in the Senate, and then departed. His belated action did not help us: a delay of twenty-four hours had been achieved, and that was all Nixon needed. S. 4106 and its companions reached the White House on the afternoon of January 2. And at 10 p.m. on January 2, unless President Nixon had signed it, S. 4106 would fail to become law. We had tried for weeks to make a pocket veto impossible, and we had lost by hours.[25]

Although Redman had failed to expedite the enrollment process, political pressure nevertheless forced President Nixon to sign the bill.

STAGE FIVE—
THE PRESIDENT

The President as Chief Legislator

As the country's founders expected legislative primacy and sought to protect the country from too strong an executive, the Constitution seemed to anticipate no role in the legislative process for the president except that of his veto power. The authors of the *Federalist Papers* were forced to defend even the presidential veto power, a power that did not exist in many eighteenth-century state legislatures:

> The propriety of a negative has, upon some occasions, been combatted by an observation, that it was not to be presumed a single man would possess more virtue and wisdom than a number of men; and that unless this presumption should be entertained, it would be improper to give the executive magistrate any species of control over the legislative body. . . .
>
> The primary inducement to conferring the power in question upon the Executive is, to enable him to defend himself; the secondary one is to increase the chances in favor of the community against the passing of bad laws, through haste, inadvertence, or design.[26]

The *Federalist* authors predicted that use of the veto would be rare, and were able to justify the veto primarily because it was qualified—two-thirds of the Congress could override it.

Even from the beginning, the president and his top officials played a more active role than the framers had anticipated. Alexander Hamilton submitted, and lobbied for, legislation, and even Thomas Jefferson himself, a member of the party that had criticized a strong presidency, presided over some party caucuses to obtain passage of his legislative packages. Subsequent to this initial aggressiveness of early presidents, the executive branch played a relatively minor role in the initial stages of the legislative process throughout most of the first 100 years of the Republic. Even Andrew Jackson, who was the first to wield the veto power effectively to gain leverage over the Congress,[27] did not attempt to manipulate and lobby the Congress in a systematic way. Nonetheless, he vetoed the bill to recharter the Second Bank of the United States as a protest against the failure of congressional committees to consult in advance the views of the administration through the Treasury Department. He provoked the ire of orator Daniel Webster: "Throughout all this history of the contest for liberty, executive power has been regarded as a lion which must be caged."[28]

Beginning primarily with Theodore Roosevelt, the president has played an

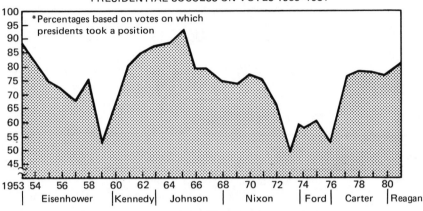

CHART 10-1
PRESIDENTIAL SUCCESS ON VOTES 1953–1981*

*Percentages based on votes on which presidents took a position

1953 54 56 58 60 62 64 66 68 70 72 74 76 78 80
Eisenhower | Kennedy | Johnson | Nixon | Ford | Carter | Reagan

SOURCE: Congressional Roll Call 1981, A Chronology and Analysis of votes in the House and Senate 97th Congress, First Session, Congressional Quarterly Inc. p. 21.

increasingly active role in developing legislative initiatives and attempting to guide the legislative process every step of the way. In large part the change has corresponded to the increased size of the country and the Congress, as well as the increased complexity of the federal government. Because the president as chief executive is elected every four years by a national electorate, his institutional incentive is to respond to the "national interest," whereas the Congress, elected by district, leans toward a more parochial, district-oriented outlook. Accordingly, leaders of Congress tend to look to the president to take the first step in solving national problems.

Today the president is viewed by many as the "Chief Legislator." President, then Senate majority leader, Lyndon B. Johnson best expressed the role of the president: "The President initiates, the legislature follows." His staff drafts legislative packages, which are sent to the Hill for passage. The president often lobbies personally for these packages. He holds breakfast meetings with legislators to persuade them to support his legislative initiatives. When a presidential initiative is in trouble, he uses his access to the media to muster public support for his views. No one has shown better recent skill at the use of the "bully pulpit" than President Reagan, who, in a dramatic address to the Congress shortly after an assassination attempt on his life, breathed new life into his tax program when most Hill savants predicted it had little chance.

Every president establishes a strongly staffed congressional relations office, and every agency has its own office to serve as a liaison to the Hill. The administration usually provides a top executive branch official as the first and most important witness to testify at hearings on any major piece of legislation. As early as 1921, the administration demanded that the Bureau of the Budget (now OMB) play a powerful role in ensuring that the administration speaks with one voice and that the left hand knows what the right is doing (President Reagan quipped in the early days of his administration that the right hand didn't know what the far right hand was doing). The president seeks to control every step of the legislative path. As the senator or congressman goes to the floor to vote, the administration lobbyists greet him at the door of the chamber. Even in the chamber, the president will sometimes send an emissary in the form of a member who is particularly close to him (for example, Senator Paul Laxalt, a close friend of President Reagan, often represented him on the floor). The president also becomes personally involved in the logrolling necessary to enact his legislation. To woo Democratic support for his budget cuts, President Reagan persuaded one Louisiana congressman in the Ninety-seventh Congress to support him in exchange for an administration commitment to support sugar price supports, a program it had previously opposed. He also agreed not to campaign against any congressman who supported his program. He flew delegations of congressmen from both parties to Camp David for barbecues—cowboy hats and all. The master of the soft sell, Reagan's personal interaction tipped the scales and gave him a tremendous victory. Thus, the role of the president in the legislative process today is hardly restricted to his use of the veto power.

Presidential Veto

The framers of the Constitution predicted little use of the veto power. As Alexander Hamilton said: "It is evident that there would be greater danger of his not using his power when necessary, than of his using it too often, or too much."[29] Hamilton's fear has proved unfounded in recent times. Franklin D. Roosevelt ushered in a new era of presidential intervention in Congress. Whereas earlier presidents had sent broad-brush policy messages to Congress, FDR sent down bills drafted by the administration. He even lobbied as to which committees his bills should be referred. Most important, when he used the veto he did it symbolically and dramatically to muster public support for his position, as opposed to that of Congress. For example, in 1935, President Roosevelt dramatized his disapproval of a measure by personally delivering his veto message to a joint session of Congress.

Recent presidents are not reluctant to use their veto power. In little more than two years in office, President Ford vetoed sixty-two public bills. Congress overrode only twelve vetoes, emphasizing the potency of the president's veto power. However, the threat of a presidential veto is sometimes dissipated by poor use. For example, after four years in office, President Carter in 1980 used the veto to override legislation providing salary increases for health-care employees, especially doctors in Veterans' Administration hospitals. That the influence of the Carter administration was waning is evident in the overwhelming vote to override. Often presidents attempt to use the threat of a veto to stall legislation or to persuade legislators to modify the legislation to comply with presidential objectives.

Vetoed legislation can become law if two-thirds of the members "present and voting" in both chambers override the veto. The president cannot veto one portion of a bill but not the rest. However, in his veto message he often explains the reason for his veto. His reasoning is rarely a great surprise to the congressional leadership, for, more often than not, the White House has, throughout the history of the bill, sent informal signals to the Hill indicating its displeasure.

Once an enrolled bill is sent to the White House, the president has ten days, excluding Sunday, to sign or veto the measure. If no action is taken in the ten-day period and Congress is in session, the bill automatically becomes law without the president's signature. If Congress adjourns before the ten-day period ends, the legislation may die by a "pocket veto." This presidential power has been curtailed to some degree by recent court decisions.

Although bill signing is often a perfunctory matter, it is often used to reward a president's friends and to get personal credit for the legislation. When President Carter signed a regulatory reform bill, which had been introduced by Iowa Senator John Culver, he held a signing ceremony much like a coronation in its extravagance. Both Carter and Culver were facing tough reelection fights. Amid the strains of violins, the guests drank punch (Carter seldom served hard liquor) and ate cakes. Such fanfare was particularly ironic, for President Carter had bitterly fought the legislation behind the scenes. Nonetheless, the president wanted to gain credit during his presidential race for a bill strongly desired by the small business community and consistent with his 1976 campaign pledge of less government regulation. Both Carter and Culver lost in November 1980.

The President as Chief Executor

The veto is not the only way in which an administration can effectively kill legislation. Even after a bill is duly enacted and in the United States Code, the administration has almost infinite weapons at its disposal to thwart the legislative aims of the Congress. First, it can nominate men and women to execute the law who are unsympathetic and will administer the programs in a hostile or lackluster way. It is a fact that the "advise and consent" powers of the Senate place some constraints on the presidential appointment power, but refusal to confirm a presidential choice is rare.

A president sometimes refuses to request funds for a program he does not want. Not believing in the efficiency of the Law Enforcement Assistance Administration, President Carter refused to include ample funds for it in the budget. Congress, of course, can appropriate funds, even without presidential request; however, when the congressional majority and the president are in the same party, such a breach is unlikely. Finally, within certain limits, the president can defer spending funds that have been appropriated, impound funds (with congressional approval), and reprogram funds among functions.

Because of President Nixon's excessive use of impoundments, Congress passed legislation to restrict presidential discretion in that area. Nonetheless, enforcement of these restrictions is difficult, and the president's power to forget legislative programs he does not like is formidable.

Furthermore, as the chief executor of the laws, the president has broad prosecutorial discretion not to enforce legislative prohibitions. Critics forecast President Reagan did not plan to enforce the mining laws vigorously when he substantially reduced the number of inspectors available to investigate mine safety violations. Similarly, the Justice Department's laxity in enforcing the Robinson–Patman Antitrust Act, which was enacted to prevent predatory pricing practices from squeezing out small business, would have rendered the act a nullity if the Federal Trade Commission—an agency independent of the president—had not vigorously prosecuted violations.

Moreover, when a president is averse to a program, he can thwart the issuance of regulations or require a reexamination of existing regulations in light of presidential priorities. As one of his first acts in office in 1981, President Reagan established a Task Force on Regulatory Relief, headed by Vice President George Bush, to target major regulations throughout the executive branch for review and revision to comply with the president's promise to "get the government off the backs of the people." More accurately, the task force mechanism permitted the president to rewrite regulations implementing laws with which he was unhappy.

Given the system of checks and balances, the president cannot go too far in defying legislative intent without inviting a court challenge or a legislative battle. Public-interest law firms became famous during the Nixon administration for going to court to force federal agencies to enforce enabling statutes. Moreover, legislative oversight is designed to castigate and pressure the administration to carry out legislative aims. Occasionally, a legislator will go into court to challenge an allegedly illegal presidential activity, like impoundment, when he can prove a diminution of his legislative power resulting from the president's actions. For all these caveats, the power of the president to thwart legislative goals is great indeed.

On the other side of the coin, the president and executive branch agencies have tremendous discretion to accomplish legislative goals that Congress never intended. Generally, when Congress enacts statutes, it delegates to agencies or departments very broadly defined powers. Most often a more precise language is not acceptable. The coalition necessary to pass a piece of legislation usually is founded on some ambiguities that permit differing interests to find a common cause. To exchange those ambiguities for more precise language, which makes clear who is helped and who is hurt by the legislation, would make the necessary coalition more difficult to build and to maintain. Consequently, the legislative history of a bill frequently contains floor debate in which supporters contend for inconsistent interpretations of the language of the bill before them. In a sense, such inconsistencies of meaning and purpose are almost inevitable in a country as pluralistic as America and in a legislative institution that reflects such pluralism with 435 House members and 100 senators, all elected locally and independently of a binding party platform or commitment. One example of an ambiguous overly broad charter is the one Congress gave to the Interstate Commerce Commission.

Based on a broad mandate to regulate trucks in the public interest, convenience, and necessity, the very complex regulatory structure devised by the Interstate Commerce Commission limited the rates charged by common carriers, restricted competition among carriers, and even governed the kind of freight that could be carried between two points. Certainly Congress did not intend that the ICC require trucks to return to their point of origin empty after delivering certain commodities—but the agency was given the discretion to issue that regulation.[30]

Between 1965 and 1975, Congress passed more regulatory legislation than ever before in its history, particularly in the health and safety areas. Congress told the Environmental Protection Agency to make the air clean, the Occupational Safety and Health Administration to make the work place safe, and the Federal Trade Commission to regulate unfair or deceptive trade practices. The mandates were broad, and the intended guidelines were few. In an effort to regulate unfair trade practices the FTC attempted to control the advertising of children's cereals. The National Transportation Safety Board proposed regulations to require mandatory seat belts and air bags to increase automobile safety. To protect endangered wildlife, the EPA went to court for the infamous snail darter and blocked construction of a major dam. Each of these agency actions prompted nationwide controversy.

Once again, checks are available to prevent an agency from carrying its mandate too far. Congress, particularly in recent years, has used its appropriations and authorizations process to curb agencies gone astray. The Federal Trade Commission was publicly drawn and quartered in the 1980 authorization bill because Congress believed it had wrongly construed its legislative mandate. Similarly, persons adversely affected by government regulation can go to court to argue that an agency has violated or transgressed its statutory authorization. Nonetheless, present doctrines of judicial construction and congressional inertia combine to give agencies great latitude in aggressively expanding their statutory powers.

Finally, through the increasing use of executive order, a president can effectively pass his own legislation, which has much the force of law.[31] President Johnson, on his own initiative, issued an executive order requiring affirmative action for government contractors. Presidents Ford, Carter, and Reagan issued executive orders, without legislative authorization, requiring all executive branch agencies to prepare cost-benefit analyses before implementing major rules. Presidents Carter and Reagan issued far-reaching executive orders and agreements dealing with the Iranian hostage crisis and settlement. Although a president cannot adopt an executive order that contravenes existing legislative directives, he has considerable discretion to issue orders, which have binding legal force, in areas not covered by the legislative branch.

STAGE SIX—THE JUDICIAL ROLE IN THE LEGISLATIVE PROCESS

Statutory Interpretation

The federal courts are more than observers of the legislative process. Article III of the Constitution provides that "the judicial power shall extend to all cases in law and equity arising under this Constitution, the laws of the United States, and treaties made, or which shall be made, under their authority." In 1803 the Supreme Court, under Federalist Chief Justice John Marshall, issued the historic landmark opinion in *Marbury* v. *Madison*,[32] asserting the power of the Court, under the Constitution, to declare statutes unconstitutional. At best, the colonial and parliamentary precedents of the assertion of the power of judicial review were spotty. The highest court in the land, in a bold and definitive stroke, preserved for itself the power not only to interpret legislative intent but also to circumscribe in their correct constitutional spheres the power of the president and of the Congress.

Under the traditional role of the court, a federal judge adjudicates claims of two or more litigants arising out of existing federal law. For example, in a private antitrust lawsuit, one company sues another under the Sherman Antitrust Act to obtain damages resulting from illegal price-fixing. The court is the interpreter of the antitrust law and, as such, has the final say on the interpretation of the law in that particular controversy. To determine legislative intent, the court consults legislative history: committee reports, floor debates, and conference reports. When the documents indicate a consideration of the problem by the Congress, the courts are able to determine the intent of Congress and thus apply the law to the case before it. However, in many situations, the heart of the problem being adjudicated has escaped the attention of Congress altogether.

How then is the court to fulfill its constitutional responsibility in deciding the case? It has several options. First, a court looks to legislative history only if the meaning of the statute is ambiguous. Random comments by legislators reflect, in all likelihood, not the sense of the Congress but merely the sense of one member. A court should therefore be wary of delving into legislative history unless the statute cannot be interpreted without it.

It is difficult to predict the response of the Supreme Court, which guides the interpretations handed down by lower federal courts and agencies, to any given statute at any given time. In previous years, the Court has been somewhat sympathetic to the notion of "implied remedies." If a statute created a right, but did not specify the means by which an individual could enforce his rights, the court concluded that remedies could be implied. Most recently, however, the Court has cut back sharply on the doctrine of "implied remedies."

Various rules govern the judicial interpretation of the history of a statute. First, a court is not to look behind the "plain meaning" of a statute. Given the use of unambiguous words, the legislation should speak for itself. To rummage around in various committee reports and floor debates denigrates the legislative process. And any deliberate effort by the use of floor speeches or colloquy to create a particular judicial interpretation should be viewed with a jaundiced eye. Although floor debate sometimes sheds light on ambiguous words and phrases, prepared speeches are more likely to lead judicial interpretation down the primrose path.

Expanding Role of the Courts

In recent years, the role of the courts in affecting government policy has expanded as litigation evolved from the so-called private interest model to the public interest model. Now, the courts, and in particular the Washington federal courts, are expected to interpret the existing statutory responsibilities of agencies while reviewing regulations promulgated by the agencies under broad legislative mandates. Public interest litigation is significantly different from private interest litigation; public interest litigation usually reflects all the complications of the legislative process and is frequently the "second bite of the apple" for those groups that lost in Congress and in the agency decision-making process.

Because major interest groups are in conflict, the law that Congress passes is frequently the product of numerous hearings and negotiations between the different groups. Almost every decision regarding nuclear energy and environmental conservation regulations, for example, inevitably ends up in court. When a business or industry is required by the Environmental Protection Agency to decrease air pollution, both the business community, complaining that it goes too far, and the environmental community, complaining that it is not strong enough, are likely to challenge that regulation in court before the rule can go into effect.

Similarly, the courts are injected into the policy-making function of virtually every major government regulation. Theoretically, at least, the court is to review regulations under carefully circumscribed standards of judicial review spelled out by Congress. The court is instructed to decide merely whether an agency decision is "arbitrary or capricious," whether the agency followed the correct procedures, and whether the decision is consistent with the agency's statutory mandate. Here again, however, the Congress, more often than not, has abdicated to the courts the responsibility for discerning legislative intent from vague statutes. Some scholars and judges have called upon the courts to revive the "nondelegation doctrine" rather than allowing Congress to leave broad and unguided power to make major policy decisions in the courts.[33]

If the Congress disagrees with a judicial interpretation of a statute, it has an easy solution: It can pass new legislation clarifying its intent.

Constitutional Questions

The resolution of constitutional questions is more intricate. To overturn a judicial ruling declaring a statute is unconstitutional, Congress can, by a two-thirds vote, initiate a constitutional amendment. To become law, the amendment must be ratified by three-fourths of the states; it is not presented to the president for his approval. However, Congress has an infinite number of ways to influence constitutional decision making. Through its power to confirm judges, the Senate ensures the appointment of judges whose political and social philosophies are consistent with the views of the majority of the chamber.[34] The two-step nominating process—the president nominates, the Senate confirms—ensures at least a rough reflection of the evolving political consensus.[35]

Although Congress cannot overturn a judicial interpretation of the Constitution, it can enact legislation to expand the guarantee of the Constitution. In *Zurcher* v. *Stanford Daily*,[36] the Supreme Court stated that the press was not guaranteed special protection from police searches by the First Amendment. Because Congress disagreed, legislation was passed requiring the use of a subpoena rather than a search warrant in investigating press offices. Similarly, in *Mapp* v. *Ohio*,[37] the Supreme Court expanded the "exclusionary rule" to prohibit the use of evidence obtained in violation of the Fourth Amendment's search and seizure arrest warrant requirements in state criminal trials. The primary purpose of the exclusionary rule is to deter the police from violating the Fourth Amendment. Chief Justice Warren Burger, in a subsequent dissenting opinion, suggested that Congress provide an alternative remedy to deter the police and thereby obviate the need for the judicially created exclusionary rule.[38] The Congress has proposed some legislative remedies, but none has been adopted.

In certain cases the Constitution explicitly permits Congress to expand upon constitutional rights. Thus, in the voting rights area,[39] Congress reduced the requirements of literacy tests far beyond the level declared constitutionally required by the courts. As its authority, the Congress and the Supreme Court cited the fifth section of the Fourteenth Amendment, which provides Congress with "power to enforce, by appropriate legislation, the provisions of this Article."

However, the ability of Congress to affect constitutional decisions is limited. In a recent bill,[40] North Carolina Senator Jesse Helms attempted to overturn the Supreme Court decision providing the right of women to abort a pregnancy by defining human life, for purposes of the Fourteenth Amendment, as beginning at the point of conception. This legislation raised profound questions about the role of Congress in interpreting the Constitution. Although the Supreme Court is the ultimate arbiter of the Constitution, certainly the Congress is also *an* arbiter of its meaning. Congressmen and senators, under oath to support and defend the Constitution of the United States, have to reconcile their own views with those of the courts in measuring the constitutionality of legislation considered by the Congress. Many noted constitutional scholars argue that each congressman has the obligation to vote against any legislation that would clearly violate existing constitutional standards. Moreover, many congressmen, with due respect to the Supreme Court's views, insist that they should vote for or against legislation based on their own views of constitutionality. However, the subject does not draw a standing-room-only audience. The population of either chamber declines suddenly when one or more members begin to debate the constitutionality of a legislative proposal. Those matters should "be left to the courts," they argue; the intricacies of the

Lull in the siege of Washington.

From *The Herblock Gallery* (Simon & Schuster, 1968)

due process clause and the equal protection clause of the Constitution are not a favorite topic of most congressmen.

Limits on Federal Court Jurisdiction and Powers

Finally, a Congress displeased with an overly intrusive judiciary can proceed to restrict the standards of judicial review, cut back on some statutory jurisdiction, and modify venue laws. Under the Constitution, Congress has the power to establish and regulate the lower, or "inferior," federal courts. Thus, when constitutional rights are not at stake, Congress can—although it rarely does—cut off judicial review. Even when specific constitutional issues are involved, some scholars argue Congress can limit the jurisdiction of the lower federal courts by requiring all such claims to be made through the state judicial system and ultimately reviewed by the United States Supreme Court. It may also be able to limit remedies available to federal courts, like busing, in effectuating constitutional rights. Many bills were introduced in recent Congresses to limit federal court jurisdiction although none has become law. The constitutionality of these limitations have not yet been tested in the courts.

STAGE SEVEN—
BACK IN CONGRESS

Ultimately, almost every piece of legislation returns to Congress, for the fine-tuning of legislation continues even after enactment.

First, and foremost, Congress reviews most statutory federal programs. Although some earlier programs were permanently authorized, more recently new federal programs expire every so often—every year, every three years, or even every ten years. At that point Congress reviews the effectiveness of the statute and rewrites the underlying legislation and legislative history to deal with problems that have emerged since the program was initially enacted. The new legislative "history" may tell the agency or court what Congress intended in the original statute or in the amendment. During hearings, congressmen pressure leading executive branch officials to pursue certain policies more assiduously or to back off from specific strategies.

Usually communications between the agencies and the authorizing committees are continuous. An agency rarely makes a major move without first doing the necessary political homework in the House and Senate committees. In committee reports, agencies often request new legislative history to help them justify in the courts new programs or initiatives. Just as frequently, an agency is forced to head in new directions as a result of a committee report.

Even a permanent authorization—that is, a legislative program or authority that continues in the absence of legislation to the contrary—goes through a yearly appropriations process, which is by no means perfunctory. The Appropriations committee—or more accurately, the Appropriations subcommittees—often reverse authorizing committees to establish different policy directions for the executive branch by cutting funds for a program of which they disapprove, earmarking funds for favored initiatives, and inserting legislative history into the report to pressure the agency to take a particular course of action. More recently the Budget committees have acted to influence legislative programs by cutting funds.

Thus, the watchdogs of the executive branch constantly scrutinize every nuance of a law's evolution and act swiftly when agency enforcement is less than that desired.

Legislation that requires little funding may languish on the statute books for years without sparking congressional interest. However, whenever a vibrant, controversial—or expensive—issue is at stake, Congress keeps its fingers in the pot and defers to the other two branches only when it is to its political advantage to pass the buck.

ELEVEN

WHO CONTROLS EXPENDITURES?

The Congress shall have power to lay and collect taxes, duties, imposts, and excises.
Article I, Section 8

No money shall be drawn from the Treasury, but in consequence of appropriations made by law.
Article I, Section 9

None of us really understands what's going on with all these numbers.
David Stockman, director
of the Office of Management
and Budget, 1981[1]

he Constitution allocates to Congress two essential fiscal responsibilities: to raise revenue and to control spending—the "power of the purse," the ultimate power over virtually every federal activity. In 1982 the federal purse controlled the largest budget in the world—$709 billion in fiscal year 1982—and the largest debt in the world—exceeding $1 trillion—resulting in a predicted budget deficit of well over $100 billion.[2]

Until the 1930s, Congress jealously had guarded its budgetary powers against encroachment by the executive branch. During the colonial period, the popularly elected state legislators used their budgetary powers to curb overly aggressive royal governors, and Congress, throughout its two centuries, similarly used budgetary control to check the presidency.

However, beginning with the New Deal in the 1930s and extending into the 1960s, congressional attention to budgetary restraints waned. The supply of money appeared endless. President Lyndon B. Johnson successfully funded his "Great Society" domestic programs and at the same time financed a costly war in Southeast Asia. As long as monies were plentiful and the competing demands of both "guns and butter" could be met in the period after World War II, the struggle to control funds was neither desperate—nor bitter.

257

TABLE 11-1
FEDERAL BUDGET REVENUES AND EXPENDITURES,
1789–1982 (in millions of dollars)

Fiscal year	Federal Revenues	Federal Expenditures	Budget surplus or deficit (−)	Fiscal year	Federal Revenues	Federal Expenditures	Budget surplus or deficit (−)
1789–1849	1,160	1,090	+70	1950	39,485	42,597	−3,112
1850–1900	14,462	15,453	−991	1951	51,646	45,546	+6,100
1901–1905	2,797	2,678	+119	1952	66,204	67,721	−1,517
1906–1910	3,143	3,196	−52	1953	69,574	76,107	−6,533
1911–1915	3,517	3,568	−49	1954	69,719	70,890	−1,170
1916–1920	17,286	40,195	−22,909	1955	65,469	68,509	−3,041
1921	5,571	5,062	+509	1956	74,547	70,460	+4,087
1922	4,026	3,289	+736	1957	79,990	76,741	+3,249
1923	3,853	3,140	+713	1958	79,636	82,575	−2,939
1924	3,871	2,908	+963	1959	79,249	92,104	−12,855
1925	3,641	2,924	+717	1960	92,492	92,223	+269
1926	3,795	2,930	+865	1961	94,389	97,795	−3,406
1927	4,013	2,857	+1,155	1962	99,676	106,813	−7,137
1928	3,900	2,961	+939	1963	106,560	111,311	−4,751
1929	3,862	3,127	+734	1964	112,662	118,584	−5,922
1930	4,058	3,320	+738	1965	116,833	118,430	−1,596
1931	3,116	3,577	−462	1966	130,856	134,652	−3,796
1932	1,924	4,659	−2,735	1967	149,552	158,254	−8,702
1933	1,997	4,598	−2,602	1968	153,671	178,833	−25,161
1934	3,015	6,645	−3,630	1969	187,784	184,548	+3,236
1935	3,706	6,497	−2,791	1970	193,743	196,588	−2,845
1936	3,997	8,442	−4,425	1971	188,392	211,425	−23,033
1937	4,956	7,733	−2,777	1972	208,649	232,021	−23,373
1938	5,588	6,765	−1,177	1973	232,225	247,074	−14,849
1939	4,979	8,841	−3,862	1974	264,932	269,620	−4,688
1940	6,361	9,456	−3,095	1975	280,997	326,151	−45,154
1941	8,621	13,634	−5,013	1976	300,005	366,418	−66,413
1942	14,350	35,114	−20,764	TQ.	81,773	94,728	−12,956
1943	23,649	78,533	−54,884	1977	357,762	402,710	−44,948
1944	44,276	91,280	−47,004	1978	401,997	450,804	−48,807
1945	45,216	92,690	−47,474	1979	465,940	493,635	−27,694
1946	39,327	55,183	−15,856	1980	520,050	579,613	−59,563
1947	38,394	34,532	+3,862	1981	599,272	657,204	−57,932
1948	41,774	29,773	+12,001	1982	617,766	728,375	−110,609
1949	39,437	38,834	+603				

DATA FOR 1789–1939 ARE FOR THE ADMINISTRATIVE BUDGET: DATA FOR 1940 AND ALL FOLLOWING YEARS ARE FOR THE UNIFIED BUDGET. IN CALENDAR YEAR 1976, THE FEDERAL FISCAL YEAR WAS CONVERTED FROM A JULY 1–JUNE 30 BASIS TO AN OCT. 1–SEPT. 30 BASIS. THE TQ REFERS TO THE TRANSITION QUARTER FROM JULY 1 TO SEPT 30, 1976. OFF-BUDGET FEDERAL ENTITY OUTLAYS BEGIN IN 1973.
SOURCE: EXECUTIVE OFFICE OF THE PRESIDENT, OFFICE OF MANAGEMENT AND BUDGET, 1982

"There's money enough to support both of you—
now, doesn't that make you feel better?"

From *The Herblock Gallery* (Simon & Schuster, 1968)

Amazingly, Congress had developed no procedures to ensure a rough equivalency of spending and revenue levels. Because funds were plentiful, there was little incentive to dampen the nationwide spurt in federal activism. But in the late 1970s, the chickens came home to roost.

Spiraling inflation, coupled with recession, unemployment, and a general malaise of the American economy, produced an overwhelming public demand to cut federal spending, to reduce the size of big government, to minimize the growth of the federal debt and deficit, and to alleviate the tax burden. President Nixon was the first to sound alarm about the need for fiscal austerity, but his high-handed efforts only infuriated members of Congress—both houses of which were controlled by the other party—who viewed his impoundment activities as an encroachment on their constitutionally guaranteed fiscal prerogatives.

Congress responded to the Nixon challenge with the Congressional Budget and Impoundment Control Act, perhaps the most significant congressional reform measure of the 1970s. President Carter, with at best modest success, attempted to use the new Budget Act procedures to control the federal budget by forming an alliance with the new chairmen of the Senate and the House Budget committees, Maine's Edmund Muskie and Connecticut's Robert Giaimo. They paved the way for the first real test of the new budget process in the Ninety-seventh Congress. The task of the Ninety-seventh Congress was not made easier by President Reagan's plan to increase defense spending, decrease tax revenues, and balance the budget simultaneously. In 1981 approximately 72 percent of the federal budget was allocated to entitlements and other "back door" spending items—for example, social security, loan guarantee funds, interest payments—which cannot be decreased easily through the budget process.[3] Thus, Congress faced a dilemma: to cut popular social programs or defy the recently elected president. These proposed budget cuts in social programs sparked major national debate, not only over the social policies underlying these programs but, just as importantly, over the budget process enacted in 1974.

The struggle, in 1981, to gain control of the shrinking federal budget prompted a congressional power reallocation. It pitted the president against Congress, interest group against interest group, Democrats against Republicans. It generated a series of battles among main committees responsible for raising and spending monies—the authorizing, Appropriations, Budget, and taxation committees. Even more important, it challenged many principles traditionally held sacrosanct by Congress. In the Senate, the struggle cast gaping holes in the most hallowed of rights: the right to filibuster. And in both chambers the omnipotence of the Budget committees decreased the traditional powers of the formerly exalted Appropriations and taxation committees. Finally and significantly, it created a war between the authorizing

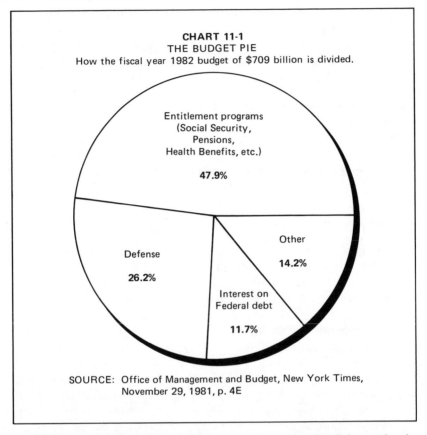

CHART 11-1
THE BUDGET PIE
How the fiscal year 1982 budget of $709 billion is divided.

Entitlement programs
(Social Security,
Pensions,
Health Benefits, etc.)

47.9%

Defense

26.2%

Interest on
Federal debt

11.7%

Other

14.2%

SOURCE: Office of Management and Budget, New York Times,
November 29, 1981, p. 4E

committees and the Budget committees over major national policies, seriously damaging the autonomy of the committee fiefdom.

Concern about the federal budget prompted other significant changes in congressional procedures for controlling federal purse strings. Congress improved its "oversight," or review, of the effectiveness of government policies and programs. Statutes enacted in the 1970s provided Congress with procedural tools to oversee, with exacting scrutiny, expenditures, particularly those in the foreign policy arena, and to limit agency regulatory discretion.

In short, Congress in the 1970s experienced a major upheaval in its traditional ways of controlling the purse. Perhaps the tremors will be short-lived, and perhaps the power bases in the Congress will be restored or shifted yet again. However, one thing is clear. Congress will continue to search for ways to improve its grip over the federal budget, for that is the source of its most enduring power.

This chapter examines the main components of congressional control over the power of the purse. A brief history of the evolution of the budget process is followed by a description of the dynamics of establishing a federal budget in the Ninety-seventh Congress. The next chapter looks at the committees responsible for raising revenue and their relationship in the overall budgetary system. The chapter also examines the "oversight" functions of congressional committees and the degree to which they control the daily activities and policies of federal agencies. Finally, the fiscal relationship between the courts and the Congress is discussed.

Each section focuses on the constant tug-of-war between the branches of government over the control of federal expenditures—perhaps the most significant power struggle in the checks-and-balances paradigm.

HISTORY OF THE FEDERAL PURSE

Congress values none of its powers more than the power of the purse. Colonial assemblies used this power as leverage over royal governors. The Massachusetts legislature, for example, refused to fix a permanent salary for the governor and insisted, instead, on funding the executive branch with such precise annual allowances that gave the governor little spending discretion. A formal statement by the Massachusetts legislature in 1728 asserted the "undoubted right of all Englishmen, by Magna Carta, to raise and dispose of money for the public service of their own free accord, without compulsion."[4]

During the Revolution, the Continental Congress examined in excruciating detail each expenditure of the Continental Army and, to the chagrin of the officers, Monday-morning quarterbacked their major strategic decisions. The Continental Congress provided for the organization and equipment of the army, issued paper money to finance military operations, and in a myriad of ways oversaw the activities of the army.

The fiscal dominance of the early Continental Congress stood in stark contrast to the fiscal helplessness of the Congress of the Confederation, which lacked the authority to secure from the states the money needed to pay the national debt and current national expenses. The inability of the Congress to raise revenues precipitated a crisis of confidence in the viability of the federal government and resulted in the Constitutional Convention. As James Madison stated in his introduction to the *Journal of the Constitutional Convention*, one "radical infirmity" of the Articles of Confederation was the "urgent demands of the Federal Treasury and the glaring inadequacy of supplying it."[5]

Indeed, the authors of the Constitution felt so strongly about ensuring the fiscal prerogatives of the Congress that a serious (although unsuccessful) movement was undertaken to make the secretary of the Treasury directly accountable to the Congress instead of to the president.[6] With a sense of urgency, Alexander Hamilton explained the need for a Congress with clear-cut financial strength in the *Federalist Papers*:

> Money is, with propriety, considered as the vital principle of the body politic, as that which sustains its life and motion, and enables it to perform its most essential functions. A complete power, therefore, to procure a regular and adequate supply of it, as far as the resources of the community will permit, may be regarded as an indispensable ingredient in every Constitution.[7]

The Constitution expressly gives Congress the authority to raise revenues and to control public expenditures by appropriation.

> The Congress shall have the power— to lay and collect taxes, duties, imposts and excises. [Article I, Section 8]
> No money shall be drawn from the Treasury, but in consequence of appropriations made by law. [Article I, Section 9]

The House and the Senate share roughly equal responsibilities for appropriating funds. But the House of Representatives was delegated the *exclusive* right to initiate revenue bills because the framers of the Constitution believed the House was closer to the electorate and could therefore better reflect public concerns.[8] Having recently fought a revolution in which the rallying cry was "no taxation without representation," the constitutional conferees were circumspect in giving too much taxation power to the Senate, which was not then directly elected. By tradition, rather than law, the House also initiated appropriation bills.

Faced with the problem of preparing a federal budget, the first Congress appointed a small Committee of Ways and Means—thirteen members, one from each state—to "prepare an estimate of supplies requisite for the service of the United States in the current year, and report thereupon."[9] However, with the establishment of a Treasury Department, the Ways and Means Committee was disbanded. Instead, Congress relied exclusively on Treasury Secretary Alexander Hamilton, who dominated fiscal matters until his resignation in 1795. With the departure of Hamilton, Congress asserted a predominance in budgetary matters that it was to retain for well over a century. It re-created the Ways and Means Committee and required an annual budget estimate from the secretary of the Treasury. The Ways and Means Committee (which was made a "standing," or permanent, committee in 1811) handled both the raising of revenue and appropriations; by the time of the Civil War, it had become the most powerful committee in Congress. As political scientists Kenneth Bradshaw and David Pring stated: "It had established by its tight and comprehensive control over finance the right to cut or reject policies and expenditures proposed by other committees and had won itself a privileged status which enabled it to enforce its views in the House."[10] The comparable Senate committee never achieved the same status because it lacked the authority to originate revenue bills.

Evolution of the
Appropriations Committees

The heavy press of business in a rapidly expanding nation in the post-Civil War era forced the Ways and Means committees in both chambers to jettison their responsibility for appropriations. However, the power of the new appropriations committees established in each chamber was short-lived. They began to encroach on the jurisdiction of the standing committees with responsibility for specific subject areas and not only aggressively cut the funds provided by these authorizing committees but also grafted substantive authorizing provisions onto appropriation bills. Not surprisingly, a coalition of standing committees successfully dismembered the appropriations committees, and between 1877 and 1885, half the jurisdiction of the appropriations committees was distributed to the relevant standing committees. Consequently, for more than fifty years the government lacked a centralized budget-making mechanism. Instead, standing committees were entrusted with the dual responsibility of establishing substantive programs and appropriating the money to pay for them.

In general, the role of the Treasury secretary in the budgetary process[11] was routine and perfunctory. Individual spending agencies transmitted their budget requests to Congress in a Book of Estimates. With some significant exceptions, presidents and Treasury secretaries were passive bystanders, forwarding the agencies' budget estimates to Congress with little revision or comment. The built-in conflict between authorizing and appropriations committees, which had imposed some restraints on spending, disappeared. Fiscal irresponsibility reigned.[12]

Role of the Executive Branch

Historically, considerable tension has existed between the executive and legislative branches over the primary allegiance of the Treasury secretary. As previously mentioned, delegates to the Constitutional Convention had attempted to make the secretary of the Treasury directly accountable to Congress as he had been under the Articles of Confederation. Losing that battle, Congress was further irritated by Alexander Hamilton, who refused to act as its agent. When Hamilton asked to come before Congress in 1792 to answer

Alexander Hamilton's years as secretary of the treasury (1789–1795) were made difficult by tension between the executive and legislative branches.

questions concerning the public debt, legislators protested Hamilton's practice of dominating the two branches. In 1793 the House passed a resolution claiming that Hamilton had violated appropriation laws, ignored instructions, failed to discharge essential duties, and had committed an indecorum against the House.[13] Legislative investigations persisted until Hamilton decided to resign in 1795. However, concern over the activities of the Treasury secretary persisted. President James Monroe was plagued by a Treasury secretary who consistently failed to advise him of Treasury requests for money that had been sent to Congress. Interestingly, however, Monroe did not fire the secretary even though communications between them at times ceased.[14]

The struggle over the allegiance of the Treasury secretary intensified during Andrew Jackson's presidency. Congress treated the Treasury secretary as its agent, delegating to him, rather than to the president, the responsibility for placing government money in either the National Bank or state banks. Jackson, who wanted the funds deposited in state banks, had to remove two secretaries before finding one willing to execute his plan. A Senate resolution censured Jackson for acting in derogation of the Constitution and the laws. Jackson, however, continued to insist that the Treasury belonged wholly to the executive branch and that the safekeeping of public funds was an executive, not a legislative, responsibility. In 1840 Whig President William Henry Harrison reversed the Jackson position, warning of the "unhallowed union of the Treasury with the Executive Department."[15] Later President John Tyler concurred. In short, the struggle for control of federal monies and the Treasury continued well into the nineteenth century, with Congress, in general, maintaining the upper hand.

By the turn of the twentieth century, it had become clear that a better method was needed to control federal spending. Without restraint, Congress passed innumerable river and harbor bills, private pension bills, and bills compensating veterans.[16] The lack of a centralized appropriations committee, with a vested institutional responsibility for setting spending priorities, had resulted in rampant fiscal irresponsibility. The executive branch sought to place some restraints on Congress. Initially, in the late nineteenth century, the president depended on the veto to keep the budget within reason. President Grover Cleveland, for example, vetoed almost 304 spending bills. President Theodore Roosevelt initiated numerous efforts to gain control of federal spending. William Howard Taft prohibited bureau officers and division chiefs from applying to Congress for legislation or appropriations except with the consent and knowledge of the department head. Furthermore, Taft specified that requests from Congress for information were to be satisfied exclusively through, or authorized by, department heads.

In the 1920s Congress instituted two major budgetary reforms. First, in 1921, it enacted the Budget and Accounting Act, which created the Bureau of the Budget, located in the Treasury Department, and authorized the president to appoint his own budget director. The Budget Bureau was given the authority to assemble, correlate, and revise department estimates but was not allowed to touch estimates prepared for Congress and the Supreme Court. In addition, the General Accounting Office (GAO) was established to help Congress devise a national budget. The comptroller general of the GAO could be removed only upon the initiative of Congress.

The 1921 act marked the congressional recognition of the central role of the executive branch in budgetary matters. Congressional leaders had long been nervous about acknowledging a role for the executive branch in establishing the budget. "Uncle Joe" Cannon, that powerful speaker of the House, had warned that an executive budget would signify the surrender of the most important element of representative government: "I think we had better stick pretty close to the Constitution with its division of powers well defined and the taxing power close to the people."[17] To ensure its own continued role in the budget process, each house quickly moved to centralize its own controls over the budget. The House consolidated jurisdiction over all appropriations into a single committee. The Senate soon followed suit. The objective of these reforms was to consolidate all appropriations in one comprehensive measure. However, these expectations were short-lived. Instead, the Appropriations committees established subcommittees to submit separate subcommittee appropriations bills to the Congress one by one—a practice that continues today. The subcommittees enjoyed a substantial degree of autonomy because of their intense specialization, and, in general, the full Appropriations committees deferred to the subcommittee recommendations. Thus instead of one appropriation bill, historically there have been about thirteen.

For fifty years after these budget reforms the executive branch played an increasingly powerful role in the budget process, largely because of the continued failure of Congress to centralize its budget activities. The Bureau of the Budget gained new powers as a central clearinghouse. It reviewed agency budget proposals to determine their accord with the fiscal program of the president; it coordinated departmental comment on legislation originating in Congress; and it advised the president as to whether a bill should be signed or vetoed. During the Franklin Roosevelt administration, the bureau grew from 40 to 600 people as its responsibilities were expanded beyond the narrow role of preparing the national budget. Entrusted with the task of controlling activities of the various executive departments, it became an instrument to promote economic stability.

The White House dominance of budgetary activities culminated in the Nixon administration when the president, through a reorganization plan submitted to Congress, replaced the Budget Bureau with the Office of Management and Budget (OMB), an office directly under the presidential thumb. Nixon explained that the new agency would no longer be primarily concerned with preparing the budget, but rather would assess "the extent to which programs are actually achieving their intended results, and delivering the intended services to the intended recipients."[18]

Recognizing the critical role of OMB, Congress insisted that its director be appointed with the advice and consent of the Senate. The battle over the allegiance of the Treasury secretary was no longer of moment. Now the key actor in the budgetary process was the OMB director—and he owed his loyalty and reporting responsibility directly to the president.

The executive branch's dominance of the budgetary decision-making process stemmed from its virtual monopoly over fiscal information. The expertise of its budget analysts, coupled in recent times with their access to computer resources, far surpassed that of the Congress. Executive agencies were forbidden to recommend budget levels to Congress (although their recommendations often were leaked to friendly staff on congressional committees). Instead, the only recommendations received by Congress were those sent by the president and defended by agency spokesmen at appropriation hearings. Any discrepancy between an agency's original request and the president's ultimate recommendation was shielded by executive secrecy. Only certain independent agencies—Federal Trade Commission and other agencies that do not report to the president but are considered "arms" of Congress—were permitted to communicate their budgetary requests directly to Congress.

Congressional budgetary expertise was in short supply. Certain outside groups, like the Brookings Institution and well-established interest groups, published budget studies, but in-house congressional expertise to counter the vast resources of the OMB was not available. The General Accounting Office was rather a watchdog auditor, not a budgetary analyst. The ready availability of White House expertise created a presumption favoring White House budgetary requests. Although these requests were not always granted, they set the parameters for budgetary debate.

In the booming economy of the early 1960s, little tension existed between the president and the Congress over spending priorities. President Lyndon Johnson confidently affirmed the ability of the United States to finance both military and domestic needs without trading one off against the other.[19] However, after the Vietnam War, the cupboard was almost bare. Budget expert Allen Schick blames insufficient funding on "uncontrollable" expenditures in his book *Congress and Money*:

Part of the reason for this deviation from past patterns was a radical change in the composition of the federal budget. . . . Before the Vietnam conflict, most of the budget was spent on the operations of government agencies. As measured in the national income accounts, 55 per cent of the fiscal 1964 outlays (the last year before significant Vietnam escalation) went for purchases of goods and services, with 25 per cent for transfer payments, and less than 10 per cent for grants to state and local governments. The distribution was quite different in fiscal 1975, the last year before implementation of the congressional budget process. Forty per cent of the 1975 budget was spent on transfer payments to individuals, and another 15 per cent was granted to states and localities.

Most transfer payments are mandatory entitlements over which Congress is extremely reluctant to exercise control. The amounts spent on a particular benefit program usually are determined by external factors such as the number of people receiving Social Security, public assistance or unemployment compensation. As the beneficiary populations increase, they generate automatic rises in federal payments. Moreover, most of the transfer programs are indexed so that the level of benefits automatically adjusts in response to changes in the cost of living or some other index. . . .

As a consequence of this growth in entitlements and transfer payments, the portion of the budget that is "uncontrollable" climbed from 60 per cent in fiscal 1968 to 72 per cent in the 1974 budget. During this period more than 90 per cent of the increase in total outlays was accounted for by uncontrollable spending.

These figures suggest that most incremental resources are committed before Congress has an opportunity to make current budget decisions. As a result, budget conflict cannot be contained merely by tapping the incremental resources of the federal government. This problem has been complicated by the sluggish performance of the economy and periodic reductions in income tax rates. The combination of spiralling expenditures, lowered tax rates, and revenue shortfalls has resulted in chronic and sizable budget deficits. . . .

Deficit spending was a political "safety valve," making it possible to soften the harsh choices of program cutbacks or tax increases. It was a convenient conflict-abatement strategy, provided that budget makers were willing to bear the political onus of high deficits. Yet despite—perhaps because of—deficit spending, budgetary conflict heated up during the pre-Budget Act years. There were repeated efforts to terminate or curtail programs, in disregard of the incremental strategy of assuring budget tranquility by continuing programs. . . .

Although many of [Nixon's] aims were thwarted by Congress, his cut-back drives precipitated intense budget strife.[20]

Various congressional devices to regain control of the budgetary process were doomed to failure because of a lack of congressional procedures and because the practice of considering spending programs separately, one by one, continued. For every device explored by Congress, another device was at hand to deflate its utility. For example, to avoid budgetary ceilings, some committees placed favored programs on "off-budget" status, thereby excluding such expenditures from not only budget totals but also spending limits.

Birth of the Budget Act

An overhaul of the congressional budgetary process was generated by a major issue of the 1972 presidential campaign. With unsurpassed bravado, President Nixon vetoed numerous appropriation bills, charging they constituted reckless spending.[21] After his reelection, Nixon used his strong national mandate to impound funds as a means to control federal spending. He vetoed Federal Water Pollution Control legislation in 1972 and threatened to impound the funds if his veto was overridden. Subsequently, $6 billion of water pollution control funds were impounded. He also withheld more than $10 billion for other domestic programs and took unilateral steps to prevent the expenditure of appropriations. In short, Nixon threw down the gauntlet to Congress. Unless

Congress devised mechanisms to control spending, the president was likely to be successful in appealing to the public for determination of his budget priorities. The message to Congress was blunt: "I don't care what you appropriate; I will decide what will be spent."[22]

Thus challenged, Congress responded with the Congressional Budget and Impoundment Control Act of 1974,[23] which created the tools necessary to regain dominance in fiscal matters. It is ironic—but perhaps a testament to our constitutional scheme of government—that a most aggressive "imperial" president should be most responsible for the reemergence of a strong Congress.

In devising the Congressional Budget Act of 1974, the members of Congress were well aware that the distribution of power within the legislative branch would be altered considerably. Because of the traditional strength of the committees, particularly the Appropriations and Senate Finance and House Ways and Means committees, the Budget Act does not eliminate their function but rather superimposes another budgetary layer through the creation of a Budget Committee in each house.

Not surprisingly, the main opponents of the budgetary reform were members of the Appropriations and tax committees, previously the dominant actors in the budget drama. Their fears of losing power to the infant Budget committees were well founded. As the new budget process developed strong roots in the congressional power structure, the Appropriations committees lost their status as the sole arbiters of spending amounts for each government program. Now such decisions are frequently made during debates over budget resolutions, thereby reducing the function of the Appropriations committees in many circumstances to administration. Similarly, the taxation committees lost their monopoly over determining revenue levels, for such determinations now are sometimes made by budget resolutions.

However, it was clear to Congress that a new budget process was necessary to respond to an increasing public demand for an end to fiscal irresponsibility. That throughout much of congressional history no procedures were available to equate the spending and revenue sides of the equation is unbelievable. Unlike even the smallest business or the most primitive household budget, no one was responsible for the so-called bottom line. The Appropriations committees spent, the revenue committees taxed, but no mechanism was available to assess the combined impact of spending and taxing on budget surpluses or deficits. Increasingly large budget deficits resulted, and in the 1970s Congress was forced to raise the public debt level to finance, by borrowing, public expenditures.

When the Congressional Budget and Impoundment Control Act finally passed, it passed overwhelmingly. In the Senate, there were no votes in opposition, and in the House only 23 nay votes. In the House–Senate conference, there were no significant issues concerning the budget process itself, but the impoundment control procedures created a temporary stalemate. The impasse was broken by dividing impoundments into two categories: rescission and deferral. A presidential "rescission of funds"—that is, a total elimination of funding—must be approved by the Congress within forty-five days after being proposed. In contrast, a presidential "deferral"—that is, a deferral of funds to another year—is automatically sustained unless disapproved by either house. And so, this compromise firmly in place, the Budget Act became a reality. Not the least salient fact of the whole debate is that legislation of such major consequence became law with such remarkable dispatch—within two years of the first specific proposals.

To assuage the residual fears of some of the House leaders, the House Budget Committee was established with a rotating chairman and membership—to preclude any development of lasting power in the Committee. The Senate Budget Committee was not subject to these limitations and was authorized to function like any other standing committee.

PRINCIPLES AND MECHANICS
OF THE BUDGET PROCESS

In practice, the budget process has evolved differently from the intended principle. In principle, the Budget Act was designed to be a procedural, not a substantive, process, based on the premise that fiscal responsibility is best achieved by an orderly consideration of the revenue and spending side of an equation according to a fixed and predictable timetable. Congress intended that the existing authorizing and Appropriations committees would retain their jurisdictional responsibilities as long as they met the mandated timetable. Within the terms of the Budget Act itself there is no built-in bias toward *less* spending. Rather, the main impetus is to ensure a budget procedure capable of spotlighting spending increases or decreases and their relationship to revenue measures.

In practice, the Budget committees have usurped substantial jurisdiction from the other committees and the budget procedure has resulted in an antispending bias. In the process, Congress has been transformed from a bumbling giant slowly meandering through major legislative changes to a lithe jogger with the procedural capability of fast-tracking perceived national mandates with but the briefest glance at the procedural safeguards so carefully built up over the years.

The budget process, a one-year cycle, begins with the submission of budget requests by the president within the first fifteen days of the new session.

Prepared by the OMB, these requests usually set the parameters for the debate on the amount of funding appropriate for each program. Before submission to Congress, the requests have been subjected to months of backbiting, rumor, innuendo, and jockeying within the executive branch. Through an elaborate appeal process, an agency can request additional funds by appealing the OMB decision. During the Carter administration, agencies often leaked their desires to friendly staff of the same party in the Congress. The Reagan administration attempted, somewhat successfully, to clamp down on such interbranch communications by threatening to impose severe sanctions on any agency official who leaked budget recommendations to the Congress before such recommendations were authorized by the OMB. David Stockman, the "iron czar" of the OMB, negotiated personally with agency heads over program reductions, using his pocket calculator to compute compromises.

The budget requests submitted to Congress by the OMB are technical documents, which are often difficult for the generalist Hill staffer to understand. Consequently, there is a significant time lag—during which the Congressional Budget Office and other special-interest experts are consulted—before the Hill and the public understand fully the ramifications of a president's budget requests.

The various authorizing committees then evaluate the programs and report the estimated spending levels of all committee programs by March 15. To retain greater control over the contents of the report, a chairman sometimes prepares the report in the form of a letter rather than a committee resolution. The letter usually responds explicitly to the president's suggested cuts or increases. In 1982, for example, Chairman Orrin Hatch refused to convene the Senate Labor and Human Resources Committee before March 15 because he feared that the ranking minority member, Senator Edward Kennedy, had formed a bipartisan majority coalition able to block certain recommendations to adopt the Reagan cuts in social programs. Instead, Hatch wrote a personal letter to the Budget Committee.

By April 1 the Congressional Budget Office (CBO) makes its own evaluation of the administration's proposed budget package, analyzing the estimates and economic assumptions and sometimes proposing its own budget package. Thus, the CBO provides countervailing expertise and an independent perspective on the OMB budget proposals. Throughout the budget process, conflict rages between the economic analyses of the executive and legislative budget analysts.

With these recommendations in mind, the Budget Committee formulates by April 15, a First Concurrent Budget Resolution, containing various spending *targets* for each authorizing committee. Supporters of the Congressional Budget Act said during the 1974 debate that the First Budget Resolution contained only "targets," not "ceilings." Thus, in theory, the estimates are advisory, not binding. In addition, the Budget Committee was to involve itself not in the substance of the programs but in the determination of overall spending targets. The Budget Committee, for example, might propose an overall budget outlay for Fiscal Year (FY) 1982 of about $4.5 billion for the Justice Department, but it would not recommend a transfer of monies from the Antitrust Division of the Justice Department to drug enforcement. Further, the authorizing committees have the authority to determine how much to spend, regardless of the "targets" in the First Resolution; however, the figure of the authorizing committee can be overturned subsequently by a majority of the Chamber in the Second Resolution. No point of order rests against a committee on the floor because it exceeds its target.

In the First Concurrent Budget Resolution the budget committees propose targets for budget "authority," that is, the actual amount of money appropriated for a program, and establish targets for "outlays," that is, the expected actual expenditures, as opposed to appropriations, in a fiscal year. The outlay figure is set by a complicated formula based in part on the agency's spending experience. For example, in the area of defense, a government agency may contract for a new nuclear carrier in one year but not actually pay for it until another year. The outlay is not recorded until it is actually spent. Thus budget outlays are usually not equal to the amount appropriated. Aggregate budget totals usually reflect "outlay" totals, not spending authority totals.

In addition to the upcoming fiscal year, the Budget resolutions set targets for the "out years," that is, the two years subsequent to the fiscal year under consideration. Thus the Ninety-seventh Congress set spending for FY82, FY83, and FY84. For example, the 1981 First Concurrent Budget Resolution[24] provided the following FY 1982 targets for the Administration of Justice "budget function," number 750, which is under the jurisdiction of the judiciary committees:

Administration of Justice (750):

(A) New budget authority, $4,300,000,000;
(B) Outlays, $4,450,000,000.[25]

In 1981, for the first time, the First Budget Resolution also specified the amounts to be cut from the Justice Department:

(10) The Senate Committee on the Judiciary shall report changes in laws within the jurisdiction of that committee sufficient to require reductions in apppropriations for programs authorized by that committee so as to achieve savings in budget authority and outlays as follows: $116,000,000 in budget authority and $13,000,000 in outlays for fiscal year 1982; 133,000,000 in

budget authority and $81,000,000 in outlays for fiscal year 1983; and $144,000,000 in budget authority and $124,000,000 in outlays for fiscal year 1984.[26]

Although the specific areas to be cut are usually not discussed, legislative history can indicate where the Congress feels the cuts should be made. For example, concerning the Judiciary Committee, the 1981 Senate Budget Committee report said:

> Reconciliation decisions affecting programs in this function assume the adoption of (1) the President's proposal to eliminate the formula and categorical grant programs of the Office of Juvenile Justice and Delinquency Prevention (OJJDP) and to authorize juvenile justice and delinquency prevention as an eligible activity under the proposed social services block grant, and (2) the President's Federal employee compensation reform package.[27]

Thus, although theoretically the Budget Committee does not have substantive expertise, it can provide signals as to the areas where it feels the cuts should be made.

The First Concurrent Resolution also recommends revenue targets. As in the case of spending cuts, the budget committees sometimes are not reticent about making their proposals clear. For example, in 1981 the Senate Budget Committee, while accepting the figure of the Senate Finance Committee, also stated its own views on tax preferences and urged the Finance Committee accordingly:

FINANCE COMMITTEE RECOMMENDATION

The Finance Committee recommended an FY 1982 revenue floor of $650.2 billion. They accepted both the economic assumptions and the revenue proposals offered by the Administration. In addition, the Finance Committee requested that $0.1 billion of revenue be allowed for miscellaneous tax and tariff bills. The Finance Committee provided no recommendation for total revenues or tax reductions in FY 1983 or FY 1984.

COMMITTEE RECOMMENDATION

The Committee recommends an FY 1982 revenue floor of $650.3 billion. This provides for the full Administration tax program including the 3 1/2-year 30 percent marginal tax rate reduction and Accelerated Cost Recovery depreciation, and increased user fees as shown in table 2. The net tax reduction would equal $51.3 billion from current law revenue of $701.6 billion. The Committee revenue recommendation also fully accommodates the President's revenue request for reductions of $97.1 billion and $144.8 billion in FY 1983 and FY 1984.

The Committee considered and rejected several proposals to reduce certain tax preference items. However, it adopted language recommending "to the Finance Committee that it consider seriously the reduction or elimination of those tax preferences which are no longer justified; provided, however, that all revenue recovered from any such amendments or eliminations would be matched by equal reductions in general tax rates."[28]

Only germane amendments relating to the amount of funds available to the various committees can be debated. However, when funds are cut, the programs they funded are likewise cut; the death knell for major social issues is often hidden in the dry, technical wording of an amendment. For example, in the debate over the First Budget Resolution in 1981, Senator Orrin Hatch introduced an amendment to cut the dollar figures of the Labor and Human Resources ceilings:

AMENDMENT NO. 72

(Purpose: To delete funding for the Legal Services Corporation)

Mr. HATCH. Mr. President, I send an amendment to the desk and ask for its immediate consideration.
The PRESIDING OFFICER. The amendment will be stated.
The assistant legislative clerk read as follows:

The Senator from Utah proposes an unprinted amendment numbered 72.

Mr. HATCH. Mr. President, I ask unanimous consent that the reading of the amendment be dispensed with.
The PRESIDING OFFICER. Without objection, it is so ordered.

The amendment is as follows:

On Page 2, Line 16, strike "$775,100,000,000" and insert "$775,000,000,000."[29]

The amendment failed: 24 to 72. Had it passed, it would have seriously endangered the continuation of the Legal Services Corporation.

The authorizing committees must report legislation with new spending authority by May 15. In authorizing new programs the committee can ignore the proposed cuts, and cut, instead, any other program under its authorization as long as the recommended target is met. Although it rarely happens in practice, the authorizing committee can even reject the budget targets altogether and enter into a floor fight to increase spending targets. Thus in the

Ninety-seventh Congress, the House Education and Labor Committee restored many of the college loan programs in excess of the spending targets. The House, and ultimately the Congress, upheld this decision by the committee.

During the Ninety-seventh Congress the Judiciary Committee failed to cut the total $116 million recommended in the First Budget Resolution. Rather than risk a Budget Committee fight, which it was doomed to lose, the Judiciary Committee reconvened and hammered out a new authorization bill to bring spending within the targets. Pennsylvania Senator Arlen Specter, chairman of the Juvenile Justice Subcommittee, persuaded the Judiciary Committee to retain the Juvenile Justice Program even though the spending targets of the Budget Committee had been based on the elimination of this program. Instead, after much juggling, a package was negotiated that took monies from two other programs within the jurisdiction of Judiciary. With few spending programs under its jurisdiction, the Judiciary Committee was able to balance its books with relative ease. However, in a committee like the Labor and Human Resources Committee, which controls billions of dollars of social service programs, deciding which programs to cut to meet budget targets often consumes days and involves many acrimonious fights.

To delay reporting out authorizing legislation until after May 15, the committee obtains a waiver from the Budget Committee. Obtaining a waiver is a routine matter unless a member of the Budget Committee has a particular substantive proposal he wants enacted. Thus, the waiver requested by the Judiciary Committee for the Department of Justice authorization bill in the Ninety-sixth Congress was originally denied because a powerful member of the Budget Committee wanted Judiciary to make certain substantive changes in the legislation.

The timetable is such that the authorizing committees report out their legislation on the same date that Congress theoretically completes action on the First Budget Resolution, a time sequence designed to indicate the non-binding intent of the first resolution. The scheduling is truly symbolic, however, for, in reality, the expected budget targets exert tremendous pressure on members of authorizing committees.

Throughout the summer, Congress considers authorizing bills providing "budget authority" which were, at least theoretically, reported out of committee by May 15. Action is completed on all thirteen appropriations bills for the following fiscal year by the seventh day after Labor Day. Appropriations committees aim for the targets set by the First Budget Resolution, but they are not required to hit the bull's-eye. Actually, Appropriations committees are expected to "scrooge" the targets, that is, to appropriate less money than that agreed to by the Budget and authorizing committees, and to determine which accounts are to receive priority attention.

The Second Budget Resolution, which is completed by September 15, is binding. At this point the Budget Committee sets overall budget "ceilings"—as opposed to "targets"—as well as ceilings for each committee. If Appropriations committees have provided funding above these ceilings, the Budget Committee, and subsequently the whole chamber, reports out "reconciliation" legislation, which instructs the committees to cut their programs to achieve the overall ceilings. Again, budget ceilings are aggregate spending figures, not program-specific. Congress is required to complete the reconciliation process by September 25, and on October 1 the new fiscal year begins. The president himself can play no formal role in the budgetary process and cannot veto the resolutions. However, he can veto reconciliation, authorization or appropriations legislation that is inconsistent with his budget priorities.

THE BUDGET ACT IN PRACTICE

As it evolved within the Ninety-seventh Congress, the budget process has dominated the congressional legislative process in a way that was unanticipated by even its most ardent supporters. The timetable is largely ignored. The budget process has matured into a mechanism that allows the achievement of social goals, spending cuts, and taxation objectives within the first six months of a congressional session. The hoops through which most spending legislation must jump have been substantially reshaped.

Of course, to accomplish these miraculous results, a strong consensus on an overall economic and budgetary philosophy is necessary. Without such a consensus, it would be virtually impossible to dissuade the myriads of public interest and business groups from clamoring for more funds. However, with a strong election mandate, such as that of the 1980 election, and the persuasive leadership of a charismatic president, the budget process permitted lightning-quick reversal of years of public policy. An examination of the sequence of events in the Ninety-seventh Congress cogently demonstrates the dramatic impact that the budget process can have on a vast array of programs.

The budget process began in the Ninety-seventh Congress with much fanfare. In early 1981 President Reagan, in a stellar Hill performance before both chambers, appealed to the Congress as well as the nation to implement his proposed budget cuts. Because his budget slashed many social programs simultaneously, each member and each interest group had to establish its own priorities, thus precluding the formation of any coalition to the contrary. The Republican leadership, under Senator Peter Domenici of New Mexico as chairman of the Budget Committee, turned the budget process topsy-turvy. Late in March 1981, long before the April 15 deadline of the First Concurrent

TABLE 11–2

THE BUDGET PROCESS ESTABLISHED BY THE 1974 BUDGET ACT

STAGE ONE	The President submits his budget by the 15th day after Congress meets, usually in early February.
STAGE TWO	The various authorizing committees must evaluate the programs within their jurisdiction and submit reports to the budget committees of the estimated spending levels of all programs. This report must be submitted by March 15.
STAGE THREE	By April 1, the Congressional Budget Office evaluates the administration's budget package and submits a report to the budget committees.
STAGE FOUR	By April 15, the budget committees report the First Concurrent Budget Resolution to their houses. This resolution contains *spending targets* for each authorizing committee. It also recommends *revenue targets* for the Finance and Ways and Means Committees.
STAGE FIVE	By May 15, Congress must complete action on the First Concurrent Budget Resolution. This resolution is *not* sent to the President. By May 15, each authorizing committee must report any bills or resolutions authorizing new spending authority to the floor of their houses. The authorizing committee may ignore the spending target set by the budget committee. Any bills not reported out by May 15 must get a budget waiver by the budget committee in order to be scheduled for floor consideration.
STAGE SIX	By the seventh day after Labor Day, Congress must complete action on all bills providing new budget authority as well as all thirteen appropriations bills.
STAGE SEVEN	By September 15, Congress must complete action on the Second Concurrent Budget Resolution which sets spending *ceilings* and revenue levels.
STAGE EIGHT	By September 25, Congress must complete action on any "reconciliation" legislation which forces committees to adjust their spending or revenue levels to those contained in the Second Concurrent Budget Resolution.
STAGE NINE	On October 1, the new fiscal year begins.

Budget Resolution, the Budget Committee brought to the floor of the Senate a reconciliation resolution to achieve cuts in the then current fiscal year of 1981 (as well as 1982 and 1983). The reconciliation resolution slashed many ongoing programs and embodied the reduced-funding policy of the administration. The tactic was risky. A defeat of the reconciliation resolution would severely jeopardize the enactment of Reagan's complete economic package. However, relying on his recent national election and his high standing in the polls, Reagan decided to gamble and the reconciliation legisation became the congressional referendum on the entire budget process. Reagan won his gamble when the reconciliation bill passed the Senate, with only 10 dissenters. The Republicans used the reconciliation resolution, technically scheduled at the very end of the process in September, to make the first budget stand.

To a degree never experienced in recent congressional history, both parties generated tremendous partisan loyalty when confronted with the politics of the reconciliation resolution. The Democratic Caucus designated certain amendments "Democratic" and on those amendments cohesion was demanded; on all other amendments members could vote their conscience. On the Republican side, utter loyalty to the proposed resolution was demanded and, with rare exceptions, attained.

The first salvo of the budget battle was launched by Senator Jesse Helms. In an amendment to transfer funds from foreign food assistance programs to domestic nutrition programs, Helms attempted to force Democrats to choose between foreign assistance for children abroad and domestic programs. In an eloquent colloquy on the budget cuts, Senator Kennedy and Senate Majority Leader Howard Baker set the tone for the entire budget debate during the first session of the Ninety-seventh Congress:

> Mr. KENNEDY. Mr. President, when we listen to the good Senator from North Carolina argue that his amendment will restore some $200 million for the school lunch program, it is important that we recognize that it was his administration which recommended a $1.6 billion reduction in the school lunch program. Fourteen and a half million children will not get school lunches under the administration program. . . .
>
> The Senator from North Carolina wants to talk about his support for school lunches and for feeding children. Let us not be mistaken about what his amendment really does. It takes away the crust of bread from starving children in Africa or in Southeast Asia under the pretense that we will teach the dictators and the totalitarian regimes over there a lesson and feed the good American kids back here at home. That is hogwash. This is absolutely hogwash. And the Senator from North Carolina understands it, and we understand it here, and the

American people are going to understand it certainly before this debate is over with. . . .

Mr. BAKER addressed the Chair.

The PRESIDING OFFICER (Mr. GRASSLEY). The Chair recognizes the majority leader.

Mr. BAKER. Mr. President, will the distinguished manager of the amendment yield 2 minutes to me?

Mr. DOLE. Mr. President, I have been authorized to yield 2 minutes to the Senator from Tennessee.

Mr. BAKER. Mr. President, more than any of the debate I have heard so far, the statement by the distinguished Senator from Massachusetts displays the difference between the minority's point of view on the state of this Nation's economy and the majority's point of view.

I believe the poor of this country would be cruelly used by any effort to try to restore to this budget full funding for programs that have failed. I believe that the proposal by the Senator from North Carolina—

Mr. KENNEDY. Will the Senator yield?

Mr. BAKER (continuing). Provides for what should be provided by a human and compassionate country, that is food for those who cannot feed themselves, and at the same time, it does not provide public funds, in this time of economic distress, to those who should not have them—to the children of the rich and the middle-income families of this country.

Mr. KENNEDY. Will the Senator yield?

Mr. BAKER. The argument of the Senator from Massachusetts shows the very essence of the difference in our points of view. The amendment that the Senator from Massachusetts refers to would really give us a chance to add to the measure before us. I am sure everyone will note it will do just that: It will add, but it will not take away anything.

Mr. President, the responsibility of this side, of the majority in the Senate, in my view, is to make sure that when we add to programs, we take away someplace else, because we have to get our economy under control. . . .

Mr. KENNEDY. I want to make a final point here, Mr. President. I think it is a sad day indeed when we pit the poorest starving people in Africa, Asia, India, and Southeast Asia—where there are about a billion on the verge of starvation—and when we pit the 15,000,000 children under 5 who die every year from hunger, disease, and malnutrition against American children. And to justify this travesty, we use the pious answer that we are going to protect the budget.

If that is what the cost of fighting inflation is, it is unacceptable. It is unacceptable. It is unacceptable for this Nation and this Congress, if that is the only area we can find to tighten the belt.[30]

As the media accurately reported, the liberals were totally unable to put a dent in the first reconciliation resolution.

Not surprisingly, the Democratic House leadership did not schedule the reconciliation for Fiscal Year 1981 programs until the debate on the First Concurrent Budget Resolution because it wanted time to compose a comprehensive package that might be acceptable to both liberal and conservative Democrats. The Democrats on the House Budget Committee, under Congressman James Jones of Oklahoma, met in caucus to determine the priorities of the Democratic membership. However, Reagan, seeing that some compromise on his proposals was necessary, co-opted a conservative Democrat, Phil Gramm of Texas, to put together a compromise budget package with Republican Delbert Latta of Ohio who served as ranking member on the Budget Committee (known as Gramm-Latta I). This package easily defeated the Democratic alternative. Speaker Tip O'Neill was roundly castigated by the press for not putting up the good fight and conceding defeat too soon. Nonetheless, the combination of the overwhelming March Senate victory and the May defection of key conservative House Democrats—not to mention the popular mandate for significant cuts in the size of big government— rendered the House leadership, with all its tools of persuasion, impotent.

The second round of the budget battle in the Senate came with the First Budget Resolution, which contained the cuts already enacted in the first reconciliation resolution. The legislative skirmishes of the first budget battle were repeated. Again and again it was hammered home to Democrats that they, like the mythical Sisyphus, were constantly pushing amendments that had no chance of success. Many of the same issues—veterans' benefits, social security, school lunches, student loans—were raised a second time. The Democrats also led several unsuccessful attempts to attack the revenue assumptions of the Reagan tax plan. The entire First Budget Resolution passed the Senate in early May. The authorizing committees were under intense pressure to follow the mandate from the floor.

Meanwhile, the third round in the budget drama began with the debate on the supplemental appropriations legislation for Fiscal Year 1981.[31] Virtually every year, Congress enacts a "supplemental appropriations bill" to fund activities that would otherwise run out of money. Such funds are often necessitated by unexpected expenses. For example, the 1981 bill provided about $24 million in additional resources for the decennial census and extra monies for private counsel fees resulting from the Iranian hostages incident. However, this supplemental appropriations bill also contained "rescissions," that is, cuts in funds already appropriated for Fiscal Year 1981, and several deferrals of expenditures, some of which Congress rejected. The supplemental appropriations bill thus provided a vehicle to cut $76,819,000 from education programs for the handicapped.[32] Even so, the committee's recommended rescission was considerably smaller than that recommended by the president.

By specifying proposed rescissions on a program-by-program basis as part of a supplemental appropriations bill, President Reagan placed Democratic senators in a bind. Failure to pass the bill would seriously curtail many important government programs, like the food stamp program. The political dynamics of the legislation, unlike those of a budget resolution, would provoke immediate repercussions. Nevertheless, the gargantuan multi-page Supplemental Appropriations bill, with its proposed recissions of more than $15 billion, passed without dissent.

Substantive policy questions were intertwined with these very difficult budgetary decisions. Theoretically, appropriations bills deal only with spending figures, not substantive provisions. However, by framing an amendment in monetary terms, a member of Congress can use the legislation to raise basic social questions. North Carolina Senator Jesse Helms proposed an amendment to prevent the use of federal monies to fund abortions except where the life of the mother is at stake. Past compromises on the issue of federal funding for abortions had permitted such funding when the pregnancy resulted from rape or incest or when the abortion was medically necessary to preserve the life of the mother. To most senators' chagrin—particularly those up for reelection in 1982—they were forced to vote on this amendment. The amendment passed. (However, a more controversial amendment prohibiting the coverage of abortions in federal employee insurance plans was not raised, although it had passed the House.) That social change was accomplished through appropriations amendments was no surprise to anyone. Despite much criticism, appropriations bills have been, and will continue to be, used in both the House and the Senate to promulgate substantive legislation.

By May 15, the authorizing committees were pressured, although not required, to report out the spending cuts specified in the First Budget Resolution. Through many political gymnastics, most—but not all—committees complied.

An entirely new and unpredictable tool was then used by the Budget Committee. To get a definitive and final vote on the budget cuts, the Budget Committee reported out a *second* reconciliation proposal.[33] Incorporating all the budget cuts proposed for fiscal years 1982, 1983, and 1984 (the first reconciliation bill dealt primarily with FY 81, 82, and 83), this reconciliation legislation, unlike the first reconciliation proposal, was a bill, not a resolution, that is, it was binding. Again, under the timetable established in the Budget Act, reconciliation legislation was scheduled for autumn, *after* the authorizing and appropriations measures were passed. The Omnibus Reconciliation Act of 1981 (the official name of the second reconciliation proposal) reiterated all the "guns and butter" issues previously debated.

A similar scenario was played out in the House of Representatives. Hoping for a rule to force separate votes on each program, Speaker Tip O'Neill was pleased when the Rules Committee reported out a rule specifying at least five different votes on the Reagan package. Not surprisingly, Reagan wanted an "up or down" vote on his entire economic package. In a major, and startling, defeat for the House leadership, the rule lost on the floor 217 to 210. The 53-vote Democratic margin had been eroded by the so-called Democratic boll weevils (southern and western conservative Democrats), who sided with Reagan.

The most dramatic innovation in the 1981 Omnibus Reconciliation Act was the successful use of the budget procedures to enact substantive legislation, particularly in the Senate. Reconciliation legislation was originally designed to enforce the mandates of the second budget resolution after all the substantive committees had completed their work on authorizations and appropriations. When a committee failed to comply with a budget ceiling, Congress could require it to make additional savings. Despite the insistence of the Budget Act authors that it was designed to deal only with spending ceilings and revenue levels, the Omnibus Reconciliation Act of 1981 contained many substantive provisions inserted by the authorizing committees hoping to circumvent and short-cut the normally tedious legislation process.[34] For example, the 1981 bill contained communications, postal service, and housing measures. Many Senate leaders questioned whether such a procedure should be permitted in the future. The Omnibus Reconciliation Bill passed in late June 1981.

The next step in the formal budget schedule, as provided by the 1974 Budget Act, was the passage of appropriations bills by the first week in September. But by September 1981 none of the thirteen appropriations bills had passed. Indeed, by Thanksgiving only one appropriations bill was enacted—the bill to fund Congress—and when the Congress recessed in December, only three of the appropriations bills had passed.

This utter failure to meet the schedule created a major fiscal and political problem. As the federal fiscal year begins on October 1, the monies to fund government operations must be enacted by September 30. But because Congress traditionally fails to pass appropriations bills on time, a mechanism, the continuing resolution, has been created to keep the government alive. In accordance with this practice, at the end of September Congress passed a continuing resolution to provide monies until November 20, 1981. However, this stopgap measure was a significant setback for the Reagan economic program because it continued funding at 1981 fiscal levels—without the budget slashes President Reagan had fought so hard to get in the spring. In addition, President Reagan had hoped to get $13 billion more in budget cuts in the appropriations bills. He threatened to veto appropriations legislation that did not provide these extra cuts, which were viewed as particularly important. With Reagan's increase in military spending, new projections predicted that Reagan would have the largest budget deficit in history—more than a trillion dollars for the four years of his administration. (Indeed, President Reagan's frustration with the budget process prompted him at one point to suggest a modification of the impoundment provisions in the Budget Act to let a president refuse to spend monies appropriated by Congress.)

The Democratic tactic of chipping away at the Republican coalition finally paid off. In their first (and only) major fiscal victory of the year House Democrats, with the aid of eighteen gypsy moths (moderate Republicans from the Northeast and Middle West), successfully defeated President Reagan's efforts to achieve additional cuts on November 16, 1981. Their victory was further enhanced by the widely publicized *Atlantic* magazine comments of OMB Director David Stockman, who impugned the soundness of the Reagan economic program.[35]

Finally, just before Thanksgiving, the Senate and the House agreed on a compromise funding measure that failed to provide $3 billion of the desired presidential cuts. On November 23, 1981, Reagan, in a daring move, vetoed the measure to regain leverage over the budget battle. The federal government threatened to grind to a halt, and Congress postponed the final resolution of the federal budget until December 15, at which time a compromise was finally reached.

The Second Budget Resolution was passed three months after the deadline—and even then it was just a pro forma reaffirmation of the first resolution. The 1981 budget cycle was over.

FUTURE OF THE BUDGET PROCESS

The 1981 budget process played very differently than anticipated by the 1974 act. The First Budget Resolution, designed to advise on spending targets, became, instead, a mandatory spending ceiling. The Second Budget Resolution, designed to be enacted by September 15 as binding legislation, became, instead, a pro forma measure on December 15. The reconciliation legislation, designed as a tool to enforce the mandate of the Second Budget Resolution, served, instead, to enforce the First Budget Resolution and to fast-track certain substantive legislation. The appropriations bills, scheduled to be enacted by early September, had not passed by Thanksgiving.

But the most interesting aspect of the budgetary mechanism, as used in the Ninety-seventh Congress, was its impact on the congressional power structure. The once powerful Appropriations committees rubber-stamped many decisions that had already been made on the floor. Although the authorizing committees retained their discretion to meet the budget ceilings in any way they saw fit, they nonetheless came under extreme pressure to adhere to the assumptions specified by the Budget committees and floor debates. On the whole, the authorizing and Appropriations committees lost some of their autonomy to determine the fate of their programs.

Did the budget process, as it evolved in the Ninety-seventh Congress, demonstrate the success or the failure of the 1974 Budget Act? From one perspective, this omnipotent budget process streamlined a bumbling Congress and made it respond effectively to a perceived national mandate. By eliminating legislative hurdles, the Ninety-seventh Congress instituted major changes in public policy within six months after it began. Between January 19 and August 7, 1981, the Reagan economic package was enacted largely intact. Perhaps this phenomenon can be explained by the sweeping changes that took place in the Congress. The Senate shifted for the first time in more than twenty years from Democratic control to Republican control. Democratic members of the House were understandably concerned about the results of the next election. However, only the dramatic Reagan electoral mandate allowed the attainment of such an easy presidential victory and the retention of party loyalty among rank-and-file members.

On the other hand, an expeditious implementation of major social change can be dangerous. The Congress was not intended to be a quick-hit institution but rather an institution of careful deliberation. In a bicameral Congress, one house is designed to check the wisdom of the other. George Washington felt that the Senate should be the "saucer" in which the coffee cools. Many politicians argue that the 1980 election signified a mandate to dump Jimmy Carter, not a mandate to alter the major social and economic policies of the last quarter century. The Budget Act, as enacted in 1974, was designed to be a slow, thoughtful process in which committees of expertise would maintain their leverage over the programs with which they were familiar. The Budget Act of 1974, as acted upon in 1981, forced decisions on all the major budget proposals before serious analysis of the president's program was possible. It seemed to be good politics, but critics challenged its usefulness to the legislative process.[36]

The debate over the reconciliation process highlights the conundrum long faced by Congress. How does a legislative institution respond promptly to popular demands without being improvident? Perhaps the diversity of congressional membership alone is sufficient to provide the necessary balance in the budget system. In the second session of the Ninety-seventh Congress the budget process did not progress with the speed or sureness of the first session. Indeed the Congress failed to pass the First Budget Resolution by the May 15 deadline with a divided House rejecting all proposals before it. Minnesota Congressman Frenzel stated: "We have been voting for ghosts and shadows, based on moonbeam, smoke and rainbow dust. What we are witnessing is a deterioration of the budget process."[37] As more members of Congress, on both sides of the aisle, became less enchanted with the Reagan economic program, the House and Senate leadership declined to use the action-forcing mechanisms of the earlier year and proceeded along the route anticipated by the Budget Act.

Regardless of the wisdom of the Draconian reconciliation tactics, there is a growing concern that the budget process consumes too much congressional time. The whole body of legislative procedure by which congressional financial decisions are made is extremely cumbersome. Theoretically, Congress is to pass every year two budget resolutions, thirteen appropriation bills, one reconciliation bill, and perhaps revenue-raising legislation. Three sets of major committees are involved in each decision—Budget, Appropriations, and Taxation committees—not to mention every authorizing committee with respect to the content of its own programs. The federal purse strings are literally strangling congressional initiative.

The future of the budget process is far from clear. Some have suggested a curbing of the reconciliation process and the elimination of the Second Budget Resolution. Still others have proposed a thorough reexamination of the committee structure. Before 1974, Appropriations committees played a critical role in controlling spending. Now that the Budget committees are entrusted with some of that role, the function of the Appropriations committees is different.

Finally, some believe that the legislative budget process will never be powerful enough. They point to ever-increasing budget deficits that even a Republican administration pledged to balance the budget by 1984 cannot halt. To balance the budget, they propose a constitutional amendment.[38] Ironically, the proposed constitutional amendment picked up the most steam at a time when the budget process was working efficiently. Under the amendment, as passed by the Senate in the Ninety-seventh Congress, the Congress would be required to enact a balanced budget except when two-thirds of the members voted to change the equation and in times of national emergency. (The amendment for a balanced budget was defeated in the House.) Although the concept of a balanced budget is politically appealing to most members of Congress— from both ends of the political spectrum—many feel that it will impose an undesirable degree of rigidity in setting the national budget. As of 1982, thirty-four of the thirty-eight states necessary had demanded a constitutional convention to pass the balanced budget amendment.

WAYS TO LOOSEN
THE PURSE STRINGS

Although Congress has established tight control over the purse with multi-step budget procedures, it also recognizes the need for flexibility in the budget system. Therefore, it has deliberately designed several safety valves to circumvent the budget process.

Reprogramming

First, Congress tolerates a practice known as "reprogramming," which allows executive agencies to use funds in an appropriation account for purposes other than those contemplated at the time of the appropriation. Reprogramming generally takes place after consultation with the pertinent congressional committees; often only the chairman and ranking member will be informed.

Congress anticipates that the executive branch will, on occasion, be forced to reallocate funds within an account for a number of reasons: unforeseen developments, changing requirements, incorrect price estimates, wage-rate adjustments, and legislation enacted after appropriations. It therefore permits an agency to "reprogram" funds. The basis for reprogramming is nonstatutory, in general, and derives from informal understandings.

In the 1960s and early 1970s many agencies cavalierly shifted funds among programs when they disagreed with congressional priorities or policies. Through reprogramming, an agency can bypass the normal authorization and appropriation stages.

Between 1956 and 1972 an estimated $2.6 billion a year was reprogrammed by the Defense Department. When an administration changed hands, the amount of reprogramming increased. President Kennedy, for example, used the reprogramming device to modify the defense budget priorities he inherited.[39]

Congressional Research Service expert Louis Fisher commented: "The opportunity for mischief is substantial. An agency could request money for a popular program, knowing that Congress will provide the funds. Later it can use the money for a program that might not have passed scrutiny of the full Congress."[40] Thus, the Pentagon has used the reprogramming device to fund programs previously cut by the Appropriations or defense committees.

Moreover, it has been used to initiate major new weapon systems. As Fisher relates:

> The electronic battlefield (the "McNamara Line") was started in the fall of 1966 by means of a reprogramming action. Not until years later did Congress as a whole learn about the project. Even Stuart Symington, a ranking member of the Senate Armed Services Committee, said that he first learned about a project when reading a weekly magazine.[41]

The new congressional emphasis on oversight has been accompanied by a renewed emphasis on curbing reprogramming. Many committees publicize reprogramming requests, through printed hearings, and committees traditionally not concerned with reprogramming have become more cognizant of the practice.

Transfer

Whereas Congress merely tolerates reprogramming, it openly delegates to certain agency officials statutory "transfer authority," which permits them to transfer funds from one appropriation "account" to another. For example, in the Lend-Lease Act of 1941, Congress appropriated $7 billion for aircraft and tanks but permitted the president to transfer as much as 20 percent of the appropriations to other categories of defense weapons. Likewise in 1972–73 the Pentagon used its broad statutory transfer authority to finance the Cambodian war.

Experts have criticized Congress for giving the executive branch a carte blanche, particularly in the defense area, to initiate major new policies and make significant financial commitments without express congressional authority. Largely as a result of the Vietnam War, and the abuses of the Pentagon in financing the war through transfer authority, Congress grew increasingly reluctant to hand out broad grants of transfer authority and scrutinized more closely defense spending. However, as the scars of the Vietnam War heal and the nation grows more defense conscious, it will be interesting to note whether both reprogramming and the transfer of defense monies once again become standard operating procedure.

Off-Budget Items

Congress frequently circumvents its own budget process by excluding certain items from budget totals. Off-budget items—referred to as "back-door programs"—are thus protected from the annual fiscal knife.

Before the passage of the 1974 Budget Act, there were five main kinds of back-door spending. First, some agencies had the authority to borrow money from the Treasury or the public without going through the appropriations process. Second, certain agencies had the authority to enter into contracts prior to the passage of the appropriations bill, thereby pressuring the Appropriations committee into providing sufficient funds to pay off the agency's debt. A third type of back-door spending included entitlement programs, like veterans benefits, health care and educational assistance, social security, which entitle a certain category of persons to benefits. The spending level of entitlement programs, which in 1981 amounted to 48 cents out of every dollar of the budget, is fixed. Fourth, Congress simply designated a program as off-budget.

The fifth back-door spending method, the credit budget, deserves special attention. The credit budget includes all the money the federal government is forced to borrow to pay the budget deficit and to provide low interest loans and loan guarantees to students, farmers, small business men, foreign governments, and others to achieve social goals. The total credit demand generated by the United States government in fiscal year 1983 was $204.7 billion.[42]

Government loan programs have their costs. Sometimes loans to special groups are as low as 1 or 3 percent even though the cost to the federal government to borrow the funds is much higher. Moreover, in a tight money market, a high government-generated credit demand plays a key role in driving up interest rates. High interest rates, in turn, make it difficult for the private sector to borrow, and thus inflation spirals. Nonetheless, without a credit budget, the federal government could not promote such goals as higher education and foreign aid.

The Budget Act did help to eliminate some back-door spending. Although existing back-door spending programs were preserved or "grandfathered," the Act provided that new contract and borrowing authority could be enacted only according to certain budget procedures. Now a credit budget must be established by Congress on an annual basis.

Entitlements remain the last major sanctuary for back-door spending in new legislation. In the Budget Act, Congress made some modest efforts toward restraining entitlement spending. Now new entitlement legislation can be considered only after the First Budget Resolution has been adopted and it cannot become effective until the next fiscal year. Moreover, the Budget Act permits the Appropriations committees to offer amendments to reduce new entitlement spending. Nonetheless, entitlements remain largely immune from the rigors of the Budget Act.[43]

Continuing Resolution

Congress frequently fails to pass authorization or appropriation bills in time to keep an agency legally afloat. Authorization and appropriations bills often

die before enactment because they become laden with extraneous materials—
everything from limitations on abortion to restrictions on the enforcement of
civil rights laws.

The odds of any authorization or appropriations bill passing the Congress
unscathed have become quite low indeed.

When appropriations bills fail to pass on time, an agency cannot pay its
employees. To allow the federal government to continue to function, a continuing resolution is usually adopted. Some agencies operate for years on a
continuing resolution. Although an unwritten rule forbids the use of continuing
resolutions as political footballs, the tacit threat that an agency will be forced
to close is always there. During the Ninety-sixth Congress, the Federal Trade
Commission was closed for three days when the Appropriations committees
refused to agree to a continuing resolution. Packages of continuing resolutions
to deal with programs whose appropriations failed to pass in time are promulgated every year.

TWELVE

REVENUE AND OVERSIGHT

THE TAXATION COMMITTEES

The tax code is probably the most labyrinthine, byzantine, convoluted—and important—statute in the United States Code. Its provisions not only raise the revenues to fill the federal coffers; they also set essential economic and social policies. The committees that control the taxation laws are, therefore, among the most powerful in Congress.

The Ways and Means Committee

Because of its exclusive power to initiate revenue bills, the Ways and Means Committee in the House of Representatives historically has been a most important congressional committee. Created in the First Congress, it is the oldest specialized committee, and its chairman traditionally has been given great procedural powers and prestige. At one time he even served as the floor leader for the majority party in the House. He was widely viewed as a major member of the House leadership and was frequently groomed for higher positions in the party. Ways and Means Committee members were the crème de la crème of the House. They were smart. They were loyal to the party. They had accumulated great seniority and expertise. They came from safe districts and were thus immune from the political pressures imposed on mere mortal members. Afforded special rules and privileges on the floor, the bills reported from the Ways and Means Committee were thus protected from political ambush. Perhaps the most important token of its esteem was the appointment of the Democratic members of Ways and Means as the sole members of the Committee on Committees, which controlled committee assignments between 1911 and 1974.

Political scientists love to write about the Ways and Means Committee, which some have claimed is the most prestigious of the three prestige committees (the other two, Appropriations and Rules committees). In 1974 Professor David R. Mayhew[1] solemnly referred to its role as "institutional maintenance" because its members could be counted on to perform "grueling, unrewarding legislative work." Although the members of Ways and Means came from safe districts and therefore could resist electoral pressures and operate for the public good—or so the theory went—there were chinks in its armor. For example, it was tough to get on the committee unless your views on the oil-depletion allowance were known. Ralph Nader, a scathing critic of the committee, argued that it did not serve the public good at all but instead protected special interests under a cloak of secrecy that hid its proceedings from scrutiny.[2]

During the congressional revolution of the 1970s, the Ways and Means Committee became a "bastille" that symbolized the inequities of the old order. The attack by the insurgents was facilitated with the downfall of Wilbur Mills, who had chaired the committee from 1957 to 1974. The power of Mills was supreme. With empire builder Mills at the helm, the Ways and Means Committee asserted and obtained jurisdiction in many areas only peripherally related to taxation. When Congress finally decided to pass the first form of medical assistance to the senior citizens—the Medicaid programs—Mills saw to it that they were administered by the Social Security Administration over which the committee had jurisdiction. As a result of this precedent, most other health proposals were claimed by Ways and Means. And because most welfare programs are administered as a part of the social security system, these too came within the jurisdiction of Ways and Means. Even when welfare became a less popular legislative subject and when rampant confusion reigned nationwide over whether social security taxes were being used to pay for welfare programs, Ways and Means held on to its jurisdiction.

Because tariffs used to regulate the flow of imports are just another form of tax, Ways and Means claimed jurisdiction and not only over tariffs per se but over most foreign trade programs as well. Unemployment compensation, financed by a tax on employers, belonged properly to Ways and Means. All of the various trust funds, financed by earmarked taxes, were part of its jurisdiction. And so highway funds, airport funds, antipollution funds, all had to receive the imprimatur of the Ways and Means Committee. Because some programs, such as highways and airports, came under the direct jurisdiction of other standing committees as well, Ways and Means insisted on "sequential referral," whereby Ways and Means would get a crack at them after they had been approved by the other committees. Co-equal jurisdiction was awarded in the case of health legislation, for which another standing committee claimed total jurisdiction.

And, of course, all revenue bills went to Ways and Means. Thus any change in the income tax laws, estate and gift tax laws, and any proposal for tax breaks went to Ways and Means. A subcommittee concerned with "miscellaneous tax measures" receives particular attention from lobbyists for special-interest groups.

Wilbur Mills' omnipotence went to his head, and in 1972 he made a stab at the presidency, calling on all those he had helped over the years to finance his bid in the New Hampshire primary. (His lavish receptions of shrimp and other delicacies were well renowned.) He was trounced, and when he returned to the Hill his career plunged downward after he was found drunk with an exotic dancer at the Tidal Basin. In 1974 when Mills announced he would not run for chairman, he left the Ways and Means Committee vulnerable to the revolutionary rank and file in the caucus.

In 1974 the Ways and Means Committee was stripped of its single most important weapon when the Democratic caucus, by a vote of 146 to 122, transferred its power of committee assignment to the newly created Steering and Policy Committee. When Ways and Means Committee Democrats functioned as the Committee on Committees, their power had extended to the very heart of the House of Representatives. (The Republican Ways and Means Committee members did not perform such assignment chores.) A newly elected member early understands that committee assignments can mean everything in terms of his congressional career. The Democrats, as the majority party, used the committee assignment power extensively to coax errant members into accepting revenue legislation. When Mills took the floor of the House on a major tax bill, he had not only the prestige of the oldest standing committee of the House behind him but also the constant awareness of his heavy influence on the future committee assignments of every Democratic member.

Another blow to the prestige and power of the Ways and Means Committee came with the adoption of a procedure in 1975 whereby the Democratic Caucus, by a petition of fifty members, could instruct the Rules Committee as to the kind of rule a tax bill should receive. Previously Mills had preached the intricacies of the tax code, so intricate that changes in it could be sculpted only by the experts of the Ways and Means Committee. And to avoid contaminating the design with amateurish floor amendments, he argued, it was necessary to consider tax bills only under closed rules. No matter that many Ways and Means Committee members also found the tax code arcane and boring and consequently paid little attention to the manipulations of the chairman and a few cohorts. No matter that most committee members, neither lawyers nor accountants nor economists, brought few skills or training in the field to their work. No matter that the Senate, with its nongermaneness rules, would be free to alter this carefully scripted product in many ways forbidden to the House. No matter. In the usual scenario for a tax bill, Mills presented the bill to an empty House chamber under a closed rule. The compliment from the ranking minority member to the chairman on his skill in bringing forth this legislative masterpiece for all to admire and support was only occasionally marred by a dissident Ways and Means Committee member, who might deferentially ask a question or even offer a complaint. Because no amendments were allowed, the bill sailed through, frequently on a voice vote.

Under the reforms, the majority caucus sometimes required the Rules Committee to permit amendments. Taxation measures no longer automatically receive an "up or down" vote but are subject to the same evaluation and amendment process as other legislation. The Ways and Means citadel was vulnerable, and in 1975 when the caucus required an open rule to consider the sacrosanct oil-depletion allowance, the allowance was finally repealed for most major oil companies.

Numerous other reforms targeted at the Ways and Means Committee, many of which were recommended by Missouri Congressman Richard Bolling, chairman of the Rules Committee, and California Congressman Phillip Burton, were adopted by the caucus. The membership was increased from 25 to 37. As a result of a committee reorganization plan, Ways and Means subcommittees were created. Whereas only four subcommittees were required, six were created—but tax legislation was kept at full committee. With the passage of sunshine rules, all committee mark-ups, hearings, and conferences were opened to the public. Congressional reformers urged that open mark-ups would reduce the influence of special-interest groups. The immediate impact of the sunshine rules seemed to bear out this hypothesis. In 1974 the ranking Republican on the Ways and Means Committee, a congressman from Pennsylvania, offered an amendment to bail out the Piper aircraft family, a longtime supporter from his home state. Bad press coverage in Pennsylvania prompted him to drop the amendment.

To somewhat hamper the open-meeting requirement, the Ways and Means Committee held some mark-ups in tiny rooms, a practice criticized by some but viewed as self-preservation by others. For example, an all-night meeting of the House–Senate Conference Committee on the Economic Recovery Tax of 1981, the biggest tax cut in history, was held in a 16- by 30-foot office. As a House aide explained: "You keep out a lot of the pirates. The physics of a small room gets the job done faster." Regardless of the size of the room, however, the special-interest lobbies managed to get their tax loopholes, turning the tax bill into a "Trojan horse."[3] No matter how small the conference room, the halls of Congress—and of the White House—are large enough for deal making. Thus, in retrospect, it is not clear whether the cloak of secrecy promotes or obstructs the passage of a "fair and equitable" tax bill.

The changeover in the chairmanship and membership of the Ways and Means Committee contributed to its decline. When Wilbur Mills retired in 1974, Congressman Al Ullman of Oregon took over. Because he lacked both the political savoir faire and the procedural powers of his predecessor and because the members of the Ways and Means Committee were less senior, less committed to the party, and less politically secure, the committee had trouble ramrodding tax bills through the House in the old manner. Nonetheless, thanks to its still considerable expertise, and benefiting from tradition, most tax bills were reported out under a closed rule and suffered few changes in the House.

The Senate Finance Committee

The shifting fortunes of the House Ways and Means Committee were accompanied by a resurgence of the Senate Finance Committee, long viewed as the poor second cousin. Theoretically, at least, the responsibility of the Finance Committee is limited to response to House revenue bills. In practice, however, the Finance Committee circumvents the constitutional mandate by pouncing on minor House tariff or taxation bills with major taxation amendments. Although in recent years it has played a co-equal role with the Ways and Means Committee in taxation matters, it has never attained its glamorous or exalted position. Its members are not handpicked mandarins. Its bills do not receive preference on the Senate floor and are fair game for Senate floor amendments. House members tend to refer disdainfully to the "Christmas tree" taxation bills that emerge from the Senate with goodies for every special-interest group in town. In the House, only those special-interest groups— like oil—that are able to get the "right" members appointed to the committee can prevail.

Much of the resurgence of the Senate Finance Committee is due to the wily and aggressive chairmanship of Senator Russell Long of Louisiana. With new players on the House side, Senator Long lost no time in asserting the power of the Senate on tax issues, even to the point of threatening to initiate an entire tax bill by way of a nongermane amendment to a minor House bill. When the new personnel on the House side precluded the House–Senate conferences from being the love feasts of old, Senator Long became the dominant force in the conference committee structure. The Finance Committee, which had only the professional staff of the Joint Tax Committee at its disposal until 1966, when Long became chairman, now boasts its own professional staff. Long also chose his colleagues on the Finance Committee very carefully, paying special attention to their activities in gas and oil legislation.[4]

A classic example of Long's prowess involved the 1977 Social Security Act amendments. The bill was desperately needed to shore up a social-security fund that was about to run out of money. Long had contrived to stall the bill in the Senate until the very close of the session, which is typical of important tax bills. Meeting over the Christmas holidays, the House members of the conference committee were still in disagreement about some features of the bill, and the senators, under Long's tutelage, were a solid phalanx, not only on the bill but on a nongermane amendment that would provide a tax credit for tuition paid to parochial and other private schools. The senators were adamant: the House conferees would agree to the controversial nongermane proposal on tuition tax credits or the social-security bill would die aborning. At a crucial point, Senator Long signaled his fellow senators, who announced an end to the conference. During the stalemate of several days' duration, Senator Long succeeded in obtaining concessions on every other point in controversy. Finally, when Chairman Ullman and his House conferees could be squeezed no further, Senator Long announced that Republican Senator William Roth of Delaware, sponsor of the tuition tax credits proposal, had graciously agreed to withdraw his amendment. Now the social security bill could become law, and the senior citizens would not be deprived of their social security benefits because of the recalcitrance of the House conferees. Long not only had picked up all the bargaining chips but had cemented the loyalty and support of a Republican member of his Finance Committee as well.

The co-equal — if not preeminent — status of the Senate Finance Committee was confirmed in the Ninety-seventh Congress when it joined forces with the Republican White House to achieve a significant victory for the so-called Kemp–Roth tax-cut package (named for its Republican co-sponsors, Congressman Jack Kemp of New York and Senator William Roth of Delaware).

The Senate Finance Committee, chaired by the acerbic, witty Robert Dole of Kansas, managed to maintain a high degree of autonomy from the White House, for, despite party ties, the tax bill included provisions not desired by the administration, most notably a provision that prevents "bracket creep" by indexing income tax brackets to inflation rates. Regardless of the merits of this controversial proposal, it represents a radical new approach to internal revenue laws.

Despite the seesawing of power between the two taxation committees, the 1974 Budget Act has resulted in reducing the powers of both. Not only is the First Budget Resolution required to specify assumptions as to revenue levels, but in the Ninety-seventh Congress the Budget Committee took this requirement as the rationale for proposing major new tax initiatives. Thus, the revenue committees are under enormous pressures to heed the instructions passed by the entire Congress in the budget resolutions. Failure to enact the instructions could, at least theoretically, prompt the Congress in the Second Budget Resolution to force the committees to comply.

Tax Expenditures

A major and very controversial taxation reform of the 1974 Budget Act involved tax expenditures. The federal income tax structure is designed to accomplish two purposes: to raise revenue by taxing individual and corporate income and to exclude certain receipts, "tax expenditures," from the concept of income to achieve economic or social objectives. A tax expenditure, frequently called a tax incentive (or loophole), is specifically designed to encourage certain types of activity.[5] For example, Congress passed certain tax breaks that it hoped would tend to encourage the preservation of historic buildings. Thus developers, because they could write off the expenses of restoration construction, were encouraged to pour money into preserving historic areas. Similarly, Congress passed a campaign contribution deduction and credit to foster political contributions.

Tax incentives, or expenditures, have the same impact on the federal budget as direct expenditures because they represent revenues foregone by the federal government. Viewed this way, they represent 25 percent of total government spending, or in 1981, $228 billion.[6]

Critics describe the tax expenditures process as a back-door mechanism for giving political gifts to special interests. They argue that "tax incentives are inimical to the equity of a tax system."[7] Instead, they urge Congress to achieve the desired social and economic objectives through direct grants, which are more immediately subject to public awareness and scrutiny.

Supporters of tax expenditures make essentially three arguments.[8] First, on a philosophical level, they argue that tax expenditures are not equivalent to government spending because, by definition, anything that is not taxable income belongs to the individual or the corporation, not the government.

Second, on a more practical level, many argue that tax expenditures are preferable because they are simple and are removed from the bureaucratic hand. Finally, there is the hard political reality that Congress will vote dollars through tax incentives that it refuses to appropriate through expenditure programs. Indeed, tax expenditures have risen 14 percent a year, compared with the 11 percent growth rate for direct budget spending.

Although tax expenditures seem here to stay, the 1974 Budget Act took a major step in increasing public awareness of their effects by requiring the revenue committees to publish a report describing all new or increased tax expenditures.[9] An effort to include tax expenditures within the budget process for the purpose of limiting public spending failed miserably, for the business community (particularly the Business Round Table, which consists of many powerful Fortune 500 corporations) remains hostile to any attempt to proceduralize consideration of tax expenditures. Consequently, the exposure of tax expenditures to political light has yet to demonstrate that brighter light results in better laws.

Tax Staff

The power of the revenue committees derives largely from their expertise, and from this perspective, their stature tends to be constant. To most members of Congress, the tax field is complicated and boring, and they are more than willing to defer on tax matters to the expertise of the revenue committees. The chairmen of the tax committees further intimidate by preaching the tax code intricacy gospel, that is, that changes can be made only by experts. Most congressmen lack the staff to understand, never mind to propose, tax measures. The revenue committees, on the other hand, have their own staff of experts and the Joint Committee on Internal Revenue Taxation, which was established in 1926.

The Joint Committee, one of the few examples of bicameral cooperation and staffing, traditionally has attracted some of the best-known authorities in the tax field. Dr. Lawrence Woodworth, for many years the staff director, enjoyed the confidence of several chairmen of both the House and the Senate committees. Shortly before his death, he became director of tax policy in the Treasury Department under the Carter administration.

His imprimatur was on much House Ways and Means tax legislation, as well as the staffers that he trained. The staff, which performs for both the House and the Senate, produces a product capable of deflecting amendments from the floor of either chamber. Some argue that the tax legislation drafted by the Joint Committee staff is superior to that drafted by the Treasury Department. Congress clearly does not intend to take a back seat in the area of taxation.

The staff members of the Joint Committee, who have become far more important than most of the committee members themselves, provide a critical bipartisan line between the tax membership in both Houses. Because they perceive themselves as serving the members of the committees, and not the Congress as a whole, they have created a monopoly on the knowledge and expertise of taxation that few Senate or House offices can match. Thus, floor amendments on most tax bills rarely succeed, for without the imprimatur of the Joint Committee staff, seat-of-the-pants proposals raised from the floor rarely enjoy the confidence of the members.

Senators and congressmen who are not on the revenue committees but who want to play a role in forging tax proposals must get information from other sources. Sometimes a staff member of the Joint Committee "leaks" proposals, information, analyses, and critiques of tax measures reported from the revenue committees to a member who shares his ideology. Other times, members have to rely on outside groups that have developed taxation expertise. For example, the AFL–CIO invested substantial resources in developing its own tax expertise, and each industry is not hesitant about preparing tax proposals to enhance its position. Although small, a few public interest groups have developed taxation expertise to represent "the public" in tax matters. Occasionally, a member cares so strongly about taxation measures that he hires staff or outside academic consultants with expertise in that area. Finally, the Treasury Department seeks out senators and congressmen to propose floor amendments desired by the administration when it is unsuccessful in committee. All in all, however, the resources available to non-committee members are scanty. The power of the revenue committees thus seems invincible.

Tax Reform and the Media

In earlier years, taxation received little media attention or public awareness. The federal government was growing by leaps and bounds, with no end in sight to the revenues available to attain both domestic and international objectives. Even after the sunshine reforms, most activities of the revenue committees generated little interest. Ralph Nader in 1975 lamented the lack of concern: "The political genius who can make the taxing and spending activities of Congress interesting to the taxpayers who make all this possible deserves an entire hall of fame."[10]

In 1982, however, with an estimated 1982 budget deficit of over $100 billion, an increasing tax burden, and double-digit inflation rates, the issue of taxation no longer seemed so arcane or remote. Taxpayer revolts at the state level in both California (Proposition 13) and Massachusetts (Proposition 2½) sparked national attention, and Ronald Reagan rode to office promising tax cuts not only to ease the burdens but also to increase incentives for business investments. No political genius was necessary to prompt public awareness of bills to reduce taxation. However, Ralph Nader's point was well put. A renewed enthusiasm for tax cutting does not presuppose public interest in the minutiae of tax bills—and that is where the bones are hidden. President Carter made tax reform, like the elimination of the three-martini lunch, an integral part of his election fight in 1976, but he failed so abysmally in Congress that he refused to support specific tax reform measures in the Democratic platform during his reelection campaign in 1980.

The media can be partially blamed for failing to expose the many tax giveaways to special interests. Without access to the media, individual members of Congress remain powerless to arouse public interest in a fair tax system. Many critics argue that the tax system should not be used as an instrument of social and economic reform—that is, the transfer of wealth from the "haves" to the "have-nots." Although this point may be valid, that today's tax code provides a principal vehicle for attaining national objectives is an established fact. When the government wants to increase national productivity, Congress passes additional tax breaks for research and development expenditures. When it wants to protect senior citizens, it levies social security taxes. When it wants to promote day care, it passes tax credits. The richer a person and the higher his or her tax liability, the more he or she benefits from most tax breaks. Given the structure of the code, no taxation legislation is neutral. The 1974 Budget Act significantly improved the taxation process by requiring the public disclosure of tax expenditures and an estimate of their budgetary impact. However, interest in streamlining the tax system has yet to be generated. Although the 1981 tax bill, with the most massive tax cuts in history, can be commended for its daring, if simplistic, approach to solving economic problems, it also should be criticized for failing both to simplify the tax laws and eliminate the clearly inappropriate and grossly irregular tax loopholes. The nation still awaits the political genius who can make tax reform succeed.

CONGRESSIONAL OVERSIGHT

To oversee the activities of the executive branch and ensure proper execution of the laws, the Legislative Reorganization Act of 1970 requires each committee to "review and study on a continuing basis, the application, administration, execution and effectiveness" of the laws and agencies within its jurisdiction. In the House, special subcommittees have been appointed to conduct oversight investigations.[11]

Although some critics claim that oversight has failed, the objective here is to demonstrate that, particularly in recent years, oversight has been effective in giving Congress control over all major activities in the executive branch. It exercises this control by: conducting oversight hearings to rewrite agency authorization bills; exercising the "legislative veto" against undesirable agency policies, a device that is particularly effective in the foreign policy area; using the confirmation process to pressure nominees into following congressional demands; attaching "riders" to appropriations bills to curb politically unacceptable agency actions; and, of course, cutting agency funds in the annual budget process.

Has Oversight Failed?

The congressional oversight function has been characterized by some congressional critics as precisely that—"oversight," that is, failure to recognize the flaws and abuses in the executive branch. The criticism of the oversight mechanism became particularly acute in the 1960s and 1970s when the federal regulatory establishment literally quadrupled in size. Increasingly, critics pointed out that, instead of spending so much money, Congress should exert more energy in determining whether federal monies were being spent wisely and efficiently and whether agency regulations were consistent with congressional desires.

Some political scientists cited the "iron triangle" theory[12] to explain the failure of oversight. The members of the "iron triangle"—the congressional committee that established the program, the constituent groups who benefit from the program, and the agency that administers the program—are bound together by a strong common interest. With these common goals, a committee has little incentive to conduct vigorous oversight of the programs under its jurisdiction.

A classic example of the "iron triangle" is the Agriculture Committee–Farmers–Agriculture Department triangle in which all three sides of the "triangle" have the common goal of protecting a certain agricultural program, like peanuts, tobacco, or wheat. The iron triangle theory works only for programs, like agricultural subsidies, in which the constituencies subject to the program all support and benefit from the program. For example, the peanut farmers strongly support peanut price support programs. But because consumer concern about the high cost of peanuts is generally too diffuse to muster a concerted, well-financed opposition to peanut price supports in Congress, pressure to "reform" the program is rare.

A different situation exists in the environmental and worker protection areas, where the group being regulated does not benefit from the regulation and has conflicting interests with those who do benefit from the regulations. The perspective of a company with hazardous waste problems is different from that of those who live near a dumping site. Therefore, oversight of the

Environmental Protection Agency is less placid than that of programs in which the conflict of interest is minor.

An evaluation of the success or failure of congressional oversight depends on one's perception of the purpose of oversight. If "oversight" means the control of agency policies and practices by congressional committees, the "iron triangle theory" highlights the success of oversight, not its failure. One can be sure that the members of the soybean subcommittee know precisely what is happening in the soybean program. In controversial areas, like environmental programs, subcommittee members are poignantly aware of the policy ramifications of every agency action. Although the members sometimes prefer to duck a controversial issue, the potential for intervention looms over every agency decision. This is particularly true in the area of policy making. For example, the evidence is compelling that the antitrust policies of the FTC are molded by every Congress in the authorization and appropriations process.[13]

The lack of public or media interest in oversight has contributed to the general perception of oversight failure. It is boring. A member rarely gets political credits for the day-to-day oversight of an agency. Few newsletters carry pictures of a congressman in an empty hearing room interrogating a lower level agency official. Particularly in the 1960s and 1970s, when abundant optimism prevailed about the ability of government to cure the woes of humanity, legislators preferred bragging about their new programs rather than about their eradication of inefficiency. However, that oversight was a quiet affair did not make it less effective or pervasive.

The New Enthusiasm for Oversight

The mood changed in the late 1970s and early 1980s, when congressional oversight of executive branch activities assumed a new and broadly publicized importance. The Ninety-sixth Congress proudly proclaimed itself "the Oversight Congress." In the first half of 1975, House committees spent two-thirds again as many days in oversight hearings and mark-ups as they had during the same period in 1973, and three times as many days as in the first half of 1971.[14] The Senate similarly showed an increase, although not as great as that in the House. Committees in both houses devoted more than one-sixth of their resources to oversight in 1975, compared with one-ninth two years earlier. Speaker O'Neill reported that in 1979 the House devoted a startling 39 percent of its hearings to oversight.

Enthusiastically, Congress tackled its oversight responsibilities. It refashioned major areas of domestic policy, for example, by deregulating the airline industry. New statutes enacted in the 1970s provided procedural tools to scrutinize expenditures in the foreign policy arena. What changed oversight into a hot image?

From a political vantage point, correctly packaged oversight, which exposes bureaucratic inefficiency or ineptitude, provides great political benefits and few negatives. What American has not screamed in frustration at the "nameless," "faceless" bureaucrat when trying to locate an Internal Revenue Service rebate or a missing social security check? Small businesses, in particular, complained of excessive paperwork and government red tape and demanded relief. Congressmen gladly agreed to come to the rescue. By pressuring the bureaucracy on behalf of businesses disgruntled with agency rules or anxious for federal handouts and by revising federal programs to provide more grants or loans for constituents, members of Congress reap campaign monies from grateful recipients. By helping a Vietnam "vet" obtain his rightful benefits, a congressman creates goodwill throughout his district. The government bureaucrat provides an easy political scapegoat upon whom to pin the economic problems of high taxes and inflation. As Professor Morris Fiorina said:

> Congressmen possess the power to expedite and influence bureaucratic
> decisions. This capacity flows directly from congressional control over what
> bureaucrats value most: higher budgets and new program authorizations. . . . The
> key to the rise of the Washington Establishment . . . is the following observation.
> The growth of an activist federal government has stimulated a change in the mix
> of congressional activities. Specifically, a lesser proportion of congressional
> effort is now going into programmatic activities and a greater proportion into
> pork-barrel and casework activities. As a result, today's congressmen make
> relatively fewer enemies and relatively more friends among the people of their
> districts.[15]

Democrats and Republicans tripped over each other in their pledges to eliminate that evil trio: waste, fraud and corruption. In short, congressional oversight evolved from a low-key activity into a potent political tool not only to control public policy but also to enhance reelection prospects.

From a substantive vantage point, oversight became a way for a member of Congress to be a policy leader without spending money. Experts in regulatory policy from major think tanks and academic institutions—Harvard, Chicago, Brookings, the American Enterprise Institute—pointed out that excessive government interference in the marketplace, especially in the area of so-called economic regulation, increased consumer prices and impeded industrial productivity. Deregulation was legitimized as an important public policy objective. Suddenly all of Congress was interested in the oversight of major agency policies, areas previously immune from scrutiny except by the oversight subcommittee.

The Airline Deregulation Act of 1978 was the first major initiative in the congressional oversight area. Beginning in 1975, Senator Edward Kennedy, then chairman of the Administrative Practice and Procedure Subcommittee of the Judiciary Committee, held a multitude of hearings on the anti-competitive effects of airline regulation. Conclusion: Airline regulation was costly not only to the consumers but also to the airline industry itself. The hearings and accompanying publicity served to forge a broad coalition of segments of the airline industry as well as consumer groups favoring airline reform. By the time legislation had been introduced, the Commerce Committee was prepared to take action. In 1978 airline deregulation legislation was enacted.

Other deregulation proposals followed on the heels of airline deregulation. Congress deregulated the trucking industry. In 1980 Congress partially deregulated the railroad industry and bank interest rates. The restructuring of the Federal Trade Commission was the first congressional effort to curb an agency's powers in the consumer protection area. Under Chairman Michael Pertschuk, a former staff director of the Commerce Committee, the FTC had aggressively issued sweeping regulations to eliminate unfair and deceptive trade practices, managing to infuriate, in the process, virtually every organized interest in Washington—the insurance companies, funeral directors, cereal manufacturers, and used-car salesmen.

The FTC authorization battle received prominent national attention. Senator Wendell Ford, chairman of the Consumer Subcommittee of the Commerce Committee, held a press conference to get maximum credit for disciplining the recalcitrant agency. (Ford was also chairman of the Democratic campaign committee and up for reelection in 1980.) A number of rules under consideration in the Federal Trade Commission were killed or substantially modified. New procedures were added. The hearings and mark-up on the legislation were covered by television and received maximum attendance. Why? Because for the first time a number of constituent interests had demanded significant changes in the agency. Congressional oversight had developed its own political rewards.

Much congressional oversight interest has focused on health and safety regulations, which multiplied primarily in the 1970s when fifty-six new regulatory statutes were enacted (more regulatory agencies were created under President Nixon than at any other time). Under these statutes, Congress delegated to the agencies broad powers to make the air clean, the workplace healthy, and consumer products safe. Little guidance was provided, however, as to how to trade off the costs and benefits of regulation. A regulation to provide extremely clean air could result in the closing of a substantial portion of an industry. Immunity of the regulatory process from political pressure, although viewed by some as desirable, insulates agency staff from the realities of business practice. As the costs of government regulation skyrocketed, so too did the demand for political accountability in the Congress.

Proposals to improve congressional control over agency decision making were not long in coming. In the Ninety-fifth and Ninety-sixth congresses sunset legislation was acclaimed the panacea to ensure a systematic review of government programs.[16] Under these proposals, each government program would be "sunseted" every ten years unless renewed by Congress. In this way, programs and agency missions are the focus of attention at least every ten years. Another proposal for congressional control, the legislative veto, allows a committee, a house, or the entire Congress to veto an agency action.[17]

Oversight Hearings

Most congressional oversight hearings are routine, dry affairs. A department or agency head comes to the Hill to discuss his agency's initiatives and spending priorities. Questioning usually focuses on agency requests for increased funding or expanded authorizations. In all-but-empty hearing rooms, the agency witness speaks in monotones to the one committee member presiding.

One main reason for the oversight hearing is to lay the predicate for an authorization bill. Many older agencies and programs have permanent authorizations. In other words, they will continue to operate unless Congress acts to terminate their authority. In recent decades, the trend has been toward periodic reauthorization, that is, the program dies unless a new authorization bill is passed. Most new health, safety, and environmental programs must be reauthorized every few years. In most situations, the debate over the reauthorization bill is limited to new powers or new spending authority that the agency desires, as opposed to questions concerning the fundamental mission of the agency. Sometimes, agency waste or stupidity is investigated.

The hearings are sometimes a forum for discussing major agency policies. A notable example occurred in 1981 when the Labor and Human Resources Committee discovered that the National Cancer Institute's grant program was providing thousands of dollars of funds to a researcher who had previously been found guilty of fabricating research data. Before whirring cameras, both Democrats and Republicans delighted in exposing this abuse of public funds to public ridicule.

Congressmen sometimes become deeply enmeshed in the nitty-gritty of an agency's activities. Unfortunately, however, this obsession with minutiae sometimes diverts congressmen from more important activities. In an oversight hearing of the Consumer Product Safety Commission (CPSC) in the Ninety-seventh Congress, a House subcommittee chaired by Henry Waxman of California examined in detail a final CPSC rule on lawn-mower safety. Several congressmen, relying on their own lawn-mowing experience, even went so far as to want to rewrite the rule themselves in an impromptu fashion. This debate demonstrates the respective roles of Congress, the agencies, and the courts in considering the validity of regulations.

Mr. Brown: Was the standard set by CPSC with or without comment from the industry?

Mr. McLaughlin: They went through the full rule-making procedures, which provide ample opportunity for comment, input, in fact judicial review after it was promulgated. The Fifth Circuit reviewed it.

Mr. Brown: The standard has been reviewed by a court?

Mr. McLaughlin: By the Fifth Circuit, and it has been upheld as both cost effective and a performance standard reasonably related to addressing a reasonable risk of injury.

Mr. Brown: Thank you, Mr. Chairman.

Mr. Dannemeyer: May I make an innocent inquiry?

Mr. Waxman: Yes.

Mr. Dannemeyer: Under our system, when is it the function of the Judicial Branch, even a Circuit Court of Appeals, to make a determination of cost effectiveness for a proposed regulation? It struck me that if that determination is to be made that is within the legislative arena, not the judicial arena. But maybe I do not understand our constitutional system.

Mr. Waxman: Do you have a comment on that?

Mr. McLaughlin: Under Section 11 of the Consumer Product Safety Act, it provides that the agency must make certain findings when they promulgate a rule. One of the findings is that the costs of the rule are justified by the benefits of the rule, by the requirements of the rule.

The agency made that finding when they promulgated the lawn-mower standard. And when it was— when judicial review was sought, it was challenged on that basis, and the court did examine that— that contention.

Mr. Waxman: So I might just recognize myself on this amendment. I have had a difficult time dealing with this amendment because I try to avoid using lawn mowers and have been pretty successful in doing that.

(Laughter.)

Mr. Waxman: No grass grows in my district. Unfortunate, at my home it grows.

(Laughter.)

Mr. Waxman: But I have avoided trying to understand how lawn mowers work and how we can make them more safe. And I have heard arguments from the people making lawn mowers that sound quite right. And then I have heard the other arguments the other way, that also sound quite right.

And I guess I am left with the fact that 80,000 injuries occur each year due to contact with the blade of lawn mowers. It is a frequent source of serious kinds of accidents. And we have a Consumer Product Safety Commission that has worked on setting a standard, receiving evidence, hearing different points of view on how best the public could be protected without placing— supposedly without placing unreasonable burden on industry and ultimately on the consumer that will pay for the standard.

And I have to reach the conclusion that the CPSC has heard all the information about this and has made its judgment. They may be incorrect. But I have not as a member of the Subcommittee heard enough in any kind of formal sense to make a judgment that the CPSC is wrong.

So I with some reluctance, Mr. Dannemeyer and others, will vote against the amendment to strike the CPSC standard to deal with lawn mowers.[18]

The proposed rule was not congressionally rewritten.

Legislative Veto

Congress has attached legislative veto provisions of one kind or another to more than 200 laws, and every president since Franklin D. Roosevelt has challenged them as an unconstitutional encroachment of executive powers. Under a typical legislative veto provision, an authorized action by an agency, for example, the issuance of regulations establishing gas prices, can be vetoed by Congress within a fixed period of time. Often a veto of only one house is sufficient to block the agency action. Most extant vetoes cover only a specific agency action, like certain immigration decisions, or a certain kind of regulation. Recent proposals, however, seek to subject every government regulation to a legislative veto. One such proposal was introduced as H.R. 1776 to symbolize a call to return government power to the hands of elected representatives.

Serious constitutional problems arise with the one- or two-house legislative veto.[19] Recent federal court decisions have struck down the veto as unconstitutional, and the Supreme Court has agreed to rule on the subject. The "presentment clause" of Article I requires all legislation to pass both houses and be presented to the president for his signature or veto. The legislative veto, however, obviates the president's powers because the veto itself is not subject to presidential rejection. Furthermore, the veto may interfere with the president's power to execute the laws, thereby contravening the "separation of powers principle" in the Constitution that divides the government into three co-equal branches.[20] A one-house veto appears to violate the bicameralism requirements of the Constitution.

Supporters argue that the legislative veto ensures the correct implementation of legislation by the executive branch. In an era when Congress is forced to rely increasingly on bureaucratic expertise to hammer out the details of broadly worded policy mandates, supporters argue that a mechanism is necessary to reverse agency decisions that contravene legislative intent.

Clearly, the legislative veto increases committee leverage over agency policies. Politically savvy agencies negotiate the substance of a regulation with the oversight committees before adoption to obviate subjecting their programs to the vagaries of congressional review. After studying the use of the veto in various regulatory programs, Professor Harold H. Bruff and Ernest Gellhorn concluded:

> Although the administrative programs in the case histories were quite different, they had certain common characteristics. Each was in an area of considerable public concern, if not controversy. In all the programs except that administered by the GSA, there was repeated major legislation during the period under study. Congress could have used such legislation to resolve issues that had emerged in rulemaking programs subject to legislative vetoes. Whether for reasons of indecision or deadlock, however, it ordinarily chose to leave these issues open in the revised statutes and to rely on the legislative veto mechanism to maintain control over agency policy initiatives. Therefore, the process of review was an active one, not one marked by congressional inattention to forthcoming rules.
>
> Given such conditions, it is not surprising that the veto power gave rise to negotiation and compromise over the substance of rules between the agencies and the congressional oversight committees. Significant negotiation occurred in all five programs despite their disparate natures, and it was often intense. Since the statutes generally created new programs requiring broad implementing regulations, the initial focus of the negotiations was correspondingly broad. As the negotiations progressed, however, the issues in controversy were reduced to a small number for ultimate consideration by Congress. This narrowing process gave the committees and especially their staff substantial power to define the issues that would be likely to receive the attention of Congress as a whole.[21]

Critics of the veto advocate greater specificity in the legislation to avoid broadly worded mandates, but legislative realists point out that the essence of the legislative process, compromise, often necessitates broad policy statements.

A possible solution to this fifty-year-old veto battle (which has spawned innumerable senior and Ph.D. theses, articles in political journals, and law review pieces) is the British lay-it-on-the-table procedure. Under this procedure, a regulation does not go into effect until Parliament has had sufficient time to review and overrule it. Congress has considered certain adaptations of this approach.

The Legislative Veto in Foreign Policy

The legislative veto has become an important tool for Congress to maintain control over foreign policy.[22]

After World War II, the president, as commander-in-chief, dominated the formation of foreign policy and relegated Congress to a subordinate role. The foreign policy committees were regarded as relatively unimportant, powerless, and unprestigious, and foreign policy matters were conducted largely in a nonpartisan manner. Popular discontent with the Vietnam War prompted a resurgence of the legislative branch in foreign policy matters. James L. Sundquist described the new congressional ascendency in 1973–76 as "the most aggressive reassertion of Congressional control of foreign policy since the era of neutrality before World War II."[23]

Using the "credibility gap" created by President Nixon during the Vietnam War and the Watergate scandal as its battle cry, the Ninety-third Congress reaffirmed the authority of the Congress to take command of foreign policy. In a series of legislative measures, Congress gained the procedural tools necessary to control presidential decisions before-the-fact. In the past, the congressional role had been reactive. In *Foreign Policy by Congress*, Thomas M. Franck and Edward Weisband described the congressional determination to regain co-equal status in foreign policy:

The War Powers Act, . . . signaled a new kind of Congressional involvement in Executive performance. This "new oversight" is significantly different from the investigative variety. It works by mandating prior consultation, not through the investigation of actions that have already taken place. Its principal object is *decision-sharing*. A new crop of laws requires the Executive to pause before implementing decisions and enlists Congress, or its committees, in the process of deciding. The new oversight tries to involve Congress in shaping, improving, or preventing a decision. Its object is prescriptive and prophylactic.

Investigatory oversight, by contrast, typically seeks information on why or how a decision came to be made—usually after it has already been implemented by the Administration. It often tries to fix blame for a bad decision made without Congressional participation, sometimes generating legislation to prevent recurrence of past mistakes.

The new oversight also differs from the investigatory variety in another respect. It aims at a higher level of authority and impact. Whereas investigative oversight typically involves a Congressional committee monitoring—or harassing—a bureau chief or Deputy Assistant Secretary, the new oversight is focused on the President and his principal cabinet officers. That is because it is concerned with "getting a handle" on the "big issues" whereas traditional investigative oversight is more oriented toward keeping the bureaucracy honest and effective in its daily routine.

Investigative oversight continues to be an important function of the Congress. Since 1973, however, a higher priority has been accorded to developing and implementing the new oversight. Of the various subjects which legislators have subjected to this process, they have had the most success with human rights, arms exports, and nuclear sales. Beginning in 1973, the Congress has gained the right to be consulted in each of these fields *before* key decisions are made or policies implemented.[24]

Congress adopted many procedures to ensure its co-equal status. In 1973 Congress enacted, over presidential veto, the War Powers Act, which was designed to recapture the congressional power to declare war. The resolution requires a president to "consult with Congress" before introducing armed forces into hostilities or into situations where imminent involvement in hostilities is "clearly indicated by the circumstances." A report has to be made within forty-eight hours. If Congress does not approve the action within sixty days, the president has to remove the troops (allowing an additional thirty days of action if the president certifies it as necessary to cover the withdrawal). In practice, the War Powers Act has had at best limited effect. Every president has resisted following its mandates. President Carter failed to consult the Congress before his abortive helicopter airlift of the Iranian hostages in April 1980 and submitted a pro forma, uninformative report after the mission's failure. Although Congress, as of 1982, had not flexed the muscles of the War Powers Act, there is no doubt that its presence has curbed the president's independence in warmaking. For example, as the hostilities in El Salvador intensified in 1982, the Congress instantly began debating the desirability of an American presence in the Latin American conflict. The administration was on notice that the Congress would not give the president a carte blanche as it had in the 1964 Tonkin Gulf Resolution, which led to active American involvement in Vietnam.

In 1974 Congress somewhat shackled the president's power over foreign aid. The Foreign Assistance Act permits Congress to veto arms sales.[25] Congress used this power to veto the decision of the Ford administration to send military supplies to Angola; to cut off military assistance to Chile, Uruguay, and South Korea for violation of human rights; and to slash aid to India because of its rejection of nuclear nonproliferation objectives. In 1974 Congress also asserted a substantial degree of control over trade policy when, in enacting a new trade agreement act in 1974, it subjected a wide range of executive actions to either a legislative veto or a requirement for affirmative congressional action. In addition to its increased use of legislative vetoes to reverse executive branch legislative policy, Congress exercises control of foreign aid in annual appropriations bills when it slashes or increases funds to nations depending on their relationship with this country.[26]

Gone are the days when the Foreign Affairs committees lacked stature and foreign policy questions lacked the drama of partisan conflict. Even under popular presidents, Congress did not relinquish its procedural tools to control foreign policy. In 1981 President Reagan proposed a sale of AWAC airplanes to Saudi Arabia, a proposal that was opposed by the many congressmen and senators who were concerned about the situation in the Middle East. President Reagan by a slight margin succeeded in blocking a two-house veto, but not until the issue was fully aired in public debate. Moreover, to the chagrin of the White House, the Ninety-seventh Congress continued to impose sanctions on countries that refused to adhere to our nonproliferation policies. In short, every president, Democrat and Republican, has resisted congressional involvement in foreign affairs and every secretary of state has complained of intervention by politicians in diplomacy. It is unlikely, however, that Congress will relinquish the reins.

Confirmation of Executive Branch Officials

Under the Constitution, certain high level presidential appointments must be confirmed by the "advice and consent" of the Senate. With few exceptions, the nominations are noncontroversial and speedily pass on the floor. Sometimes hearings are not even held; rarely is a report written. But, on occasion, the confirmation process is used effectively to influence policy in the executive branch. A senator sometimes threatens to delay and obstruct a nomination until the desired policy commitments have been obtained. In the Ninety-seventh Congress, the nomination of Ernest Lefever to head the Human Rights

Commission triggered a national debate over human rights as a foreign policy goal. Lefever wanted to reverse the Carter policy of denying aid to countries that violated human rights. By his critical statements, Lefever polarized the human-rights issue and antagonized Republicans and Democrats on the Foreign Affairs committees. Rather than face defeat on the floor, the administration withdrew his name.

The Lefever confirmation fight is the rare exception. Most nominees, even the most extreme, are confirmed overwhelmingly because senators believe that, in the absence of compelling circumstances to the contrary, the president is entitled to his choice. Nonetheless, the confirmation hearings provide important forums to sensitize nominees to the issues deemed vital by Congress.

Appropriations

Under the Constitution, every dollar spent by the federal government must be appropriated by the Congress. The Senate and House Appropriations committees are responsible for determining the level of expenditures proper for each federal function. Each year, the Appropriations subcommittees review the programs within their jurisdiction and propose the budget authority for the following fiscal year. Theoretically, thirteen annual appropriations bills are passed. In practice, however, some programs, like entitlements, have permanent appropriations, and others exist from year to year by congressional resolution, in particular those controversial programs that require an annual review.

Historically, as pointed out earlier, Appropriations committees, which controlled the budget, were among the most powerful in Congress. The authorization committees could establish new programs, but only the Appropriations committees could fund them. New programs sometimes were unable to begin functioning because funds had not been appropriated. Well-heeled and wise Capitol Hill lobbyists contributed to the campaign funds of members of the relevant Appropriations subcommittees, not without cause.

Even though the Budget committees have siphoned off a lot of power, the Appropriations committees continue to wield considerable influence on agency policies. After spending targets have been set by the First Budget Resolution, the Appropriations committees become a second bite of the apple for many constituencies. Moreover, the Appropriations "riders"—to restrict the use of funds by agencies—provide major vehicles for public policy making. Appropriations committees also influence agency policies by earmarking funds for specific purposes. For example, the Food and Drug Administration wanted to use some of its funds to encourage greater public participation in its drug safety hearings. Although the FDA did not have statutory authority to conduct this program, it persuaded the Appropriations Committee to earmark $250,000 in funds on a pilot basis. When the FDA expenditures were challenged in court as being unauthorized, the FDA was upheld because of the clear congressional intent apparent in the Appropriations Committee Report. Because reports are generally written by the staff, it is quite possible that no senator or congressman ever focused on such earmarking. Nonetheless, despite the tenuous nature of legislative history in the appropriations process, the agencies are careful not to transgress too far from the expectations of the Appropriations Committee. To do so would be to risk the ire of the committee the next time around.

Thus, appropriations bills remain, even after the passage of the Budget Act, a major tool for congressional control of executive branch policies and activities.

OVERSIGHT OF
THE JUDICIAL BRANCH

Congressional oversight of the judicial branch differs from that of the executive branch. Because the framers of the Constitution were concerned about protecting the independence of the judicial branch from dominance by the legislature, a common phenomenon in early state governments, they provided little congressional financial leverage over the judges of the judicial branch.

Article III provides that judges shall hold their offices "during good behavior, and shall, at stated times, receive for their services a compensation, which shall not be diminished during their continuance in office." Thus Congress cannot exert pressure on the courts by threatening to cut their salaries. Furthermore, there is no traditional congressional oversight of the courts. Hearings are rarely (if ever) held to review the efficiency of court programs or to urge the courts to spend more money on magistrates, for example, than on law clerks. Of course, Congress sometimes refuses to increase judicial salaries and to provide funds for more law clerks or larger offices. However, compared with its firm grip over the executive purse, the Congress has little control over the judicial bank account.

Historically, however, the Congress has not been reluctant to express displeasure with the courts. It can refuse to establish new judgeships; it can consider "packing" courts that are in disfavor and pass legislation to transfer certain categories of cases from liberal to conservative courts or vice versa. In rare moments of pique, Congress has even initiated impeachment hearings. For example, some of the opinions of Supreme Court Justice William O.

Douglas so aroused the ire of Congressman Gerald Ford that he seriously attempted to bring impeachment proceedings against him in the House.

Congressional unhappiness with the role of the courts is reflected, in the long run, in the philosophies of the judges placed on the bench. Under the Constitution, judges are nominated by the president and confirmed with the "advice and consent" of the Senate. By well-established custom, which has prevailed since about 1840, federal district court judges are selected by the senators from the state in which the district is situated, provided the senators and the president belong to the same party. When they belong to different parties, the president turns to the party organization for recommendations. In general, the president has a freer hand in the appointment of judges of circuit courts of appeal, whose jurisdiction spans several states, than of district court judges, who serve within individual states.

Congress has taken its confirmation power seriously. Of the 116 persons nominated by presidents to be justices of the Supreme Court, 21 failed to receive the approval of the Senate, a far higher proportion than for any other federal office. By tradition and precedent, the senators within whose state a nominee resides are given, as "senatorial courtesy," a virtual blackball rejection power over a nominee. If a senator does not like a presidential nominee, he sends in his "blue slip," and the Judiciary Committee generally honors the rejection.

Senatorial courtesy has in more recent times come to mean that senators will give serious consideration to, and be favorably disposed to support, an individual senator of the president's party who opposes a nominee to an office in his state. But as a chief clerk of the Senate Judiciary Committee observed: "He just can't incant a few magic words like 'personally obnoxious' and get away with it. He must be prepared to fight, giving reasons for opposing the nominee. If his reasons are not persuasive to other senators or if he is not a respected member of the Senate, he stands a chance of losing his fight."[27]

Professor Harold Chase discussed the emergence of "senatorial courtesy" as we know it today:

> Senators, whether chosen by state legislators, as they were at an earlier time, or by the voters of the state, must continuously nurture their political support back home; that is, if they hope for additional terms in office—and it is a rare senator who does not. In this connection, senators from the First Congress on have recognized that one or two senators have a much greater stake in a particular appointment than others. It is, of course, exceedingly helpful to a senator to be able to reward supporters with good posts in the federal government. Conversely, it is enormously damaging to a senator's prestige if a president of his own party ignores him when it comes to making an appointment

from or to the senator's own state. What is even more damaging to a senator's prestige and political power is for the president to appoint to high federal office someone who is known back home as a political opponent to the senator. It was easy for senators to see that if they joined together against the president to protect their individual interests in appointments, they could to a large degree assure that the president could only make such appointments as would be palatable to them as individuals. Out of such considerations grew the custom of senatorial courtesy.[28]

In 1979 Judiciary Committee Chairman Edward Kennedy abrogated some of the traditional "blue slip" rights by claiming that the Judiciary Committee should examine all judicial nominees, even those who receive the blue slip (an innovation continued by the new chairman, Strom Thurmond). However, the blue slip remains a considerable factor.

For a short period of time President Jimmy Carter, supported by such groups as the American Bar Association and Common Cause, attempted to minimize the political nature of appointments by establishing a Merit Selection Commission system. Although many senators argue that a nominee's integrity, not his political views, should determine his qualifications to judge, their vote does not always reflect that philosophy. Ultimately, the political nature of the nomination and confirmation process ensures that the views of nominees change as the political consensus changes.

In evaluating federal programs, courts are aware that the Constitution directs Congress to control the public purse. Hence, courts historically have shown great sensitivity to those programs. The reluctance of the courts to force the Congress to appropriate monies for programs derives from the Andrew Jacksonesque retort: "Now you have made your decision—you enforce it." Consequently, the courts mandate appropriations only when a case has firm constitutional roots, for example, the federal taking of property without due process. And in certain cases involving women's rights, the courts have held that women are entitled to the same social benefits accorded to men, thereby increasing federal costs. However, the preferred approach is to invalidate a statute on the grounds that it is unconstitutional, rather than to require Congress to encompass a new class of beneficiaries.

Far less sensitivity has been shown to state legislatures and local governments. Many major civil rights decisions of the Supreme Court have required the expenditure of monies by state and local governments. The busing of schoolchildren to force integration, for example, placed considerable financial burden on state and local governments. Moreover, the federal courts have held that inhumane living conditions in many state mental and correctional institutions are violations of the Constitution, thus forcing the expenditure of monies to correct such situations. Some federal judges, like Arthur Garrity, a federal judge in Boston, actually had to run the daily activities of the Boston school system because he had found intentional discrimination against black children and teachers.

Historically the courts and the Congress have stepped warily in imposing fiscal restraints on one another; the truce was eroded somewhat in the 1980s as the federal courts imposed difficult, controversial, and expensive remedies on home-district constituents.

THIRTEEN

THE CONGRESSMAN
AS REPRESENTATIVE

Τ he Constitution enumerates with great care the various responsibilities of the Congress: to declare war, appropriate monies, raise revenues. Yet the most profound responsibility of the Congress—to represent the people—is never explicitly mentioned. Despite this conspicuous absence, the Constitutional Convention nevertheless focused extensively on structuring the Congress to maximize its ability to respond to public sentiments and needs. Indeed, the goal of a government based on "the right of Representation in the Legislature, a right inestimable . . . and formidable to tyrants only"[1] is so inherent in the constitutional scheme of government that any study of Congress would be remiss if it did not examine this most fundamental responsibility.

This chapter examines the congressman as an elected representative. The first section discusses the various theories of representation: Should a congressman vote for his district's parochial interests or the national good, his conscience or his constituency? It also examines how a congressman defines his constituency, especially in light of the many national constituencies that provide campaign financing.

The second section describes the services a congressman provides his constituents. It looks at the congressman as the ombudsman, who helps his constituents deal with the federal government, and as the logroller, who bargains in the Congress to provide dams and parks and public works for the home district. The following chapter focuses on the congressman as political animal facing election and reelection and, in particular, the impact of campaign financing on a congressman's political behavior. Finally, Chapter 15 looks at what the Congress likes to do least, oversee the ethical behavior of its members.

THEORIES OF REPRESENTATION

Constitutional Role of Representation

The framers of the Constitution counted on the House of Representatives to reflect changing public sentiments. As the delegates to the Continental Congress were regarded as advocates for their colony or state, so too the members of the House of Representatives were expected to represent the regional, parochial interests of their congressional district. As *The Federalist Paper No. 52* explained: "As it is essential to liberty that the government in general should have a common interest with the people, so it is particularly essential that the branch of it under consideration should have an immediate dependence on, and an intimate sympathy with, the people."[2]

The senators, on the other hand, elected every six years by the state legislatures, were to be the representatives of the sovereign states. To quote from *The Federalist* again: "The equal vote allowed to each State is at once a constitutional recognition of the portion of sovereignty remaining in the individual States, and an instrument for preserving that residuary sovereignty."[3] Moreover, the Senate was to be the deliberative body, able to check the "sudden and violent" passions of more popular assemblies.[4] The method of electing senators was changed in 1913 by the Seventeenth Amendment to the Constitution, which provided for the direct election of senators for six-year terms. (In fact, by 1913, most states had already shifted to the popular election of senators; the Constitution allowed either direct election or legislative selection before the Seventeenth Amendment.) Nonetheless, the luxury of running for reelection every six, rather than every two years, still enables senators to fulfill the constitutional hope that the Senate would remain somewhat aloof from rapidly changing political currents.

Poignantly aware, even then in a much smaller nation, of the vast divergence of interests in a rapidly growing country, the framers recognized that the nation's survival depended on the representation of each major faction in Congress. Although factionalism and political parties were feared as the nem-

The first woman member of Congress, elected in
1916, Jeannette Rankin (Republican of Montana)
opposed entry into World War I and II.

esis of democracy, the inevitability of partisan conflict was recognized and methods were sought to institutionalize it in constitutionally useful ways. Thus James Madison opined that individual liberties could be protected from the tyranny of a majority by ensuring the representation of a vast diversity of interests in the Congress:

> The only remedy is to enlarge the sphere, and thereby divide the community into so great a number of interests and parties, that . . . a majority will not be likely at the same moment to have a common interest separate from that of the whole or of the minority . . . and in the case they should have such an interest, they may not be apt to be united in the pursuit of it. It was incumbent on us then to try this remedy, and with that view to frame a republican system on such a scale and in such a form as will control all the evils which have been experienced.[5]

Could a Congress designed to represent a full spectrum of economic and social interests also solve national problems? Local issues, the framers were confident, would be handled by state legislatures. But could a national legislature representing parochial interests legislate in the national interest?

Political scientists and social commentators continue to argue that question. Some argue that Congress has erred on the side of nearsighted parochialism. Acerbic political commentator Walter Lippmann articulated this perspective:

> With exceptions so rare they are regarded as miracles of nature, successful democratic politicians are insecure and intimidated men. They advance politically only as they placate, appease, bribe, seduce, bamboozle, or otherwise manage to manipulate the demanding threatening elements in their constituencies. The decisive consideration is not whether the proposition is good but whether it is popular—not whether it will work well and prove itself, but whether the active talking constituents like it immediately.[6]

Others argue that the compromise resulting from the clash of competing parochial interests in the legislative arena represents the success, not the failure, of democracy. Professor Robert Dahl of Yale reflects this Madisonian theory:

> The theory and practice of American Pluralism tend to assume, as I see it, that the existence of multiple centers of power, none of which is wholly sovereign, will help (may indeed be necessary) to tame power, to secure the consent of all, and to settle conflicts peacefully. . . . To win national elections, even to win influence over national policies, every group must participate somehow in the politics of coalition building. To be sure it can pursue its own goals; and it must engage in conflict; but it must also conciliate, compromise, negotiate, bargain—

and in the process often forego its lesser goals for its greater objectives. In this sense, no single group can win national elections—only a heterogeneous combination of groups can.[7]

Thus, in representing the parochial, regional needs of his district in the legislative process, each congressman helps to forge a nationwide consensus acceptable to a heterogeneous nation with conflicting and incompatible needs.

Still other political scientists refuse to comment on the desirability of parochialism; instead, they look at its impact on a congressman's behavior. Political science professor David Mayhew argues that congressmen are "single-minded seekers of re-election."[8] Representing the home district well is not simply a constitutional duty, it is a political necessity and the key to reelection.

Irrespective of whether congressmen should be lampooned as "intimidated men," lauded as effective representatives, or viewed as good politicians, the fact is that congressmen exert most of their time and energy in constituent-oriented and reelection activities. They conduct polls to determine their electorate's views on the issues before the Congress; they help individual constituents obtain federal benefits; they assist the home district in obtaining federal grants to build highways, dams, and parks. The quality of his casework or the quantity of his benefit programs may not put his name in the history books, but without performing these basic services, he may not get reelected. A congressman who becomes too "national" in focus to concentrate on local needs loses sight of both his primary constitutional responsibility and his dependence on his home district for reelection.

The Dilemma of a Representative

A most frequent congressional debate on twentieth-century college and high school campuses, whether a legislator should vote his constituents' instructions or his own conscience, is also the oldest dilemma of representative government. The dilemma has been expressed best, perhaps, by an apocryphal French general who cynically proclaimed: "There go my troops; I am their leader, so I best follow them." In 1774 Edmund Burke argued: "Your representative owes you, not his industry only, but his judgment; and he betrays instead of serving you if he sacrifices it to your opinion."[9]

The jargon of political scientists divides the members of Congress into three categories: the "delegate," who discerns the will of his constituents and votes accordingly; the "trustee," who uses his own judgment to determine the best path; and the "politico," who determines his vote by calculating the degree of "heat" a yea or nay vote will generate in his home district.

Some "delegates," with their mandates clearly and narrowly spelled out by the previous election, keep "books" that record, chapter and verse, their campaign promises. Although most members of Congress keep track of their mail on controversial issues, the self-pronounced delegate can recite precise numbers and the geographical origin of every letter he receives. Polling techniques and questionnaires are used to check on, and supplement, the mail count. The questionnaire is a particularly attractive device that can be used for good or evil. A valid questionnaire—that is, a questionnaire that does not suggest desired answers or reflect the bias of the legislator—can determine valid popular sentiment. However, "Do you think that we should let the Russians walk all over us, or do you think I should vote for an adequate military budget to keep them in their place?" is not a valid question. When a congressman who uses such "guided" questionnaires solemnly announces on the floor that an overwhelming percentage of his constituents favor his voting record, it is unlikely to affect his peers.

"Trustees," who do what they think is best regardless of their constituents' position, argue that they are United States congressmen *from* a particular district of a particular state, not delegates of a constituency *to* the Congress. Congressman Robert Eckhardt, a representative from an oil-producing district in Texas, courageously carried the trustee theory to its political extreme. He voted against the parochial interests of his constituency, arguing that the national energy interests were more important than the interests of the oil industry and that his constituency would be better off with his votes. Their popular perception was to the contrary, and he lost his next election. Similarly, during the August 1981 tax fight, many Democrats voted against President Reagan's tax package even though their mail averaged 4 to 1 for the president; they believed that the bill would destroy the capacity to ever balance the budget or to fund necessary government programs.

The late President John Kennedy published an exciting set of vignettes about public officials who put national and long-range issues ahead of their own political well-being. Like Robert Eckhardt of Texas, they shared the common experience of losing their public office at a subsequent election. Kennedy's book, entitled *Profiles in Courage*, sums up the trustee theory of congressional representation in its preface:

> It is difficult to accept such a narrow view of the role of United States
> Senator—a view that assumes the people of Massachusetts sent me to
> Washington to serve merely as a seismograph to record shifts in popular
> opinion. I reject this view not because I lack faith in the "wisdom of the
> people," but because this concept of democracy actually puts too little faith in
> the people. Those who would deny the obligation of the representative to be
> bound by every impulse of the electorate—regardless of the conclusions that

his own deliberations direct—do trust in the wisdom of the people. They have faith in their ultimate sense of justice, faith in their ability to honor courage and respect judgment, and faith that in the long run they will act unselfishly for the good of the nation. It is that kind of faith on which democracy is based, not simply the often frustrated hope that public opinion will at all times under all circumstances promptly identify itself with the public interest.

The voters selected us, in short, because they had confidence in our judgment and our ability to exercise that judgment from a position where we could determine what were their best interests, as a part of the nation's interests. This may mean that we must on occasion lead, inform, correct and sometimes even ignore constituent opinion, if we are to exercise fully that judgment for which we were elected. But acting without selfish motive or private bias, those who follow the dictates of an intelligent conscience are not aristocrats, demagogues, eccentrics or callous politicians insensitive to the feelings of the public. They expect—and not without considerable trepidation—their constituents to be the final judges of the wisdom of their course; but they have faith that those constituents—today, tomorrow or even in another generation—will at least respect the principles that motivated their independent stand.[10]

Most members show traits endemic to both schools of thought; they are, to use the jargon, "politicos" who balance the needs of their district against national concerns. Almost every member acknowledges that he or she has "ducked out" on some issues. Some insist that they only "vote for the home folks" on issues of little moment, that on an issue important to the national welfare, they are prepared to take the heat from parochial opposition within the district. The importance of the issue nationwide is a barometer of how to vote because the media pay more attention to roll-call votes on such issues. A parochial vote on national issues is not likely to be quiescent.

Most congressmen, regardless of the polls, are paranoid about defeat. Horror stories abound of congressmen who were defeated for being too "national" and those who lost to a bad economy or long presidential coattails. As Richard Fenno points out in his book *Home Style*, virtually every member of Congress looks over his shoulder, especially as election time nears:

Once having gone through a testing election, early or late, a member will entertain the possibility of its recurrence forever. Even when he is being spared, it will be happening to someone he knows. And he will take it as a warning signal to himself. These frequent warning signals also remind the member that his security is not proportionate to the rise and fall of national electoral tides. He will be more affected, for better or for worse, by his efforts to help himself.[11]

This paranoia is reflected in a member's voting record. How a vote will subsequently be interpreted at election time is difficult to predict, particularly when the needs of the district are not directly at stake.

A similar dilemma faced some twenty-six members of Congress who voted against the Organized Crime Act of 1970. The centerpiece of President Nixon's anti-crime package, even its title militated against any effective opposition. A "no" vote was a vote for organized crime. After much surgery in the House Judiciary Committee, the bill was finally allowed a rule for floor consideration. Through the efforts of the committee chairman and several senior committee members, various "bargains" had been struck with the Senate to delete some of the controversial provisions. For example, preventive detention, under which persons accused of crime can be temporarily denied bail because they are determined to be dangerous to the community, was limited to the District of Columbia. By the time the bill came up for final House passage, much of the national attention had been diverted to other causes. The members who voted against the bill were surprised that so little negative mail was generated. But their relief was short-lived. At the next election, their opponents made their nay vote a major issue. Although the dire predictions of neither the proponents nor the opponents of the Organized Crime Act of 1970 came to pass, many who voted yea would have had easier consciences had they voiced their opposition and those who voted nay would have had easier reelection races in stifling their opposition. Organized crime did not seem to care much one way or the other, judging by crime statistics.

Luckily, most legislation does not pose the dilemma of choosing between the public interest and the interest of the home district. With the exception of extremely controversial and publicized issues—abortion, the death penalty, school prayer—there is little lobbying, little public awareness, and considerable apathy on the part of the electorate with respect to most legislative issues. A member is not lobbied by any interest group on 30 percent of the votes and is lobbied by only one relevant interest group on 36 percent of the votes.[12] Academic studies on the degee to which members attempt to reflect the will of their constituents indicate that on cutting social issues, like civil-rights legislation, members tend to vote with their constituencies; but on issues like foreign aid, members vote along party lines.[13] However, in recent years, even the foreign policy area has been more political with each ethnic group lobbying vociferously for the needs of its place of national origin. Thus, the Irish, the Greeks, the Jews, the Lebanese, all have organized political groups committed to ensure that members vote with their ethnic constituencies on foreign aid.

On issues that have a direct impact on the district, representatives invariably vote with the district. John Kennedy wrote:

These, then, are some of the pressures which confront a man of conscience. He cannot ignore the pressure groups, his constituents, his party, the comradeship of his colleagues, the needs of his family, his own pride in office, the necessity for compromise and the importance of remaining in office. He must judge for himself which path to choose, which steps will most help or hinder the ideals to which he is committed. He realizes that once he begins to weigh each issue in terms of his chances for reelection, once he begins to compromise away his principles on one issue after another for fear that to do otherwise would halt his career and prevent future fights for principle, then he has lost the very freedom of conscience which justifies his continuance in office. But to decide at which point and on which issue he will risk his career is a difficult and soul-searching decision.[14]

Each member of Congress must make his own calculus: Should he follow his own conscience, his party, or his constituents? Fortunately, most votes do not necessitate these stark choices.

Constituencies are not, of course, homogeneous groups. In casting a difficult vote, a congressman must consider his geographic constituency, his general election constituency, his primary election constituency. Members also consider their nationwide constituency. Richard Fenno elaborated on the problem of multiple constituencies:

> More frequent, we think that this kind of choice is one in which the Congressman must choose among constituencies within the district. Also, when studies of party voting conclude that a member of Congress can vote independently because he or she "knows the constituency isn't looking," we need to ask again, which constituency? One of the several constituencies may very well be looking.[15]

When a congressman's primary election and general election constituencies are different, the choice is particularly difficult. Senator Daniel Moynihan of New York faced a dilemma in his 1982 election strategy. Should he lean to the left to stave off possible liberal candidates in the primary or remain moderate to challenge right-wing Republican insurgent candidates in a state that in 1980 had elected the extremely conservative Alfonse D'Amato? Which constituents should he look to for instruction? Certain so-called national members of Congress, like Senator Jesse Helms, receive strong support and financing from constituents across the nation. What happens when his national constituents disagree with his constituents at home? Jesse Helms actually jeopardized the financial welfare of his own home state of North Carolina when his leadership of the far right infuriated many senators on both sides of the aisle. To teach Helms a lesson, Republican Senator Mark Hatfield of

Oregon and Democratic Senator Tom Eagleton of Missouri offered amendments to eliminate tobacco price supports for the tobacco grown in North Carolina. Tobacco barely survived, 45 to 43. Even "safe" senators, like Republican Paul Laxalt of Nevada, are faced on occasion with this conundrum. Although the national Republican constituency clearly supported an MX missile system, the Nevada residents did not want it in their backyards; to avoid the dilemma, Laxalt tried unsuccessfully to prevail upon a close friend, President Ronald Reagan, to devise an airborne alternative to the MX missile.

TASKS OF A CONGRESSMAN

Ombudsman

Service to the constituency is the most time-consuming activity of any congressional office. As government has grown more complex, the ombudsman role has assumed much greater importance. There was a time when most people had little involvement with their federal government. Aside from paying income taxes and getting drafted, there was little contact necessary between the average citizen and his government. With the advent of the New Deal and the Great Society programs, that limited contact changed dramatically. Every citizen today has reason or necessity for contacting the federal government. The days of fulfilling ombudsman obligations by sending out "baby books" to appropriate constituents are over; constituent needs and demands have progressed geometrically with the years since 1930. Baby books are out, or at least inadequate. (And at one time, at least, a tool for revenge. Upon being fired by his member-employer, an irate staffer conveniently arranged to confuse the mailings so that the graduates of parochial schools for girls received baby books instead of the traditional congratulatory notes from their congressman.) Everything from a small loan for a local business to medical care for a deserving veteran involves the discretionary attention of a federal agency. Can members of Congress get such attention swiftly and maybe even favorably? At least so most citizens think, and most congressmen advertise.

Many members devote a substantial portion of their staff and funds to performing the ombudsman role. Referred to as casework, it is the stuff of which successful politicians build large and grateful pluralities. Indeed, concerned caseworkers often succeed even when they fail by making the constituent feel that his congressman is "fighting the pointy-headed bureaucracy" that keeps him from getting his due. Most important, many commentators argue that good casework can counteract a congressman's unpopular votes and positions. Indeed, some political scientists, most notably Morris Fiorina of Yale, believe that congressmen create bureaucracy to allow themselves the opportunity of helping their constituents wade through it.[16]

A variation on the individual casework is the "pork-barrel" role that members of Congress play. No district is without institutional needs. Districts need money for grants to the local college, new post offices, dams—every geographical region of the country wants the federal government to do something. An energetic and astute member of Congress can deflect many legislative bullets by carefully playing the role of Member Bountiful when it comes to projects and grants. The late Mendel Rivers of South Carolina used his position as chairman of the House Armed Services Committee to provide many military installations for his district. His slogan at campaign time was "Rivers Delivers." With one more naval installation, some wags insisted, South Carolina would sink into the Atlantic Ocean. The capacity of Mendel Rivers to deliver made it very hard for opponents to concentrate on his voting record.

More liberal members soften the opposition of the business community by providing such projects as new buildings and internal improvements for the district. Conversely, more conservative members divert their opposition by providing grants to community organizations and institutions involved with private-sector benevolence. Given the extensive role played by the federal government in the shape and health of local communities, it is hard to argue that the pork-barrel function is not an appropriate part of the representative's job.

Savvy White House operators use the announcement of new projects to forge closer links between a congressional delegation and the administration. Sometimes the president himself or the appropriate cabinet officer announces the grant or project with the congressman by his side, always with an appropriate "photo opportunity." The delegation receives advance notice of the upcoming award to allow the official announcement to come from the congressional office. Although advance notice is usually reserved for congressmen who are members of the administration's party, the White House sometimes uses the opportunity to forge alliances on the opposite side of the aisle. A member of Congress, especially one of the opposition party, does not wait to be asked to participate in the announcement of the forthcoming pork. Aggressive inquiry at the executive agency involved usually pries loose the information. Thus, the congressman does his own grant announcing. A congressman does not even have to vote for a project to take credit for it. Congressional offices often issue press releases taking credit for public grants with which they had nothing to do. As a congressman, OMB Director David Stockman played this game:

> Indeed, as a congressman, Stockman himself had worked hard to make certain that his Fourth District constituents exploited the system. His office maintained a computerized alert system for grants and loans from the myriad agencies, to make certain that no opportunities were missed. "I went around and cut all the ribbons and they never knew I voted against the damn programs," he said.[17]

In all events, the image the member seeks to portray back home is that he carries enough clout in Washington and works hard enough at his job so that these federal goodies, which might have been delivered anywhere in the country, are wending their way to his district or state.

The delivery of programs, monies, and grants back home is almost always universally acclaimed in the district. The lecture about government waste almost never extends to projects that benefit the home turf. Senator William Proxmire, a Democrat from Wisconsin, proudly portrays himself as the opponent of government waste. As the author of the Golden Fleece award, he regularly designates for public ridicule federal research projects that appear inane. (For example, he lambasted a study by the National Science Foundation on why men and women fall in love.) Moreover, he assiduously votes against federal pay hikes, arguing the need for fiscal austerity. Nonetheless, when it comes to the multibillion dollar dairy subsidy program—a program that is widely criticized by Democrats and Republicans alike —Proxmire is quiet. The program is vital to the economy of his home state and he votes consistently with the dairy lobby. Similarly, during the budget-cutting spree of the Ninety-seventh Congress, western senators who lashed out at social service programs were the first to come to the defense of expensive federal water projects. Northern liberals, quick to criticize water projects, are the first to defend unnecessary military installations or defense contracts vital to the economy of their state.

No one, not even the press, is immune from some political contradiction. The *Chicago Tribune*, which has traditionally opposed "government waste" and lamented the amount of pork-barrel projects emanating from the federal government, never saw reason to include Illinois items in their strictures against waste. As director of the Office of Management and Budget, David Stockman was considered ruthless in his efforts to weed out waste and fat from the federal budget, including a proposal to abolish the Community Services Agency. He insisted that the grants made by this agency were a prime example of unnecessary federal spending. However, earlier, as a congressman from Michigan, he had vigorously joined an effort to get funds from that agency for Michigan. Asked to reconcile his views, he insisted that his prime duty as a congressman was to make sure that Michigan received its share of whatever was going out and that, without his action, the money only would have gone somewhere else. No one in Michigan complained about his efforts to steer federal funds Michigan's way. (The CSA was abolished in 1981, the first federal agency to be eliminated since World War II.)

It is a hard fact of political life that a member of Congress can hardly find an issue on which the people of his constituency will not choose up sides. However he votes or speaks, he will draw some flak, some support. Unanimous approval is bestowed only on the award of grants and programs.

The Congress has always maintained a suitable climate for raising pork and sending it out in barrels, and the institutional structure is well established to preserve the pork-barrel system. Thus, the chairman of the Public Works Committee is a man to be courted. Even critics of the pork barrel agree that a congressman who brings the bacon home to the district significantly enhances his chance for reelection. Senator Daniel Patrick Moynihan of New York and Senator Robert Stafford of Vermont, the ranking Democrat and Republican, respectively, on the Senate Committee for the Environment and Public Works, have attempted to provide a system that will better coordinate the use of public funds for federal buildings and expose these expenditures to public sunshine. Not surprisingly, their bills have not been received with open arms.

Use of Forum to Represent Constituencies

Another way to represent constituencies is the effective use of the forum by effective use of the media. Members use floor speeches to publicize problems of great local concern to the district—a flood, a crisis in an industry, the impact of acid rain on the district's lakes and streams. Then again, the subject matter is not always quite so serious. In 1981 when the Boston Celtics won the national basketball championship, Senator Edward Kennedy and Senator Paul Tsongas, the junior senator from Massachusetts, introduced a joint Senate resolution commending the Boston Celtics for their victory against Houston. Not to be outdone, Senator John Tower from Texas, hearing a challenge to his team, charged down to the floor to make flattering comments about his home team. A lively debate ensued. This is not the weighty stuff that one usually thinks the United States Senate spends its day doing, but this is the stuff about which everyone back home loves to read. One-minute speeches are permitted at the start of every House session to allow discourse on whatever is current and choice. If the speaker likes what the member is saying or is distracted, the minute can lengthen into several. If the speaker is not favorably inclined to the remarks, the minute can be on the short side. In addition, a member can ask for permission, a "Special Order," to address the House at the close of legislative business for up to thirty minutes. As mentioned earlier, the longer speeches, both in the Senate and in the House, are frequently not made in person. They are inserted in the *Congressional Record* even if the member never appeared in the chamber on the day of the address.

If the speech is newsworthy, the press and other media pick it up. Although the soliloquies given under special orders are not usually well attended, they can be read in the *Record*, of course. In addition, House floor proceedings are televised. The media-conscious member sends out press releases to all and sundry, announcing that the member has forthrightly told the American people his views on a burning issue of the day. Should the press fail to print or otherwise report the speech, the member broadsides a copy to his constituents in newsletters sent via franked mail. The audience reached is clearly larger than that reached by a letter to the editor. That the newsletter often exaggerates beyond recognition the congressman's contribution is accepted fact. According to the newsletter of a Democratic congressman from Massachusetts, his legislation on regulatory reform in the Ninety-seventh Congress was the cornerstone of anti-regulatory efforts in the House of Representatives. Needless to say, his legislation was not under serious consideration by any committee or subcommittee. But he was no exception. Virtually every congressman puffs his performance. The Truth in Advertising Laws do not apply to Congress, and the mailing price is free.

Sometimes, however, special orders and one-minute speeches are used to generate real dialogue about national problems in the Congress and the country. To initiate a debate on the Vietnam War in the late 1960s, a group of members, led by Democratic Congressmen Benjamin Rosenthal of New York and Andrew Jacobs of Indiana, took a series of special orders designed to keep the House in session all night while they bespoke their opposition to the war. Because the effort was well publicized in advance, the galleries were full, with people waiting to get in. Democratic Congressman Wayne Hays of Ohio, a hawk on the war, called sufficient quorum calls to break up the session. The media gave full coverage to the views of the anti-war members, as well as to Congressman Hays' opinion that the sponsors were "agents of Hanoi" and dupes of the Communists.

Many other kinds of forums are also available. An active and articulate member has numerous opportunities to speak, both in the home district or state and nationally. (These allow an opportunity not only to promote pet issues but also to receive an honorarium, one of the few ways a member can legitimately supplement his congressional salary.) Key members are sought by the media for comments on pending legislation and issues. Some are invited to appear on "Meet the Press," "Face the Nation," and other talk and news shows. Their views get substantial coverage, at least in their home turf and frequently coast to coast.

Some members view their manipulation of the media to get favorable nationwide coverage for critical issues as the single most important part of their representative function. Democratic Congresswoman Bella Abzug of New York became a national figure by her articulate use of the forum for equal rights for women. The late Congressman Allard Lowenstein, also of New York, used the forum to advance his views against the Vietnam War and his "Dump Johnson" movement. Senator Charles Percy of Illinois became a household name long before he became chairman of the Senate Foreign Relations Committee because of his effective use of the electronic and print media. Congressman Les Aspin of Wisconsin is teased about having the "fastest mimeograph machine in the West," but he has, without a doubt, used the media to advance his views to a national audience. The members who excel in media coverage are subjected to a good deal of envious needling by their colleagues. At one Presidential Inauguration two camera-conscious members of the House were eager to get closer to the television cameras that were being trained on the president while he delivered the Inaugural Address. As they sought to elbow each other out of the way, New York's Governor Hugh Carey, then a member of the House, quipped that "they are going to have to use a split screen for those two."

The use of the forum is effective not only for representing the views of constituents but also for creating a political environment that will identify a member as a leader on key issues. By a sophisticated use of the forum, a member does not have to choose between his own views and those of his constituents. He can ensure that the two are compatible. He can package his views in a favorable light. He can educate his voters.Every member uses the media to further his views, at election time under duress, and at other times with eagerness and enthusiasm. In all events, using the public forum as a catalyst for advancing social and economic change is part of the job of being a congressman. It is almost impossible to get elected in the first place without knowing how to use the forum, and many members find its use an attractive and ego-satisfying way of trying to stay in Congress and to accomplish policy objectives.

Casting a Vote

Casting a vote in the House or the Senate is very much the hardest task, as John Kennedy so accurately described:

> Lawyers, businessmen, teachers, doctors, all face difficult personal decisions involving their integrity—but few, if any, face them in the glare of the spotlight

as do those in public office. Few, if any, face the same dread finality of decision that confronts a Senator facing an important call of the roll. He may want more time for his decision—he may believe there is something to be said for both sides—he may feel that a slight amendment could remove all difficulties—but when that roll is called he cannot hide, he cannot equivocate, he cannot delay—and he senses that his constituency, like the Raven in Poe's poem, is perched there on his Senate desk, croaking "nevermore" as he casts the vote that stakes his political future.[18]

Most members are nagged by the feeling that all the good and thoughtful votes cast do not add to one's political capital. Most of the time most of the public does not know and does not care how their elected representatives vote. In 1979 a member of the House of Representatives voted approximately 672 times, and a senator, 497 times. Most recorded votes are unnoticed by the average constituent; only a small number of votes receive media coverage.

On "media-attended" issues, the individual member must watch in frustration as his position is framed in the inevitable shorthand of the press and television. Congressman Columbus, a well-known conservative in the House, cast his expected vote in favor of declaring the earth flat today. For Congressman Columbus to try to explain that he is not really a conservative, that the issue was not about whether the earth is flat, but rather involved a procedural issue in which party loyalty was a factor, and that in any event he really believes the earth is round, will be in vain.

In the Ninety-seventh Congress where sensitive social issues provoked heated floor debates and votes, the superficiality of media coverage, particularly that on the evening news, was sometimes blatantly damaging. When Senator Jesse Helms sponsored an amendment to eliminate federal funding for all abortions (except where the life of the mother was at stake), the media reported the votes in terms of pro- and anti-abortion. That many of those who voted against the amendment believed federal funding should be provided in extreme situations was not made clear to the television audience. Such a broad-brush characterization can have devastating political ramifications.

The media can control the public's appraisal of a legislative battle and a legislator's performance. During the debate over the president's budget cuts in 1981, the president floated a proposal to cut back on social security benefits. The reaction in the Senate was instantly hostile, and Democratic Senator Daniel Moynihan of New York proposed a resolution expressing the sense of the Senate that social security benefits should be left intact. Because of the high probability that Moynihan's resolution would succeed and embarrass the Reagan administration, the Republican leadership, led by Senator Robert

Dole, the chairman of the Finance Committee, introduced a resolution in support of social security substantively similar to the Moynihan resolution, thereby giving the Republicans a chance to undercut the Democrats and cast a symbolic vote for social security. The Moynihan resolution lost narrowly; the Dole resolution passed with no votes against it. The next day the press reported on the Dole victory, and virtually no one in the nation realized that Senator Moynihan was the primary initiator of the resolution.

The press can be devastating. Former Democratic Senator and presidential contender Eugene McCarthy once described reporters as blackbirds lined up on a wire—when one flies off the rest follow. During the August 1981 debate on the Reagan tax legislation, Senator Edward Kennedy objected to the House–Senate conference report giving a $33 billion tax break to the oil industry, a particularly newsworthy item as the administration had just eliminated the $122 monthly minimum social security benefits. Unfortunately, the conference report had been reported to the floor Saturday evening, and Senator Kennedy's objection was phoned in from Cape Cod, which had the effect of delaying the final vote on the tax package until the following Monday, when an air traffic controller's strike was scheduled to take place. Many senators were furious at having to return after the weekend, to say nothing of the possibility of being stranded in Washington, D.C., during the August recess. The press reported the story almost exclusively from the vantage point of furious senators. One headline actually said: "Kennedy suns, while Senate stews." The merits of his objection received little comment until weeks later when columnists and cartoonists pointed out the unfairness of the tax package.

It is neither electorate indifference nor media oversimplification, however, that makes taking a position so difficult and impolitic. Indeed, it is the lack of indifference by some portion of the constituency that causes members of Congress to agonize over the rightness of their vote. Special-interest constituencies are especially attentive to the vote of their representatives. Social security recipients may not know where El Salvador is, but one way or another they will find out that someone in Congress moved to change the way that the cost of living adjustments are figured for social security benefits, and on *that* issue they will very much want to know where their representatives stand. "We are watching you" is the warning delivered, and the members know that, no matter how much good they may do for the Republic on the other issues, their level of support or opposition from the social security recipient constituency will be determined by that vote. If the media or a special-interest group does not focus public attention on a controversial vote, a member's political opponents will. They wait like birds of prey for one false step. In 1982 a Minnesota Democrat who was challenging a moderate Republican sent a statewide mailing to the elderly in an envelope similar to those used to mail social security benefits. The envelope contained a political announcement, in the color and size of a federal paycheck. His opponent, the message said, had voted to cut social security benefits.

The views of individual voters are not the only force to be reckoned with when a vote on the floor is nigh. Political action committees (PACs), which have multiplied like amoebas in recent years, cannot be ignored. The relationship between the PAC position and a congressman's vote is often critical. A "wrong" vote can mean loss of PAC support in the next election, and loss of support for one means gain of support for the opposition. The combined impact on voting behavior of individual business and interest-group PACs has only begun to be measured. Although the media are quick to point out that a particular subcommittee chairman has accepted money from a PAC that has an issue before the subcommittee, a measurement of linkage between the campaign contributions and voting patterns has not been undertaken. Proponents of public financing to replace in whole or in part the role played by the PACs insist that the entire legislative process is being distorted by the PACs, causing many kinds of public issues to be deflected or deferred because of their influence.

Contributions are only one way to influence a member's stand. Ratings compiled by numerous groups who monitor the Hill—Americans for Democratic Action and Americans for Constitutional Action, for example—are used to measure the poles for voting behavior. Members with a "high" rating from one of these groups are immediately type-cast as liberals or conservatives by the media, by their colleagues, and by other lobbying groups in Washington. Some members have cast votes to bring down their scores on the polar rating charts so as to appear more moderate to their constituents and their colleagues. Other ratings make a conscious effort to cover the spectrum of issues that surface in any given session of Congress. The ratings of the League of Women Voters and the Ripon Society are two examples. But the range of the "spectrum" of issues is in the eye of the beholder. To some constituents, there is only one issue.

The single-interest groups terrorize incumbents. Anti-abortion groups, pro-gun groups, groups advocating prayer in the schools, anti-busing groups—all can make life miserable for any member of Congress who seeks to be a statesman and a generalist on the issues. In most sessions of Congress more than one vote is taken on each of these explosive issues. Votes on such emotional issues are impossible to explain. As Massachusetts Congressman Barney Frank described the congressional attitude on abortion: Most members of Congress are neither passionately for nor against abortion; they passionately want to avoid the issue. Incumbents who hope to soften the opposition of these groups by trying to explain their contrary votes are dreamers. Consistent opposition to the special-interest point of view increases the odds of being targeted by those groups in the next election. Depending on their plurality, members take their future in their hands each time they vote on an explosive issue, or so they think.

With few exceptions, like busing, most divisive issues of the last two decades do not enjoy a majority support as vigorous as that of the sponsoring special-interest groups. Thus, although poll after poll has shown a more permissive attitude on abortion, anti-abortion groups continue to succeed in countless elections and legislative battles. Unfortunately, the majority view is not as passionately held on these issues as is the minority view. The majority of constituents may or may not consider the votes on these issues in deciding how to vote in the next election. To the single-interest voter, however, a vote means life or death. Because they are more vocal and determined, the influence of single-interest voters is felt in even nonmarginal districts; in marginal districts, they can make or break.

The party label is generally not a helpful benchmark in instructing members how to vote, particularly on controversial or parochial issues. The so-called social issues, like busing and prayer in the schools, are much more influenced by geography than by party label. Southern Democrats and southern Republicans vote the issue, not the party, on social legislation. Indeed, the parochial influence is always greater than the party influence. The party has its greatest effect on procedural votes. The vote for speaker is a strict party-line vote, as is a vote on an appeal from the decision of the chair, or the adoption of committee ratios or rules at the beginning of the session. Because procedural votes hardly ever cause ripples back home, most members are quite ready to give their party leaders the requested support.

The congressional party has little leverage on votes of great importance in the home district. As a more cynical member expressed it in the House cloakroom: "I'm a strong party man, as long as it doesn't affect my district." The congressional party has rarely imposed sanctions on its errant members. It makes little or no effort to correlate its campaign finance contributions with a member's voting record. Members who consistently thwart the party will not lose seniority (except on the rarest of occasions), committee memberships, or congressional "perqs," like the frank or travel expenses. At most, errant members may feel a bit of peer pressure or lose out on a "boondoggle" congressional junket. Because the congressional party recognizes its inability to compete with the demands of the home district, arms are rarely twisted to persuade members to vote against their campaign promises.

Although generally the party cannot protect members who choose to vote with it and against their districts, a president with a strong national mandate can occasionally lessen the impact of such votes by campaigning for the congressmen and helping them to raise funds. During the budget-cutting spree of the Ninety-seventh Congress in early 1981, a conservative western Republican senator lamented that he was sure he had infuriated every interest group in his state by voting to cut all their programs. However, to vote against the party on these cuts, he poignantly acknowledged, would have jeopardized his relationship with both the newly emerging party finance committee and the strong and popular president.

FOURTEEN

REELECTION

INCUMBENCY

As indicated earlier, Professor David Mayhew suggested, with the usual academic caveats, that a congressman's voting behavior can be analyzed solely in terms of his desire to be reelected.[1] Although that explanation is a bit broad, no one argues that the itch for reelection is irrelevant. The successful politician is the reelected politician. The politicians profiled by John Kennedy as courageous lost their next political effort. To be effective for the causes held dear (including one's ego), a legislator must balance courage against constituency.

Reelection strategies clearly loom large in the congressional office. Almost from the day the oath of office is administered congressmen begin to worry about the next election. Their concern is not tempered by the knowledge that mortality rates are favorable to incumbents, in the House at least, where in 1978 more than 93.7 percent of those seeking reelection were successful. In the Senate, especially in recent years, incumbents have had more to worry about. In 1978 only some 60 percent of the incumbents were reelected.[2] Statistics notwithstanding, most members live from election to election. They simply do not believe the statistics. Horror stories of members who took their reelection for granted abound. Members assume an underdog status no matter what the statistics show. And they are afraid of defeat. Author Robert Caro wrote that as a young congressman from Texas Lyndon Johnson's greatest fear was that he would not be reelected. Johnson once met a former congressman who was operating an elevator, an image that haunted Johnson throughout his career.[3]

Many factors in the reelection battle are beyond a member's control. The reapportionment of congressional districts by the legislature is a threat that usually occurs every ten years. But interval reapportionment is sometimes attempted or accomplished. In a move that would have destroyed the coauthor's district, Mayor Richard Daley of Chicago came within two votes of persuading the state legislature to reapportion congressional seats in 1975, the midway point between reapportionment dates. Because of legislative and court reapportionments that drastically changed his district's boundaries, Congressman Sam Stratton of New York has represented four different districts.

The popularity of the administration and the resultant "coattails," or "draft," effect are also factors in a member's quest for reelection. In 1974 many an incumbent, especially Republican incumbents, went down to defeat because of Watergate. (Even so, 87.7 percent of House members seeking reelection were successful.) And in 1980 many an incumbent, especially Democratic incumbents, may have met defeat because of the unpopularity of President Carter. Nothing is more frustrating to those seeking reelection than an electorate soured by the White House performance, or by the stock-market performance, or by the job-market performance. Pointing with pride to all the votes cast seeking to correct those problems is a thankless task. The incumbent was in Congress when the bad news occurred; the incumbent is held responsible.

Incumbents win most of the time because these "uncontrollables" are more than offset by the benefits of incumbency. By identifying himself throughout his district as "The Congressman," the incumbent creates an almost "Pavlovian" reaction in the voters. Name recognition is an invaluable political asset that most challengers can never overcome. The federal "goodies" that were delivered more often than not balance out the uncontrollables. When the nation was imperiled, the incumbent was on the floor (and in the mailboxes with a franked copy of the speech) denouncing "the enemy" in a forthright speech. An incumbent's capacity to create "hard news" for the media provides access to the local press. Seniority spells media attention: A hearing conducted by a subcommittee chairman on the exploitation of tenants by condominium converters just when the issue is "hot" in the district is not without political overtones. To denounce the incumbent for grandstanding persuades few voters to join the challenger's camp. With the rare exception of a former member making a comeback, most challengers are new to the national arena. Prior experience at the state or local level does not equip the challenger with knowledge of the Washington press corps and the other national media people. A successful member of Congress knows how to get good publicity—and knowing the schedules and work habits of the press corps is primary. A former newspaperman, Congressman Roman Pucinski of Illinois knew that weekends were usually dull news periods. He scheduled his press releases to hit the "lull" in the press schedules. He frequently called up radio stations on weekends to offer them comments on anything that might interest them, again to take up the "slack" in news time.

Congressional newsletters and responses to constituent mail are in reality campaign literature. Because the taxpayer pays for the postal frank, the use of it by the incumbent for reelection purposes has been severely criticized. The limitations imposed by Congress on the use of the frank illustrate, more than anything else, the kind of problems that incumbency poses for the challenger. The House rules now prohibit more than one picture per page of a franked newsletter. The rules also preclude any "political" news or announcements. The incumbent is "limited" to having only one picture with the president of the United States, or the speaker, or the president of Egypt. The incumbent cannot ask people to vote for him in the next election, but he can describe all the great things he has done for the people of the Tenth District. Indeed, because of the unfairness to the challenger, the Congress finally passed a rule that prohibits the use of franked newsletters within a certain time period before the next election. Of course, that rule is easily circumvented by putting stamps on the newsletter. And stamped, the newsletter can become a veritable photo essay in which the incumbent is pictured with dozens of notables.

The congressional staff is the ongoing campaign organization. Although the law precludes the use of the staff or offices for reelection activity, it is the rare incumbent who does not expect his staff to be at the ready on nights and weekends when the campaign heats up. And the legitimate daytime activities of the staff enhance the incumbent's bid for reelection: staffers write speeches, answer mail, help constituents, schedule the incumbent's activities, send out congratulatory notes to the high school graduates, research the issues—their equivalent in paid campaign workers is far more than most challengers can muster. Obviously, the advantages of incumbency more than outweigh the disadvantages.

ELECTION YEAR PRIORITIES

An incumbent gearing up for reelection reorders his priorities. A year or two before reelection, a senator beefs up his attendance record to provide some "cushion" for expected absences during the campaign season. As the election draws near, tensions arise between the campaign staff eager to schedule him at home and the legislative staff concerned about substantive floor issues. Scheduling takes on a heavier local flavor. Senators and House members minimize their role as "national" figures, particularly when the local challenger back home is denouncing them for having caught "Potomac fever" and gone over to the "Eastern Establishment." The expected fence-mending with local party officials and functionaries and a desire to reestablish the appropriate measure of national party identification varies from area to area and from administration to administration. A southern incumbent seeking reelection during a Kennedy administration might soft-pedal his Democratic label more than he would during a Nixon administration, especially after Watergate. A northern Democrat might be less party-minded during a Carter administration than during a Franklin Delano Roosevelt administration. The incumbent seeks to identify himself as the "leader" of whatever the local party claims as its identity so as to forestall any serious primary election challenger.

Campaign finance is a persistent concern of the incumbent throughout his term. Some members literally consult campaign contribution lists to decide which constituents merit attention. A $1,000 donor usually enters through the front door. Incumbency is a most important asset in getting funds. Depending on his committee assignments and his voting record, he has established some kind of national and Washington constituency. If he is for the oil industry, he has the oil lobbyists and their clients. If he is against the oil industry, he has the consumer lobbyists and their clientele. If he is dextrous and on the House Ways and Means Committee or the Senate Finance Committee, he may have both. Unless he has been a complete cipher, he has pleased at least some groups.

A Washington, D.C., fund raiser is an almost standard event for any incumbent, and during the season as many as three or four a night occur at various watering spas and hotels. The traditional procedure involves a cocktail party for the incumbent, a party sponsored by the speaker, the majority leader, the chairmen of key committees, a cabinet official, or leading lobbyists or citizens. A dinner or other "sit-down" affair is rare, for custom dictates easy access, and easy exit after making a contribution. Washington fund raisers provide substantial sums, as well as access to corporate and labor PACs and their larger contributions down the line.

The national PAC is also fair game. The finance committees of incumbents sometimes solicit the political action arm of every organization doing business in Washington. The solicitation, on behalf of a sitting member of Congress, particularly one with a powerful committee seat, has an inherent appeal to any group with legislative concerns. The advantages of incumbency extend to the kinds of people who agree to sign the solicitation for funds and to the kinds of speakers who agree to adorn a fund-raising event.

The House and the Senate Republican campaign committees have begun to play a much larger role in financing campaigns. Again, the incumbent has an edge in getting party funds simply because he is a known quantity within the party. In addition to protecting the Republican flock in the 1980 election, the House Republican Campaign Committee financed several upset victories over incumbent Democratic members. The Democratic Campaign Committee, particularly in the Senate, has been relatively ineffective. In 1980 it contributed 10 percent of the money contributed by its counterpart. Instead of developing a grass-roots base of contributors, it relied on an annual dinner to provide funds. The Democratic staff was less than half the size of that of the Republicans. After the humiliation of the Democratic party in the 1980 election, the Democratic campaign committees in both houses geared up for more aggressive fund raising, prompted, in part perhaps, by the Republican success.

Even the title of incumbent wears well in a reelection campaign. "Senator" Blank calling some captain of industry or labor is much more likely to get through than "Candidate" Blank. Equally important, ensuing discussion can be pertinent to the prospective contributor. The senator or the congressman can talk sympathetically about the high prime interest rate and dazzle the constituent by describing his recent conversation with the Federal Reserve chairman at a committee hearing. Indeed, the crass subject of money may never need to be mentioned by the incumbent, for a grateful constituent is frequently a generous constituent. A challenger cannot match that conversation.

Reelection strategy also involves the identification of the key groups of support and opposition likely to be active in the campaign. An incumbent usually hires a pollster to develop a reelection profile, showing the incumbent's strengths and weaknesses in the district, the opponent likely to give him the most trouble, and constituent perceptions of the incumbent. A good profile indicates the areas to accentuate and/or camouflage. Not infrequently, a member shifts his voting pattern and legislative activities dramatically when the poll shows a close contest coming up and a negative perception of the incumbent's activities. The poll also shows the impact of single-interest groups in the district. Unfortunately, a profile only shows the state of the political health of the incumbent on a given day, like an electrocardiogram. Pollsters do not guarantee that the reading will hold good through election day. Many an incumbent has "died" at election time when the rating six months earlier had indicated excellent political health.

In the end, however, the most important election "activity" is the image: "the senator" or "the congressman." A popular campaign button advised: "Reelect the Congressman." It was used nationwide. As a cloakroom veteran once remarked: "I'd rather be 'incumbent' than 'outlooking.'"

In setting an election strategy, a candidate has to differentiate between primary and general election constituencies. Candidates strong in party support do not have to fear primary opposition, whereas candidates in a one-party state are significantly challenged only in the primary. Most congressmen, however, have to campaign in both elections. They cannot gear their policy stands to a more liberal or a more conservative constituency without losing the ability to woo the support of the other constituency during the general election. A fine balance must be drawn.

Approximately a year before an election, a candidate begins to think seriously about the nuts and bolts of reelection. He hires a pollster, a campaign manager to organize a grass-roots effort and initiate fund raising, and sometimes a consulting firm. Senators, endowed with more lavish financial resources, also hire advertising consultants to prepare the all-important image.

Although electoral activity and organizing simmer throughout the summer, Labor Day marks the real start-up for the general election. As the election draws near, the incumbent is amazed to discover and rediscover that his finely crafted voting record is almost irrelevant. He has anguished over the "hard" votes in vain. Most voters neither know nor care. What emerges from his incumbency is an ephemeral perception: the Liberal, the Conservative, the Big Spender, the Effective Leader, the Hack. What he gains from his incumbency is name recognition and better access to the resources with which all elections are won or lost: money, workers, media attention, and the means to identify his constituency.

CAMPAIGN FINANCE LAWS

Reform Efforts

When Daniel Webster died, an embarrassing set of correspondence came to light.[4] It detailed how Senator Webster had received extensive retainer fees from the Bank of the United States while he was defending its cause on the floor of the United State Senate. The most compromising document threatened the withdrawal of the senator's representation unless the bank substantially upped the retainer fee. Similar tales of other American folk heroes are constantly embellished in the cloakrooms of Congress—from stories about Abraham Lincoln as a state legislator in Illinois to Everett Dirksen as a United

States senator after whom the Senate Office Building was named. The common thread in all such stories is the difficulty some elected officials have in distinguishing between private interests and the public interest. Nowhere does that line blur more easily than during the contemplation of reelection. Because contributions are the mainstay of reelection, an incumbent can only hope that his opponent is less successful than he in raising funds.

In an era when huge sums are absolutely essential to election, it is not surprising that the methods of financing election campaigns have become the focus of much congressional attention and "reform." In the decade of the 1970s alone, four significant pieces of campaign finance legislation were introduced. Much concern was centered on large campaign contributions from well-funded special interests. Were such sums contributions or bribes? A $25 contribution from one's neighbor is quite different from a $95,000 contribution to a member of Ways and Means from the commodities industry seeking the preservation of a tax loophole. Democratic Congressman Dan Glickman of Kansas recounts how a House colleague turned to him on a floor vote on legislation involving the used car industry and confessed, "I got a $10,000 check from the Automobile Dealers' Association. I can't change my vote now."[5] Between 1978 and 1981 this association contributed more than $1 million to incumbent congressmen. A campaign contribution from a person seeking support of his financial interests is not illegal, but should such contributions and more altruistic contributions be treated differently? Is disclosure of campaign sources sufficient or should limits be placed on the sources and amounts of outside funding?

Until the reforms of the 1970s, campaign finance was regulated by the Federal Corrupt Practices Act, enacted in 1925, which bore little relation to modern campaign practices. For example, it did not even apply to primaries. Lyndon Johnson called it "more loophole than law." Motivated in part by the desire to restore congressional dignity and prodded in part by gadfly organizations such as Common Cause, Congress enacted "reforms."

The first modern effort allowed a $1 check-off on income tax forms ($2 on a joint return) for presidential races. Invented in 1966 by Louisiana Senator Russell Long, the Democratic chairman of the Finance Committee, this proposal was included in a tax bill without too much national attention and actually never took effect. Barely a year later, Senator Robert Kennedy of New York and Senator Albert Gore of Tennessee led a successful fight to repeal the provision on the ground that it would mischievously interfere with normal fund-raising efforts without solving any of the real problems in campaign financing. But in 1971, the Democrats re-created the dollar check-off fund and attached it to an extension of the debt ceiling, a bill viewed as veto-proof because the government can grind to a halt unless it passes. Because President Nixon believed the effort was aimed at complicating his 1972 re-election campaign, he refused to agree to this provision until the sponsors reluctantly postponed the effective date until after the 1972 election.[6]

The first efforts at sweeping reforms of the campaign financing of congressional races, supported by a bipartisan coalition led by Republican John Anderson from Illinois and Morris Udall, a Democrat from Arizona, floundered in a queasy Congress. In 1971 Congress passed a modest bill to limit the amount spent on media by a federal candidate. In 1973 a comprehensive bill providing public financing for congressional races was attached to an extension of a debt-ceiling bill in the Senate. The provisions were so far-reaching that a frightened House sent the entire matter back to the Senate where the provisions were withdrawn.

Senator Hart of Michigan introduced a comprehensive campaign reform bill in 1973. It called for public financing and spending ceilings. Initially, not a single senator would cosponsor the bill. As the Watergate scandal unfolded, however, the proposal generated more attention and concern.

In 1974 a comprehensive campaign reform bill passed the Senate. In its pristine form, it limited contributions and campaign spending and created public financing for congressional and presidential races. Although substantially modified in the House, including the removal of public financing for congressional races, the 1974 act, as finally passed, was the first major campaign reform in modern time.

Congress enacted four campaign finance bills in 1971, 1974, 1976, and 1979. The most sweeping was the Federal Election Campaign Act Amendment of 1974, enacted after the Watergate scandal to regulate both presidential and congressional campaign financing. A bipartisan six-member Federal Election Commission (FEC), appointed by the president and confirmed by the Senate, was established to oversee the new campaign finance requirement. To accomplish its responsibility, the FEC was to issue advisory opinions, conduct audits and investigations, issue subpoenas, and sue for civil injunctions. To retain an iron grip over the FEC, Congress provided that FEC regulations, and sections of regulations, are subject to legislative veto. Congress used this veto to reject the first set of FEC regulations. Regardless of the veto, however, the FEC overseers are careful not to anger the congressional overseers who are in a position to cut their funds.

The 1974 campaign reforms were subsequently modified by the 1976 Supreme Court decision in *Buckley* v. *Valeo*[7] and to a lesser extent by the 1976 and 1979 legislation, which cleaned up issues left open by the Supreme Court opinion and alleviated somewhat the paper-work burden.

Campaign Finance Provisions

Disclosure

The cornerstone of campaign finance reform is the disclosure of the sources of contributions, which is based on the theory that public scrutiny is the best way to prevent corruption and ugly political alliances. Congressional candidates must report significant contributions, identities of contributors, and campaign expenditures. In election years, candidates must submit preelection, postelection and quarterly reports; in nonelection years,[8] reports must be filed semiannually. Each candidate must designate a single "political committee" and a "treasurer" to be responsible for the financial reporting aspects of a campaign.[9]

Although the disclosure concept has widespread support, the complexity of FEC "red tape" is not to be denied. The regulations are so complicated and the penalties (both civil fines and criminal sanctions) for violating them potentially so severe that candidates increasingly rely on lawyers and accountants to fulfill the requirements. Some even speculate that the regulations have discouraged political newcomers from running for office. Regardless of their difficulty, the regulations have reinforced the trend toward more centralized, professional campaigns and may have altered campaign spending priorities. As Congressman Richard B. Cheney of Wyoming said about presidential races:

> No discussion of the subject can begin without first pointing out the obvious—that the requirements of the law have added significantly to the administrative and regulatory costs of campaigning. A significant portion of the funds available to a candidate have to go for accountants, lawyers, and report filing. One recent news account estimated that the costs of compliance—accountants to keep records, copiers to copy records, and lawyers to interpret regulations and sometimes to get around them—will run at least $1.5 million for each campaign that makes it to the 1980 nominating conventions. That is roughly five times what each candidate will be allowed to spend in New Hampshire, the first and traditionally the most important primary.[10]

Spending Limits

Between 1964 and 1968 campaign spending rose by 50 percent; between 1974 and 1978 it had doubled. With this exponential increase in campaign expenditures, Congress became increasingly interested in placing caps on campaign spending.

The most dramatic increase in campaign costs came in the area of television advertising.[11] A 1970 bill proposed a formula to limit the amount federal candidates could spend on political advertising. Although President Nixon vetoed the bill, it was revived in 1971 and passed overwhelmingly, 334 to 20, in the House and 88 to 2 in the Senate. The spending formula was 10 cents times the voting-age population or $50,000, whichever was greater; and of the amount so determined not more than 60 percent could be spent for broadcast media use. With such a strong showing, Nixon did not bother to veto, and the members of Congress had won round one against Madison Avenue and the television industry. But the legislation was effective for only three years, 1972 to 1975.

In 1974 Congress extended spending limits even further by expanding coverage to all expenditures in federal elections, and presidential campaign spending was also restricted under a public funding scheme.

The spending limits worked to the advantage of incumbents, because challengers do well only if they spend a great deal of money—usually more than allowed under the formulas enacted.[12] The campaign spending limits were ultimately overturned by the Supreme Court in *Buckley* v. *Valeo* on the grounds that they interfered with the rights of political expression guaranteed by the First Amendment. This court challenge was brought by an alliance of members from both ends of the political spectrum, liberal Democrat Eugene McCarthy and conservative Republican William Buckley. The court was careful to specify that such limitations were valid in presidential elections only if the presidential candidate accepted public financing. If a candidate refused public assistance, no limits could be imposed.

The costs of running congressional campaigns are prohibitive. In 1974 the co-author had the dubious distinction of being a participant in the most costly congressional race in history, when both candidates each spent more than a half million dollars. The record did not last through the next election, and by 1980 campaign costs well in excess of a million dollars for a single House seat were fairly common. The amount spent in the most expensive Senate elections was much, much higher. Between 1974 and 1980 the average expenditure in the House and the Senate races grew significantly, from $54,000 to $157,128 (109%) for House candidates and from $437,000 to $1,075,495 (146%) for senatorial aspirants.[13] In 1980, the average House campaign in a suburban district cost $197,000 and the average urban district race cost $155,000.[14] The increasing costs of campaigning coupled with the limits on campaign contributions force congressional candidates to rely increasingly on such external sources of funding as political action committees.

Contribution Limits

Congress has placed severe restrictions on the size of campaign contributions, restrictions that were upheld by the Supreme Court as an appropriate remedy against the reality, or appearance, of improper influence by large donors. The limitations on contributions vary depending on the nature of the contributor. Individuals can give no more than $1,000 to a candidate for a primary or general election campaign and no more than $25,000 in any year to all candidates.

Originally candidates had to comply with strict limitations on the amount they could contribute to their own campaigns. These limitations reflected congressional concern about the rash of millionaires running for office. When the Supreme Court struck down these limits, personal financing became a key factor in congressional races. It is not surprising, then, that the House and the Senate have such large numbers of millionaires.

Independent Expenditures

Independent expenditures are made on behalf, but independent, of the candidate. They were originally limited by Congress, but the Supreme Court struck down the limit, again on First Amendment grounds. As a result, such expenditures have become an essential component of modern-day elections, permitting special-interest groups, or "issue purists," to have a disproportionate influence on congressional campaigns. The first to experiment with this form of campaign activity was the sophisticated American Medical Association (AMPAC); their lead was subsequently followed effectively by conservative groups like the National Conservative Political Action Committee (NCPAC), which targeted five senatorial candidates in the 1980 election and defeated four of them. Often it is difficult to determine whether an expenditure is independent. For example, an anti-abortion pamphlet attacking a Democratic senatorial candidate was copied verbatim by the Republican candidate. Coincidence or good advance planning?

Independent expenditures are subject to minimal disclosure regulation, and so far the penalties for violating even these minimal requirements have been less than harsh.[15] Professor Xandra Kayden has concluded that independent expenditures should be more clearly regulated and monitored. She has explained the role such expenditures play in a two-party political system:

> One reason for the existence of campaign spending is because campaign finance laws have restricted many who would like to participate actively in elections. In addition, independent expenditures are responses to very real issues in American politics.[16]

Perhaps, then, independent expenditures are a necessary escape valve for those groups that do not find an adequate means of expression within the Democratic and Republican parties.

There is a $5,000 limit on contributions to political action committees

(PACs). No PAC can give more than $5,000 to any one candidate,[17] but there are no limitations on the amount of independent expenditures by PACs.

Party Expenditures

Although the amount parties can spend on campaigns is limited, it was hoped that campaign finance legislation would strengthen parties in relation to other sources of expenditures. The law permits higher contributions to parties ($20,000 per person to national party committees) than to campaigns or other nonparty multi-candidate committees like PACs. National and state parties can spend 2 cents per vote or $20,000, whichever is greater, in Senate races and in House races in states with only one congressman. Otherwise, the House race limit is $10,000. Parties are permitted to use two-cent postage, thus equalizing the cost of direct-mail solicitation to that of special-interest groups, which often qualify for special rates. Moreover, to encourage grass-roots political activity, the law distinguishes between national and local party committees for purposes of campaign contributions as well as other things.[18]

Incumbency Protection

One result of congressional campaign financing reform has been to preserve incumbency. It has been cynically termed incumbency protection legislation, and the statistics tend to bear this out (see Table 14-1). In 1978, in the House, 93.7 percent of the incumbents were reelected, and in the Senate, 60 percent. Incumbents were getting reelected even before campaign reform laws were passed, but the new laws have enhanced this tendency. Professor Gary Jacobson makes a persuasive case that the main impetus behind campaign reform is the discouragement of congressional competition.[19] Had the Supreme Court not knocked down spending limitations, the incumbency rate would probably be even more dramatic.

PACs

Campaign finance reforms spawned a phenomenal growth in the number of PACs. An estimated 608 PACs existed in 1974. That number increased to more than 2,300 in 1980. The amount spent by PACs in congressional races has grown even more phenomenally (see Table 14-2): PACs contributed an estimated $58 million to congressional campaigns in the 1980 elections, an increase of 60 percent over 1978.

PACs are the unexpected result of a minor change in campaign laws. In 1970 corporate and union gifts to political campaigns were forbidden. Labor unions circumvented this prohibition by establishing groups (like the Committee on Political Education, or COPE) to collect "voluntary" contributions from their membership to be given to political candidates, a political activity

TABLE 14-1
INCUMBENCY SUCCESS RATE:
HOUSE AND SENATE INCUMBENTS AND ELECTION OUTCOMES, 1954-1982

Year	Incumbents Running	Primary Defeats		General Election Defeats		Re-elected	
	(N)	(N)	%	(N)	%	(N)	%
House							
1954	(407)	(6)	1.5	(22)	5.4	(379)	93.1
1956	(410)	(6)	1.5	(15)	3.7	(389)	94.9
1958	(394)	(3)	0.8	(37)	9.4	(354)	89.8
1960	(405)	(5)	1.3	(25)	6.7	(375)	92.6
1962	(402)	(12)	3.0	(22)	5.5	(368)	91.5
1964	(397)	(8)	2.0	(45)	11.3	(344)	86.6
1966	(411)	(8)	1.9	(41)	10.0	(362)	88.1
1968	(409)	(4)	1.0	(9)	2.2	(396)	96.8
1970	(401)	(10)	2.5	(12)	3.2	(379)	94.5
1972	(392)	(13)	3.3	(13)	3.3	(366)	93.4
1974	(391)	(8)	2.0	(40)	10.2	(343)	87.7
1976	(383)	(3)	0.8	(12)	3.1	(368)	96.1
1978	(382)	(5)	1.3	(19)	5.0	(358)	93.7
1980	(398)	(6)	1.5	(31)	7.8	(361)	90.7
1982	(402)	(4)	1.0	(29)	7.2	(369)	91.8
Senate							
1954	(27)	(0)	—	(4)	17	(23)	83
1956	(30)	(0)	—	(4)	13	(26)	87
1958	(26)	(0)	—	(9)	35	(17)	65
1960	(28)	(0)	—	(1)	4	(27)	96
1962	(30)	(0)	—	(3)	10	(27)	90
1964	(30)	(0)	—	(2)	7	(28)	93
1966	(29)	(2)	7	(1)	3	(26)	90
1968	(28)	(4)	14	(4)	14	(20)	71
1970	(28)	(1)	4	(3)	11	(24)	86
1972	(26)	(1)	4	(5)	19	(20)	77
1974	(26)	(1)	4	(2)	8	(23)	88
1976	(25)	(0)	—	(9)	36	(16)	64
1978	(22)	(1)	5	(6)	27	(15)	68
1980	(29)	(4)	4	(9)	31	(16)	55
1982	(30)	(0)	—	(2)	7	(28)	93

SOURCE: PAUL R. ABRAMSON, JOHN H. ALDRICH, AND DAVID W. RONDE, *CHANGE AND CONTINUITY IN THE 1980 ELECTIONS* (WASHINGTON, D.C.: CONGRESSIONAL QUARTERLY PRESS, 1982), P. 192

CHART 14-1
THE GROWTH OF PACs

Total number of political action committees and their contributions to political
campaigns. Figures are for election years.

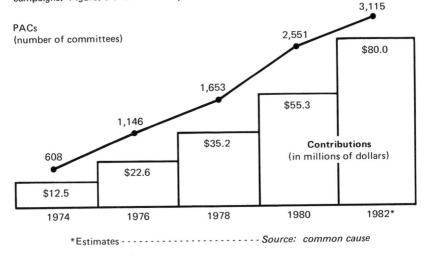

*Estimates - *Source: common cause*

SOURCE: The New York Times, April 4, 1982, p. F3

that gave labor great leverage in Congress. But labor grew concerned about
the legality of their political committees when contributions by government
contractors to federal candidates were banned. Unions feared this prohibition
might be extended to cover manpower training contracts, which they administered. Business groups, moreover, were eager to establish their own PACs.
In 1976 labor and management joined hands in legitimizing the role of PACs
in financing congressional campaigns. This turned out to be an unwise strategy
for labor unions, for they were soon outstripped by businesses in both the
size and influence of PACs. In 1974 labor PAC contributors amounted to
one-half of all PAC contributions, whereas business-related PACs contributed
38 percent. By 1978 labor contribution constituted only 29.3 percent, whereas
business had jumped to 61 percent.[20] Labor had lost its edge in Congress.

Given the unpredictable results of the earlier efforts at reform, it would
have been understandable for Congress to ignore the whole PAC issue. But
the relentless drumbeat of newspaper stories reporting congressional over-
reliance on special-interest PAC money made ostrich behavior untenable.
Moreover, PACs have had a major impact on the electoral process. First,
PAC money from trade association groups with a financial stake in the out-

TABLE 14-2
PAC CONTRIBUTIONS TO CONGRESSIONAL CANDIDATES, 1979–1980*

PAC Type	Distribution To Incumbents	Distribution To Challengers	Distribution To Open Seats
House			
Labor	71%	16%	12%
Corporate	67	21	12
Trade	68	19	12
Not Connected to Other Organizations	33	45	20
Senate			
Labor	74%	17%	10%
Corporate	46	44	11
Trade	58	31	11
Not Connected to Other Organizations	30	55	15

*Percentages may not add to 100 because of rounding off.

SOURCE: NORMAN J. ORNSTEIN, THOMAS E. MANN, MICHAEL J. MALBIN, AND JOHN F. BIBBY, *VITAL STATISTICS ON CONGRESS, 1982* (WASHINGTON, D.C.: AMERICAN ENTERPRISE INSTITUTE, 1982), PP. 80–81.

come of the legislative process tends to go to incumbents, particularly those who sit in important committee spots. Democrats have historically received more money than Republicans from PACs because, until the 1980 election, they controlled all the powerful chairmanships. After the political turnaround in the Senate in 1980, a shift in the proportion of PAC funds going to the respective parties is likely. Thus, business PACs tend to be not opinion leaders but protectors of the status quo.

Second, when there is no incumbent, PAC money tends to be "late" money, not "seed" money. PAC managers are, on the whole, conservative; they provide money only where it is likely to reap reward. Thus PAC money has less of an impact on election results where there are no clear winners.

Third, the PAC use of independent expenditures, which are ideological—as opposed to financial—in purpose, has increased, thereby giving minorities or one-issue purists a disproportionate influence on the political process. The net effect of independent expenditures in special policy areas is unclear. Efforts to challenge PAC independent expenditures in the courts have been

TABLE 14–3
TOP 10 PAC CONTRIBUTORS TO CANDIDATES (1979–1980)

1. Realtors Political Action Committee (National Association of Realtors)	$ 1,536,573
2. UAW-V-CAP (United Auto Workers)	$ 1,422,731
3. American Medical Political Action Committee (American Medical Association)	$ 1,348,985
4. Automobile and Truck Dealers Election Action Committee (National Automobile Dealers Association)	$ 1,035,276
5. Machinists Non-Partisan Political League (Int. Association of Machinists & Aerospace Workers)	$ 847,708
6. AFL-CIO COPE Political Contributions Committee (AFL-CIO)	$ 776,577
7. Committee for Thorough Agricultural Pol. Education (Associated Milk Producers)	$ 738,289
8. Seafarers Political Activity Donation "SPAD" (Seafarers Int'l Union of North America)	$ 685,248
9. United Steel Workers of America Political Action Fund (United Steelworkers of America)	$ 681,370
10. National Association of Life Underwriters PAC (National Association of Life Underwriters)	$ 652,112

SOURCE: FEDERAL ELECTION COMMISSION 2/21/82

unsuccessful to date. In 1980 the Carter–Mondale presidential campaign committee and Common Cause, the self-styled citizens' lobby, filed suit against a group called Americans for Change, which was founded by Senator Harrison Schmitt of New Mexico for the purpose of making independent expenditures on behalf of Ronald Reagan's presidential campaign. The suit was unsuccessful, and the ability of conservatives to use independent expenditures to promote their own candidates has stimulated a growth in independent groups on both the liberal and conservative sides. Political scientists predict that independent expenditures will ultimately not tilt the process to any particular ideology but only increase the amount of money poured into already expensive campaigns. However, political observers have proposed remedies to prevent the disproportionate influence of special-interest PACs, for example, that each candidate be given equal time in the media, without charge, to respond to the accusations made by independent PACs.[21]

The role of PACs in the legislative process is significant. Obviously, no member admits that his vote was bought or even influenced by contributions.

Nonetheless, business clearly believes that its voice can be enhanced in the public sector through PAC activity. Business publications are replete with articles instructing readers how to set up PACs, and PAC managers publicly brag about their invitations to cocktail parties and dinners from congressmen who are trying to woo money. With embarrassing frequency, a member's vote can be equated with the PAC contributions for or against him. Fact: A congressman from Oregon fought against the confirmation of the general counsel of Louisiana Pacific as the assistant secretary of agriculture. Fact: The PACs of the Louisiana Pacific contributed a tremendous sum to his opponent in the preceding election. Fact: A congressman from Illinois fought to preserve the commodity tax "straddle." Fact: The congressman had received thousands in campaign funds from the PACs of the commodities industry. And PACs consciously try to affect the voting records of the recipients of their largesse. COPE, the AFL-CIO's PAC, withdraws support from candidates who do not toe the labor legislative line.[22] (The co-author of this book lost his COPE funding because maritime labor leaders were angry over his vote against a subsidy for shipping companies.) Because both congressmen and PAC managers are political animals and because both act pragmatically to maximize their self-interest in the money game, the kind of rational political behavior just described is expected. However, from the viewpoint of good public policy, it is unwise to expose the legislative process to such pressure. Special interests have always been a political reality, but now, as a result of recent "reforms," they have the means to increase their clout in proportion to individual voters.

As a serious side effect of PAC growth, the impact of party campaign financing has diminished, at both the presidential and congressional levels. Although recent statutes were designed to maintain and enhance the role of national parties in campaign financing, the realities of the amounts obtainable through the PACs and nonparty financing deny the statutory goals.

Political party organizations are less important now than previously in funding House and Senate campaigns. In 1980 only 6 percent of the money raised for House races came from parties, compared with 17 percent in 1972. Similarly, in the Senate races, the contributions of the party dropped from 14 percent of the total in 1972 to only 9 percent of the total in 1980.[23]. PAC growth has diminished the influence of the congressional campaign committee. The occasional complaints by national party leaders about the impact of such independent money-raising activities have little effect. Chairman Richard Richards of the Republican National Committee criticized the early targeting of Democratic candidates for defeat in the 1982 elections by the National Conservative Political Action Committee, pointing out that such activities created a blacklash and siphoned money from more legitimate political ac-

TABLE 14-4

A COMPARISON OF CONTRIBUTIONS TO THE
DEMOCRATIC AND REPUBLICAN PARTIES

	1979–80	1981–82
Democratic National Committee	$15,112,775	$12,543,489
Senate Democratic Campaign Committee	1,653,849	1,327,704*
House Democratic Campaign Committee	2,094,109	6,800,000
Total	$18,860,733	$20,671,193
Republican National Committee	$ 63,231,442	73,383,778
Senate Republican Campaign Committee	20,603,452	44,748,230
House Republican Campaign Committee	27,940,000	57,940,000
Total	$111,774,894	$176,072,008

*AS OF NOVEMBER 22, 1982.

tivities, particularly the national parties. Fred Wertheimer, president of Common Cause, echoed his concerns:

> By nature PACs are fragmenters, and PACs have been a major contributor to the increasing fragmentation of our political system. In this way, PACs today serve to substantially weaken an already-weakened political party system. They are a major and ongoing challenge to party responsibility and party responsiveness in Congress. They will do increasing damage to the political parties, particularly in Congress, until their power is harnessed.[24]

To respond to the PAC distortion, the congressional and national parties have stepped up their own fund-raising efforts. Because Republicans traditionally have received less PAC money than their Democratic counterparts, the Republican party took the lead in grass-roots fund-raising to fill the money gap. Their initiative paid off, for party fund raising was instrumental in advancing the 1980 Republican party electoral victories. Democrats struggled to follow their lead (see Table 14-5).

Moreover, groups within each party formed their own PACs to assist candidates who were campaigning from a specific ideological perspective. In addition, potential presidential contenders in the 1984 election created PACs in 1981 to assist Democratic congressional candidates in 1982. (As political observers point out, such organizations also keep the financial irons in the fire for potential presidential challenges.) Similar PACs exist to help conservative Republican candidates.

Public Financing

The PAC problem prompted campaign finance legislation to curb PAC expenditures in congressional races. In 1975 Democratic Congressman Phillip Burton of California devised a bill for public financing of congressional campaigns. Some of the 225 co-sponsors evidently had second thoughts, for the bill received only 123 votes. In the following Congress, Congressman John Anderson of Illinois and a co-author of this book teamed up to sponsor a similar bill. Although the cast of characters was not dissimilar, the opposition in the House had become more organized. The support of the chairman of the House Administration Committee, Frank Thompson of New Jersey, and the entire Democratic leadership was not sufficient; the bill died in committee. In 1978 an attempt was made to offer public financing as an amendment to another bill. The debate was spirited, but unsuccessful.

On October 17, 1979, the House passed the Campaign Contribution Reform Act by a vote of 217 to 198. Sponsored by Representatives David Obey of Wisconsin and Tom Railsback of Illinois, the act passed as an amendment to the Federal Election Commission authorization bill. The act, which dealt with only House races, limited the total PAC contributions to a single candidate to $70,000 in a two-year election cycle and capped any single PAC contribution to a candidate in a primary or general election. Otherwise, it did not address the problem of public financing, for the sponsors had to drop such provisions to get the bill up for a vote at all. Even though the Obey–Railsback bill dealt only with House races, Senate opponents threatened to filibuster. The bill was not considered in the Senate.

On the Senate side, public-financing legislation was even less successful.[25] In the Ninety-fifth Congress, public-financing legislation reported from the Rules and Administration Committee was dropped after a filibuster. The legislation proposed a general election spending limit of $250,000 plus 10 cents times the voting-age population of the state; major party candidates were to be eligible for 25 percent of this total as a flat grant; contributions of up to $100 per donor were to be matched up to the spending limit. Candidates accepting public money were to spend no more than $35,000 of their own money on the campaign. Third party and independent candidates were not eligible for the flat grant, but they were to receive matching funds where they raised 10 percent of the spending limit or $100,000, whichever was less, in individual gifts of $100 or less. Primary elections were not to be covered.

In the Ninety-sixth Congress, while Obey–Railsback was gathering steam in the House of Representatives, similar legislation introduced in the Senate never saw the light of day.[26]

There are compelling arguments for and against the public financing of congressional campaigns. Proponents argue that it will eliminate the conspicuous advantage of wealthy individuals who may, after the Supreme Court's decision in *Buckley* v. *Valeo*, spend unlimited amounts of their own money on campaigns. Moreover, because the *Buckley* opinion left the other contribution limits intact, raising large amounts of money from individuals has become increasingly difficult (an especially acute problem in the more expensive Senate elections); candidates are consequently forced to rely heavily on contributions from special-interest PACs. Public funding would stop spiraling campaign costs and diminish the reliance on special-interest PACs.

Opponents make three basic arguments. First, Congressman Bill Frenzel of Minnesota argued that public financing would eliminate a valuable barometer of a candidate's popularity: "Private financing functions in a manner similar to the free market. It has been one of the traditional ways of determining the popularity and attractiveness of a candidate."[27] Second, opponents argue that public financing is unfair to, or encourages, the minority party and independent candidates, depending on the provisions for the distribution of funds. Third, public financing by providing direct grants to candidates may hurt the party system. Although the proportionate share of funds provided by parties has been small historically, the national party leadership has begun to seriously consider the funding of congressional races, which may prove to be the key to the party's revival.

Because public financing will probably protect incumbents, that is, the status quo, minority parties will be less likely to support public financing. As Professor Gary Jacobson said:

> The Republican position was that (public financing) favored incumbents—
> hence, mainly, Democrats—because the spending limits that would accompany
> public funds would not permit challengers to conduct competitive campaigns.
> The argument that spending limits protect incumbents has been offered every
> time the issue has come up; the critical difference in 1977 was that Republican
> senators adopted it as their own, speaking, in effect for Republican challengers
> rather than themselves as incumbents.[28]

The recent shift in political power may result in a similar shift on the public-financing issue. However, the question of public financing of congressional races is presently in limbo. Critics claim this is still "the best government money can buy," and this phenomenon is likely to continue.

FIFTEEN

CONGRESSIONAL ETHICS

The Congress that convened in January 1979 was to have inaugurated a new era of Congressional integrity. The preceding Congress had initiated more ethics reforms than ever before. Both the House and the Senate had enlarged their codes of conduct. Congressmen and senators were required to disclose their financial worth and to limit their outside earned income. The reforms were intended to be, as Speaker Tip O'Neill said, "the toughest code of ethics of any legislative body in the country."[1]

Ironically, in the final hours of the Ninety-sixth Congress, Michael (Ozzie) Myers of Pennsylvania was expelled from the House, following his bribery and conspiracy conviction in the Abscam investigation. On that same October day, Congressman Robert Bauman of Maryland was charged with soliciting sex from a 16-year-old boy and agreed to enter a court-supervised rehabilitation program. One week later, Congressman John Jenrette of South Carolina was convicted of bribery and conspiracy charges in connection with the Abscam investigation. Four other "Abscam" congressmen were awaiting trial. A few months earlier, Representative Daniel Flood resigned from Congress and pleaded guilty to bribery charges, and Congressman Charles Diggs of Michigan was sentenced to a prison term for mail fraud and payroll cheating.

The scandals of the Ninety-sixth Congress were not confined to the House of Representatives. Herman Talmadge of Georgia was denounced by the Senate for mishandling campaign funds, and Harrison Williams of New Jersey was under an investigation in the Abscam probe, which later led to his conviction in federal court and resignation from the Senate.

SCANDALS NOT A NEW PHENOMENON

Congressional corruption is hardly a new phenomenon. In the 1870s Congressman Oakes Ames of Massachusetts rocked the Congress with the Credit Mobilier scandal. Credit Mobilier, a construction company organized to build the Union Pacific Railroad, distributed shares of its stock to numerous influential congressmen at bargain prices to prevent an investigation of its corrupt practices and to obtain favors. Ames was censured.[2]

In the 1870s, Speaker James G. Blaine received $64,000 for using his influence on behalf of a railroad. Blaine did not go to jail; instead, he became Secretary of State. The scandal did destroy his chances of becoming president, however.[3] In 1912 the Senate expelled William E. Lorimer of Illinois for selling votes. His indiscretion was not in vain, however, for publicity over the scandal prompted the Senate to approve the Seventeenth Amendment, which provides for the direct election of senators.[4]

Congressional misbehavior is not necessarily more profligate today than in earlier years, but unethical conduct is much more likely to be exposed, because of the increased aggressiveness of political reporting. In *The Powers That Be*, David Halberstam described the radical metamorphosis of the Washington press corps during the Franklin Roosevelt administration in the 1930s. Before the New Deal, Halberstam wrote, journalism in Washington was a gentleman's profession. Journalists were "properly dressed men who wore fedoras and carried walking sticks."[5] Correspondents were not inclined to vigorously pursue and report on the unsavory aspects of Washington political life:

> They all carried calling cards, they never rushed from one office to another; they knew all the people they spoke to by name and they as rarely as possible used the telephone, the telephone was a sign of being rushed, it seemed a mark of discourtesy. Besides there was always time to visit news sources in person, the government was so small, there were so few sources of information. . . . One reporter covered the entire executive branch in those days—The White House, State, War, Interior, Commerce—so if a colleague covered the Congress the two men might make up the entire bureau.[6]

According to Halberstam, the enhanced role of the Washington press corps is directly related to Franklin Roosevelt:

As he used the media more often and more directly, they became more influential; they became more and more the architects of the national agenda making more decisions on what the great issues were rather than just responding to the decisions of others. The press corps was becoming a different, more serious, and better informed body.[7]

Since the Roosevelt years the Washington press establishment has continued to increase in prestige and stature. The role of the press in uncovering Watergate has been widely praised, and it has continued aggressive investigation of corruption and misconduct in Washington politics. Norman J. Ornstein, professor of political science at Catholic University, in an interview about the homosexual scandal involving Congressman Robert Bauman of Maryland, argued that since 1974 when Wilbur Mills plunged into the Tidal Basin with Fanne Fox, the press has investigated not only corruption but the personal conduct of congressmen as well with much greater scrutiny. "After the Tidal Basin incident," Ornstein maintained, "it became respectable to report events of that kind. If rumors about Bauman had circulated 10 years ago, most reporters would have been reluctant to report the story."[8]

Law enforcement authorities, like the press, have also become more aggressive in pursuit of congressional wrongdoing. Until recent times, clear abuses of discretion and blatant conflicts of interest were tolerated to a much greater degree by law enforcement authorities. Daniel Webster's arrangement with the Bank of the United States, as described earlier, is a classic example of the acceptance of unlawful conduct in an earlier era. Treatment of such cases was less severe as late as the 1960s. When Senator Thomas Dodd of Connecticut was accused of the misuse of more than $160,000 in campaign funds and the double billing of the federal government for travel and other expenses, he was not prosecuted. Mark Green, in *Who Runs Congress?*, wrote: "The Justice Department was part of Johnson's administration, and Johnson was one of Dodd's friends; even the FBI was suspect, since Dodd had once been an agent."[9] The Senate censured Dodd for misuse of campaign funds but in spite of the evidence refused to censure him for double billing. The Adam Clayton Powell affair in the late 1960s is another example of prosecutorial reticence. Although investigated by the Justice Department and censured by the House in 1967, Powell was not indicted for his misdeeds.

The Abscam investigation is evidence of the more assertive, perhaps too assertive, role that law enforcement authorities can assume in uncovering congressional scandal. In its Abscam operation, the FBI did not simply pursue crimes that had already been committed; rather it was seeking to determine which congressmen were likely to engage in criminal activity. Abscam marked the first time that a congressional probe of this nature had been undertaken.

RELUCTANCE TO
PUNISH MISCONDUCT

Why congressional misconduct continues regardless of the ethics reforms in recent years remains a troubling question. One explanation of the problem can be traced back nearly two hundred years to the Constitutional Convention of 1787. The framers of the Constitution decided that each house of Congress should have the responsibility of disciplining its misbehaving members. The founding fathers expected congressmen and senators to be, like themselves, statesmen of impeccable character totally devoted to public service. In their essays in the *Federalist Papers* James Madison and Alexander Hamilton expressed confidence that the intelligence of the American people would naturally lead them to choose only men of virtue to represent them. Madison argued that members of the House would be so honored at the opportunity to serve that out of sheer gratitude to their constituents they would strive to prove themselves worthy. "There is in every breast a sensibility to marks of honor, of favor, of esteem, and of confidence, which apart from all considerations of interest is some pledge for grateful and benevolent returns." Madison also thought that the necessity of running for reelection would deter representatives from abusing their office. In seeking reelection "they must descend to the level from which they were raised; there forever to remain unless a faithful discharge of their trust shall have established their title to a renewal of it."[10]

The founding fathers feared that the sacred separation of powers principle would be jeopardized by outside oversight. Thomas Jefferson later wrote in his *Manual of Parliamentary Practice* that when a member of Congress is accused of a crime

> the case is first to be laid before the House, that it may judge of the fact and of the grounds for the accusation, and how far forth the manner of the trial may concern their privilege; otherwise it would be in the power of other branches of the government . . . to take any man from his service in the House, and so, as many, one after another, as would make the House what he pleaseth.[11]

Traditionally, both houses of Congress have been reluctant to use their power under the Constitution to discipline misbehaving members. Although the House Ethics Committee was formed in 1969, it did not conduct a formal investigation until the case involving Congressman Robert Sikes of Florida in 1976. That investigation was undertaken only after Common Cause had already compiled extensive evidence against Sikes for conflict of interest. Sikes was reprimanded, not disciplined. (The reprimand had no legal effect, but it did hasten Sikes' decision not to run for reelection.) The recent expulsion of Congressman Michael Myers marked the first expulsion action by the House since the Civil War. The decisive action in that case was atypical, for the motivating factor behind the House's overwhelming vote to expel Myers was undoubtedly a desire to appease disenchanted constituents before an election.

During the Koreagate scandal in 1977, the House Ethics Committee held only a minimum number of sessions. The committee's special counsel ultimately resigned in protest. The members of the Ethics Committee, far from pursuing a thorough investigation, even refused to swear under oath that they too had not been recipients of Korean lobbyist Tongsun Park's largesse. The committee sluggishly sent out questionnaires to members of Congress requesting information about their relationship with Park and other South Korean lobbyists. Many congressmen did not bother to respond.[12] The Ethics Committee was deemed the most "moribund" committee in the House. "One sure way to get a smirk on Capitol Hill," *U.S. News & World Report* editorialized, "is to refer to the House Committee on Standards of Official Conduct as the Ethics Committee. Seldom—if ever—has this body demanded high rectitude of House members."[13]

A lack of commitment to matters of ethics is apparent in the Senate as well. That august body even has difficulty in finding members willing to serve on its Ethics Committee. The committee was operating at half capacity early in the Ninety-sixth Congress because the Senate leadership could not persuade senators to fill the positions. When the leadership attempted to draft freshmen, several southern senators protested, because the committee was scheduled to take action on the Talmadge matter. Southern senators wanted a committee composed of members who had known Talmadge longer and who would, in Russell Long's words, give Talmadge "the benefit of the doubt."[14] The leadership finally persuaded three non-freshmen—Mark Hatfield, Jesse Helms, and Quentin Burdick—to complete the committee roster. Senators Stevenson and Schmitt, however, agreed to stay on the committee only until the Talmadge investigation had been completed. When they resigned, the leadership again could not find anyone to take the jobs. Finally two freshmen, Senators Heflin and Wallop, were drafted. Heflin became the first senator to become chairman of a standing committee in his first year in office.[15] In the Ninety-seventh Congress, with the changeover to the Republicans, Senator Wallop became chairman.

Reluctance about passing judgment on a fellow member is a primary reason for the unpopularity of the Ethics committees. Senators and congressmen believe that misbehaving members should be judged by their constituents, not their colleagues. When Charles Diggs was convicted in 1979 and then reelected, Congressman Parren Mitchell of Maryland saw no reason to take punitive action. "If they [the people] want to elect Hitler, that's their right," he analogized.[16] Sanford Watzman, in *Conflict of Interest, Politics, and the Money Game*, took a different position. Watzman argued that the misdeeds of a congressman transcend the boundaries of his particular district. "We shouldn't be forced to stand at the perimeter sniping perhaps at our own representatives but finding the others out of our range. The integrity of *every* lawmaker, including those in neighboring districts and other states, is important to us because every member of Congress answers roll calls affecting the entire country."[17]

The Supreme Court in *Powell* v. *McCormack*[18] ruled that the Constitution does not empower Congress to exclude a member. However, Congress does have the right to punish a member for misconduct. A rule that has been implemented by the House Democratic Caucus automatically strips party members of their committee or subcommittee chairmanships when they are censured by the full House or indicted for a felony that could result in imprisonment for two years or more. Under this rule, Congressmen Charles Wilson (who was censured), John Murphy, and Frank Thompson relinquished committee chairmanships. The rule, however, does not affect Republican members of Congress.[19]

RECENT REFORMS

All the widely publicized ethics reforms of the Ninety-fifth Congress have proved ineffective. The financial disclosure forms, which senators and congressmen have been required to file since 1977, allow the use of vague and misleading statements. Members are not required to reveal the exact amount of their financial holdings, and many have taken advantage of the broad categories on the forms to conceal their true worth. In 1978 one congressman from Pennsylvania listed "none" in every space on the form pertaining to income. He even failed to disclose his congressional salary.[20] On the House disclosure form, the highest category for holdings was $100,000 or over. Thus, Representative Frederick Richmond of New York listed his shares of the Walco National Corporation in the $100,000 or over category, whereas in reality they were worth more than $18 million.[21]

The 1977 ethics reforms were, for the most part, halfhearted measures enacted in response to the public outcry over Koreagate. Both houses have already begun to retreat from their much publicized 1977 commitment. The Senate and the House have eased their financial disclosure rules. In 1979 the

Senate voted to postpone until 1983 the new limitation on outside earned income.[22] In 1982, the limitation was removed entirely. And the financial disclosure forms in the Senate are no longer subject to a General Accounting Office audit.

Neither the House nor the Senate rules provide clear guidelines as to what constitutes a conflict of interest. The Senate in 1977 tabled a proposed amendment by John Durkin of New Hampshire that would have prohibited a member from initiating legislation that would aid his own financial interests. Instead, the Senate passed a weaker resolution that prohibited a senator from aiding a bill only if it could be proved that his primary motivation was to promote his own financial interests. The burden of proving improper motivation was left to the Senate Ethics Committee.[23]

The completed 1978 financial disclosure forms revealed potential conflicts of interest among a substantial number of congressmen. According to the 1978 Congressional Quarterly Report study, eight members of the House Ways and Means Committee and six members of the House Banking and Urban Affairs Committee reported holding bank stock and sixteen members of the House Agricultural Committee reported agricultural interests.[24] Common Cause has suggested that the Ethics committees of both houses devise a divestiture rule that would require congressmen sitting on a particular committee to divest themselves of financial interest in the area of that committee's jurisdiction.[25] Neither committee has shown any sign of formulating such a rule.

Observers believe that the public financing of presidential campaigns has resulted in substantial reform of presidential politics. Congressional campaigns, however, are still privately funded, and special-interest money formerly earmarked for presidential campaigns has in recent years been transferred to congressional races. John Gardner, founder of Common Cause, wrote in 1976: "A lot of Congressmen were bought and sold in 1976, just like the good old days except the going rates were higher. . . . The money-heavy special interests couldn't buy themselves a President so they tried to buy as many members of Congress as they could."[26]

Every time a Koreagate or an Abscam scandal rocks the Capitol, Congress as an institution loses credibility, and its ability to act as a co-equal branch is diminished.

Clearly, ethical violations need to be punished with more rapidity and force, and greater restrictions need to be placed on the financial power of special-interest groups; nonetheless, it is easy to overstate the incidence and importance of corruption on the Hill. Indeed, in light of the vast monied influence of special-interest groups in Washington and the high political stakes involved, it is surprising that the scandals in Congress have been so few.

SIXTEEN

CONGRESS
WORKS

Let us develope the resources of our land, call forth its powers, build up its institutions, promote all its great interests and see whether we also in our day and generation may not perform something worthy to be remembered.

Daniel Webster quotation,
appearing above
the speaker's rostrum

Does it work? Is Congress the primary branch, as intended by those constitutional craftsmen?

If the measure of viability is popular conception, then Congress has been the first failure rather than the first branch. Poll after poll shows that the integrity of the institution of Congress is rated at or below that of the proverbial used-car salesman. Even the exception drawn for the citizen's own congressman is slowly eroding away. The spate of Abscam scandals coupled with the unseemly and self-conscious method by which Congress monitors its ethics confirms Mark Twain's punditry as far as the average voter is concerned: "It could probably be shown by facts and figures that there is no distinctly native American criminal class except Congress."

However, public perception aside, Congress does serve effectively as a representative body. The legitimacy of a statute passed by Congress is unquestioned. Courts may strike down a law as being beyond the Constitution; the president or the administrative agency may poorly execute the law. But seldom is doubt cast upon the overall faithfulness of the legislative process to popular will. Indeed, the criticism frequently comes about because Congress does not always respond as quickly to popular will as some would like.

The secret of this legitimacy lies in the parochial nature of the election process. As we have seen, a member is first and foremost a representative of his district and state. His party label, his loyalty to an administration, his commitment to issues, all come second to his concern for his constituency. His ombudsman efforts may appear to be incidental to the role of representative, but the member cannot escape knowledge of the machinations of the federal government when he performs as the interlocutor between government and its citizens. The rise of sophisticated polling methods, used by both the media and the politicians, allows an even greater awareness of the perceptions of people at home about the laws under consideration and the vote of their member on those laws.

The frequency of elections to the House of Representatives ensures a short time-lag between congressional action and citizen reaction. Whereas pure parliamentary bodies rely on special elections to detect changes in popular mood between national elections, no legislator (and no president) can ignore the biennial message that the voters send Washington, D.C. The entire institution has been designed to allow the member to represent his constituency in the safest way possible. The emphasis on public works, on doing "more" for one's district, transcends the ideological and national goals that the administration or the national party may espouse. Service on the Foreign Affairs or the Judiciary Committee may be prestigious in the Congress and *The New York Times*, but service on the Agriculture, Rural Development, and related appropriations subcommittees plays much better at home. Whatever his penchant for oratorical flights of fancy rhetoric, the average member is extremely conservative about his votes and his priorities. Consequently, when Congress does move, it usually moves the way the majority of the country wants to move.

In its very strength as the representative of the people's will lies its weakness as a leader-policymaker-initiator. The size of the two bodies, which ensures a reflection of the pluralism of the country, makes it most difficult to fashion an initiative from within the Congress. Even in the House, where members tend to become more specialized and expert in a small area of government, there is a need to know a little bit about everything. Rare is the occasion when members totally defer to the expertise of any small group within their midst on any important issue. Building a coalition around a new idea initiated within the Congress thus becomes most difficult.

In all events, it is hard to rival the president as chief policymaker. As one

Reagan White House adviser commented during the 1982 budget battles: "Look, there are 535 guys up there. How are they going to agree on anything?" The president's "bully pulpit," his staff of experts who are not concerned about reelection, his claim of representing the whole country and therefore speaking for everybody—all are unmatchable assets when it comes to floating a new idea and moving it forward. It is little wonder that the legislative process has been described: "The President proposes, the Congress disposes."

The president's forum is perhaps the most difficult for congressmen to match. When the president speaks, the world listens. The media are always at the ready. The president commands the attention of the American people simply by being president and announcing that he has something important to say. A Franklin Roosevelt or a Ronald Reagan can further maximize that presence by being a Great Communicator. But even bad communicators, the Jimmy Carters and the Gerald Fords, are easily heard and seen.

The individual member of Congress, with very few exceptions, has a totally different chore in getting his ideas across to the American people. Typically, the individual member of the House and, in most instances, the individual senator have difficulty getting the attention of the national media. While the local press, radio, and to a lesser extent television pick up on a member's message, seldom can that coverage be replicated at the national level. Most members of Congress go through their entire service in Congress without ever appearing on network television or in *The New York Times*. Most congressional speeches and most congressional press releases are prepared for home consumption. The Congress of the 1980s does not have the stature of the Congress of 1789. The delicate constitutional balance has been tipped by the media, and a challenge to Congress today is to get national recognition for its actions.

Limited access to national media has at least two consequences for congressional behavior. Some members command attention by taking extreme positions. Senator Joseph McCarthy was the leading exponent of that school. Others use "catchy" proposals and dramatic press conferences to get the attention of national media moguls. Some members develop newsworthy awards (Wisconsin Senator William Proxmire's Golden Fleece Award) or take unexpected trips (Congressman George Hansen of Idaho went to Iran while the hostages were still captive) or wear noteworthy costumes (New York Congresswoman Bella Abzug's floppy hats or Illinois Congressman Ken Gray's white "ice-cream" suits). Political confrontation gets better media coverage than polite commentary. New York Congressman John LeBoutillier gained more media attention by calling Tip O'Neill a "fat Democrat" than some hardworking congressmen get their entire career. Commanding this unusual "corner" on the media market can sometimes overcome the president's natural advantage as a communicator.

A more orthodox approach to media access is the formation of coalitions within and without the Congress. News coverage can be substantially multiplied when legislation is co-sponsored by sufficient members representing a geographic or ideological mix. Elaborate press conferences are staged for important proposals with the purpose of including a goodly number of members, each with access to his own media market. Sometimes a special order is sought to permit a large coalition of members to make floor speeches for a proposal. All this and more is done to get some of the attention that is automatically given to the president when he makes a speech, holds a press conference, or sends a written message up to the Hill.

Year after year the out-of-power, out-of-the-White House congressional party tries to offset the impact of the president's State of the Union message. Often opposition congressional leadership requests and obtains "equal time" from the television networks to respond. Outside media experts, the new elite of political organizations, help the out-of-office party prepare its response. But compelling format and solid preparation cannot compete. The news is what the president said.

To think of Congress as a noncreative force of government is a serious mistake. A more valid judgment would grant that Congress does not initiate policy easily, but that, given sufficient cause and provocation, it rises to the challenge. Ending the war in Vietnam is a classic modern example.

Although the Congress of the 1960s was unwilling to resist President Lyndon B. Johnson's heavy military buildup in Vietnam, the Congress of the 1970s was sufficiently determined and stubborn to end the war over President Gerald Ford's opposition. The manner in which Congress seized the initiative was exactly the manner contemplated by the constitutional founders. In 1974 and then again in 1975 Congress refused to appropriate the more than half a billion dollars requested by the president; without funds, the war could not be prosecuted further, according to the president, and the fall of South Vietnam would follow (and the consequent domino effect would operate on the rest of Southeast Asia). The confrontation was frontal and complete. It was painfully apparent to the members of the Congress that the war in Vietnam enjoyed little public support; the war became the rallying point of opposition to members who had previously supported the war. Member after member publicly recanted through appropriate "mea culpas" for their previous support. The 1974 midterm elections were as much a referendum on the war as they were on Watergate. Both the Senate and the House conducted numerous hearings and investigations to assess blame and criticism for the exposure in Vietnam. Some members filed lawsuits seeking to have the courts declare further prosecution of the war outside the presidential powers. (The lawsuits were unsuccessful.) The War Powers Act was passed to prevent future Vietnams. Although all these legislative activities impacted the congressional mood, the termination of the war was expressly ordained by the roll-call vote in the House, which refused to appropriate the requested additional money.

Even in the absence of constitutional crises, Congress participates at all stages in the legislative process. Much fanfare may accompany presidential packages, but rarely do such packages emerge from Congress without substantial substantive revision. When OMB Director David Stockman dared to suggest to Budget Chairman Peter Domenici and Finance Chairman Robert Dole that they accept verbatim the Reagan budget package, a package replete with high defense spending and major domestic slashes, they not-so-politely reminded him of the co-equal status of Congress and proceeded to reprioritize national spending. In the recent past Congress has completely rewritten national refugee policy, deregulated the trucking industry, restricted wide-scale busing as a remedy for school segregation, cut federal funding for abortions, provided "indexing" to reduce "bracket-creep" in national taxes, continuously denied foreign aid for countries not abiding by nuclear nonproliferation policies, rejected anti-human rights administration nominees, extended the Voting Rights Act, preserved the social security system, alleviated regulatory burdens on small businesses, and curbed American involvement in El Salvador. Although the merits of each measure can be debated, the measures themselves are evidence of an active Congress, a Congress intent on performing its responsibilities—the trouble is in getting credit for them.

The president has tremendous inherent legislative powers of his own. Every year the executive branch issues volumes of federal regulations that often have greater substantive impact than the legislation from which they are derived. Some of the greatest strides in civil rights were achieved through the president's ability to issue executive orders. But, in measuring the breadth of the president's constitutional power, the courts have said that the president has maximum power when his exercise of power is expressly ratified by congressional action. The courts prefer the president to handle international crises with the active involvement of Congress, rather than through presidential fiat, as in the Iranian hostage crisis. The absence of legislative activity diminishes the legitimacy of executive action. The interplay of Congress with the executive, then, is not a hamstringing of executive initiative but rather a support mechanism to ensure nationwide acceptance of presidential actions.

When presidential leadership collapses, Congress fills the vacuum. Sometimes the breakdown is swift and unexpected, as when President Lincoln was assassinated. Whatever Andrew Johnson's strengths or weaknesses, history records that he was not capable of uniting the country as Lincoln had envisioned. Although many historians criticize Congress for its vindictive Reconstruction policies, the more important lesson was that Congress did bridge the gap—it did lead the country until the next presidential election restored some measure of confidence in the executive branch. During the decline of

Woodrow Wilson in the later years of his presidency, Congress again filled the vacuum. Although Congress began to assert itself, in some measure, because of substantive disagreements with Wilson's postwar proposals, the ultimate take-over of foreign policy initiatives came about because Wilson lost his strength—both political and physical. But for the aggressive posture of Senator Henry Cabot Lodge and others, the country could have foundered during the long period when Wilson was not performing. Although history may find the Lodge substitutes inadequate, a supine Congress coupled with an ailing chief executive could have plunged the country into a far greater chaos.

The most recent example of Congress coming to the rescue of a presidential inadequacy is, of course, the abrupt end of the Nixon administration. Prior to the 1972 election, an appointed president was beyond contemplation. The national disillusionment caused by the disgrace of Vice-President Spiro Agnew and President Nixon brought about a virtual collapse of respect for the national government. The likelihood that Congress would restore the national spirit was not high. Throughout the entire first term of the Nixon administration, Congress had been unable to offer any opposition to executive initiatives. Even though the economy was far from stable, and the war in Vietnam was causing domestic and fiscal problems of the highest order, Congress could not agree on any program. Consequently, Nixon ruled by congressional default.

It was Congress, however, that precipitated the fall of the Nixon administration and the road back from Watergate. Constitutional scholar Senator Sam Ervin conducted the Senate inquiry that confronted President Nixon with the incriminating recording tapes, and Harvard Law Professor Archibald Cox was appointed a special prosecutor. New Jersey Congressman Peter Rodino chaired the Judiciary Committee of the House, which brought forth Articles of Impeachment in a national television spectacle that reassured the overwhelming majority of viewers that Congress could function and function well. Democrats and Republicans alike on the Judiciary Committee rose to levels of responsibility—and prominence. The confirmation by the Senate of Gerald Ford as vice president contributed to the legitimacy of that appointment. That Ford himself was a creature of the Congress helped to check the notion when he became president that an unelected unknown without mandate or authority was occupying the White House.

The unlikely congressional heroes who stopped the national bleeding over the Watergate scandals were summed up by Elizabeth Drew in *Washington Journal*:

It is difficult under any circumstances to mobilize the Congress for significant action. The Congress is composed of five hundred and thirty-five egos—not a situtation conducive to collective work. The Congress is essentially a reactive branch. Fewer and fewer enterprises are initiated by the Congress. . . . The Congress has a limited attention span. It wearies of issues. Its primary instinct is to play it safe, and its primary motivation is to get reelected. . . . But. . . . there . . . were instinctive reactions to the President's weakened position. The Congress has a kind of animal instinct about changes in the flow of power.[1]

Perhaps, in the future, it will be clear that what was decisive was the action taken by the thirty-eight members of the Judiciary Committee of the House of Representatives. It was these men and women who, by what they did, compelled the President to give up his office, established what Presidential conduct was intolerable, and handed down the tablets for the future. . . . In the course of reaching their conclusions, the elected representatives on the Judiciary Committee conducted the most fateful deliberations about the meaning of the Constitution since the document was drafted at the Philadelphia convention in 1787.[2]

The renaissance of the Congress in the post-Watergate, post-Vietnam decade is reflected most dramatically in its renewed emphasis on controlling the federal purse strings. The new, and still evolving, budget process enables Congress to systematically correlate federal revenues with federal expenditures. The Congressional Budget Office provides an independent evaluation of the administration's budget numbers. New devices are available to control "back-door" spending, like federal entitlement programs, and to limit the insidious and pervasive executive branch practice of reprogramming funds from congressionally authorized to unauthorized projects.

Long recognizing that a meaningful control of the purse strings by Congress is dependent on an adequate congressional review of executive expenditures and functions, Congress has developed specialized staffs to oversee the executive branch. Given the near anonymity of the oversight function, the intense scrutiny of agency activities by congressional subcommittees in recent years is to be commended. Both the appropriating committees and the authorizing committees have observed the executive branch and its agencies with more interest and sometimes even more expertise than the reviewing agencies of the executive branch itself. While the Office of Management and Budget, for example, can claim credit for a tough and sharp review of spending activities, the OMB has little interest in reviewing the substantive activities of the agency, particularly after the budgeting decision is made and confirmed or modified by Congress.

New enthusiasm for oversight derives largely from the legislator's sense of political self-preservation. As government programs expand and regulation increases, constituents increasingly need a friend in Washington, and the member will happily accommodate. Locating Aunt Tillie's social security check or castigating a government bureaucrat for harassing a local industry, particularly if that local industry has its own political action committee, makes friends, not enemies. Moreover, as committee staffs increase and federal money decreases, national leadership is derived not by establishing yet another program but by cutting out the fat in programs already in existence. Better to be known as "Cap the Knife" than "Mr. Big Spender."

Is Congress fulfilling the expectation of the constitutional founders that it be first among equals? In the short run it is overshadowed by a popular president, as it was during Franklin Roosevelt's era. But over any meaningful period of time, it certainly holds its own with either of the other two branches of government. Although the courts may frustrate an occasional legislative enactment, they are, with rare exceptions, incapable of denying supremacy to a Congress supported by a majority of the nation. Again, the Roosevelt era is the best example of the inability of the courts to check a congressional objective. Thus, the effort to ban child labor, twice knocked down as beyond the constitutional powers of Congress, was finally upheld when it became part of the New Deal's Fair Labor Standards Act. The same was true of most other progressive legislation that had originally been invalidated on the grounds that it violated "substantive" due process under the Constitution.

Constantly plagued by the "bad apple" syndrome, a congressional reputation for integrity, intelligence, and initiative is difficult to maintain. The corruption of a very few of the members tars the entire institution.

The Abscam scandals unleashed an as yet unresolved moral dilemma. An elaborately staged, well-executed plan, which federal authorities captured on film and sound, resulted in the conviction of six House members and one senator for accepting bribes. Most lost the next election, and the few who were still members were either ousted by, or resigned from, their respective bodies. Left unresolved was the question: how far can the executive branch go, via law enforcement authorities, in "targeting" certain members of Congress? More important, is the independence and primacy of the legislative branch threatened by such actions? Amid complicated legal arguments concerning "entrapment," some members hypothesized that a beleaguered administration might use this method to either oust or control contentious members of Congress.

Seemingly in vain, the majority of members have sought to restore their good name by ethics reforms, by institutional reforms, by efficiency studies. Most reform efforts, even if successful within the Congress, impact little on the image of Congress. Congress struggled through financial reforms following the Wilbur Mills and the Wayne Hayes sex-related scandals (though paradoxically neither former member was accused of financial wrongdoing). In 1976 a commission, chaired by Democratic Congressman David Obey of Wisconsin, spent a year trying to find a more efficient and less corruptible method of handling office allowances and reporting on and limiting outside income. The subsequent package of reforms passed by the House was accompanied by a sizable pay increase from $42,500 to $54,500 to offset the financial difficulties imposed by the reforms on certain members. The country objected strongly to the pay increase but awarded no credit for the reform spirit that had moved the House.

The Congress does not change institutionally without substantial pressure from both outside and within, but it does change and sometimes quite dramatically. When Alexander Hamilton threatened to dominate the Congress in financial matters in the first decade of the Republic, the Congress established its own countervailing finance committees. When "Uncle Joe" Cannon, the czarist speaker of the House of Representatives, used his ironclad control of the legislative agenda to block desired progressive legislation in 1909-11, rank-and-file membership revolted and resurrected the party structure, the committees, and the seniority system to redistribute power.

In the 1960s, when the House Rules Committee was out of step with the majority of the country, a majority in the Congress (however reluctantly) decided to break the logjam of civil rights legislation. A patient and tradition-minded speaker took on the entrenched leadership of the Rules Committee and forced through a rules change. The change allowed the speaker to pack the Rules Committee and thus end the power of the chairman to bottle up legislation even over the speaker's objections. The reform restored control of the Rules Committee to the speaker and denied the speaker and other members the convenient cover previously provided by the committee—failure to act on legislation that the leadership found embarrassing to bury but inconvenient or dangerous to call up had been blamed on the committee. But the reform did accomplish the agenda for change heralded by the civil rights movement and the 1964 election.

That the 1975 seniority reforms of the Ninety-fourth Congress probably restored much of the power structure of the House that had been in place before the revolt against Speaker Cannon only confirms the cyclical nature of institutional reform. The perfect way to distribute power and privileges equally and fairly among 535 disparate and competitive members remains to be discovered. Yesterday's excesses are tomorrow's reforms.

Congress works in much the way it was intended by the framers of the Constitution. They viewed Congress as the branch of government that could preserve the Republic, one nation indivisible, and it is in that sense that it has been successful as the primary and permanent source of political power in this country. The model was intended to be pluralistic, resistant to quick action, and a means for legitimizing the actions of the federal government to the states. Over the two centuries of its existence, Congress has been faithful to that model. It works.

APPENDIX 1

THE CONSTITUTION
OF THE
UNITED STATES

We the people of the United States, in Order to form a more perfect Union, establish Justice, insure domestic Tranquility, provide for the common defence, promote the general Welfare, and secure the Blessings of Liberty to ourselves and our Posterity, do ordain and establish this CONSTITUTION for the United States of America.

ARTICLE I

Section 1. All legislative Powers herein granted shall be vested in a Congress of the United States, which shall consist of a Senate and House of Representatives.

Section 2. The House of Representatives shall be composed of Members chosen every second Year by the People of the several States, and the Electors in each State shall have the Qualifications requisite for Electors of the most numerous Branch of the State Legislature.

No Person shall be a Representative who shall not have attained to the Age of twenty-five Years, and been seven Years a Citizen of the United States, and who shall not, when elected, be an Inhabitant of that State in which he shall be chosen.

Representatives and direct Taxes shall be apportioned among the several States which may be included within this Union, according to their respective Numbers, which shall be determined by adding to the whole Number of free Persons, including those bound to Service for a Term of Years, and excluding Indians not taxed, three fifths of all other Persons. The actual Enumeration shall be made within three Years after the first Meeting of the Congress of the United States, and within every subsequent Term of ten Years, in such Manner as they shall by Law direct. The Number of Representatives shall not exceed one for every thirty Thousand, but

373

each State shall have at least one Representative; and until such enumeration shall be made, the State of New Hampshire shall be entitled to chuse three, Massachusetts eight, Rhode-Island and Providence Plantations one, Connecticut five, New-York six, New Jersey four, Pennsylvania eight, Delaware one, Maryland six, Virginia ten, North Carolina five, South Carolina five, and Georgia three.

When vacancies happen in the Representation from any State, the Executive Authority thereof shall issue Writs of Election to fill such Vacancies.

The House of Representatives shall chuse their Speaker and other Officers; and shall have the sole Power of Impeachment.

Section 3. The Senate of the United States shall be composed of two Senators from each State, chosen by the Legislature thereof, for six Years; and each Senator shall have one Vote.

Immediately after they shall be assembled in Consequence of the first Election, they shall be divided as equally as may be into three Classes. The Seats of the Senators of the first Class shall be vacated at the Expiration of the second Year, of the second Class at the Expiration of the fourth Year, and of the third Class at the Expiration of the sixth Year, so that one-third may be chosen every second Year; and if Vacancies happen by Resignation, or otherwise, during the Recess of the Legislature of any State, the Executive thereof may make temporary Appointments until the next Meeting of the Legislature, which shall then fill such Vacancies.

No Person shall be a Senator who shall not have attained to the Age of thirty Years, and been nine Years a Citizen of the United States, and who shall not, when elected, be an Inhabitant of that State in which he shall be chosen.

The Vice President of the United States shall be President of the Senate, but shall have no vote, unless they be equally divided.

The Senate shall chuse their other Officers, and also a President pro tempore, in the absence of the Vice President, or when he shall exercise the Office of the President of the United States.

The Senate shall have the sole Power to try all Impeachments. When sitting for that purpose, they shall be on Oath or Affirmation. When the President of the United States is tried, the Chief Justice shall preside: And no person shall be convicted without the Concurrence of two thirds of the Members present.

Judgment in Cases of Impeachment shall not extend further than to removal from Office, and disqualification to hold and enjoy any Office of honor, Trust, or Profit under the United States: but the Party convicted shall nevertheless be liable and subject to Indictment, Trial, Judgment, and Punishment, according to Law.

Section 4. The Times, Places and Manner of holding Elections for Senators and Representatives, shall be prescribed in each state by the Legislature thereof; but the Congress may at any time by Law make or alter such Regulations, except as to the Places of Chusing Senators.

The Congress shall assemble at least once in every Year, and such Meeting shall be on the first Monday in December, unless they shall by Law appoint a different Day.

Section 5. Each House shall be the Judge of the Elections, Returns and Qualifications of its own Members, and a Majority of each shall constitute a Quorum to do Business; but a smaller number may adjourn from day to day, and may be authorized to compel the Attendance of absent Members, in such Manner, and under such Penalties, as each House may provide.

Each House may determine the Rules of its Proceedings, punish its Members for disorderly Behavior, and, with the Concurrence of two thirds, expel a Member.

Each House shall keep a Journal of its Proceedings, and from time to time publish the same, excepting such Parts as may in their Judgment require Secrecy; and the Yeas and Nays of the Members of either House on any question shall, at the Desire of one fifth of those Present, be entered on the Journal.

Neither House, during the Session of Congress, shall, without the Consent of the other, adjourn for more than three days, nor to any other Place than that in which the two Houses shall be sitting.

Section 6. The Senators and Representatives shall receive a Compensation for their Services, to be ascertained by Law, and paid out of the Treasury of the United States. They shall in all Cases, except Treason, Felony, and Breach of the Peace, be privileged from Arrest during their Attendance at the Session of their respective Houses, and in going to and returning from the same; and for any Speech or Debate in either House, they shall not be questioned in any other Place.

No Senator or Representative shall, during the Time for which he was elected, be appointed to any civil Office under the Authority of the United States, which shall have been created, or the Emoluments whereof shall have been increased, during such time; and no Person holding any Office under the United States shall be a Member of either House during his continuance in Office.

Section 7. All Bills for raising Revenue shall originate in the House of Representatives; but the Senate may propose or concur with Amendments as on other bills.

Every Bill which shall have passed the House of Representatives and the Senate, shall, before it become a Law, be presented to the President of the United States; If he approve he shall sign it, but if not he shall return it, with his Objections, to that House in which it shall have originated, who shall enter the Objections at large on their Journal, and proceed to reconsider it. If after such Reconsideration two thirds of that House shall agree to pass the bill, it shall be sent, together with the objections, to the other House, by which it shall likewise be reconsidered, and if approved by two thirds of that House, it shall become a Law. But in all such Cases the Votes of both Houses shall be determined by Yeas and Nays, and the Names of the Persons voting for and against the Bill shall be entered on the Journal of each House respectively. If any Bill shall not be returned by the President within ten Days (Sundays excepted) after it shall have been presented to him, the Same shall be a Law, in like Manner as if he had signed it, unless the Congress by their Adjournment prevent its Return, in which Case it shall not be a Law.

Every Order, Resolution, or Vote to which the Concurrence of the Senate and House of Representatives may be necessary (except on a question of Adjournment) shall be presented to the President of the United Sates; and before the Same shall take Effect, shall be approved by him, or being disapproved by him, shall be repassed by two thirds of the Senate and House of Representatives, according to the Rules and Limitations prescribed in the Case of a Bill.

Section 8. The Congress shall have Power to lay and collect Taxes, Duties, Imposts and Excises, to pay the Debts and provide for the common Defence and general Welfare of the United States; but all Duties, Imposts and Excises shall be uniform throughout the United States;

To borrow money on the credit of the United States;

To regulate Commerce with foreign Nations, and among the several States, and with the Indian Tribes;

To establish an uniform Rule of Naturalization, and uniform Laws on the subject of Bankruptcies throughout the United States;

To coin Money, regulate the Value thereof, and of foreign Coin, and fix the Standard of Weights and Measures;

To provide for the Punishment of counterfeiting the Securities and current Coin of the United States;

To establish Post Offices and post Roads;

To promote the Progress of Science and useful Arts, by securing for limited Times to Authors and Inventors the exclusive Right to their respective Writings and Discoveries;

To constitute Tribunals inferior to the Supreme Court;

To define and punish Piracies and Felonies committed on the high Seas, and Offences against the Law of Nations;

To declare War, grant Letters of Marque and Reprisal, and make Rules concerning Captures on Land and Water;

To raise and support Armies, but no Appropriation of Money to that Use shall be for a longer Term than two Years;

To provide and maintain a Navy;

To make Rules for the Government and Regulation of the land and naval forces;

To provide for calling forth the Militia to execute the Laws of the Union, suppress Insurrections and repel Invasions;

To provide for organizing, arming, and disciplining the Militia, and for governing such Part of them as may be employed in the Service of the United States, reserving to the States respectively, the Appointment of the Officers, and the Authority of training the Militia according to the discipline prescribed by Congress;

To exercise exclusive Legislation in all Cases whatsoever, over such District (not exceeding ten Miles square) as may, by Cession of particular States, and the acceptance of Congress, become the Seat of Government of the United States, and to exercise like Authority over all Places

purchased by the Consent of the Legislature of the State in which the Same shall be, for the Erection of Forts, Magazines, Arsenals, dock-Yards, and other needful Buildings;—And

To make all Laws which shall be necessary and proper for carrying into Execution the foregoing Powers, and all other Powers vested by this Constitution in the Government of the United States, or in any Department or Officer thereof.

Section 9. The Migration or Importation of such Persons as any of the States now existing shall think proper to admit, shall not be prohibited by the Congress prior to the Year one thousand eight hundred and eight, but a tax or duty may be imposed on such Importation, not exceeding ten dollars for each Person.

The privilege of the Writ of Habeas Corpus shall not be suspended, unless when in Cases of Rebellion or Invasion the public Safety may require it.

No Bill of Attainder or ex post facto Law shall be passed.

No capitation, or other direct, Tax shall be laid unless in Proportion to the Census or Enumeration herein before directed to be taken.

No Tax or Duty shall be laid on Articles exported from any State.

No Preference shall be given by any Regulation of Revenue to the Ports of one State over those of another: nor shall Vessels bound to, or from, one State, be obliged to enter, clear, or pay Duties in another.

No Money shall be drawn from the Treasury, but in Consequence of Appropriations made by Law; and a regular Statement and Account of the Receipts and Expenditures of all public Money shall be published from time to time.

No Title of Nobility shall be granted by the United States: And no Person holding any Office of Profit or Trust under them, shall, without the Consent of the Congress, accept any present, Emolument, Office, or Title, of any kind whatever, from any King, Prince, or foreign State.

Section 10. No State shall enter into any Treaty, Alliance, or Confederation; grant Letters of Marque and Reprisal; coin Money; emit Bills of Credit; make any Thing but gold and silver Coin a Tender in Payment of Debts; pass any Bill of Attainder, ex post facto Law, or Law impairing the Obligation of Contracts, or grant any Title of Nobility.

No State shall, without the Consent of the Congress, lay any Imposts or Duties on Imports or Exports, except what may be absolutely necessary for executing its inspection Laws: and the net Produce of all Duties and Imposts, laid by any State on Imports or Exports, shall be for the Use of the Treasury of the United States; and all such Laws shall be subject to the Revision and Control of the Congress.

No State shall, without the Consent of Congress, lay any duty of Tonnage, keep Troops, or Ships of War in time of Peace, enter into any Agreement or Compact with another State, or with a foreign Power, or engage in War, unless actually invaded, or in such imminent Danger as will not admit of delay.

ARTICLE II

Section I. The executive Power shall be vested in a President of the United States of America. He shall hold his Office during the Term of four years, and, together with the Vice-President, chosen for the same Term, be elected, as follows:

Each State shall appoint, in such Manner as the Legislature thereof may direct, a Number of Electors, equal to the whole Number of Senators and Representatives to which the State may be entitled in the Congress; but no Senator or Representative, or Person holding an Office of Trust or Profit under the United States, shall be appointed an Elector.

The Electors shall meet in their respective States, and vote by Ballot for two persons, of whom one at least shall not be an Inhabitant of the same State with themselves. And they shall make a List of all the Persons voted for, and of the Number of Votes for each; which List they shall sign and certify, and transmit sealed to the Seat of the Government of the United States, directed to the President of the Senate. The President of the Senate shall, in the Presence of the Senate and House of Representatives, open all the Certificates, and the Votes shall then be counted. The Person having the greatest Number of Votes shall be the President, if such Number be a Majority of the whole Number of Electors appointed; and if there be more than one who have such Majority, and have an equal Number of Votes, then the House of Representatives shall immediately chuse by Ballot one of them for President; and if no Person have a Majority, then from the five highest on the List the said House shall in like Manner chuse the President. But in chusing the President, the Votes shall be taken by States, the Representation from each State having one Vote; a quorum for this Purpose shall consist of a Member or Members from two-thirds of the States, and a Majority of all the States shall be necessary to a Choice. In every Case, after the Choice of the President, the Person having the greatest Number of Votes of the Electors shall be the Vice Pesident. But if there should remain two or more who have equal votes, the Senate shall chuse from them by Ballot the Vice-President.

The Congress may determine the Time of chusing the Electors, and the Day on which they shall give their Votes; which Day shall be the same throughout the United States.

No person except a natural-born Citizen, or a Citizen of the United States, at the time of the Adoption of this Constitution, shall be eligible to the Office of President; neither shall any Person be eligible to that Office who shall not have attained to the Age of thirty-five years, and been fourteen Years a Resident within the United States.

In Case of the Removal of the President from Office, or of his Death, Resignation, or Inability to discharge the Powers and Duties of the said Office, the same shall devolve on the Vice President, and the Congress may by Law provide for the Case of Removal, Death, Resignation, or Inability, both of the President and Vice President, declaring what Officer shall then act as President, and such Officer shall act accordingly, until the disability be removed, or a President shall be elected.

The President shall, at stated Times, receive for his Services a Compensation, which shall neither be increased nor diminished during the Period for which he shall have been elected, and he shall not receive within that Period any other Emolument from the United States, or any of them.

Before he enter on the execution of his Office, he shall take the following Oath or Affirmation:—"I do solemnly swear (or affirm) that I will faithfully execute the Office of President of the United States, and will, to the best of my Ability, preserve, protect, and defend the Constitution of the United States."

Section 2. The President shall be Commander in Chief of the Army and Navy of the United States, and of the Militia of the several States, when called into the actual Service of the United States; he may require the Opinion, in writing, of the principal Officer in each of the executive Departments, upon any subject relating to the Duties of their respective Offices, and he shall have Power to Grant Reprieves and Pardons For Offences against the United States, except in Cases of Impeachment.

He shall have Power, by and with the Advice and Consent of the Senate, to make Treaties, provided two thirds of the Senators present concur; and he shall nominate, and by and with the Advice and Consent of the Senate, shall appoint Ambassadors, other public Ministers and Consuls, Judges of the supreme Court, and all other Officers of the United States, whose Appointments are not herein otherwise provided for, and which shall be established by Law: but the Congress may by Law vest the Appointment of such inferior Officers, as they think proper, in the President alone, in the Courts of Law, or in the Heads of Departments.

The President shall have Power to fill up all Vacancies that may happen during the Recess of the Senate, by granting Commissions which shall expire at the End of their next Session.

Section 3. He shall from time to time give to the Congress Information of the State of the Union, and recommend to their Consideration such Measures as he shall judge necessary and expedient; he may, on extraordinary occasions, convene both Houses, or either of them, and in Case of Disagreement between them, with respect to the Time of Adjournment, he may adjourn them to such Time as he shall think proper; he shall receive Ambassadors and other public Ministers; he shall take Care that the Laws be faithfully executed, and shall Commission all the Officers of the United States.

Section 4. The President, Vice President and all civil Officers of the United States, shall be removed from Office on Impeachment for, and Conviction of, Treason, Bribery, or other high Crimes and Misdemeanors.

ARTICLE III

Section 1. The judicial Power of the United States, shall be vested in one supreme Court, and in such inferior Courts as the Congress may from time to time ordain and establish. The Judges, both of the supreme and inferior Courts, shall hold their Offices during good Behaviour, and shall, at stated Times, receive for their

Services, a Compensation, which shall not be diminished during their Continuance in Office.

Section 2. The judicial Power shall extend to all Cases, in Law and Equity, arising under this Constitution, the Laws of the United States, and treaties made, or which shall be made, under their Authority;—to all Cases affecting ambassadors, other public ministers and consuls;—to all cases of admiralty and maritime Jurisdiction;—to Controversies to which the United States shall be a Party;—to Controversies between two or more States;—between a State and Citizens of another State;—between Citizens of different States,—between Citizens of the same State claiming Lands under Grants of different States, and between a State, or the Citizens thereof, and foreign States, Citizens or Subjects.

In all Cases affecting Ambassadors, other public Ministers and Consuls, and those in which a State shall be Party, the supreme Court shall have original Jurisdiction. In all the other Cases before mentioned, the supreme Court shall have appellate Jurisdiction, both as to Law and Fact, with such Exceptions, and under such Regulations as the Congress shall make.

The trial of all Crimes, except in Cases of Impeachment, shall be by Jury; and such Trial shall be held in the State where the said Crimes shall have been committed; but when not committed within any State, the Trial shall be at such Place or Places as the Congress may by Law have directed.

Section 3. Treason against the United States, shall consist only in levying War against them, or in adhering to their Enemies, giving them Aid and Comfort. No Person shall be convicted of Treason unless on the Testimony of two Witnesses to the same overt Act, or on Confession in open Court.

The Congress shall have power to de-clare the Punishment of Treason, but no Attainder of Treason shall work Corruption of Blood, or Forfeiture except during the Life of the Person attainted.

ARTICLE IV

Section 1. Full Faith and Credit shall be given in each State to the public Acts, Records, and judicial Proceedings of every other State. And the Congress may by general Laws prescribe the Manner in which such Acts, Records and Proceedings shall be proved, and the Effect thereof.

Section 2. The Citizens of each State shall be entitled to all Privileges and Immunities of Citizens in the several States.

A Person charged in any State with Treason, Felony, or other Crime, who shall flee from Justice, and be found in another State, shall on demand of the executive Authority of the State from which he fled, be delivered up, to be removed to the State having Jurisdiction of the crime.

No Person held to Service or Labour in one State, under the Laws thereof, escaping into another, shall, in Consequence of any Law or Regulation therein, be discharged from such Service or Labour, but shall be delivered up on Claim of the Party to whom such Service or Labour may be due.

Section 3. New States may be admitted by the Congress into this Union; but no new State shall be formed or erected within the Jurisdiction of any other State; nor any State be formed by the Junction of two or more States, or parts of States, without the Consent of the Legislatures of the States concerned as well as of the Congress.

The Congress shall have Power to dispose of and make all needful Rules and Regulations respecting the Territory or other Property belonging to the United States; and nothing in this Constitution shall be so construed as to Prejudice any

Claims of the United States, or of any particular State.

Section 4. The United States shall guarantee to every State in this Union a Republican Form of Government, and shall protect each of them against Invasion; and on Application of the Legislature, or the Executive (when the Legislature cannot be convened) against domestic Violence.

ARTICLE V

The Congress, whenever two-thirds of both Houses shall deem it necessary, shall propose Amendments to this Constitution, or, on the Application of the Legislatures of two-thirds of the several States, shall call a Convention for proposing Amendments, which, in either Case, shall be valid to all Intents and Purposes, as part of this Constitution, when ratified by the Legislatures of three-fourths of the several States, or by Conventions in three-fourths thereof, as the one or the other Mode of Ratification may be proposed by the Congress; Provided that no Amendment which may be made prior to the Year One thousand eight hundred and eight shall in any Manner affect the first and fourth Clauses in the Ninth Section of the first Article; and that no State, without its Consent, shall be deprived of its equal Suffrage in the Senate.

ARTICLE VI

All Debts contracted and Engagements entered into, before the Adoption of this Constitution, shall be as valid against the United States under this Constitution, as under the Confederation.

This Constitution, and the Laws of the United States which shall be made in Pursuance thereof; and all Treaties made, or which shall be made, under the Authority of the United States, shall be the supreme Law of the Land; and the Judges in every State shall be bound thereby, any Thing

in the Constitution or Laws of any State to the Contrary notwithstanding.

The Senators and Representatives before mentioned, and the Members of the several State Legislatures, and all executive and judicial Officers, both of the United States and of the several States, shall be bound by Oath or Affirmation to support this Constitution; but no religious Test shall ever be required as a qualification to any Office or public Trust under the United States.

ARTICLE VII

The Ratification of the Conventions of nine States shall be sufficient for the Establishment of this Constitution between the States so ratifying the same.

Done in Convention by the Unanimous Consent of the States present the Seventeenth Day of September in the Year of our Lord one thousand seven hundred and Eighty seven, and of the Independence of the United States of America the Twelfth. In Witness whereof We have hereunto subscribed our Names. *Articles in Addition to, and Amendment of, the Constitution of the United States of America, Proposed by Congress, and Ratified by the Legislatures of the Several States, Pursuant to the Fifth Article of the Original Constitution.*

AMENDMENT I [1791]

Congress shall make no law respecting an establishment of religion, or prohibiting the free exercise thereof; or abridging the freedom of speech, or of the press; or the right of the people peaceably to assemble, and to petition the Government for a redress of grievances.

AMENDMENT II [1791]

A well regulated Militia, being necessary to the security of a free State, the right of the people to keep and bear Arms shall not be infringed.

AMENDMENT III [1791]

No Soldier shall, in time of peace, be quartered in any house, without the consent of the Owner, nor in time of war, but in a manner to be prescribed by law.

AMENDMENT IV [1791]

The right of the people to be secure in their persons, houses, papers, and effects, against unreasonable searches and seizures, shall not be violated, and no Warrants shall issue, but upon probable cause, supported by Oath or affirmation, and particularly describing the place to be searched, and the persons or things to be seized.

AMENDMENT V [1791]

No person shall be held to answer for a capital or otherwise infamous crime, unless on a presentment or indictment of a Grand Jury, except in cases arising in the land or naval forces, or in the Militia, when in actual service in time of War or public danger; nor shall any person be subject for the same offence to be twice put in jeopardy of life or limb; nor shall be compelled in any criminal case to be a witness against himself, nor be deprived of life, liberty, or property, without due process of law; nor shall private property be taken for public use, without just compensation.

AMENDMENT VI [1791]

In all criminal prosecutions, the accused shall enjoy the right to a speedy and public trial, by an impartial jury of the State and district wherein the crime shall have been committed, which district shall have been previously ascertained by law, and to be informed of the nature and cause of the accusation; to be confronted with the witnesses against him; to have compulsory process for obtaining witnesses in his favor, and to have the Assistance of Counsel for his defence.

AMENDMENT VII [1791]

In suits at common law, where the value in controversy shall exceed twenty dollars, the right of trial by jury shall be preserved, and no fact tried by a jury, shall be otherwise reexamined in any Court of the United States, than according to the rules of the common law.

AMENDMENT VIII [1791]

Excessive bail shall not be required, nor excessive fines imposed, nor cruel and unusual punishments inflicted.

AMENDMENT IX [1791]

The enumeration in the Constitution, of certain rights, shall not be construed to deny or disparage others retained by the people.

AMENDMENT X [1791]

The powers not delegated to the United States by the Constitution, nor prohibited by it to the States, are reserved to the States respectively, or to the people.

AMENDMENT XI [1798]

The Judicial power of the United States shall not be construed to extend to any suit in law or equity, commenced or prosecuted against one of the United States by Citizens of another State, or by Citizens or Subjects of any Foreign State.

AMENDMENT XII [1804]

The Electors shall meet in their respective States and vote by ballot for President and Vice-President, one of whom, at least, shall not be an inhabitant of the same State with themselves; they shall name in their ballots the person voted for as President, and in distinct ballots the person voted for as Vice-President, and they shall make distinct lists of all persons voted for as President, and of all persons voted for as Vice-President, and of the number of votes for each, which lists they shall sign and certify, and transmit sealed to the seat of the government of the United States, directed to the President of the Senate;— The President of the Senate shall, in the presence of the Senate and House of Representatives, open all the certificates and the votes shall then be counted;—The person having the greatest number of votes for President, shall be the President, if such number be a majority of the whole number of Electors appointed; and if no person have such majority, then from the persons having the highest number not exceeding three on the list of those voted for as President, the House of Representatives shall choose immediately, by ballot, the President. But in choosing the President, the votes shall be taken by states, the representation from each state having one vote; a quorum for this purpose shall consist of a member or members from two-thirds of the states, and a majority of all the states shall be necessary to a choice. And if the House of Representatives shall not choose a President whenever the right of choice shall devolve upon them, before the fourth day of March next following, then the Vice-President shall act as President, as in the case of the death or other constitutional disability of the President.—The person having the greatest number of votes as Vice-President, shall be the Vice-President, if such number be a majority of the whole number of Electors appointed, and if no person have a majority, then from the two highest numbers on the list, the Senate shall choose the Vice-President; a quorum for the purpose shall consist of two-thirds of the whole number of Sen-

ators, and a majority of the whole number shall be necessary to a choice. But no person constitutionally ineligible to the office of President shall be eligible to that of Vice-President of the United States.

AMENDMENT XIII [1865]
Section 1. Neither slavery nor involuntary servitude, except as a punishment for crime whereof the party shall have been duly convicted, shall exist within the United States, or any place subject to their jurisdiction.
Section 2. Congress shall have power to enforce this article by appropriate legislation.

AMENDMENT XIV [1868]
Section 1. All persons born or naturalized in the United States, and subject to the jurisdiction thereof, are citizens of the United States and of the State wherein they reside. No State shall make or enforce any law which shall abridge the privileges or immunities of citizens of the United States; nor shall any State deprive any person of life, liberty, or property, without due process of law; nor deny to any person within its jurisdiction the equal protection of the laws.
Section 2. Representatives shall be apportioned among the several States according to their respective numbers, counting the whole number of persons in each State, excluding Indians not taxed. But when the right to vote at any election for the choice of electors for President and Vice-President of the United States, Representatives in Congress, the Executive and Judicial officers of a State, or the members of the Legislature thereof, is denied to any of the male inhabitants of such State, being twenty-one years of age, and citizens of the United States, or in any way abridged, except for participation in rebellion, or other crime, the basis of rep-

resentation therein shall be reduced in the proportion which the number of such male citizens shall bear to the whole number of male citizens twenty-one years of age in such State.

Section 3. No person shall be a Senator or Representative in Congress, or elector of President and Vice-President, or hold any office, civil or military, under the United States, or under any State, who, having previously taken an oath, as a member of Congress, or as an officer of the United States, or as a member of any State legislature, or as an executive or judicial officer of any State, to support the Constitution of the United States, shall have engaged in insurrection or rebellion against the same, or given aid or comfort to the enemies thereof. But Congress may by a vote of two-thirds of each House, remove such disability.

Section 4. The validity of the public debt of the United States, authorized by law, including debts incurred for payment of pensions and bounties for services in suppressing insurrection or rebellion, shall not be questioned. But neither the United States nor any State shall assume or pay any debt or obligation incurred in aid of insurrection or rebellion against the United States, or any claim for the loss or emancipation of any slave; but all such debts, obligations, and claims shall be held illegal and void.

Section 5. The Congress shall have the power to enforce, by appropriate legislation, the provisions of this article.

AMENDMENT XV [1870]
Section 1. The right of citizens of the United States to vote shall not be denied or abridged by the United States or by any State on account of race, color, or previous condition of servitude—

Section 2. The Congress shall have power to enforce this article by appropriate legislation.

AMENDMENT XVI [1913]
The Congress shall have power to lay and collect taxes on incomes, from whatever source derived, without apportionment among the several States, and without regard to any census or enumeration.

AMENDMENT XVII [1913]
The Senate of the United States shall be composed of two Senators from each State, elected by the people thereof, for six years; and each Senator shall have one vote. The electors in each State shall have the qualifications requisite for electors of the most numerous branch of the State legislatures.

When vacancies happen in the representation of any State in the Senate, the executive authority of such State shall issue writs of election to fill such vacancies: *Provided,* That the legislature of any State may empower the executive thereof to make temporary appointments until the people fill the vacancies by election as the legislature may direct.

This amendment shall not be so construed as to affect the election or term of any Senator chosen before it becomes valid as part of the Constitution.

AMENDMENT XVIII [1919]
Section 1. After one year from the ratification of this article the manufacture, sale, or transportation of intoxicating liquors within, the importation thereof into, or the exportation thereof from the United States and all territory subject to the jurisdiction thereof for beverage purposes is hereby prohibited.

Section 2. The Congress and the several States shall have concurrent power to enforce this article by appropriate legislation.

Section 3. This article shall be inoperative unless it shall have been ratified as an amendment to the Constitution by the legislatures of the several States, as provided in the Constitution, within seven years from the date of the submission hereof to the States by the Congress.

AMENDMENT XIX [1920]

The right of citizens of the United States to vote shall not be denied or abridged by the United States or by any State on account of sex.

Congress shall have power to enforce this article by appropriate legislation.

AMENDMENT XX [1933]

Seciton 1.   The terms of the President and Vice-President shall end at noon on the 20th day of January, and the terms of Senators and Representatives at noon on the 3d day of January, of the years in which such terms would have ended if this article had not been ratified; and the terms of their successors shall then begin.

Section 2.   The Congress shall assemble at least once in every year, and such meeting shall begin at noon on the 3d day of January, unless they shall by law appoint a different day.

Section 3.   If, at the time fixed for the beginning of the term of the President, the President elect shall have died, the Vice-President elect shall become President. If a President shall not have been chosen before the time fixed for the beginning of his term, or if the President elect have failed to qualify, then the Vice-President shall act as President until a President shall have qualified; and the Congress may by law provide for the case wherein neither a President elect nor a Vice-President elect shall have qualified, declaring who shall then act as President, or the manner in which one who is to act shall be selected, and such person shall act accordingly until a President or Vice-President shall have qualified.

Section 4.   The Congress may by law provide for the case of the death of any of the persons from whom the House of Representatives may choose a President whenever the right of choice shall have devolved upon them, and for the case of the death of any of the persons from whom the Senate may choose a Vice-President whenever the right of choice shall have devolved upon them.

Section 5.   Sections 1 and 2 shall take effect on the 15th day of October following the ratification of this article.

Section 6.   This article shall be inoperative unless it shall have been ratified as an amendment to the Constitution by the legislatures of three-fourths of the several States within seven years from the date of its submission.

AMENDMENT XXI [1933]

Section 1.   The eighteenth article of amendment to the Constitution of the United States is hereby repealed.

Section 2.   The transportation or importation into any State, Territory, or possession of the United States for delivery or use therein of intoxicating liquors, in violation of the laws thereof, is hereby prohibited.

Section 3.   This article shall be inoperative unless it shall have been ratified as an amendment to the Constitution by conventions in the several States, as provided in the Constitution, within seven years from the date of the submission hereof to the States by the Congress.

AMENDMENT XXII [1951]

No person shall be elected to the office of the President more than twice, and no person who has held the office of President, or acted as President, for more than two years of a term to which some other person was elected President shall be elected to the office of the President more than once.

But this Article shall not apply to any

person holding the office of President when this Article was proposed by the Congress, and shall not prevent any person who may be holding the office of President, or acting as President, during the term within which this Article becomes operative from holding the office of President or acting as President during the remainder of such term.

AMENDMENT XXIII [1961]

Section 1. The District constituting the seat of Government of the United States shall appoint in such manner as the Congress may direct:

A number of electors of President and Vice President equal to the whole number of Senators and Representatives in Congress to which the District would be entitled if it were a State, but in no event more than the least populous State; they shall be in addition to those appointed by the States, but they shall be considered, for the purposes of the election of President and Vice President, to be electors appointed by a State; and they shall meet in the District and perform such duties as provided by the twelfth article of amendment.

Section 2. The Congress shall have power to enforce this article by appropriate legislation.

AMENDMENT XXIV [1964]

Section 1. The right of citizens of the United States to vote in any primary or other election for President or Vice President, for electors for President or Vice President, or for Senator or Representative in Congress, shall not be denied or abridged by the United States or any State by reason of failure to pay any poll tax or other tax.

Section 2. The Congress shall have the power to enforce this article by appropriate legislation.

AMENDMENT XXV [1967]

Section 1. In case of the removal of the President from office or his death or resignation, the Vice President shall become President.

Section 2. Whenever there is a vacancy in the office of the Vice President, the President shall nominate a Vice President who shall take the office upon confirmation by a majority vote of both houses of Congress.

Section 3. Whenever the President transmits to the President pro tempore of the Senate and the Speaker of the House of Representatives his written declaration that he is unable to discharge the powers and duties of his office, and until he transmits to them a written declaration to the contrary, such powers and duties shall be discharged by the Vice President as Acting President.

Section 4. Whenever the Vice President and a majority of either the principal officers of the executive departments, or of such other body as Congress may by law provide, transmit to the President pro tempore of the Senate and the Speaker of the House of Representatives their written declaration that the President is unable to discharge the powers and duties of his office, the Vice President shall immediately assume the powers and duties of the office as Acting President.

Thereafter, when the President transmits to the President pro tempore of the Senate and the Speaker of the House of Representatives his written declaration that no inability exists, he shall resume the powers and duties of his office unless the Vice President and a majority of either the principal officers of the executive departments, or of such other body as Congress may by law provide, transmit within four days to the President pro tempore of the Senate and the Speaker of the House of Representatives their written declaration that the President is unable to discharge the powers and duties of his office.

Thereupon Congress shall decide the issue, assembling within 48 hours for that purpose if not in session. If the Congress, within 21 days after receipt of the latter written declaration, or, if Congress is not in session, within 21 days after Congress is required to assemble, determines by two-thirds vote of both houses that the President is unable to discharge the powers and duties of his office, the Vice President shall continue to discharge the same as Acting President; otherwise, the President shall resume the powers and duties of his office.

AMENDMENT XXVI [1971]

Section 1.   The right of citizens of the United States, who are 18 years of age or older, to vote shall not be denied or abridged by the United States or any state on account of age.

Section 2.   The Congress shall have the power to enforce this article by appropriate legislation.

APPENDIX 2

COMMITTEES
AND SUBCOMMITTEES
OF THE NINETY-SEVENTH
CONGRESS

U.S. SENATE
Standing Committees and Subcommittees

AGRICULTURE, NUTRITION, AND FORESTRY
Soil and Water Conservation
Agricultural Credit and Rural Electrification
Agricultural Production, Marketing, and Stabilization of Prices
Agricultural Research and General Legislation
Rural Development, Oversight, and Investigation
Foreign Agricultural Policy
Nutrition
Forestry, Water Resources, and Environment

APPROPRIATIONS
Agriculture, Rural Development, and Related Agencies
Defense
District of Columbia

Energy and Water Development
Foreign Operations
HUD-Independent Agencies
Interior, and Related Agencies
Labor, HHS, Education, and Related Agencies
Legislative Branch
Military Construction
State, Justice, Commerce, the Judiciary, and Related Agencies
Transportation and Related Agencies
Treasury, Postal Service, and General Government

ARMED SERVICES
Military Construction
Tactical Warfare
Strategic and Theater Nuclear Forces
Preparedness
Sea Power and Force Projection
Manpower and Personnel

BANKING, HOUSING, AND URBAN AFFAIRS
Housing and Urban Affairs
Financial Institutions
Securities
International Finance and Monetary Policy
Economic Policy
Consumer Affairs
Rural Housing and Development

BUDGET
(No Subcommittees)

COMMERCE, SCIENCE, AND TRANSPORTATION
Aviation
Business, Trade, and Tourism
Communications
Consumer
Merchant Marine
Science, Technology, and Space
Surface Transportation
National Ocean Policy Study

ENERGY AND NATURAL RESOURCES
  Energy Conservation and Supply
  Energy Regulation
  Energy Research and Development
  Energy and Mineral Resources
  Water and Power
  Public Lands and Reserved Water

ENVIRONMENT AND PUBLIC WORKS
  Environmental Pollution
  Nuclear Regulation
  Water Resources
  Transportation
  Toxic Substances and Environmental Oversight
  Regional and Community Development

FINANCE
  Taxation and Debt Management
  International Trade
  Savings, Pensions, and Investment Policy
  Economic Growth, Employment, and Revenue Sharing
  Energy and Agricultural Taxation
  Health
  Social Security and Income Maintenance Programs
  Estate and Gift Taxation
  Oversight of the Internal Revenue Service

FOREIGN RELATIONS
  International Economic Policy
  Arms Control, Oceans, International Operations, and Environment
  African Affairs
  European Affairs
  East Asian and Pacific Affairs
  Near Eastern and South Asian Affairs
  Western Hemisphere Affairs

GOVERNMENTAL AFFAIRS
  Permanent Subcommittee on Investigations
  Governmental Efficiency and the District of Columbia
  Energy, Nuclear Proliferation, and Government Processes

Federal Expenditures, Research, and Rules
Intergovernmental Relations
Civil Service, Post Office, and General Services
Oversight of Government Management
Congressional Operations and Oversight

JUDICIARY
Agency Administration
The Constitution
Courts
Criminal Law
Immigration and Refugee Policy
Juvenile Justice
Regulatory Reform
Security and Terrorism
Separation of Powers

LABOR AND HUMAN RESOURCES
Labor
Education, Art and Humanities
Employment and Productivity
Handicapped
Alcoholism and Drug Abuse
Aging, Family, and Human Services
Investigations and General Oversight

RULES AND ADMINISTRATION
(No Subcommittees)

COMMITTEE ON SMALL BUSINESS
Capital Formation and Retention
Government Regulation and Paperwork
Urban and Rural Economic Development
Government Procurement
Productivity and Competition
Innovation and Technology
Export Promotion and Market Development
Advocacy and the Future of Small Business

VETERANS' AFFAIRS
(No Subcommittees)

Select Committees of the U. S. Senate

SELECT COMMITTEE ON ETHICS
(No Subcommittees)

SELECT COMMITTEE ON INDIAN AFFAIRS
(No Subcommittees)

SELECT COMMITTEE ON INTELLIGENCE
Budget
Analysis and Production
Legislation and the Rights of Americans
Collection and Foreign Operations

SELECT COMMITTEE TO STUDY LAW ENFORCEMENT UNDERCOVER
ACTIVITIES OF COMPONENTS OF THE DEPARTMENT OF JUSTICE
(No Subcommittees)

Special Committees of the U. S. Senate

SPECIAL COMMITTEE ON AGING
(No Subcommittees)

U.S. HOUSE OF REPRESENTATIVES
Standing Committees and Subcommittees

AGRICULTURE
Conservation, Credit, and Rural Development
Cotton, Rice and Sugar
Department Operations, Research, and Foreign Agriculture
Domestic Marketing, Consumer Relations, and Nutrition
Forests, Family Farms, and Energy
Livestock, Dairy, and Poultry
Tobacco and Peanuts
Wheat, Soybeans, and Feed Grains

APPROPRIATIONS
Agriculture, Rural Development and Related Agencies
Commerce, Justice, State, and Judiciary
Defense
District of Columbia
Energy and Water Development
Foreign Operations
HUD—Independent Agencies
Interior
Labor—Health and Human Services—Education
Legislative
Military Construction
Transportation
Treasury—Postal Service—General Government

ARMED SERVICES
Investigations
Military Installations and Facilities
Military Personnel and Compensation
Procurement and Military Nuclear Systems
Readiness
Research and Development
Seapower and Strategic and Critical Materials

BANKING, FINANCE AND URBAN AFFAIRS
Consumer Affairs and Coinage
Domestic Monetary Policy
Economic Stabilization
Financial Institutions Supervision, Regulation and Insurance
General Oversight and Renegotiation
Housing and Community Development
International Development Institutions and Finance
International Trade, Investment and Monetary Policy

BUDGET
(No Subcommittees)

DISTRICT OF COLUMBIA
Fiscal Affairs and Health
Government Operations and Metropolitan Affairs
Judiciary and Education

EDUCATION AND LABOR
Elementary, Secondary, and Vocational Education
Employment Opportunities
Health and Safety
Human Resources
Labor-Management Relations
Labor Standards
Postsecondary Education
Select Education

ENERGY AND COMMERCE
Commerce, Transportation, and Tourism
Energy Conservation and Power
Fossil and Synthetic Fuels
Health and the Environment
Oversight and Investigations
Telecommunications, Consumer Protection, and Finance

FOREIGN AFFAIRS
Africa
Asian and Pacific Affairs
Europe and the Middle East
Human Rights and International Organizations
Inter-American Affairs
International Economic Policy and Trade
International Operations
International Security and Scientific Affairs

GOVERNMENT OPERATIONS
Commerce, Consumer, and Monetary Affairs
Environment, Energy, and Natural Resources
Government Activities and Transportation
Government Information and Individual Rights
Intergovernmental Relations and Human Resources
Legislation and National Security
Manpower and Housing

HOUSE ADMINISTRATION
Accounts
Contracts and Printing
Office Systems

Personnel and Police
Services
Policy Group on Information and Computers

INTERIOR AND INSULAR AFFAIRS
Energy and the Environment
Insular Affairs
Mines and Mining
Oversight and Investigations
Public Lands and National Parks
Water and Power Resources

JUDICIARY
Administrative Law and Governmental Relations
Civil and Constitutional Rights
Courts, Civil Liberties, and the Administration of Justice
Crime
Criminal Justice
Immigration, Refugees, and International Law
Monopolies and Commercial Law

MERCHANT MARINE AND FISHERIES
Coast Guard and Navigation
Fisheries and Wildlife Conservation and the Environment
Merchant Marine
Oceanography
Panama Canal and Outer Continental Shelf

POST OFFICE AND CIVIL SERVICE
Census and Population
Civil Service
Compensation and Employee Benefits
Human Resources
Investigations
Postal Operations and Services
Postal Personnel and Modernization

PUBLIC WORKS AND TRANSPORTATION
Aviation
Economic Development
Investigations and Oversight
Public Buildings and Grounds

Surface Transportation
Water Resources

RULES
Rules of the House
The Legislative Process

SCIENCE AND TECHNOLOGY
Energy Development and Applications
Energy Research and Production
Investigations and Oversight
Natural Resources, Agriculture Research and Environment
Science, Research and Technology
Space Science and Applications
Transportation, Aviation and Materials

SMALL BUSINESS
Antitrust and Restraint of Trade Activities Affecting Small Business
Energy, Environment and Safety Issues Affecting Small Business
Export Opportunities and Special Small Business Problems
General Oversight
SBA and SBIC Authority, Minority Enterprise and General Small Business
Problems
Tax, Access to Equity Capital and Business Opportunities

STANDARDS OF OFFICIAL CONDUCT
(No Subcommittees)

VETERANS' AFFAIRS
Compensation, Pension, and Insurance
Education, Training and Employment
Hospitals and Health Care
Housing and Memorial Affairs
Oversight and Investigations

WAYS AND MEANS
Health
Oversight
Public Assistance and Unemployment Compensation
Select Revenue Measures
Social Security
Trade

Select committees of the House of Representatives

SELECT COMMITTEE ON AGING
    Health and Long-Term Care
    Housing and Consumer Interests
    Human Services
    Retirement Income and Employment

PERMANENT SELECT COMMITTEE ON INTELLIGENCE
    Legislation
    Oversight and Evaluation
    Program and Budget Authorization

SELECT COMMITTEE ON NARCOTICS ABUSE AND CONTROL
    (No Subcommittees)

JOINT COMMITTEES OF THE CONGRESS (97th CONGRESS)

JOINT ECONOMIC COMMITTEE
    International Trade, Finance, and Security Economics
    Investment, Jobs, and Prices
    Economic Goals and Intergovernmental Policy
    Monetary and Fiscal Policy
    Trade, Productivity, and Economic Growth
    Agriculture and Transportation

JOINT COMMITTEE ON THE LIBRARY
    (No Subcommittees)

JOINT COMMITTEE ON PRINTING
    (No Subcommittees)

JOINT COMMITTEE ON TAXATION
    (No Subcommittees)

APPENDIX 3

SPEAKERS OF
THE HOUSE
OF REPRESENTATIVES

CONGRESS	YEARS	SPEAKER
58th	1903–1904	Joseph G. Cannon, of Ill.
59th	1905–1906	"
60th	1907–1908	"
61st	1909–1910	"
62nd	1911–1912	Champ Clark, of Missouri
63rd	1913–1914	"
64th	1915–1916	"
65th	1917–1918	"
66th	1919–1920	Frederick H. Gillett, of Mass.
67th	1921–1922	"
68th	1923–1924	"
69th	1925–1926	Nicholas Longworth, of Ohio
70th	1927–1928	"
71st	1929–1930	"
72nd	1931–1932	John N. Garner, of Texas
73rd	1933–1934	Henry T. Rainey, of Illinois
74th	1935–1936	Joseph W. Byrns, of Tennessee
75th	1937–1938	William B. Bankhead, of Alabama

CONGRESS	YEARS	SPEAKER
76th	1939–1940	William B. Bankhead, of Alabama
77th	1941–1942	Sam Rayburn, of Texas
78th	1943–1944	"
79th	1945–1946	"
80th	1947–1948	Joseph W. Martin, Jr., of Mass.
81st	1949–1950	Sam Rayburn, of Texas
82nd	1951–1952	"
83rd	1953–1954	Joseph W. Martin, Jr., of Mass.
84th	1955–1956	Sam Rayburn, of Texas
85th	1957–1958	"
86th	1959–1960	"
87th	1961–1962	"
88th	1963–1964	John W. McCormack, of Mass.
89th	1965–1966	"
90th	1967–1968	"
91st	1969–1970	"
92nd	1971–1972	Carl B. Albert, of Oklahoma
93rd	1973–1974	"
94th	1975–1976	"
95th	1977–1978	Thomas P. O'Neill, Jr., of Mass.
96th	1979–1980	"
97th	1981–1982	"
98th	1983–1984	"

NOTES

Chapter 1 REVOLUTION IN CONGRESS

1. Arthur M. Schlesinger, Jr., *The Imperial Presidency* (Boston: Houghton Mifflin, 1973).

2. Donald R. Matthews, "Folkways of the United States Senate," in Leroy N. Rieselbach, ed., *The Congressional System* (Belmont, Calif.: Duxbury Press, 1970), p. 171. See generally, Donald R. Matthews, *U. S. Senators and Their World* (Chapel Hill: University of North Carolina Press, 1960).

3. Barbara Hinckley, *Stability and Change in Congress*, 2nd ed. (New York: Harper & Row, 1978), pp. 66–67.

4. Mark Green, *Who Runs Congress?* 3rd ed. (New York: Bantam Books, 1979), pp. 253–54.

5. See, e.g., Hedrick Smith, "Senate Republicans Decide To Postpone 'Emotional' Debates," *The New York Times*, March 27, 1981, p. A1; Helen Dewar, "Helms Maneuvers Senate Democrats Into Voting To Cut Foreign Aid," *Washington Post*, March 28, 1981, pp. A1, A11.

6. In his early days Rayburn himself had never gone along with the views of his party's leaders: "As a young Congressman he had 'gone along' with no one—not even the President, the President of his own party, whom he idolized." Robert

A. Caro, "The Years of Lyndon Johnson: Lyndon and Mr. Sam," *The Atlantic*, Vol. 248 (November, 1981), p. 50.

7. Charles L. Clapp, *The Congressman: His Work as He Sees It* (New York: Doubleday Anchor, 1964), pp. 254–55.

8. Congressional Budget and Impoundment Control Act of 1974, Pub. Law 93–344, 88 Stat. 297 (July 12, 1974), 31 U.S.C. sec. 1301 et seq.

9. Randall B. Ripley and Lewis A. Froman, Jr., "Conditions for Party Leadership," in Rieselbach, ed., *The Congressional System*, p. 128.

10. Clapp, *The Congressman*, p. 353.

11. David S. Broder, "Those Wayward Democrats," *Washington Post*, July 12, 1981, p. C7.

12. Broder, "Those Wayward Democrats," p. C7.

13. Senate Committee on Government Operations, *Study on Federal Regulation*, S. Doc. No. 95–25, Vol. II, 96th Cong., 1st sess. (1977).

14. See David R. Mayhew, *Congress: The Electoral Connection* (New Haven: Yale University Press, 1974), p. 131. Hinckley, *Stability*, p. 92. Douglas Cater, *Power in Washington* (New York: Random House, 1964), p. 18.

15. Morris P. Fiorina, *Congress: Keystone of the Washington Establishment* (New Haven: Yale University Press, 1977), p. 3.

16. Airline Deregulation Act of 1978, Pub. Law 95–504, 92 Stat. 1705 (October 24, 1978); see 49 U.S.C. sec. 1301 et seq.

17. War Powers Act, Pub. Law 93–148, 87 Stat. 555 (November 7, 1973); see 50 U.S.C. sec. 1541 et seq.

18. Pub. Law 93–559, 88 Stat. 1813, 1814 (Dec. 30, 1974), 22 U.S.C. sec. 2776. Thomas M. Franck and Edward Weisband, *Foreign Policy by Congress* (New York: Oxford University Press, 1979), p. 99. See James L. Sundquist, *The Decline and Resurgence of Congress* (Washington, D.C.: Brookings Institution, 1981), p. 289.

19. Nuclear Non-Proliferation Act of 1978, Pub. Law 95–242, 92 Stat. 120 (March 10, 1978). See 22 U.S.C. sec. 3201 et seq. See Franck and Weisband, *Foreign Policy*, p. 112.

20. See generally, James L. Sundquist, *The Decline and Resurgence of Congress* (Washington, D.C.: Brookings Institution, 1981), pp. 273–314.

21. Federal Election Campaign Act of 1971, Pub. Law 92–225, 86 Stat. 3 (February 7, 1972). It has been amended three times: Pub. Law 93–443 (1974); Pub. Law 94–283 (1976); Pub. Law 96–187 (1980); see 2 U.S.C. sec. 431 et seq.; 18 U.S.C. secs. 591, 600, 608, 610, 611; 47 U.S.C. secs. 312, 315, 802–805.

Chapter 2 ORIGINS OF CONGRESS

1. Alexander Hamilton or James Madison, *The Federalist, A Commentary on the*

Constitution of the United States (New York: Random House, 1937), *The Federalist*, No. 51, p. 338. Cited hereafter as *Commentary*.

2. Madison, *The Federalist*, No. 48, in *Commentary*, p. 322.

3. Alexis de Tocqueville, *Democracy in America*, ed. J. P. Mayer and Max Lerner (New York: Harper & Row, 1966), p. 110.

4. Woodrow Wilson, *Congressional Government: A Study in American Politics* (Boston: Houghton Mifflin, 1913), p. 11. (Originally published 1885.)

5. Wilson, *Congressional Government*, p. 23.

6. Madison, *The Federalist*, No. 47, in *Commentary*, p. 313.

7. Hamilton or Madison, *The Federalist*, No. 51, in *Commentary*, pp. 337–38.

8. Merrill D. Peterson, *Thomas Jefferson and the New Nation: A Biography* (New York: Oxford University Press, 1970), p. 46.

9. Peterson, *Thomas Jefferson*, p. 61.

10. *Works*, Vol. 6, p. 467: "Letter to Jno. Taylor," as quoted in Wilson, *Congressional Government*, p. 13.

11. Hamilton or Madison, *The Federalist*, No. 51, in *Commentary*, pp. 337ff.

12. Joseph S. Clark, *Congress: The Sapless Branch* (New York: Harper & Row, 1964).

13. Marjorie J. Fribourg, *The United States Congress: Men Who Steered Its Course, 1787–1867* (Philadelphia: Smith, 1972), p. vi.

14. Lloyd N. Cutler, "To Form a Government," *Foreign Affairs* (Fall 1980), p. 126.

15. Richard F. Fenno, Jr., *Home Style: House Members in Their Districts* (Boston: Little, Brown, 1978), p. 168.

16. *Commemoration Ceremony in Honor of the Two Hundredth Anniversary of the First Continental Congress*, 93rd Cong., 2d sess. (1975), House Doc. No. 93–413 (Washington, D.C.: Government Printing Office, 1975), p. 11. Cited hereafter as *Anniversary*.

17. Merrill Jensen, *The Articles of Confederation: An Interpretation of the Social-Constitutional History of the American Revolution, 1774–1781* (Madison: University of Wisconsin Press, 1940), p. 107.

18. R. R. Palmer and Joel Cotton, *A History of the Modern World*, 3rd ed. (New York: Knopf, 1965), p. 251.

19. Jack P. Greene, "Such an Assembly as Never Before Came Together," address in *Anniversary*, p. 42.

20. Merrill Jensen, "Historical Origins of the First Continental Congress," address in *Anniversary*, p. 12.

21. In many state legislatures today, when the two chambers cannot agree on adjournment, the governor can take the initiative to "prorogue" them.

22. Allan Nevins, *The American States During and After the Revolution, 1775–1789* (New York: Kelley, Publishers, 1969), p. 35.

23. Greene, "Such an Assembly," p. 41.

24. "Instructions for the Province of New Hampshire," in *Anniversary*, p. 79. See

generally, Lynn Montross, *The Reluctant Rebels: The Story of the Continental Congress* (New York: Barnes & Noble, 1950), p. 26.

25. "Instructions for South Carolina," in *Anniversary*, p. 85.

26. "Instructions for Rhode Island," in *Anniversary*, p. 80.

27. "A Summary View of the Rights of British America," in Julian P. Boyd, ed., *The Papers of Thomas Jefferson* (Princeton: Princeton University Press, 1950), Vol. I, pp. 131–35. Peterson, *Thomas Jefferson*, p. 27.

28. Jensen, *The Articles of Confederation*, p. 56.

29. Cecelia Kenyon, "Ideological Origins of the First Continental Congress," address in *Anniversary*, p. 9.

30. Jensen, "Historical Origins," p. 13.

31. Greene, "Such an Assembly," p. 45.

32. Greene, "Such an Assembly," p. 44.

33. "Demand for the Redress of Grievances: Declaration and Resolves," in *Anniversary*, p. 97.

34. "Demand for the Redress of Grievances," p. 97.

35. Jensen, *The Articles of Confederation*, p. 72.

36. Jack N. Rakove, *The Beginning of National Politics: An Interpretative History of the Continental Congress* (New York: Knopf, 1979), p. 49.

37. Greene, "Such an Assembly," p. 43.

38. "The Galloway Plan of Union, September 28, 1774," in *Anniversary*, p. 93.

39. "Memorial to the Inhabitants of the Colonies," in *Anniversary*, p. 920.

40. Carl Brent Swisher, *American Constitutional Development* (Boston: Houghton Mifflin, Riverside Press, 1954), pp. 15–16.

41. Jensen, *The Articles of Confederation*, pp. 108–109.

42. James Madison, *Journal of the Constitutional Convention*, ed. E. H. Scott (Chicago: Albert, Scott, 1893), p. 31. Charles Tansill, ed., *The Making of the Great Republic: The Great Documents 1774–1789* (Washington, D.C.: 1972), pp. 109ff.

43. Madison, *Journal*, p. 32.

44. This concern exists even now. For example, in the Ninety-fourth Congress, the new class of seventy-five members refused to elect a "class" officer for more than a month at a time lest anyone gain too much power.

45. Jensen, *The Articles of Confederation*, p. 135.

46. Swisher, *American Constitutional Development*, pp. 22–23.

47. William F. Swindler, "Our First Constitution: The Articles of Confederation," *American Bar Association Journal*, Vol. 67 (February, 1981), pp. 166, 168–169.

48. Madison, *Journal*, p. 34.

49. Hamilton, *The Federalist*, No. 15, in *Commentary*, p. 87.

50. Hamilton, *The Federalist*, No. 15, in *Commentary*, p. 87.

51. Jensen, *The Articles of Confederation*, p. 240.

52. Jensen, *The Articles of Confederation*, p. 5, n. 7. Jensen believed that *The Federalist Papers* overstated the case for the ineffectiveness of the Articles of Confederation. As evidence, he cited populist James Wilson: *"The Federalist* is itself the frankest, the baldest and boldest propaganda—but what of it?" (*Selected Political Essays of James Wilson*, ed. Randolph G. Adams [New York: 1930], p. 24.)

53. Nevins, *The American States*, pp. 1–7.

54. Nevins, *The American States*, p. 4.

55. Nevins, *The American States*, p. 11.

56. Robert Luce, *Legislative Assemblies: Their Framework, Make-up, Character, Characteristics, Habits and Manners* (Boston: Houghton Mifflin, Riverside Press, 1924), p. 13.

57. Luce, *Legislative Assemblies*, p. 25, quoting John Adams, "Thoughts on Government," *Works* (1776), Vol. 4, p. 195.

58. Nevins, *The American States*, p. 3.

59. Wilfred E. Binkley, *President and Congress*, 3rd ed. (New York: Vintage Books, 1962), p. 4.

60. Leroy D. Clark, *The Grand Jury: The Use and Abuse of Political Power* (New York: New York Times Book, 1976), p. 14.

61. Nevins, *The American States*, pp. 139–140.

62. John Locke, "Treatise Concerning Civil Government: An Essay Concerning the True Original, Extent, and End of Civil Government," in Edwin A. Burtt, ed. *The English Philosophers from Bacon to Mill* (New York: Modern Library, 1939), pp. 456–57.

63. Locke, "Treatise," p. 462.

64. Locke, "Treatise," p. 462.

65. Nevins, *The American States*, p. 121.

66. Nevins, *The American States*, pp. 123–24.

67. Nevins, *The American States*, p. 166.

68. Nevins, *The American States*, p. 168.

69. Rakove, *The Beginning of National Politics*, p. 84.

Chapter 3 THE CONSTITUTION AND THE NEW CONGRESS

1. James Madison, *Journal of the Constitutional Convention*, ed. E. H. Scott (Chicago: Albert, Scott, 1893), p. 46.

2. Max Farrand, *The Framing of the Constitution of the United States* (New Haven: Yale University Press, 1965), p. 9.

3. Broadus Mitchell and Louise Mitchell, *A Biography of the Constitution of the United States: Its Origin, Formation, Adoption, Interpretation*, 2nd ed. (New York: Oxford University Press, 1975), p. 2.

4. John Adams, "Our Thoughts on Government, in a letter from a Gentleman to His Friend [Philadelphia 1776]," in Merrill D. Peterson, *Thomas Jefferson and the New Nation: A Biography* (New York: Oxford University Press, 1970), p. 96.

5. Madison, *Journal*, p. 62.

6. Madison, *Journal*, p. 69.

7. Allan Nevins, *The American States During and After the Revolution, 1775–1789* (New York: Kelley, Publishers, 1969), p. 151, quoting John Adams, *Works*, (1776), Vol. 2, p. 507.

8. Alexander Hamilton or James Madison, *The Federalist, A Commentary on the Constitution of the United States* (New York: Random House, 1937), *The Federalist*, No. 58, p. 379. Cited hereafter as *Commentary*.

9. *U.S. Constitution*, Art. I, Sec. 2.

10. Madison, *Journal*, p. 79.

11. George Haynes, *The Senate of the United States: Its History and Practice* (Boston: Houghton Mifflin, 1938), p. 2. See also Roy Swanstrom, *The United States Senate, 1787–1801*, 87th Cong., 1st sess. (1966), S. Doc. No. 64.

12. Robert Luce, *Legislative Assemblies: Their Framework, Make-up, Characteristics, Habits and Manners* (Boston: Houghton Mifflin, Riverside Press, 1924), pp. 43–47.

13. For an excellent discussion of the role of the Roman Senate as "council of elders," from which the Senate was derived, see Wolfgang Kunkel, *An Introduction to Roman Legal and Constitutional History* (Oxford: Clarendon Press, 1972), p. 19.

14. Hamilton or Madison, *The Federalist*, No. 47, in *Commentary*, pp. 312–20.

15. Haynes, *The Senate of the United States*, p. 25.

16. Wilfred E. Binkley, *President and Congress*, 3rd ed. (New York: Vintage Books, 1962), p. 165.

17. Haynes, *The Senate of the United States*, p. 23.

18. Haynes, *The Senate of the United States*, p. 22.

19. Haynes, *The Senate of the United States*, p. 31.

20. Hamilton or Madison, *The Federalist*, No. 52, in *Commentary*, p. 343.

21. The House of Representatives is also entrusted with the sole power of impeachment (Art. I, Sec. 2). The Senate has the sole power to try impeachments (Art. I, Sec. 3).

22. Hamilton or Madison, *The Federalist*, No. 58, in *Commentary*, p. 380.

23. Madison, *Journal*, p. 85.

24. National League of Cities v. Usery, 426 U.S. 833 (1976).

25. Hamilton or Madison, *The Federalist*, No. 46, in *Commentary*, p. 308.

26. Forrest McDonald, *The Presidency of George Washington* (Lawrence, Kansas: Regents Press of Kansas, 1974), quoted in Senator Robert C. Byrd, "The United States Senate: First Congress," *Congressional Record*, 97th Cong., 1st sess. (1981), S 4287.

27. See generally, Kenneth Bowling, "Politics in the First Congress," unpublished dissertation, University of Wisconsin, 1968, pp. 15–17; Linda Grant DePauw, ed., *Documentary History of the First Federal Congress* (Baltimore, 1972).

Chapter 4 POLITICS ON THE HILL

1. Wilfred E. Binkley, *President and Congress*, 3rd ed. (New York: Vintage Books, 1962), p. 77.

2. James Fenimore Cooper, *The American Democrat*, quoted in George Seldes, *The Great Quotations* (New York: Pocket Books, 1969), p. 713.

3. Terry Sanford, *A Danger of Democracy: The Presidential Nominating Process* (Boulder, Colo.: Westview Press, 1981), p. 8.

4. David B. Truman, *The Congressional Party* (New York: Wiley, 1959).

5. David S. Broder, *The Party's Over: The Failure of Politics in America* (New York: Harper & Row, 1971).

6. James D. Barber, *The Pulse of Politics: Electing Presidents in the Media Age* (New York: Norton, 1980), p. 7.

7. David R. Mayhew, *Congress: The Electoral Connection* (New Haven: Yale University Press, 1975), p. 27.

8. Charles L. Clapp, *The Congressman: His Work as He Sees It* (New York: Doubleday, 1964), p. 397.

9. Binkley, *President and Congress*, pp. 255–56.

10. Lloyd N. Cutler, "To Form a Government," *Foreign Affairs* (Fall, 1980).

11. George B. Galloway, *History of the United States House of Representatives* (Washington, D.C.: Government Printing Office, 1965), p. 120.

12. Binkley, *President and Congress*, pp. 65–70.

13. Sanford, *A Danger*, pp. 8–10.

14. Congressional Quarterly, *Origins and Development of Congress* (Washington, D.C.: Congressional Quarterly, 1976), p. 91.

15. Binkley, *President and Congress*, p. 71.

16. Binkley, *President and Congress*, p. 71.

17. Binkley, *President and Congress*, p. 257.

18. Congressional Quarterly, *Origins and Development*, p. 113.

19. Senator Robert C. Byrd, *Congressional Record*, 96th Cong., 2nd sess. (May 9, 1980), S 5046; 96th Cong., 2nd sess. (May 16, 1980), S 5525.

20. Mayhew, *Congress*, pp. 20–22.

Chapter 5 PARTY LEADERSHIP

1. This tradition differs from the dynamics of various state legislatures, where House speakers are frequently chosen by coalitions of majority and minority factions. California and Illinois are recent examples.

2. Wilfred E. Binkley, *President and Congress*, 3rd ed. (New York: Vintage Books, 1962), p. 70.

3. George B. Galloway, *History of the United States House of Representatives* (Washington, D.C.: Government Printing Office, 1965), p. 109.

4. Congressional Quarterly, *Origins and Development of Congress* (Washington, D.C.: Congressional Quarterly, 1976), p. 90.

5. William Holmes Brown, *Constitution, Jefferson's Manual, and Rules of the House of Representatives*, House Doc. No. 94–663, Sec. 54 (Washington, D.C.: Government Printing Office, 1977), p. 24.

6. United States v. Ballin, 144 U.S. 1 (1892).

7. Congressional Quarterly, *Origins and Development*, p. 107.

8. Binkley, *President and Congress*, p. 238.

9. Binkley, *President and Congress*, p. 257. See also Charles O. Jones, "Joseph G. Cannon and Howard W. Smith: An Essay on the Limits of Leadership in the House of Representatives," in *Congressional Behavior*, ed. Nelson W. Polsby, (New York: Random House, 1971), p. 203.

10. Morris K. Udall, *Education of a Congressman: The Newsletters of Morris K. Udall*, ed. Robert L. Peabody (New York: Bobbs-Merrill, 1972), pp. 295–96.

11. Udall, *Education*, pp. 296–97.

12. Udall, *Education*, p. 309.

13. Udall, *Education*, pp. 312–13.

14. Udall, *Education*, p. 325.

15. S. 299, 96th Cong., 1st sess. (1979), now Publ. Law 96–354, 96th Cong., 2nd sess. (September 19, 1980).

16. Doris Kearns, *Lyndon Johnson and the American Dream* (New York: New American Library, Signet, 1976), pp. 234–35.

17. David Rogers, "A Lesson in Civics: Reagan's March Through Congress," *Boston Globe*, August 14, 1981, p. 2.

18. Steven Roberts, "Democrats Rediscover Their Power," *The New York Times*, April 11, 1982, p. E4.

19. The Ralph Nader Congress Project, *Ruling Congress: How the House and Senate Rules Govern the Legislative Process* (New York: Penguin Books, 1975), pp. 45–46.

20. Jones, "Joseph G. Cannon and Howard W. Smith," p. 203.

21. Clem Miller, *Member of the House, Letters of a Congressman* (New York: Scribners, 1962), pp. 85–86.

22. Mark Green, *Who Runs Congress?* 3rd. Ed. (New York: Bantam Books, 1979), p. 95.

23. See generally, Jones, "Joseph G. Cannon and Howard W. Smith," p. 217. Barbara Hinckley, *Stability and Change in Congress*, 2nd ed. (New York: Harper & Row, 1978), pp. 132–33.

24. Green, *Who Runs Congress?* p. 99.

25. Green, *Who Runs Congress?* p. 98.
26. Green, *Who Runs Congress?* p. 99.
27. *The Baron Report*, No. 118, February 16, 1981.
28. Randall B. Ripley, "The Party Whip Organizations in the United States," in *Congressional Behavior*, ed. Nelson W. Polsby (New York: Random House, 1971), p. 242, n. 8.
29. Nelson W. Polsby, ed., *Congressional Behavior* (New York: Random House, 1971), p. 225.
30. Ripley, "The Party Whip," p. 241.
31. *U.S. Constitution*, Art. I, Sec. 3, Cl. 4.
32. *U.S. Constitution*, Art. I, Sec. 3, Cl. 5.
33. Alexander Hamilton or James Madison, *The Federalist, A Commentary on the Constitution of the United States* (New York: Modern Library, 1937), *The Federalist*, No. 68, p. 445.
34. George H. Haynes, *The Senate of the United States: Its History and Practice* (Boston: Houghton Mifflin, 1938), Vol. 1, p. 223.
35. *U.S. Constitution*, Art. II, Sec. 1, Cl. 3.
36. Haynes, *The Senate of the United States*, p. 210.
37. *Standing Rules of the United States Senate* (Washington, D.C.: Government Printing Office, 1979), Rule 1, Sec. 3.
38. Senator Robert C. Byrd, *Congressional Record*, 96th Cong., 2nd sess. (April 18, 1980), S 3920.
39. Kearns, *Lyndon Johnson*, p. 117.
40. Burton Hersh, *The Education of Edward M. Kennedy: A Family Biography* (New York: Morrow, 1972), p. 456. Green, *Who Runs Congress?* pp. 99–100.
41. John G. Stewart, "Two Strategies of Leadership: Johnson and Mansfield," in *Congressional Behavior*, ed. Nelson W. Polsby (New York: Random House, 1971), pp. 61–92.
42. Stewart, "Two Strategies," pp. 61–92.
43. The Ralph Nader Congress Project, p. 56.
44. See Walter J. Oleszek, *Congressional Procedures and the Policy Process* (Washington, D.C.: Congressional Quarterly, 1978), p. 137.
45. Martin Tolchin, "Howard Baker: Trying to Tame an Unruly Senate," *The New York Times Magazine*, March 28, 1982, p. 74.

Chapter 6 COMMITTEES—CREATURES OF CONVENIENCE

1. Max Weber, *The Theory of Social and Economic Organization* (New York: Free Press, 1969), p. 339.
2. Thomas P. Murphy, *The Politics of Congressional Committees: The Power of Seniority* (New York: Barron's, 1978), p. 20.

3. Kenneth Bradshaw and David Pring, *Parliament and Congress* (Austin: University of Texas Press, 1972), pp. 208–10.

4. Congressional Quarterly, *The Origins and Development of Congress* (Washington, D.C.: Congressional Quarterly, 1976), pp. 83–84. See also Congressional Quarterly, *Guide to Congress*, 2nd ed. (Washington, D.C.: Congressional Quarterly, 1976), pp. 35–37.

5. Woodrow Wilson, *Congressional Government: A Study in American Politics* (Boston: Houghton Mifflin, 1913), p. 69. (Originally published 1885.)

6. Wilson, *Congressional Government*, p. 79.

7. Legislative Reorganization Act of 1946, Pub. Law 753, 79th Cong., 2nd sess., (August 2, 1946). See Congressional Quarterly, *Origins and Development*, p. 4.

8. This story is told in most political science books to demonstrate the dictatorial powers of the Rules Committee during that time period. See, e.g., Congressional Quarterly, *Origins and Development*, p. 145.

9. David Bruck, "Strom Thurmond's Roots," *New Republic*, Vol. 186 (March 3, 1982), p. 15.

10. Legislative Reorganization Act of 1970, Pub. Law 91–510, 91st Cong., 2nd sess., 84 Stat. 1140 (October 26, 1970), sec. 108(a), 2 U.S.C. sec. 190a–2.

11. Pub. Law 91–510, sec. 107(a).

12. See 2 U.S.C. sec. 190a(b). The sunshine requirements, adopted in 1973 in the House and in 1975 in the Senate, are contained in the House and Senate Rules: Rule XXV, sec. 7(b) (1975) of the *Standing Rules of the United States Senate* (Washington, D.C.: Government Printing Office, 1979), cited hereafter as "Senate Rules," and Rule XI, cl. 2(g)(1) sec. 708 (1973) of the Rules of the House of Representatives in William Holmes Brown, *Constitution, Jefferson's Manual, and Rules of the House of Representatives*, House Doc. No. 94–663 (Washington, D.C.: Government Printing Office, 1977), cited hereafter as "House Rules."

13. Walter J. Oleszek, *Congressional Procedures and the Policy Process* (Washington, D.C.: Congressional Quarterly Press, 1978), pp. 64–65.

14. "House Rules": Rule X, 6(c), sec. 701(c).

15. See generally, Congressional Quarterly, *Guide to Congress*, p. 28.

16. "House Rules": Rule XXIII, 1.

17. "Senate Rules": Rule XXIV.

18. "House Rules": Rule X, 6(e).

19. See Ada C. McCown, *The Congressional Conference Committee* (New York: Columbia University Press, 1927). Although a bit dated, this book provides an interesting history of conference committees. The conference committee originated in England in the fourteenth century.

20. Carl Sandburg, *Abraham Lincoln: The War Years 1861–1864* (New York: Dell, 1963), Vol. 2, p. 134.

21. Congressional Quarterly Service, *Congress and the Nation*, Vol. 1, *1945–1964* (Washington, D.C.: Congressional Quarterly, 1965), p. 1680.

22. Murphy, *The Politics of Congressional Committees*, pp. 117–18.

23. "House Rules": Rule XI, cl. 2(k), sec. 712. These provisions were adopted in 1955. Gerald Gunther, *Cases and Materials on Individual Rights in Constitutional Law*, 2nd ed. (New York: Foundation Press, 1976), p. 1019.

Chapter 7 COMMITTEES—THE STANDING COMMITTEES

1. Helen M. Ingram and Scott J. Ullery, "Policy Innovation and Institutional Fragmentation," *Policy Studies Journal*, Vol. 8 (Spring 1980), pp. 664–82.

2. Another example is the legislation proposed by the Carter administration to respond to a recent Supreme Court case, Zurcher v. Stanford Daily, 436 U.S. 547 (1978), which held that the First and Fourth Amendments to the Constitution do not provide additional protection to the press and other innocent third persons not suspected of a crime. While the Justice Department was willing to support only a modest bill, at the insistence of Senator Birch Bayh of Indiana, the bill was expanded to provide additional protections for individual rights. S. 1790, 96th Cong., 1st sess. (1979).

3. David R. Mayhew, *Congress: The Electoral Connection* (New Haven: Yale University Press, 1974), p. 141.

4. David Mayhew castigated the Congress for what he calls clientelism: "Congressmen protect clientele systems—alliances of agencies, Hill committees and clienteles—against the incursions of Presidents and Cabinet Secretaries." Mayhew, *Congress*, p. 3. See also Morris P. Fiorina, *Congress: Keystone of the Washington Establishment* (New Haven: Yale University Press, 1977). Going one step further than Mayhew, Fiorina claims that members of Congress keep regulatory programs alive to provide opportunities for "casework," which helps individual constituents and thereby enhances the chances for reelection.

Chapter 8 THE PEOPLE WHO WORK ON THE HILL

1. Congressional Quarterly, *Origins and Development of Congress* (Washington, D.C.: Congressional Quarterly, 1976), p. 19, quoting L. H. Butterfield, ed., *Adams Family Correspondence* (Cambridge: Harvard University, Belknap Press, 1963), Vol. 1.

2. Merrill D. Peterson, *Thomas Jefferson and the New Nation: A Biography* (New York: Oxford University Press, 1970), p. 81.

3. James Madison's admiration for the personal talents, abilities, and dedication of the representatives was obvious: "Of the Ability and Intelligence of those who composed the Convention the debates and proceedings may be a test." James

Madison, *Journal of the Constitutional Convention*, ed. E. H. Scott (Chicago: Albert, Scott, 1893), p. 51.

4. Wilfred E. Binkley, *President and Congress*, 3rd ed. (New York: Vintage Books, 1962), pp. 35–37.

5. Carl Brent Swisher, *American Constitutional Development* (Boston: Houghton Mifflin, Riverside Press, 1954), p. 23. See Malbin, *Unelected Representatives*, pp. 9–15.

6. Library of Congress, Congressional Research Service, *Congressional Staffing: 1947–1978*, Judy Schneider, CRS No. 28, August 24, 1979, reprinted in U.S., Congress, House, Select Committee on Committees, *Final Report*, 96th Cong., 2nd sess. (April 1, 1980), pp. 531–32.

7. Schneider, *Congressional Staffing*, pp. 531–32.

8. Michael J. Malbin, *Unelected Representatives: Congressional Staff and the Future of Representative Government* (New York: Basic Books, 1980), p. 13. See Commentary to Rule XI, cl. 5 of the Rules of the House of Representatives, in William Holmes Brown, *Constitution, Jefferson's Manual, and Rules of the House of Representatives*, House Doc. No. 94–663, Sec. 732(d) (Washington, D.C.: Government Printing Office, 1977). See generally, Library of Congress, Congressional Research Service, *Congressional Salaries and Allowances: Current Authorities and Amounts*, Paul E. Dwyer, Mini Brief No. MB80206, July 20, 1981.

9. Schneider, *Congressional Staffing*, p. 533.

10. Harrison W. Fox and Susan W. Hammond, *Congressional Staffs: The Invisible Force in American Lawmaking* (New York: Free Press, 1977), pp. 4–5.

11. Fox and Hammond, *Congressional Staffs, p. 5*.

12. S. Res. 97, 97th Cong., 1st sess. (March 17, 1981). See U.S., Congress, Senate, *Congressional Record*, Vol. 127, No. 43, 97th Cong., 1st sess. (March 17, 1981), S 2316.

13. Michael S. Robinson, "Three Faces of the Media," in *The New Congress*, eds. Thomas E. Mann and Norman J. Ornstein (Washington, D.C.: American Enterprise Institute, 1981), p. 65.

14. Elizabeth B. Moynihan, "Mail Call on Capitol Hill," *The New York Times Magazine*, November 15, 1981, p. 136.

15. Fox and Hammond, *Congressional Staffs*, p. 92.

16. Thomas E. Mann, Norman J. Ornstein, Michael J. Malbin, and John F. Bibby, *Vital Statistics on Congress, 1982* (Washington, D.C.: American Enterprise Institute, 1982), p. 112.

17. Richard F. Fenno, Jr., *Home Style: House Members in Their Districts* (Boston: Little, Brown, 1978), pp. 46–50.

18. Testimony of Iris Mitgang before the Senate Committee on Labor and Human Resources, 97th Cong., 1st sess. (January 28, 1981).

19. General Accounting Office, *Annual Report* 1 (1980).

20. Schneider, *Congressional Staffing*.

21. United Press International, "MX Environmental Study Challenged," *Washington Post*, March 13, 1981, p. A2.

22. Malbin, *Unelected Representatives*, p. 144.

23. Congressional Budget and Impoundment Act of 1974, 31 U.S.C. sec. 1401 et seq.

24. Allen Schick, *Congress and Money: Budgeting, Spending and Taxing* (Washington, D.C.: Urban Institute, 1980), pp. 407–408.

25. Paperwork Reduction Act of 1980, Pub. Law 96–511, 94 Stat. 2812 (December 11, 1980); see 44 U.S.C. sec. 3501 et seq.

26. Malbin, *Unelected Representatives*, p. 257.

27. Schick, *Congress and Money*, p. 132.

28. Testimony of Alice M. Rivlin in hearings held before the House Subcommittee on Legislative Committee Appropriations, 97th Cong., 1st sess. (February 4, 1981).

29. Rivlin, testimony, p. 1.

30. Schick, *Congress and Money*, p. 143.

31. See Rowland Evans and Robert Novak, "Captain General of the Tax Counterrevolution," *Washington Post*, February 11, 1981, p. A18.

32. "CBO Analysis To Show Administration Falling Short of Budget Goals," *Washington Post*, March 23, 1981, p. A2.

33. Technology Assessment Act of 1972, Pub. Law 92–484, 86 Stat. 797 (October 13, 1972); see 2 U.S.C. secs. 471–481.

34. Malbin, *Unelected Representatives*, p. 16.

35. Malbin, *Unelected Representatives*, pp. 28ff.

36. Malbin, *Unelected Representatives*, p. 130.

37. Malbin, *Unelected Representatives*, pp. 239–40.

38. Malbin, *Unelected Representatives*, p. 240.

39. Malbin, *Unelected Representatives*, p. 242.

40. Malbin, *Unelected Representatives*, p. 243.

41. Malbin, *Unelected Representatives*, pp. 243–44.

42. Malbin, *Unelected Representatives*, p. 245.

43. Alexander Hamilton or James Madison, *The Federalist, A Commentary on the Constitution of the United States* (New York: Random House, 1937), *The Federalist*, No. 51, p. 337.

Chapter 9 RITES OF PASSAGE

1. Richard Hofstadter, *The American Political Tradition: And the Men Who Made It* (New York: Vintage Books, 1973), p. 332.

2. Elizabeth Drew thoroughly canvassed the problems in "Politics and Money," *New Yorker* (December 6 and December 13, 1982). The concern about special interests has not, however, been limited to the impact of PACs. See, e.g., Drew Pearson and Jack Anderson, *The Case Against Congress: A Compelling Indictment of Corruption on Capitol Hill* (New York: Simon & Schuster, 1968), p. 22.

3. Mark Green, *Who Runs Congress?* 3rd ed. (New York: Bantam Books, 1979), pp. 143–44.

4. S. 158, 97th Cong., 1st sess. (1981).

5. Another example is the airline deregulation bill which was generated in large part by Professor Stephen Breyer of Harvard Law School, acting as consultant to a Senate Judiciary Subcommittee chaired by Senator Kennedy. See, e.g., Stephen Breyer, "Analyzing Regulatory Failure: Mismatches, Less Restrictive Alternatives, and Reform," *Harvard Law Review* Vol. 92 (1979), pp. 549, 604.

6. Timothy B. Clark, "After a Decade of Doing Battle, Public Interest Groups Show Their Age," *National Journal*, July 12, 1980, p. 1136.

7. Morton Mintz and Merrill Brown, "AT&T Spending on '80 Elections Tops Firms," *Washington Post*, April 16, 1981, p. A16.

8. Lester M. Salamon, "Federalism and Third Party Government: The Challenge to Public Management," unpublished manuscript, Urban Institute, May 8, 1982.

9. Voting Rights Act Amendments of 1982, S. 1992, 97th Cong., 1st sess. (1981). Pub. Law 97-205, 96 Stat. 131 (June 29, 1982), 42 U.S.C. sec. 1973.

10. H.R. 31, 97th Cong., 1st sess. (1981).

11. Barbara Hinckley, *Stability and Change in Congress*, 2nd ed. (New York: Harper & Row, 1978), p. 138.

12. Phyllis Schlafly, testimony, U.S., Congress, Senate, Committee on Labor and Human Resources (hearings), 97th Cong., 1st sess. (April 12, 1981).

13. Woodrow Wilson, *Congressional Government: A Study in American Politics* (Boston: Houghton Mifflin, 1913), p. 69 (originally published 1885), cited in Congressional Quarterly, *Origins and Development of Congress* (Washington, D.C.: Congressional Quarterly, 1976), p. 104.

14. S. 158, 97th Cong., 1st sess. (1981).

15. See, e.g., the acerbic interchange between Senator John Culver and Charles Schultze, chairman of the Panel of Economic Advisers, in hearings on S. 262 before the Senate Committee on the Judiciary, 96th Cong., 1st sess. (May, 1979), pp. 37–41.

16. For example, Senator Birch Bayh of Indiana anticipated opposition to his bill, S. 1790, to protect the press from police searches, and asked the chairman of the Judiciary to hold hearings at full committee, which he would chair.

17. 2 U.S.C. sec. 190b (a); see also Rule XI, cl. 2(m) (1) (B), sec. 718 in William Holmes Brown, *Constitution, Jefferson's Manual, and Rules of the House of Representatives*, House Doc. No. 94–663, secs. 293–299 (Washington, D.C.: Government Printing Office, 1977). Cited hereafter as "House Rules."

18. 2 U.S.C. sec. 192. See Gerald Gunther, *Cases and Materials on Individual Rights in Constitutional Law*, 2nd ed. (New York: Foundation Press, 1976), p. 1018. "House Rules": secs. 293–299.

19. Green, *Who Rules Congress*? p. 10.

20. David R. Mayhew, *Congress: The Electoral Connection* (New Haven: Yale University Press, 1974), p. 141.

21. Gary Orfield, *Congressional Power: Congress and Social Change* (New York: Harcourt Brace Jovanovich, 1975), pp. 35–36.

22. "House Rules": Rule XXVII, sec. 908.

23. "House Rules· Rule XXIV, sec. 898.

24. Walter J. Oleszek, *Congressional Procedures and the Policy Process* (Washington, D.C.: Congressional Quarterly Press, 1978), p. 98.

Chapter 10 RITES OF PASSAGE II

1. Max M. Kampelman, "Congress, the Media and the President," in *Congress Against the President*, ed. Harvey C. Mansfield (New York: Praeger, 1975), pp. 85, 87.

2. *Standing Rules of the United States Senate* (Washington, D.C.: Government Printing Office, 1979), Rule IX. Cited hereafter as "Senate Rules."

3. Walter J. Oleszek, *Congressional Procedures and the Policy Process* (Washington, D.C.: Congressional Quarterly Press, 1978), p. 136.

4. S. 299, 96th Cong., 1st sess. (1979).

5. Federal Courts Improvement Act of 1980, S. 1477, 96th Cong., 2nd sess. (1980).

6. Paperwork Reduction Act of 1980, Pub. Law 96–571, 94 Stat. 2812 (December 11, 1980); see 44 U.S.C. secs. 3501–3520.

7. S. 509, 97th Cong., 1st sess. (1981).

8. *Congressional Record*, Vol. 127, No. 47 (March 24, 1981), S 2569.

9. Often a senator does not need all the time he is entitled to under a unanimous consent agreement, and the time is "yielded back" to the floor manager.

10. *Congressional Record*, Vol. 127, No. 69 (May 7, 1981), S 4542.

11. Oleszek, *Congressional Procedures*, p. 165. "Senate Rules": XIII.

12. Congressional Quarterly, *The Origins and Development of Congress* (Washington, D.C.: Congressional Quarterly, 1976), p. 219.

13. Congressional Quarterly, *Guide to Congress*, 2nd ed. (Washington, D.C.: Congressional Quarterly, 1976), p. 101.

14. Gary Orfield, *Congressional Power: Congress and Social Change* (New York: Harcourt Brace Jovanovich, 1975), p. 41.

15. Civil Rights of Institutionalized Persons Act. S. 10, 96th Cong., 1st sess. (1979), Pub. Law 96–247, 84 Stat. 349 (May 23, 1980); see 42 U.S.C. sec. 1997 et seq.

16. *Congressional Record*, Vol. 127, No. 60 (April 18, 1981), S 3617.

17. Warren Weaver, Jr. *Both Your Houses: The Truth About Congress* (New York: Praeger, 1972), p. 21.

18. *Washington Report*, August 10, 1981, p. 2.

19. *Congressional Record*, Vol. 127, No. 48 (March 25, 1981), H 1073.

20. Oleszek, *Congressional Procedures*, p. 98.

21. Oleszek, *Congressional Procedures*, p. 83.

22. Oleszek, *Congressional Procedures*, p. 86.

23. William Holmes Brown, *Constitution, Jefferson's Manual, and Rules of the House of Representatives*, House Doc. No. 94–663, Rule XIX, sec. 822 (Washington, D.C.: Government Printing Office, 1977). Cited hereafter as "House Rules."

24. "House Rules": Rule XXIII, sec. 874.

25. Eric Redman, *The Dance of Legislation* (New York: Simon & Schuster, 1973), p. 259.

26. Alexander Hamilton, *The Federalist*, No. 73, in *A Commentary on the Constitution of the United States* (New York: Random House, 1937), p. 477.

27. Wilfred E. Binkley, *President and Congress*, 3rd ed. (New York: Vintage Books, 1962), p. 86.

28. Binkley, *President and Congress*, p. 100.

29. Hamilton, *The Federalist*, No. 73, in *Commentary*, p. 479.

30. See generally, Senate Committee on the Judiciary, *Federal Restraints on Competition in the Trucking Industry: Antitrust Immunity and Economic Regulation*, 96th Cong., 2nd sess. (1980).

31. Youngstown Sheet & Tube Co. v. Sawyer, 343 U.S. 579, 634–655 (1952). (Jackson, J. concurring.)

32. Marbury v. Madison, 1 Cranch. 137 (1803).

33. See, e.g., AFL-CIO v. American Petroleum Institute, 448 U.S. 607, 671 (1980). (Rehnquist, J., concurring.)

34. Sheldon Goldman, "Carter's Judicial Opponents: A Lasting Legacy," *Judicature*, Vol. 64 (March 1981) p. 344.

35. For a discussion of the Court as a political institution, see Martin Shapiro, *Law and Politics in the Supreme Court: New Approaches to Political Jurisprudence* (New York: Free Press, 1964); Robert G. McCloskey, *The Modern Supreme Court* (Cambridge: Harvard University Press, 1972); Bob Woodward and Scott Armstrong, *The Brethren* (New York: Avon Books, 1979).

36. Zurcher v. Stanford Daily, 436 U.S. 547 (1978).

37. Mapp v. Ohio, 367 U.S. 643 (1961).

38. Bivens v. Six Unknown Named Agents, 403 U.S. 388 (1971). (Burger, C.J., dissenting.)

39. Katzenbach v. Morgan, 384 U.S. 641 (1966). See general discussion in G.

Gunther, *Cases and Materials on Individual Rights in Constitutional Law* (New York: Foundation Press, 1976), p. 614.

40. S. 158, 97th Cong., 1st sess. (1981).

Chapter 11 WHO CONTROLS EXPENDITURES?

1. William Greider, "The Education of David Stockman," *The Atlantic*, Vol. 248 (December 1981), p. 27.

2. Congressional Quarterly *Weekly Report*, June 12, 1982, p. 1387.

3. Robert Pear, "War on Poverty Is Difficult To Call Off," *The New York Times*, November 29, 1981, p. E4.

4. Allan Nevins, *The American States During and After the Revolution, 1775–1789* (New York: Kelley, Publishers, 1969), p. 3.

5. James Madison, *Journal of the Constitutional Convention*, ed. E. H. Scott (Chicago: Albert, Scott, 1893), p. 34.

6. Madison, *Journal*, p. 62.

7. Alexander Hamilton, *The Federalist*, No. 30, in *A Commentary on the Constitution of the United States* (New York: Random House, 1937), pp. 182–83.

8. *U.S. Constitution*, Art. I, Sec. 7.

9. Kenneth Bradshaw and David Pring, *Parliament and Congress* (Austin: University of Texas Press, 1972), p. 311, citing Journal of the House of Representatives, 24 July and 17 September 1789.

10. Bradshaw and Pring, *Parliament and Congress*, p. 312.

11. Louis Fisher, *Presidential Spending Power* (Princeton: Princeton University Press, 1975), p. 9.

12. Bradshaw and Pring, *Parliament and Congress*, p. 312.

13. Fisher, *Presidential Spending Power*, p. 13.

14. Fisher, *Presidential Spending Power*, pp. 14–15.

15. Fisher, *Presidential Spending Power*, p. 17.

16. Fisher, *Presidential Spending Power*, pp. 24–26.

17. Fisher, *Presidential Spending Power*, p. 33.

18. Fisher, *Presidential Spending Power*, p. 47.

19. Allen Schick, *Congress and Money: Budgeting, Spending and Taxing* (Washington, D.C.: Urban Institute, 1980), p. 25.

20. Schick, *Congress and Money*, pp. 27–29.

21. Schick, *Congress and Money*, p. 440.

22. Schick, *Congress and Money*, p. 48.

23. Congressional Budget and Impoundment Control Act of 1974, Pub. Law 93–344, 88 Stat. 297 (July 12, 1974).

24. H. Con. Res. 115, 97th Cong., 1st sess. (1981), cited hereafter as H. Con. Res. 115. See also S. Con. Res. 19, 97th Cong., 1st sess. (1981).

25. H. Con. Res. 115, Title II, Sec. 202 (14).

26. H. Con. Res. 115, Title III, Sec. 302 (10).

27. Senate Committee on the Budget, Report on the First Concurrent Resolution on the Budget, FY 82, 97th Cong., 1st sess. (1981), Report No. 97–49, pp. 137–38, cited hereafter as First Concurrent Resolution Senate Report.

28. First Concurrent Resolution Senate Report, pp. 37–39.

29. *Congressional Record*, Vol. 127, No. 69, 97th Cong., 1st sess. (May 7, 1981), S 4522 (unprinted Amendment No. 72: To delete funding for the Legal Services Corporation).

30. *Congressional Record*, Vol. 127, No. 50, 97th Cong., 1st sess. (March 27, 1981), S 2851–S 2854.

31. H.R. 3512, Report No. 97–67, 97th Cong., 1st sess. (1981) (Calendar No. 93).

32. Conference Report, H.R. 3512, Report No. 97–124, 97th Cong., 1st sess. (1981), p. 77.

33. S. 1377, Report No. 97–130, 97th Cong., 1st sess. (1981).

34. In its forward to the Omnibus Reconciliation Act Report, the Budget Committee warned about the inclusion of extraneous matter as "damaging the credibility of the budget process." Report of the Committee on the Budget, S. 1377, 97th Cong., 1st sess (1981), p. 3.

35. Greider, "Education of David Stockman," pp. 27ff.

36. For a contemporary debate on the merits of reconciliation, see Richard Bolling and John E. Barriere, *Washington Post*, June 28, 1981, p. D7; Stuart E. Eizenstat, "The Hill's Budget Stampede: Misuse of the 1974 Reforms Could Turn Congress into a Rubberstamp Parliament," as reprinted in the *Congressional Record* (June 22, 1981), S 6614; and Donald T. Rotunda, "Reconciliation Not Better the Second Time Around," *Washington Post*, June 28, 1981, p. D5.

37. David Rogers, "The Budget, Capitol's Ongoing Horror Show," *Boston Globe*, June 6, 1982, pp. A33, A36.

38. S. J. Res. 58, Committee on the Judiciary, *Report on Balanced Budget-Tax Limitation Constitutional Amendment*, Report No. 97–151, 97th Cong., 1st sess. (1981).

39. Fisher, *Presidential Spending Power*, pp. 86–87.

40. Fisher, *Presidential Spending Power*, pp. 75–98.

41. Fisher, *Presidential Spending Power*, p. 92.

42. William Barry Furlong, "America's Other Budget," *The New York Times Magazine*, February 21, 1982, pp. 32, 62.

43. Schick, *Congress and Money*, pp. 78, 371–72.

Chapter 12 REVENUE AND OVERSIGHT

1. David R. Mayhew, *Congress: The Electoral Connection* (New Haven: Yale University Press, 1974), p. 141.
2. Ralph Nader, *The Revenue Committees* (New York: Viking Press, Grossman, 1975), p. xiii.
3. William Greider, "The Education of David Stockman," *The Atlantic*, Vol. 248 (December, 1981), pp. 46–47.
4. John R. Manley, "Congressional Staff and Public Policy Making: The Joint Committee on Internal Revenue Taxation," in *Congressional Behavior*, ed. Nelson W. Polsby (New York: Random House, 1971), pp. 42, 45.
5. Karen W. Arenson, "The 25% of Expenditures Washington Never Sees," *The New York Times*, February 7, 1982, p. E4.
6. Arenson, "The 25% of Expenditures," p. E4.
7. S. Surrey, W. Warren, P. McDaniel, and H. Ault, *Federal Income Taxation* (Mineola, N.Y.: Foundation Press), Vol. I, p. 257.
8. Surrey et al, *Federal Income Taxation*, p. 270.
9. 31 U.S.C. sec. 1329(a)(2).
10. Nader, *The Revenue Committees*, p. xxiii.
11. Rule X, 2(a) and (f) of the Rules of the House of Representatives in William Holmes Brown, *Constitution, Jefferson's Manual, and Rules of the House of Representatives*, House Doc. No. 94–663, sec. 692 (Washington, D.C.: Government Printing Office, 1977).
12. See chapter 1, footnote 14.
13. William E. Kovacic, "Federal Trade Commission Competition Programs (1969–1980)," revised draft September 1981; manuscript, FTC Planning Office.
14. James L. Sundquist, *The Decline and Resurgence of Congress: To Tighten Control Over Administration Oversight* (Washington, D.C.: Brookings Institution, 1981), p. 315.
15. Morris P. Fiorina, *Congress: Keystone of the Washington Establishment* (New Haven: Yale University Press, 1977), p. 46.
16. These sunset proposals have lost much of their popularity. S. 2, 96th Cong., 1st sess. (1979); Sunset Act of 1980, *Report of the Committee on Governmental Affairs*, Report No. 96–865, 96th Cong., 2nd sess. (1980). See generally, Judith H. Parris, "Sunset and Program Review Legislation: Some Congressional Options," Congressional Research Service, Library of Congress, Report. No. 79–152 (July 17, 1979).
17. H.R. 1776, 96th Cong., 1st sess. (1979); H.R. 1776, 97th Cong., 1st sess. (1981).
18. Transcript of mark-up before the House Subcommittee on Health and the Environment, 97th Cong., 1st sess. (May 13, 1981) (unpublished).

19. Consumer Energy Council of America v. Federal Energy Regulatory Commission, 673 F. 2d 425 (D.C. Cir. 1982).

20. See generally, Louis Fisher, "A Political Context for Legislative Vetoes," *Political Science Quarterly* (Summer 1978); see generally, C. F. Norton, "Congressional Review, Deferral and Disapproval of Executive Actions: A Summary and Inventory of Statutory Authority," Congressional Research Service, Library of Congress, Multilith No. 76–88G (April 30, 1976).

21. Harold H. Bruff and Ernest Gellhorn, "Congressional Control of Administrative Regulation: A Study of Legislative Vetoes," *Harvard Law Review*, Vol. 90 (1977), pp. 1369–1409.

22. Thomas M. Franck and Edward Weisband, *Foreign Policy by Congress* (New York: Oxford University Press, 1979), pp. 83ff.

23. Sundquist, *Decline and Resurgence of Congress*, p. 275.

24. Franck and Weisband, *Foreign Policy by Congress*, pp. 83–84.

25. Amendments to the Foreign Assistance Act of 1961, Pub. Law 93–559, 88 Stat. 1813, 1814 (1974).

26. Sundquist, *Decline and Resurgence of Congress*, pp. 273–314.

27. Harold W. Chase, *Federal Judges: The Appointing Process* (Minneapolis: The University of Minnesota Press, 1972), p. 7.

28. Chase, *Federal Judges*, p. 6.

Chapter 13 THE CONGRESSMAN AS REPRESENTATIVE

1. Declaration of Independence (1776).

2. Alexander Hamilton or James Madison, *The Federalist, A Commentary on the Constitution of the United States* (New York: Random House, 1937), *The Federalist*, No. 52, p. 343. Cited hereafter as *Commentary*.

3. Hamilton or Madison, *The Federalist*, No. 62, in *Commentary*, p. 402.

4. Hamilton or Madison, *The Federalist*, No. 62, in *Commentary*, p. 403.

5. James Madison "Debates in the Federal Convention of 1787," in *Documents Illustrative of the Formation of the Union of the American States* (Washington, D.C.: Government Printing Office, 1927), p. 163, as quoted in Robert A. Dahl, *Pluralist Democracy in the United States: Conflict and Consent* (Chicago: Rand McNally, 1966), pp. 41–42.

6. See generally, Ronald Steel, *Walter Lippmann and the American Century* (New York: Vintage Books, 1981).

7. Robert A. Dahl, *Pluralist Democracy in the United States: Conflict and Consent* (Chicago: Rand McNally, & Co. 1966), pp. 24, 455–56.

8. David R. Mayhew, *Congress: The Electoral Connection* (New Haven: Yale University Press, 1974), p. 5.

9. Edmund Burke, Speech to The Electors of Bristol, 1774.

10. John F. Kennedy, *Profiles in Courage* (New York: Pocket Books, 1957), p. 14.

11. Richard F. Fenno, Jr., *Home Style, House Members in Their Districts* (Boston: Little, Brown Co, 1978), p. 13.

12. Barbara Hinckley, *Stability and Change in Congress*, 2nd ed. (New York: Harper & Row, 1978), pp. 52–54, citing John Kingdon, *Congressmen's Voting Decisions* (New York: Harper & Row, 1973).

13. Hinckley, *Stability and Change*, p. 185. See also Donald E. Stokes and Warren E. Miller, "Constituency Influence in Congress; (1963), Leroy N. Rieselbach, ed., *The Congressional System* (Belmont, Calif.: Duxbury Press, 1970), p. 432.

14. Kennedy, *Profiles*, p. 10.

15. Fenno, *Home Style*, p. 28.

16. Morris P. Fiorina, *Congress: Keystone of the Washington Establishment* (New Haven: Yale University Press, 1977), p. 346.

17. William Greider, "The Education of David Stockman", *The Atlantic*, Vol. 248 (December, 1981), p. 30.

18. Kennedy, *Profiles*, p. 6.

Chapter 14 REELECTION

1. David R. Mayhew, *Congress: The Electoral Connection* (New Haven: Yale University Press, 1974), p. 5.

2. John F. Bibby, Thomas E. Mann, and Norman J. Ornstein, *Vital Statistics on Congress, 1980* (Washington, D.C.: American Enterprise Institute, 1980), pp. 15–16.

3. Robert A. Caro, "The Years of Lyndon Johnson," *The Atlantic*, Vol. 248 (October, 1981).

4. Mark Green, *Who Runs Congress?* 3rd ed. (New York: Viking Press, 1979), p. 167.

5. "Did Congressman Sell His Vote?" *Boston Globe*, June 11, 1982, p. 4.

6. Gary C. Jacobson, *Money in Congressional Elections* (New Haven: Yale University Press, 1980), pp. 177–78. See generally, Thomas M. Durbin, *Report on Campaign Financing* (Washington, D.C.: Congressional Research Service, 1980).

7. Buckley v. Valeo, 424 U.S. 1 (1976).

8. 2 U.S.C. sec. 434(a).

9. 2 U.S.C. sec. 432.

10. Michael J. Malbin, ed. *Parties, Interest Groups and Campaign Finance Laws* (Washington, D.C.: American Enterprise Institute, 1980), p. 239.

11. Hearings before the House Committee on Rules and Administration, Federal Election Campaign Act of 1971, p. 172; cited in Jacobson, *Money*, p. 184.
12. Jacobson, *Money*, pp. 1, 187–190.
13. Thomas E. Mann, Norman J. Ornstein, Michael J. Malbin, and John F. Bibby, *Vital Statistics on Congress, 1982* (Washington, D.C.: American Enterprise Institute, 1982), pp. 63–64.
14. Bill Peterson, "Republicans May Show What Money Can Do in November Races," *Washington Post*, May 30, 1982, p. A2.
15. Xandra Kayden, "Campaign Under Seige, One Senator's Defeat" *New York University Review of Law and Social Change*, Vol. 67 (1980).
16. Kayden, "Campaign Under Seige," p. 79.
17. 2 U.S.C. sec. 441a(a) (2).
18. 2 U.S.C. sec. 441a(d) (3). See generally, Malbin, *Parties*, p. 261.
19. Jacobson, *Money*, p. 1.
20. Richard Reeves, "When Reform Backfires," *Esquire* (March 1980), pp. 7, 11.
21. David S. Broder, "Equal Time for Targets," *Washington Post*, August 26, 1981, p. A25.
22. Malbin, *Parties*, pp. 272–73.
23. Mann, Ornstein, Malbin, and Bibby, *Vital Statistics*, pp. 69–70.
24. Fred Wertheimer, "The 'PAC' Phenomenon in American Politics," *Arizona Law Review*, Vol. 22 (1980), p. 616.
25. Jacobson, *Money*, p. 200.
26. S. 623, 96th Cong., 1st sess. (1979).
27. Jacobson, *Money*, p. 203.
28. Jacobson, *Money*, p. 207.

Chapter 15 CONGRESSIONAL ETHICS

1. *1977 Congressional Quarterly Almanac*, p. 763.
2. Arthur M. Schlesinger, Jr., and Roger Bruns, eds., *Congress Investigates: A Documented History, 1792–1974* (New York: Bowker, 1975) Vol. 3, pp. 1849ff.
3. George H. Mayer, *The Republican Party, 1854–1964* (New York: Oxford University Press, 1964), pp. 210–12.
4. Richard N. Current, T. Harry Williams, and Frank Freidel, *American History: A Survey*, 3rd ed. (New York: Knopf, 1971), p. 552.
5. David Halberstam, *The Powers That Be* (New York: Knopf, 1979), p. 6.
6. Halberstam, *The Powers That Be*, p. 7.
7. Halberstam, *The Powers That Be*, p. 13.
8. Ward Sinclair, "A Muddy Stream," *Washington Post*, October 4, 1980, pp. A1, A9.

9. Mark Green, *Who Runs Congress?* 3rd ed. (New York: Bantam Books, 1979), p. 178.

10. Alexander Hamilton or James Madison, *The Federalist, A Commentary on the Constitution of the United States* (New York: Random House, 1937), *The Federalist*, No. 57, p. 372.

11. Thomas Jefferson, *Manual of Parliamentary Practice*, cited in Irwin B. Arieff, "House Democrats' New Rule on Punishment May Imperil Congressional Autonomy," *Congressional Quarterly Weekly Report*, Vol. 38, No. 2 (October 18, 1980), pp. 3154–3155.

12. Marvin Stone, "A Sordid Example," *U.S. News and World Report* Vol. LXXXIII, No. 5 (August 1, 1977), p. 68.

13. Stone, "A Sordid Example," p. 68.

14. *1979 Congressional Quarterly Almanac*, p. 568.

15. *1979 Congressional Quarterly Almanac*, p. 568.

16. *1979 Congressional Quarterly Almanac*, p. 563.

17. Sanford Watzman, *Conflict of Interest, Politics, and the Money Game*, (New York: Cowles, 1971), p. 79.

18. Powell v. McCormick, 395 U.S. 486 (1969).

19. Irwin B. Arieff, "House Democrats' New Rule on Punishment May Imperil Congressional Autonomy," *Congressional Quarterly Weekly Report*, Vol. 38, No. 2 (October 18, 1980), p. 3154.

20. John Felton, "The Wealth of Congress," *Congressional Quarterly Weekly Report*, Vol. 36, No. 35 (September 2, 1978), p. 2314.

21. Felton, "The Wealth of Congress," p. 2321.

22. *1979 Congressional Quarterly Almanac*, p. 541.

23. Felton, "The Wealth of Congress," p. 2316.

24. Felton, "The Wealth of Congress," pp. 2315–2316.

25. "How Money Talks in Congress: A Common Cause Study of the Impact of Money on Congressional Decisionmaking" (1979), p. 27.

26. *1977 Congressional Quarterly Almanac*, p. 803.

Chapter 16 CONGRESS WORKS

1. Elizabeth Drew, *Washington Journal* (New York: Random House, 1974), pp.9–10.

2. Drew, *Washington Journal*, p. 401.

SELECTED BIBLIOGRAPHY

The authors recommend the following books and articles, each of which provided us with a unique insight into the workings of the Congress:

Binkley, Wilfred E. *President and Congress*, 3rd ed. New York: Vintage Books, 1962

Clapp, Charles L. *The Congressman: His Work as He Sees It*. New York: Doubleday Anchor, 1964.

Congressional Record. Washington, D.C.: Government Printing Office. (Any issue is worth the time.)

Cutler, Lloyd N. "To Form a Government." *Foreign Affairs*, Fall, 1980.

Drew, Elizabeth, "Politics and Money," *New Yorker*, December 6 and 13, 1982.

The Federalist, A Commentary on the Constitution of the United States. New York: Random House, 1937.

Fenno, Richard F., Jr. *Home Style: House Members in Their Districts*. Boston: Little, Brown, 1978.

Fiorina, Morris P. *Congress: Keystone of the Washington Establishment*. New Haven: Yale University Press, 1977.

Fisher, Louis. *Presidential Spending Power*. Princeton: Princeton University Press, 1975.

Franck, Thomas M. and Weisband, Edward. *Foreign Policy by Congress*. New York: Oxford University Press, 1979.

423

Green, Mark. *Who Runs Congress?* 3rd ed. New York: Bantam Books, 1979.

Greider, William. "The Education of David Stockman." *The Atlantic*, Vol. 248, December, 1981.

Hinckley, Barbara. *Stability and Change in Congress*, 2nd ed. New York: Harper & Row, 1978.

Jacobson, Gary C. *Money in Congressional Elections*. New Haven: Yale University Press, 1980.

Madison, James. *Journal of the Constitutional Convention*, ed. E. H. Scott. Chicago: Albert, Scott, 1893.

Malbin, Michael J. *Unelected Representatives: Congressional Staff and the Future of Representative Government*. New York: Basic Books, 1980.

Mann, Thomas E. and Ornstein, Norman J., eds. *The New Congress*. Washington, D.C.: American Enterprise Institute, 1981.

Mann, Thomas E., Ornstein, Norman J., Malbin, Michael J., and Bibby, John F. *Vital Statistics on Congress, 1982*. Washington, D.C.: American Enterprise Institute, 1982.

Mayhew, David R. *Congress: The Electoral Connection*. New Haven: Yale University Press, 1974.

Miller, Clem. *Member of the House, Letters of a Congressman*. New York: Charles Scribner's Sons, 1962.

Oleszek, Walter J. "Congressional Procedures and the Policy Process." Washington, D.C.: *Congressional Quarterly*, 1978.

Orfield, Gary. *Congressional Power: Congress and Social Change*. New York: Harcourt Brace Jovanovich, 1975.

Rakove, Jack N. *The Beginning of National Politics: An Interpretative History of the Continental Congress*. New York: Knopf, 1979.

Redman, Eric. *The Dance of Legislation*. New York: Simon & Schuster, 1973.

Rieselback, Leroy N., ed. *The Congressional System*. Belmont, California: Duxbury Press, 1970.

Schick, Allen. *Congress and Money: Budgeting, Spending and Taxing*. Washington, D.C.: Urban Institute, 1980.

Sundquist, James L. *The Decline and Resurgence of Congress*. Washington, D.C.: Brookings Institution, 1981.

Udall, Morris K. *Education of a Congressman: The Newsletters of Morris K. Udall*, ed. Robert L. Peabody. New York: Bobbs-Merrill, 1972.

Wilson, Woodrow. *Congressional Government: A Study in American Politics*. Boston: Houghton Mifflin, 1913.

INDEX

DATE DUE